Takane & Hana

4

STORY AND ART BY

Yuki Shiwasu

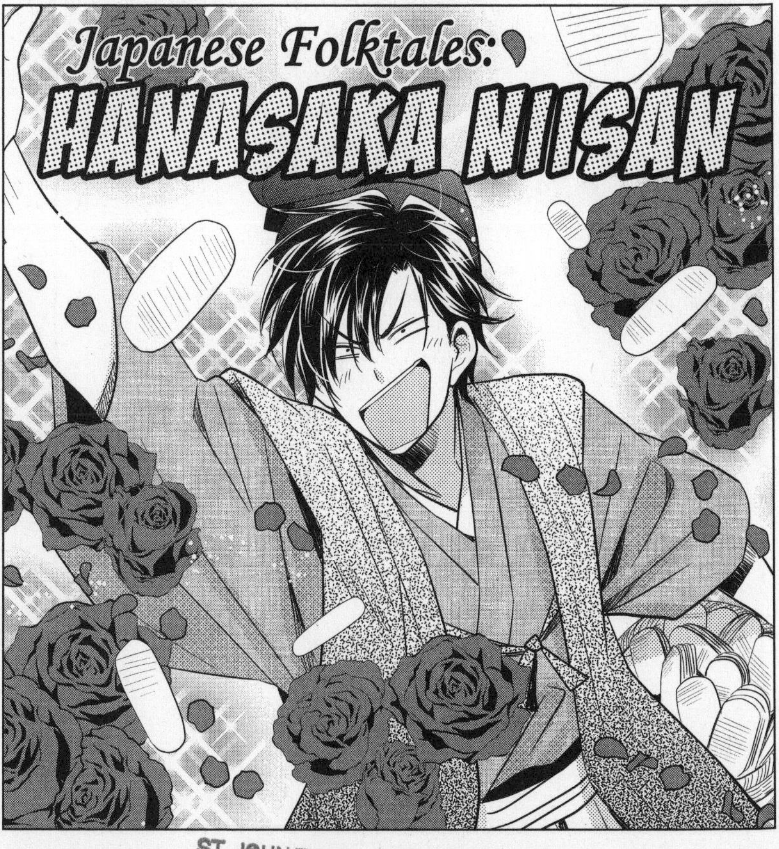
Japanese Folktales:
HANASAKA NIISAN

Takane & Hana

4

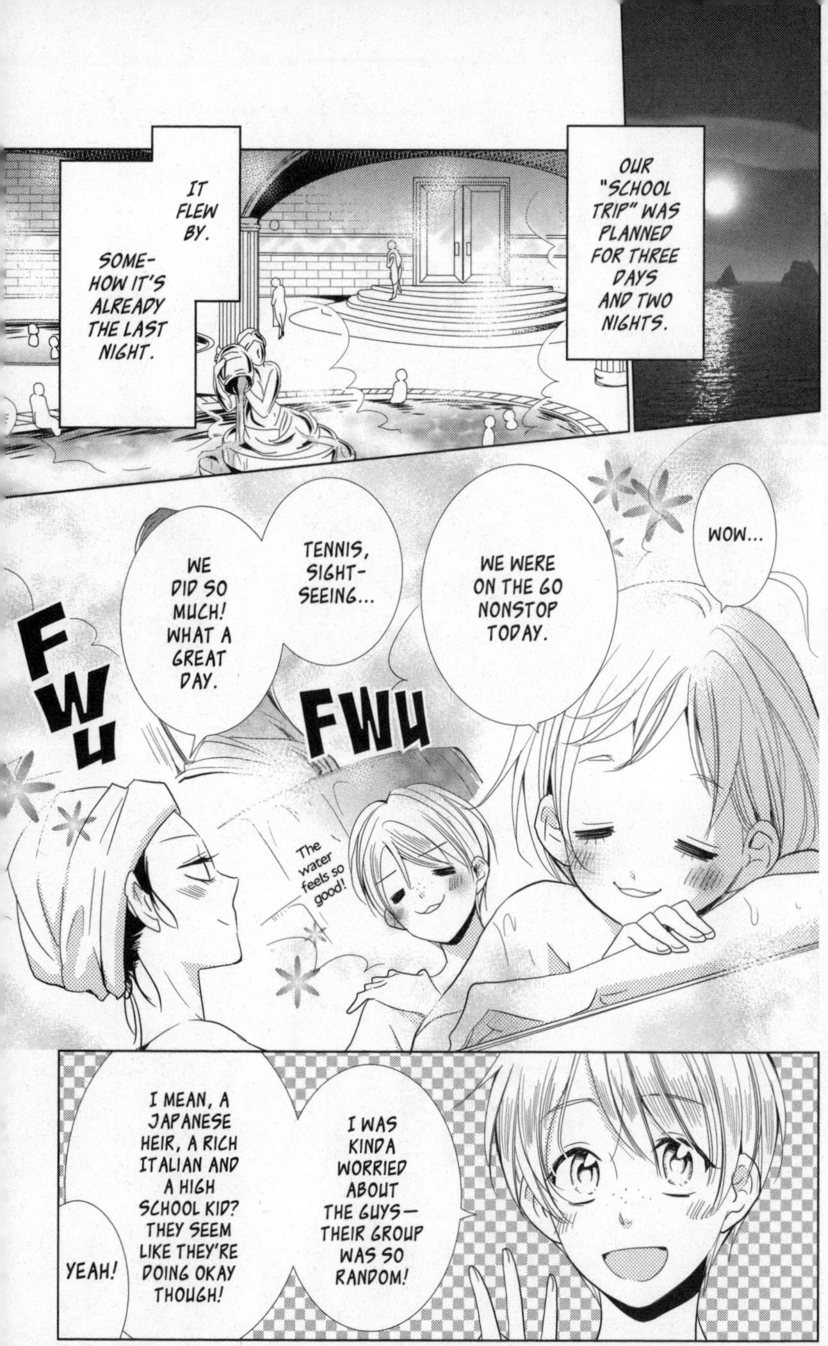
OUR "SCHOOL TRIP" WAS PLANNED FOR THREE DAYS AND TWO NIGHTS.
IT FLEW BY.
SOME-HOW IT'S ALREADY THE LAST NIGHT.
WOW...
WE WERE ON THE GO NONSTOP TODAY.
TENNIS, SIGHT-SEEING...
WE DID SO MUCH! WHAT A GREAT DAY.
FWU
FWU
The water feels so good!
I WAS KINDA WORRIED ABOUT THE GUYS—THEIR GROUP WAS SO RANDOM!
I MEAN, A JAPANESE HEIR, A RICH ITALIAN AND A HIGH SCHOOL KID? THEY SEEM LIKE THEY'RE DOING OKAY THOUGH!
YEAH!

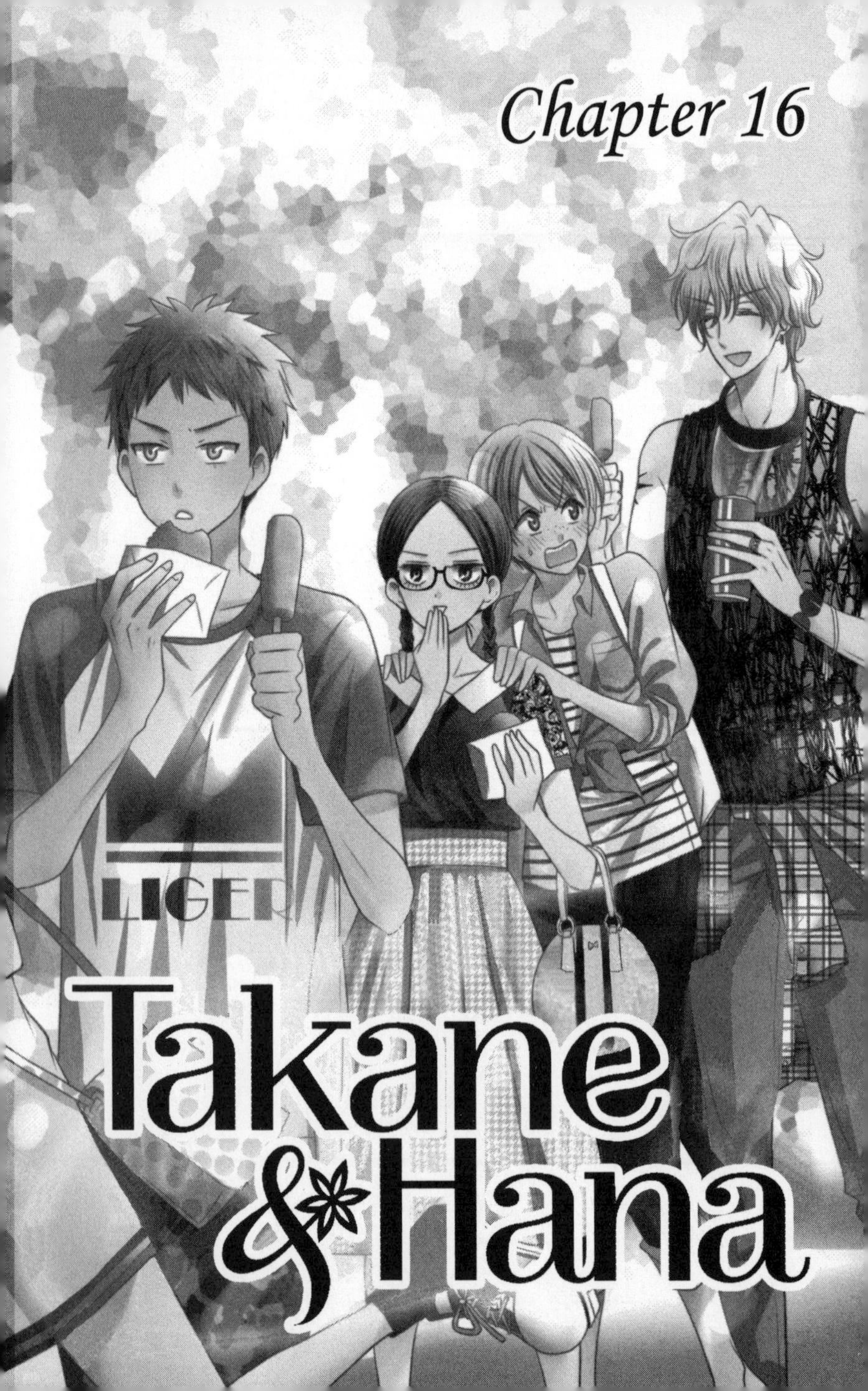
Chapter 16
LIGER
Takane & Hana

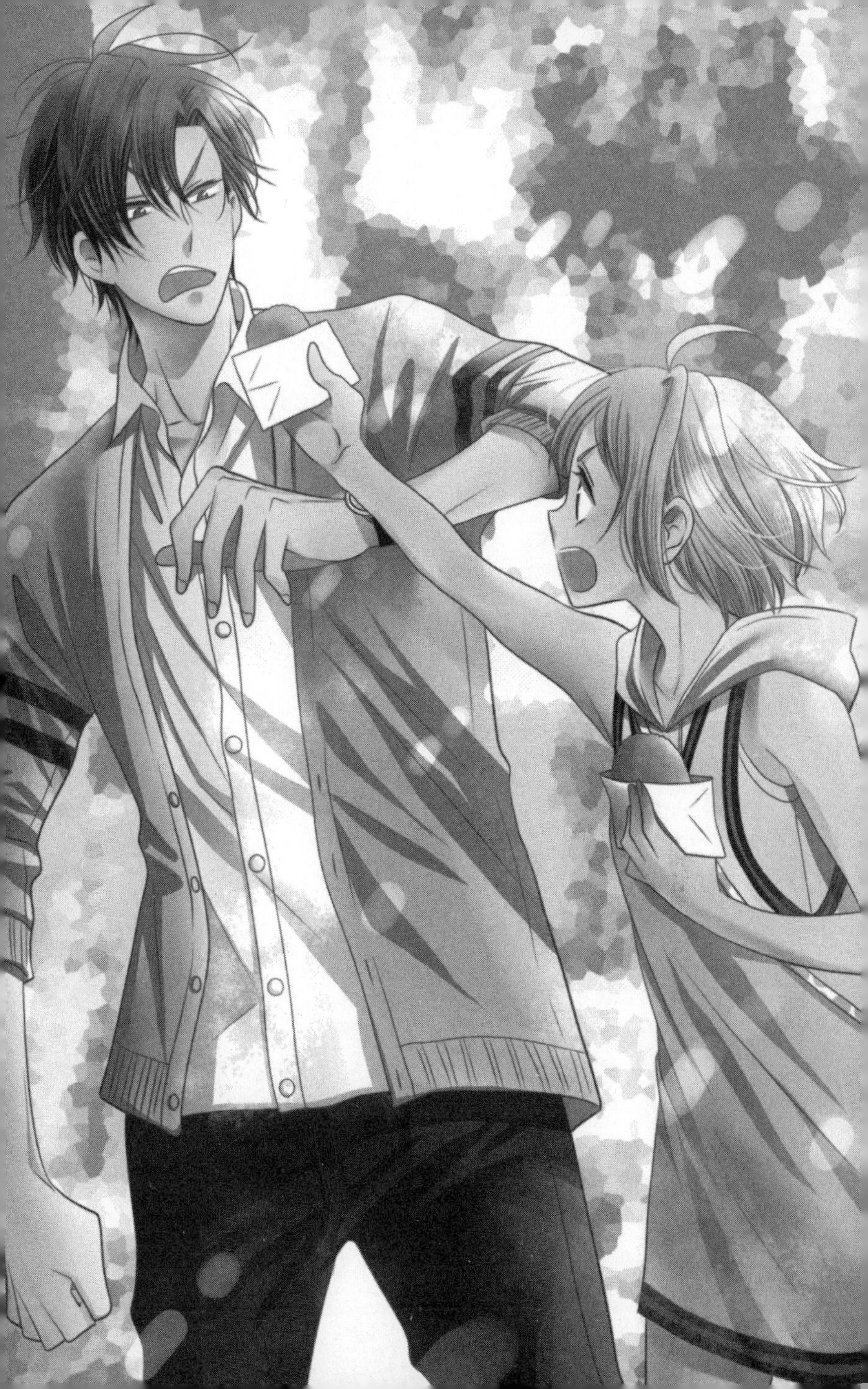

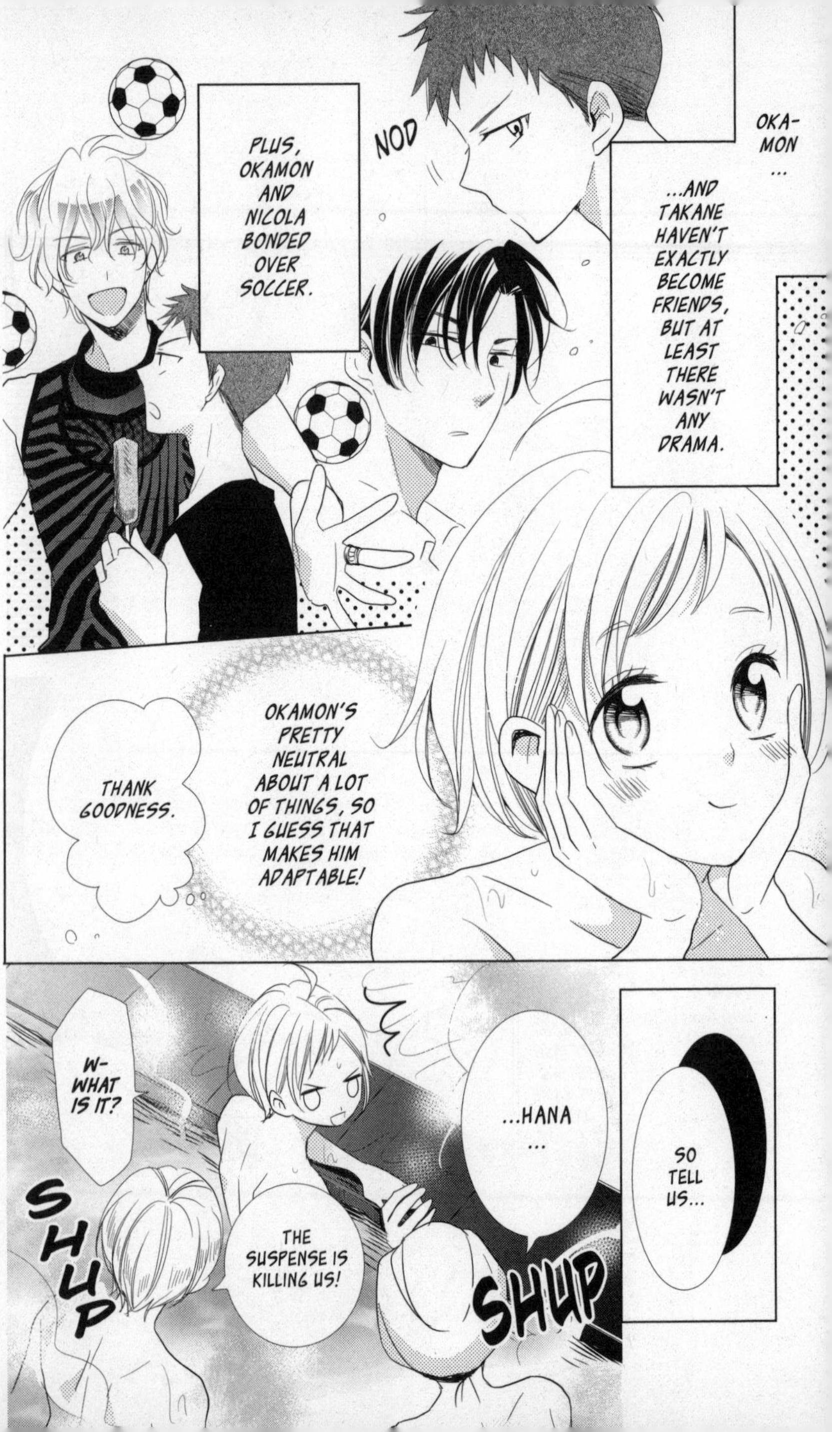
OKA-MON...
...AND TAKANE HAVEN'T EXACTLY BECOME FRIENDS, BUT AT LEAST THERE WASN'T ANY DRAMA.
NOD
PLUS, OKAMON AND NICOLA BONDED OVER SOCCER.
OKAMON'S PRETTY NEUTRAL ABOUT A LOT OF THINGS, SO I GUESS THAT MAKES HIM ADAPTABLE!
THANK GOODNESS.
SO TELL US...
...HANA...
W-WHAT IS IT?
SHUP
THE SUSPENSE IS KILLING US!
SHUP

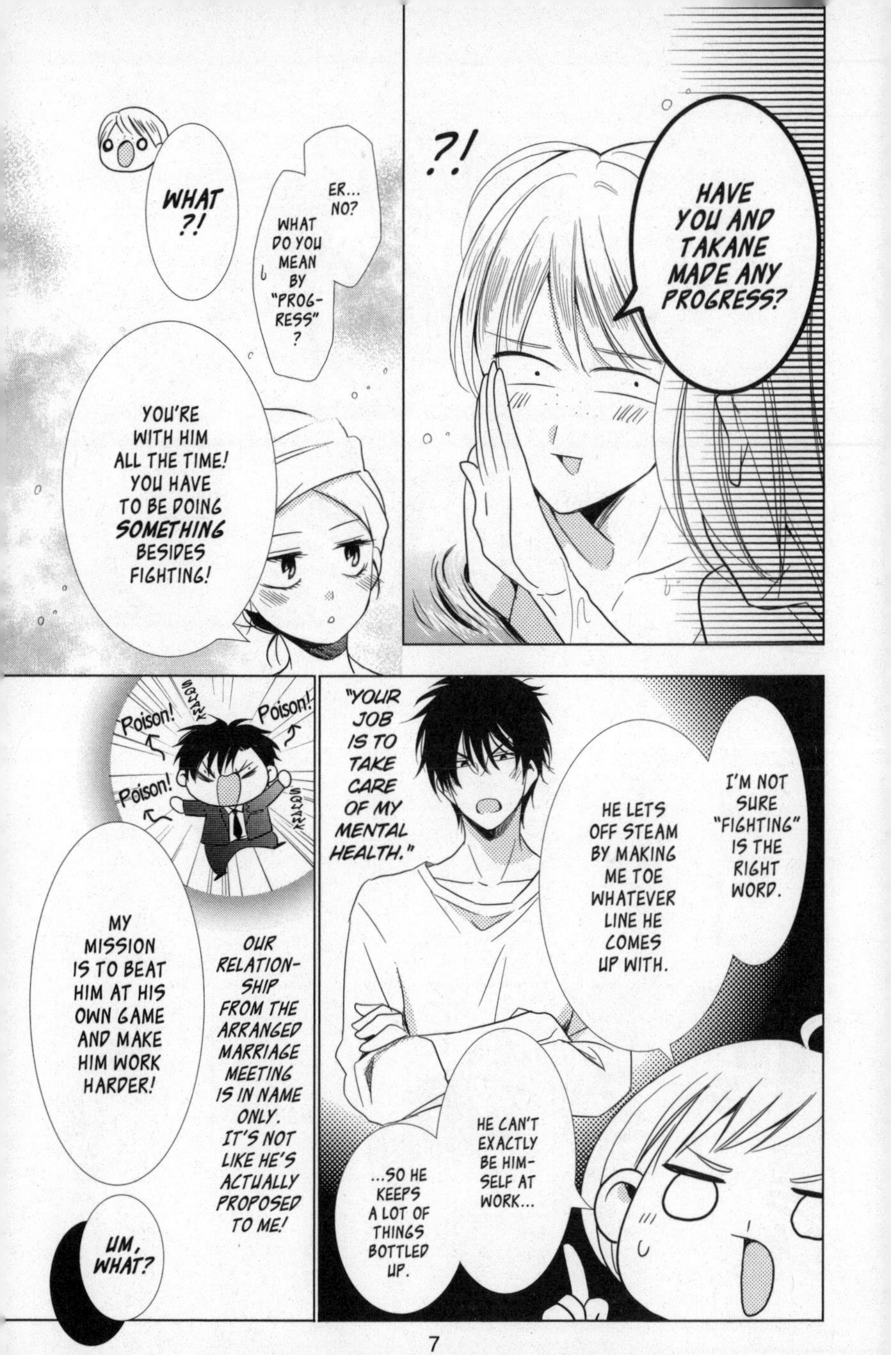
HAVE YOU AND TAKANE MADE ANY PROGRESS?
?!
ER... NO?
WHAT DO YOU MEAN BY "PROG-RESS"?
WHAT ?!
YOU'RE WITH HIM ALL THE TIME! YOU HAVE TO BE DOING SOMETHING BESIDES FIGHTING!
I'M NOT SURE "FIGHTING" IS THE RIGHT WORD.
HE LETS OFF STEAM BY MAKING ME TOE WHATEVER LINE HE COMES UP WITH.
"YOUR JOB IS TO TAKE CARE OF MY MENTAL HEALTH."
HE CAN'T EXACTLY BE HIM-SELF AT WORK...
...SO HE KEEPS A LOT OF THINGS BOTTLED UP.
Poison!
Poison!
Poison!
SQUAWK
SQUAWK
OUR RELATION-SHIP FROM THE ARRANGED MARRIAGE MEETING IS IN NAME ONLY. IT'S NOT LIKE HE'S ACTUALLY PROPOSED TO ME!
MY MISSION IS TO BEAT HIM AT HIS OWN GAME AND MAKE HIM WORK HARDER!
UM, WHAT?

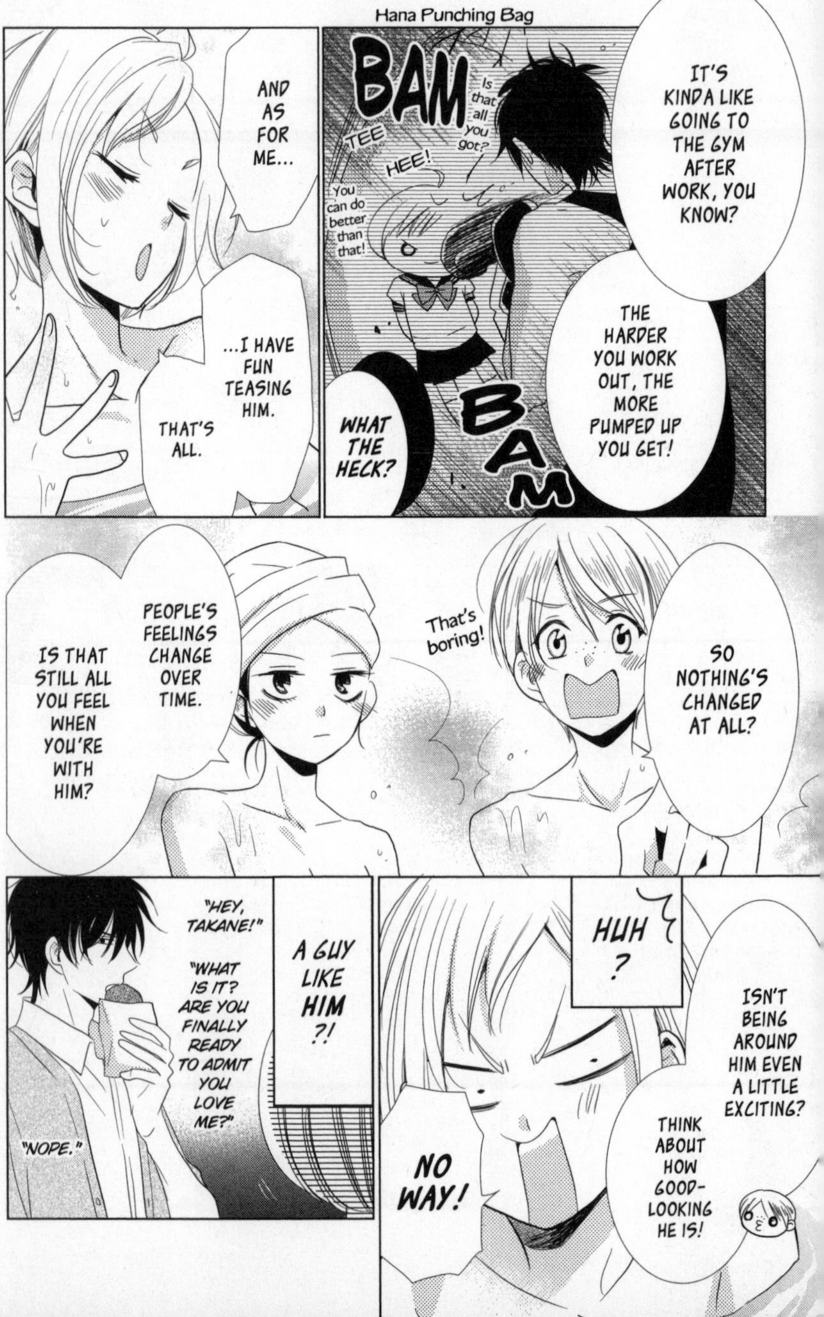
Hana Punching Bag
IT'S KINDA LIKE GOING TO THE GYM AFTER WORK, YOU KNOW?
THE HARDER YOU WORK OUT, THE MORE PUMPED UP YOU GET!
BAM
Is that all you got?
TEE HEE!
You can do better than that!
BAM
WHAT THE HECK?
AND AS FOR ME...
...I HAVE FUN TEASING HIM.
THAT'S ALL.
SO NOTHING'S CHANGED AT ALL?
That's boring!
PEOPLE'S FEELINGS CHANGE OVER TIME.
IS THAT STILL ALL YOU FEEL WHEN YOU'RE WITH HIM?
ISN'T BEING AROUND HIM EVEN A LITTLE EXCITING?
THINK ABOUT HOW GOOD-LOOKING HE IS!
HUH?
NO WAY!
A GUY LIKE HIM?!
"HEY, TAKANE!"
"WHAT IS IT? ARE YOU FINALLY READY TO ADMIT YOU LOVE ME?"
"NOPE."

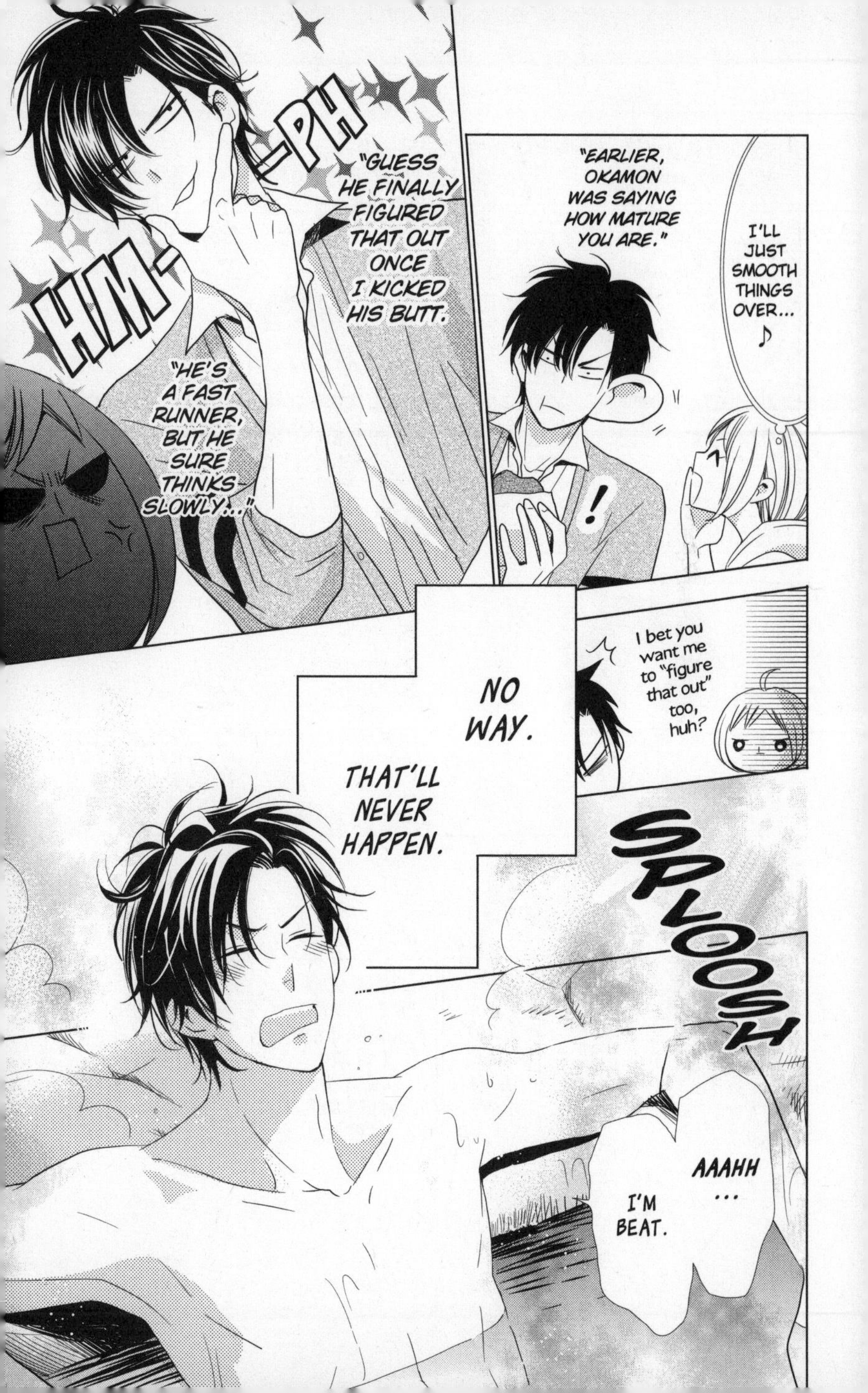

I'LL JUST SMOOTH THINGS OVER... ♪
"EARLIER, OKAMON WAS SAYING HOW MATURE YOU ARE."
!
HM--PH
"GUESS HE FINALLY FIGURED THAT OUT ONCE I KICKED HIS BUTT.
"HE'S A FAST RUNNER, BUT HE SURE THINKS SLOWLY..."
I bet you want me to "figure that out" too, huh?
NO WAY.
THAT'LL NEVER HAPPEN.
SPLOOSH
AAAHH ...
I'M BEAT.

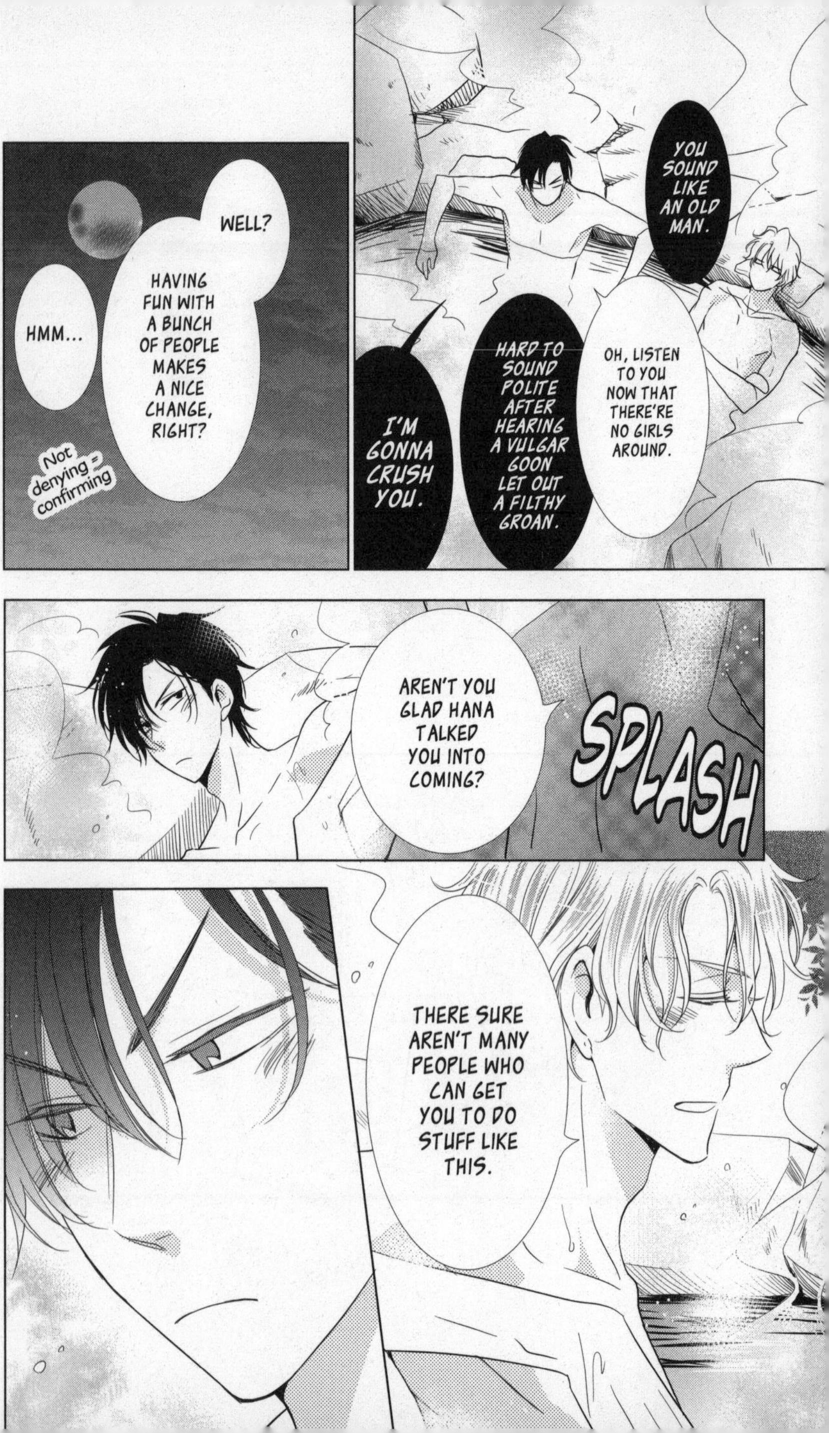
YOU SOUND LIKE AN OLD MAN.
OH, LISTEN TO YOU NOW THAT THERE'RE NO GIRLS AROUND.
HARD TO SOUND POLITE AFTER HEARING A VULGAR GOON LET OUT A FILTHY GROAN.
I'M GONNA CRUSH YOU.
WELL?
HAVING FUN WITH A BUNCH OF PEOPLE MAKES A NICE CHANGE, RIGHT?
HMM...
Not denying = confirming
SPLASH
AREN'T YOU GLAD HANA TALKED YOU INTO COMING?
THERE SURE AREN'T MANY PEOPLE WHO CAN GET YOU TO DO STUFF LIKE THIS.

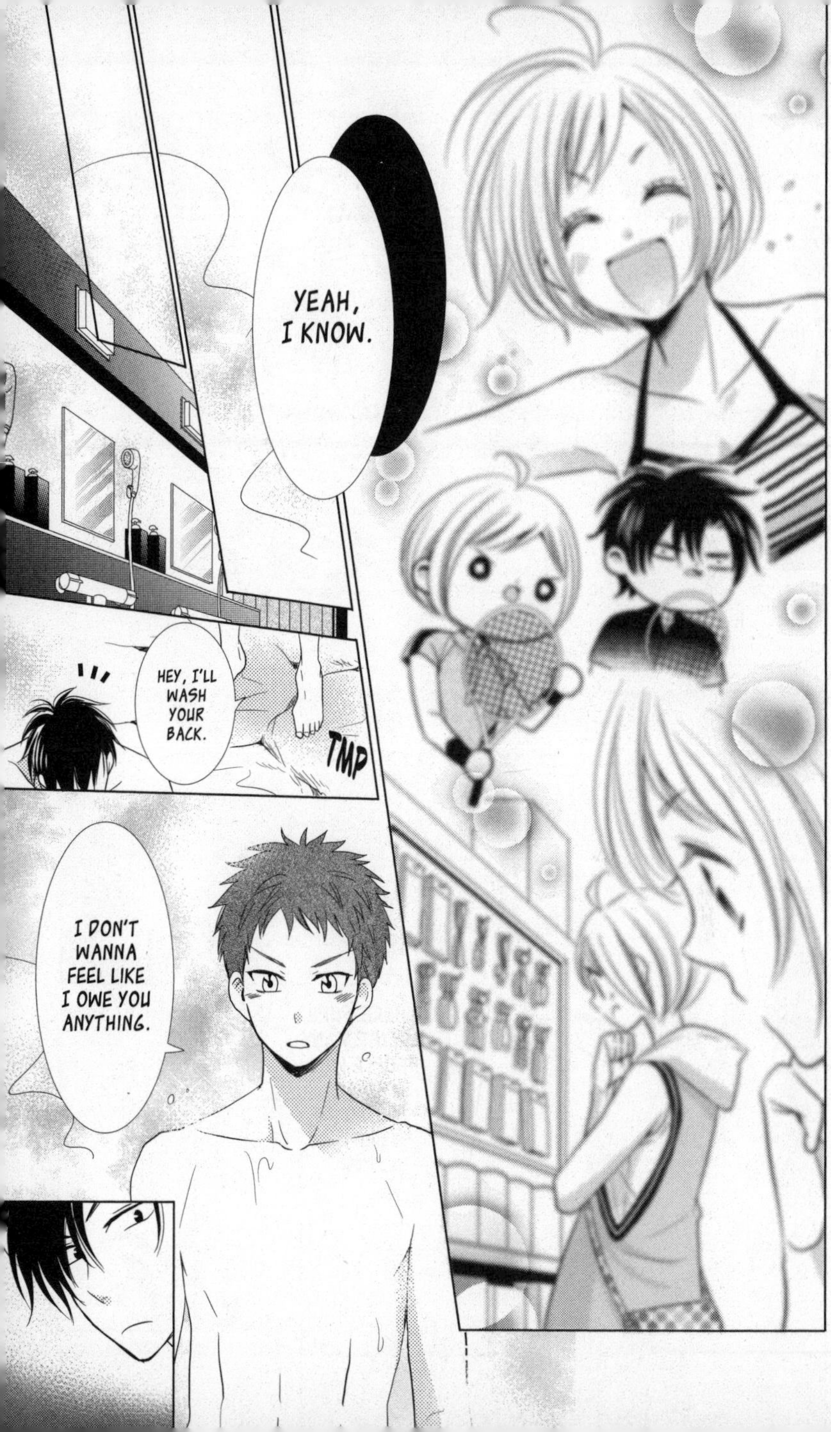
YEAH, I KNOW.
HEY, I'LL WASH YOUR BACK.
TMP
I DON'T WANNA FEEL LIKE I OWE YOU ANYTHING.

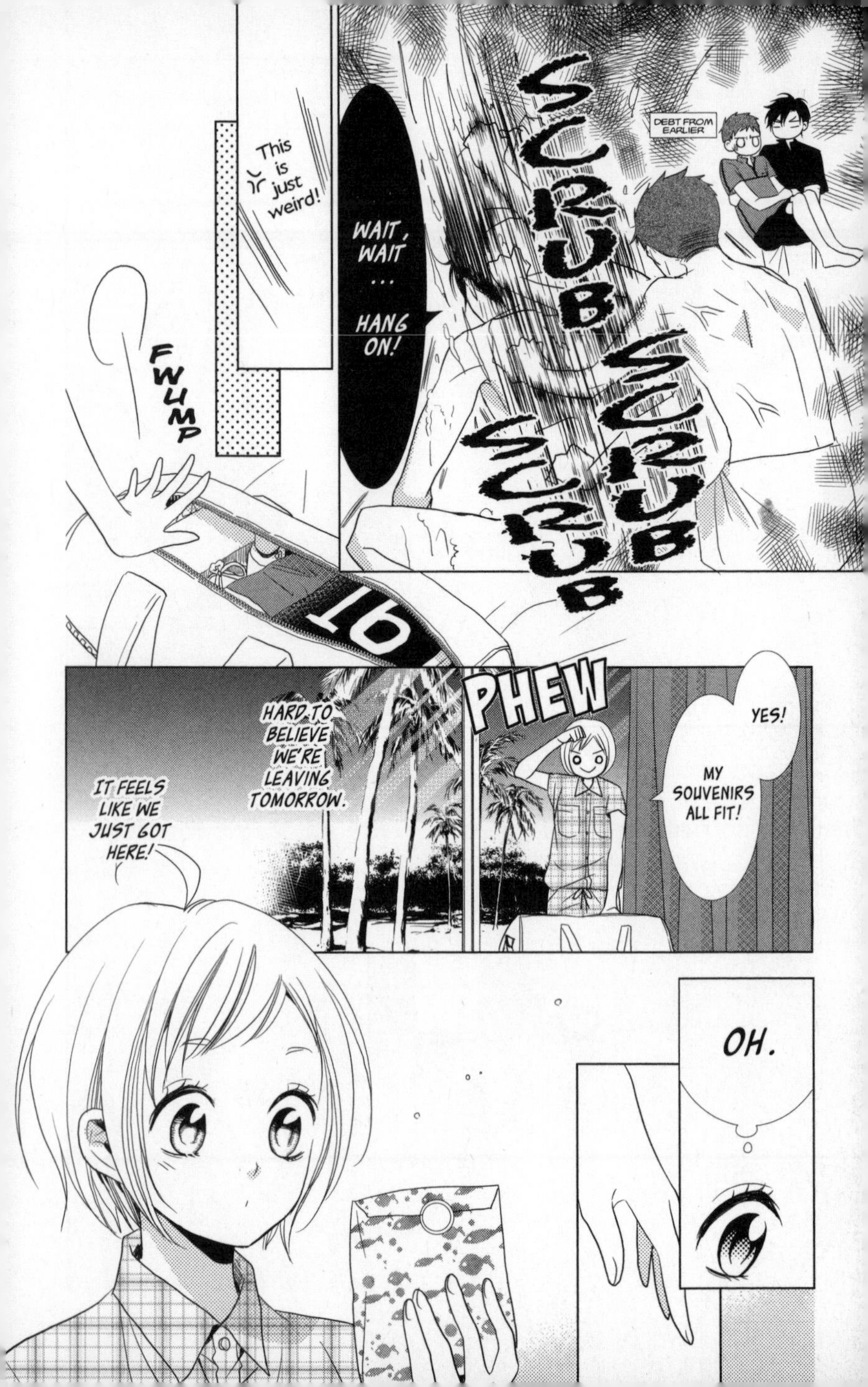
SCRUB
SCRUB
SCRUB
DEBT FROM EARLIER
WAIT, WAIT... HANG ON!
This is just weird!
FWUMP
YES!
MY SOUVENIRS ALL FIT!
PHEW
HARD TO BELIEVE WE'RE LEAVING TOMORROW.
IT FEELS LIKE WE JUST GOT HERE!
OH.

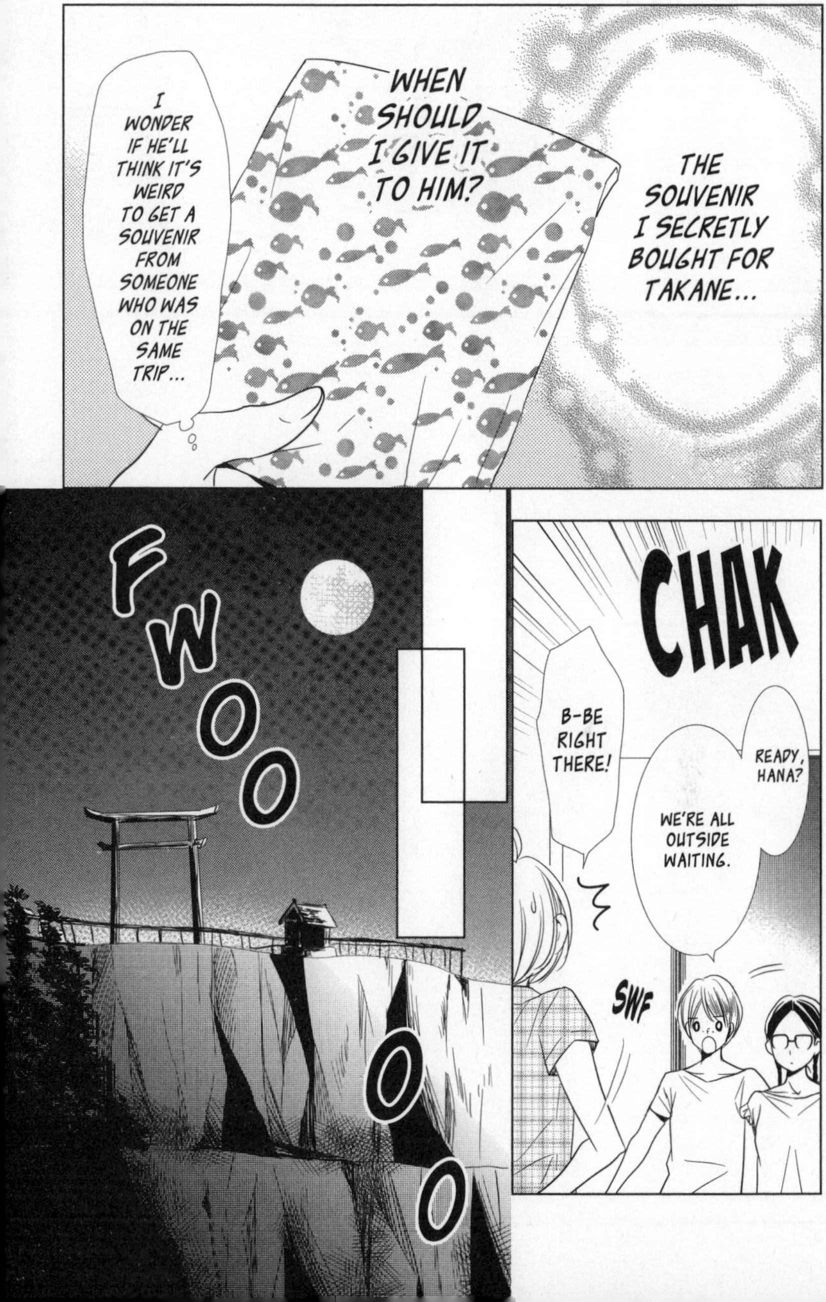
THE SOUVENIR I SECRETLY BOUGHT FOR TAKANE...
WHEN SHOULD I GIVE IT TO HIM?
I WONDER IF HE'LL THINK IT'S WEIRD TO GET A SOUVENIR FROM SOMEONE WHO WAS ON THE SAME TRIP...
CHAK
READY, HANA?
WE'RE ALL OUTSIDE WAITING.
B-BE RIGHT THERE!
SWF
FWOOOOO

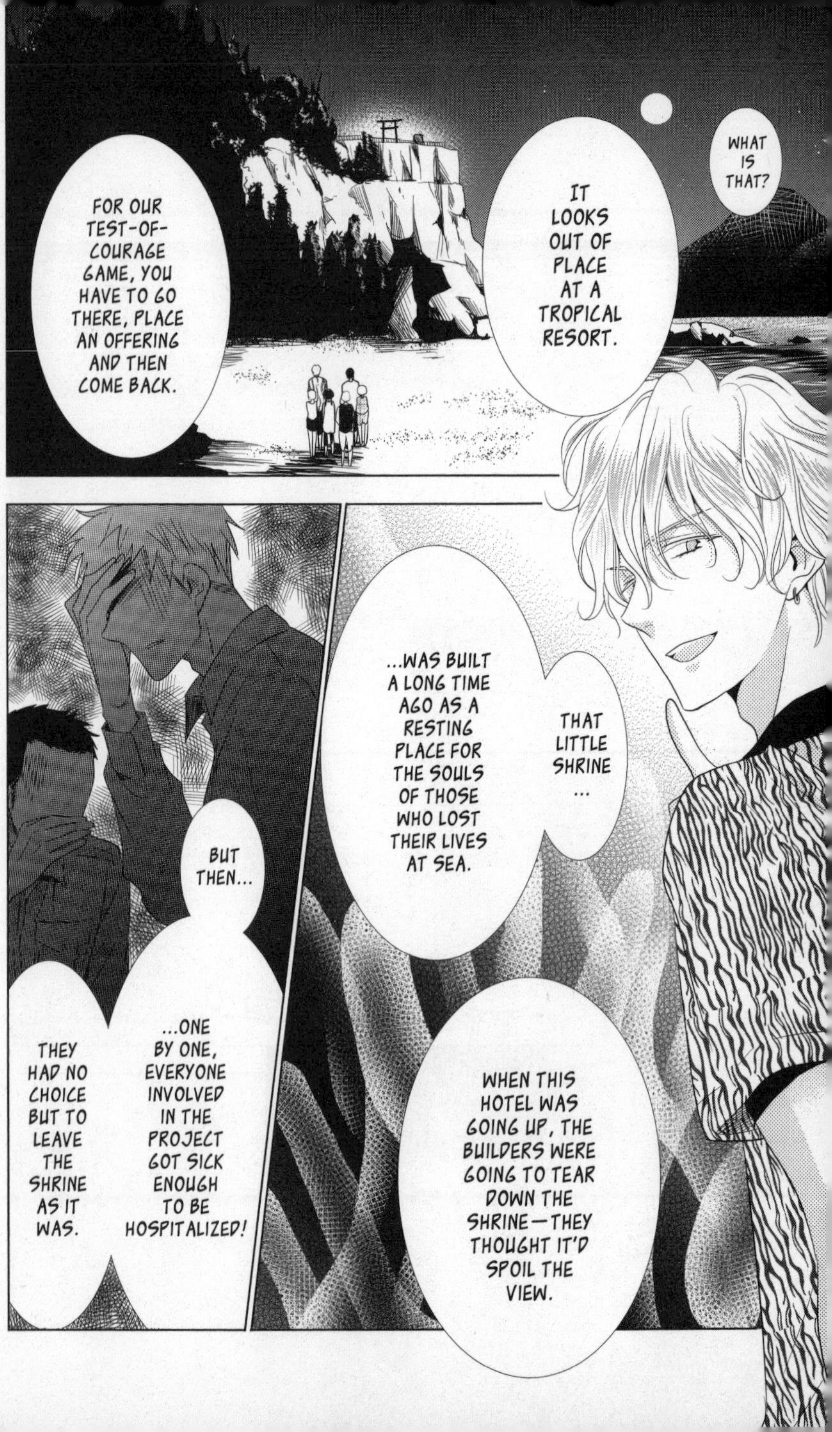
WHAT IS THAT?
IT LOOKS OUT OF PLACE AT A TROPICAL RESORT.
FOR OUR TEST-OF-COURAGE GAME, YOU HAVE TO GO THERE, PLACE AN OFFERING AND THEN COME BACK.
THAT LITTLE SHRINE ...
...WAS BUILT A LONG TIME AGO AS A RESTING PLACE FOR THE SOULS OF THOSE WHO LOST THEIR LIVES AT SEA.
WHEN THIS HOTEL WAS GOING UP, THE BUILDERS WERE GOING TO TEAR DOWN THE SHRINE—THEY THOUGHT IT'D SPOIL THE VIEW.
BUT THEN...
...ONE BY ONE, EVERYONE INVOLVED IN THE PROJECT GOT SICK ENOUGH TO BE HOSPITALIZED!
THEY HAD NO CHOICE BUT TO LEAVE THE SHRINE AS IT WAS.

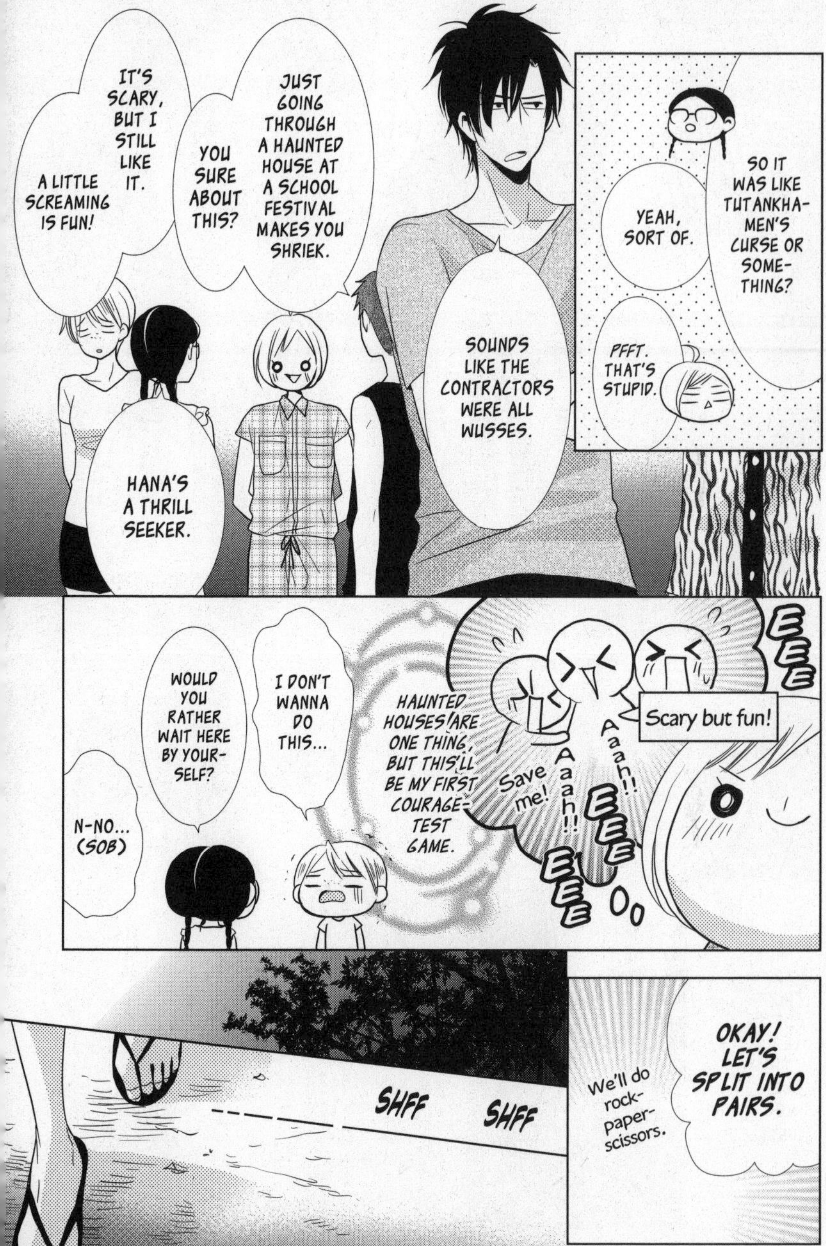

So it was like Tutankhamen's curse or something?
Yeah, sort of.
Pfft. That's stupid.
Sounds like the contractors were all wusses.
Just going through a haunted house at a school festival makes you shriek.
You sure about this?
It's scary, but I still like it.
A little screaming is fun!
Hana's a thrill seeker.
EEE
Scary but fun!
Aaaah!!
Save me!
Aaah!!
EEE
EEE
OO
Haunted houses are one thing, but this'll be my first courage-test game.
I don't wanna do this...
Would you rather wait here by yourself?
N-no... (sob)
Okay! Let's split into pairs.
We'll do rock-paper-scissors.
SHFF
SHFF

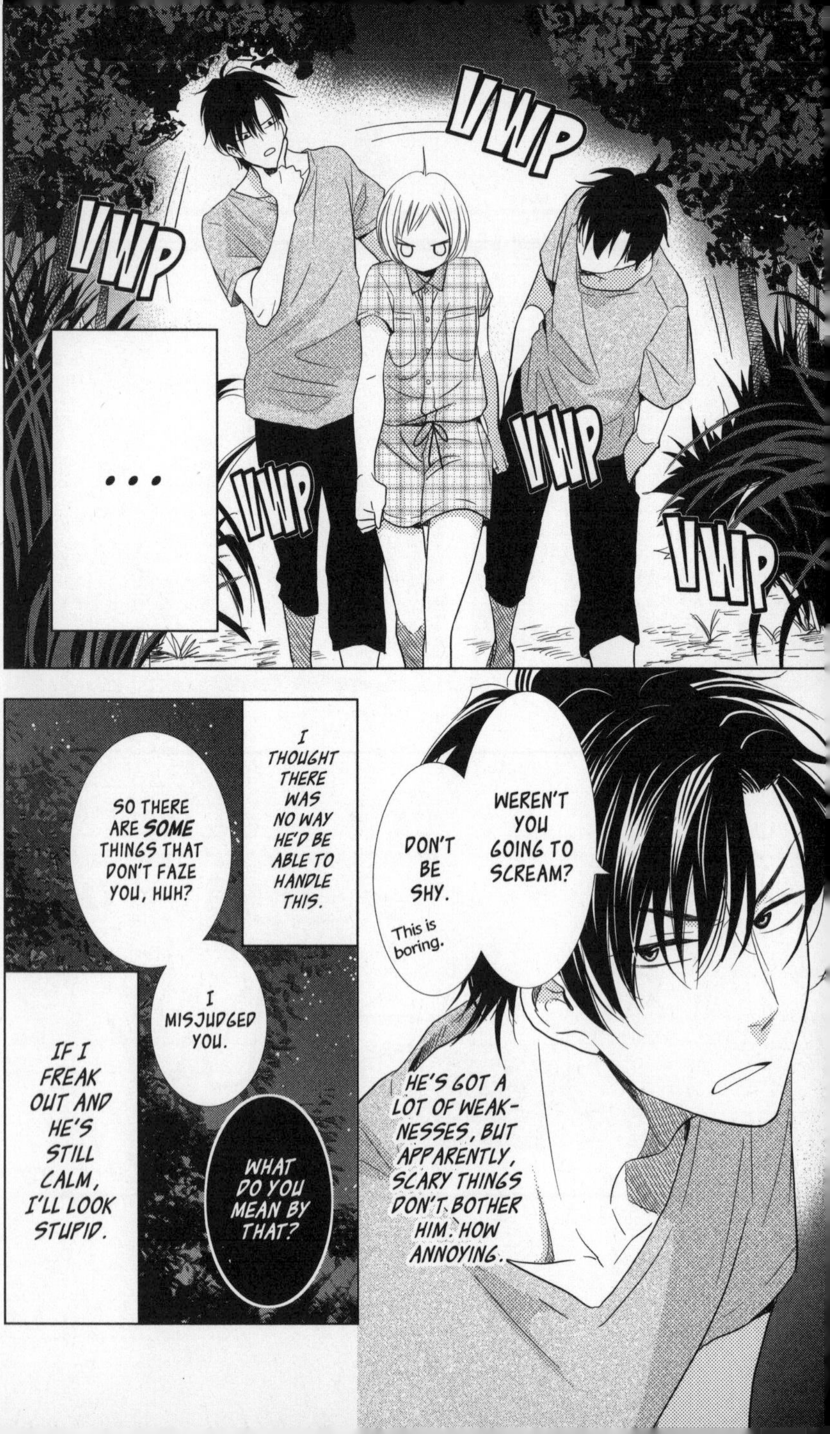
VWP
VWP
VWP
VWP
VWP
...
WEREN'T YOU GOING TO SCREAM?
DON'T BE SHY.
This is boring.
HE'S GOT A LOT OF WEAKNESSES, BUT APPARENTLY, SCARY THINGS DON'T BOTHER HIM. HOW ANNOYING.
I THOUGHT THERE WAS NO WAY HE'D BE ABLE TO HANDLE THIS.
SO THERE ARE **SOME** THINGS THAT DON'T FAZE YOU, HUH?
I MISJUDGED YOU.
WHAT DO YOU MEAN BY THAT?
IF I FREAK OUT AND HE'S STILL CALM, I'LL LOOK STUPID.

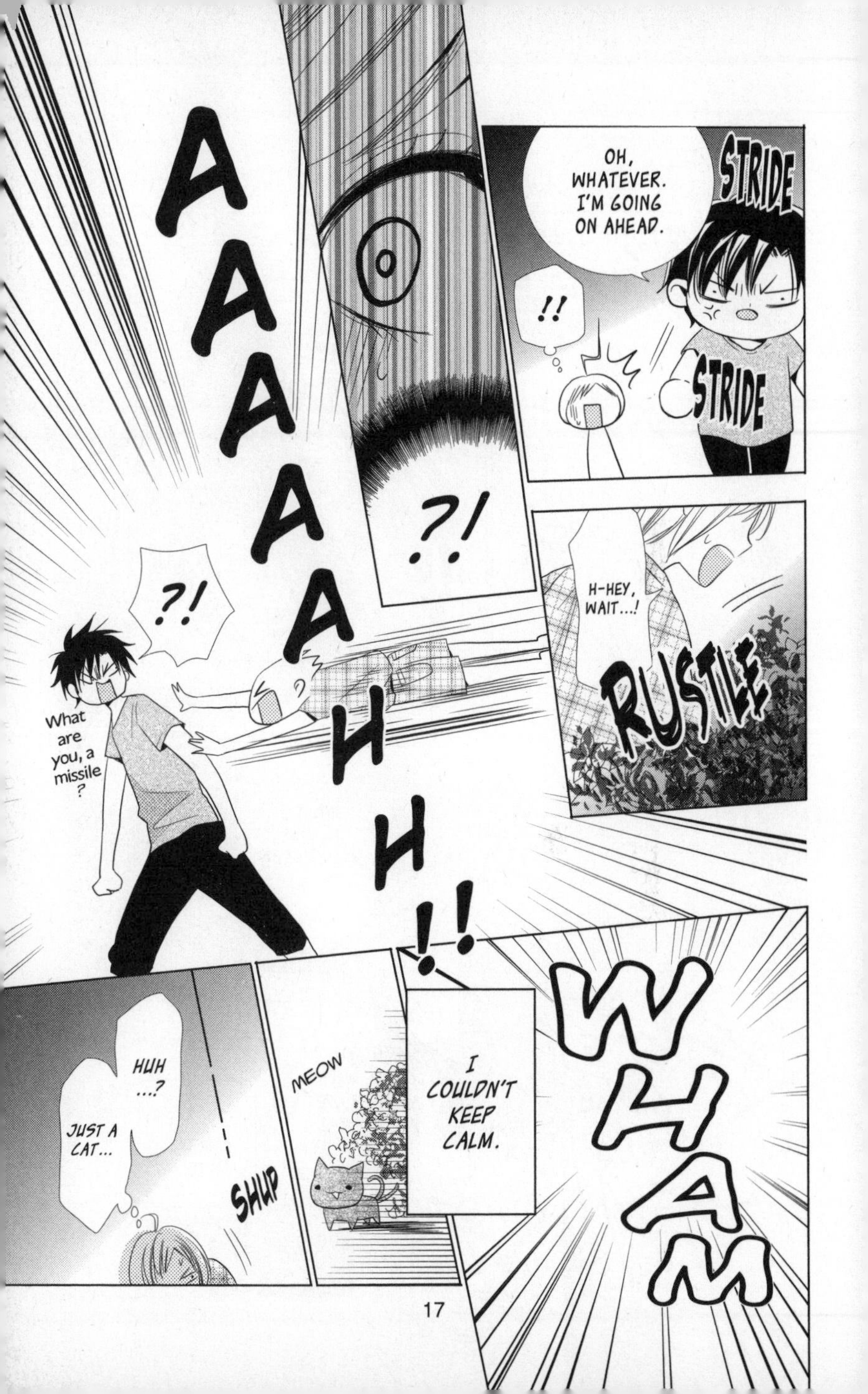

STRIDE
OH, WHATEVER. I'M GOING ON AHEAD.
!!
STRIDE
H-HEY, WAIT...!
RUSTLE
?!
AAAAHH!!
?!
What are you, a missile?
WHAM
I COULDN'T KEEP CALM.
MEOW
SHUP
HUH...?
JUST A CAT...

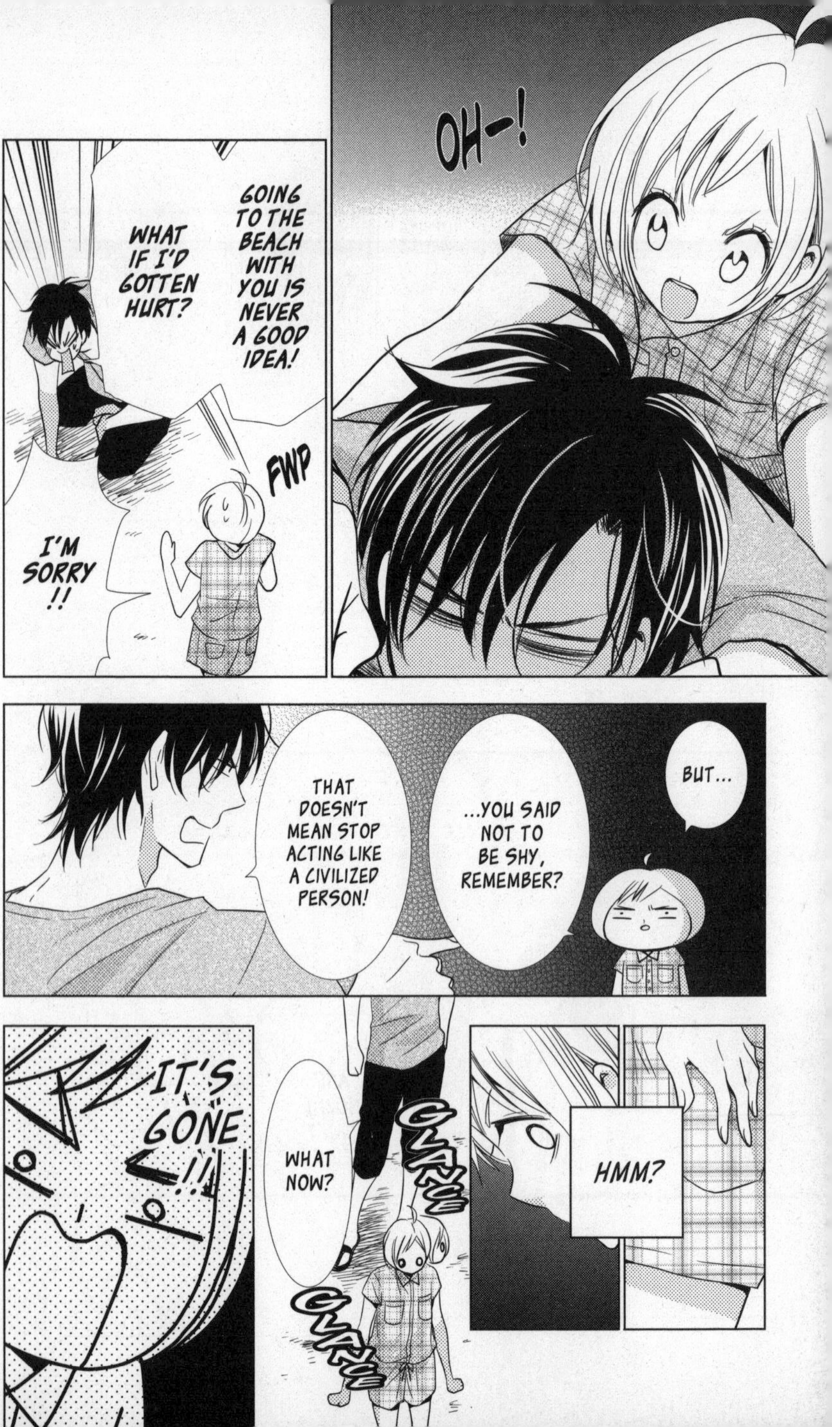
OH—!
GOING TO THE BEACH WITH YOU IS NEVER A GOOD IDEA!
WHAT IF I'D GOTTEN HURT?
FWP
I'M SORRY!!
BUT...
...YOU SAID NOT TO BE SHY, REMEMBER?
THAT DOESN'T MEAN STOP ACTING LIKE A CIVILIZED PERSON!
HMM?
WHAT NOW?
IT'S GONE!!

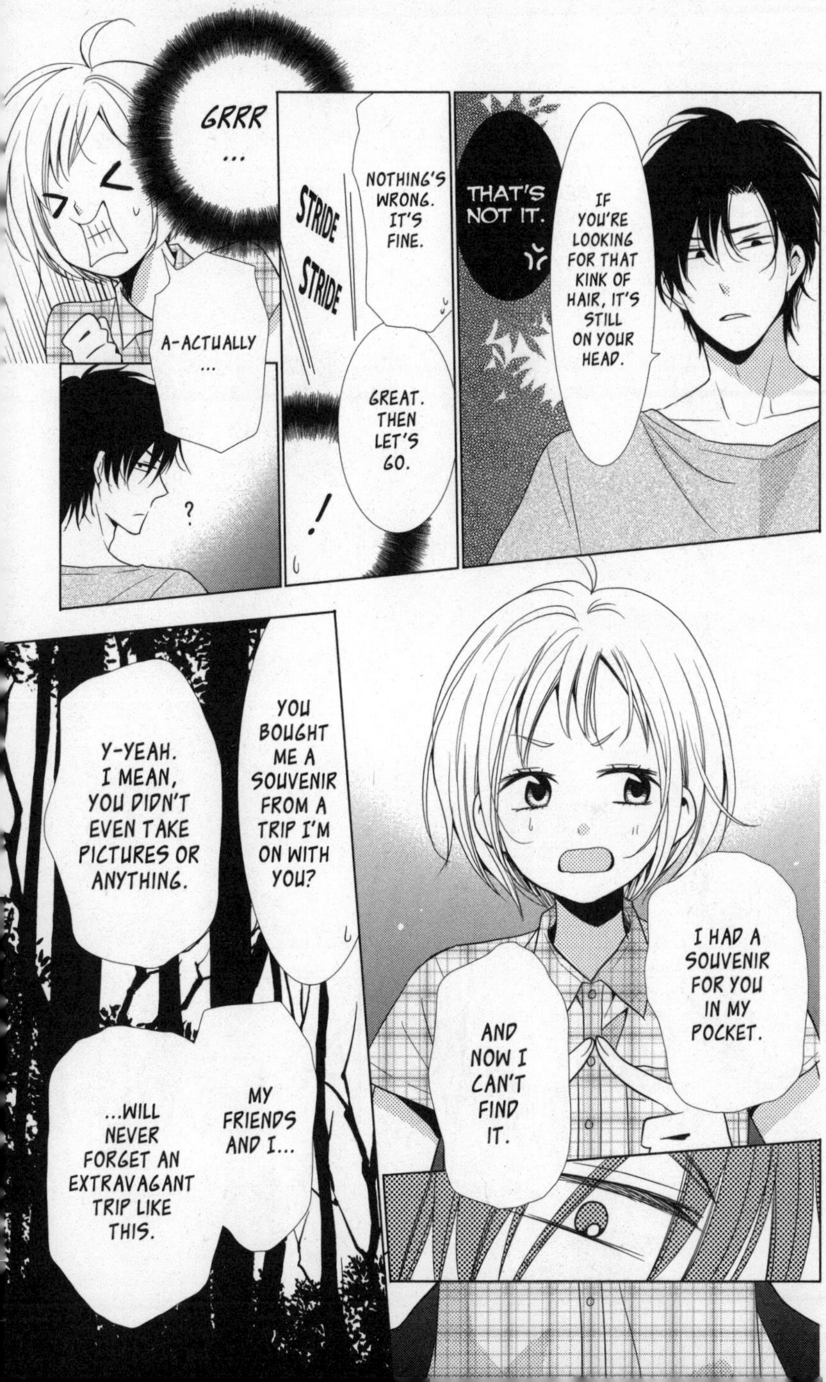
IF YOU'RE LOOKING FOR THAT KINK OF HAIR, IT'S STILL ON YOUR HEAD.
THAT'S NOT IT.
NOTHING'S WRONG. IT'S FINE.
STRIDE
STRIDE
GREAT. THEN LET'S GO.
!
GRRR ...
A-ACTUALLY ...
?
I HAD A SOUVENIR FOR YOU IN MY POCKET.
AND NOW I CAN'T FIND IT.
YOU BOUGHT ME A SOUVENIR FROM A TRIP I'M ON WITH YOU?
Y-YEAH. I MEAN, YOU DIDN'T EVEN TAKE PICTURES OR ANYTHING.
MY FRIENDS AND I...
...WILL NEVER FORGET AN EXTRAVAGANT TRIP LIKE THIS.

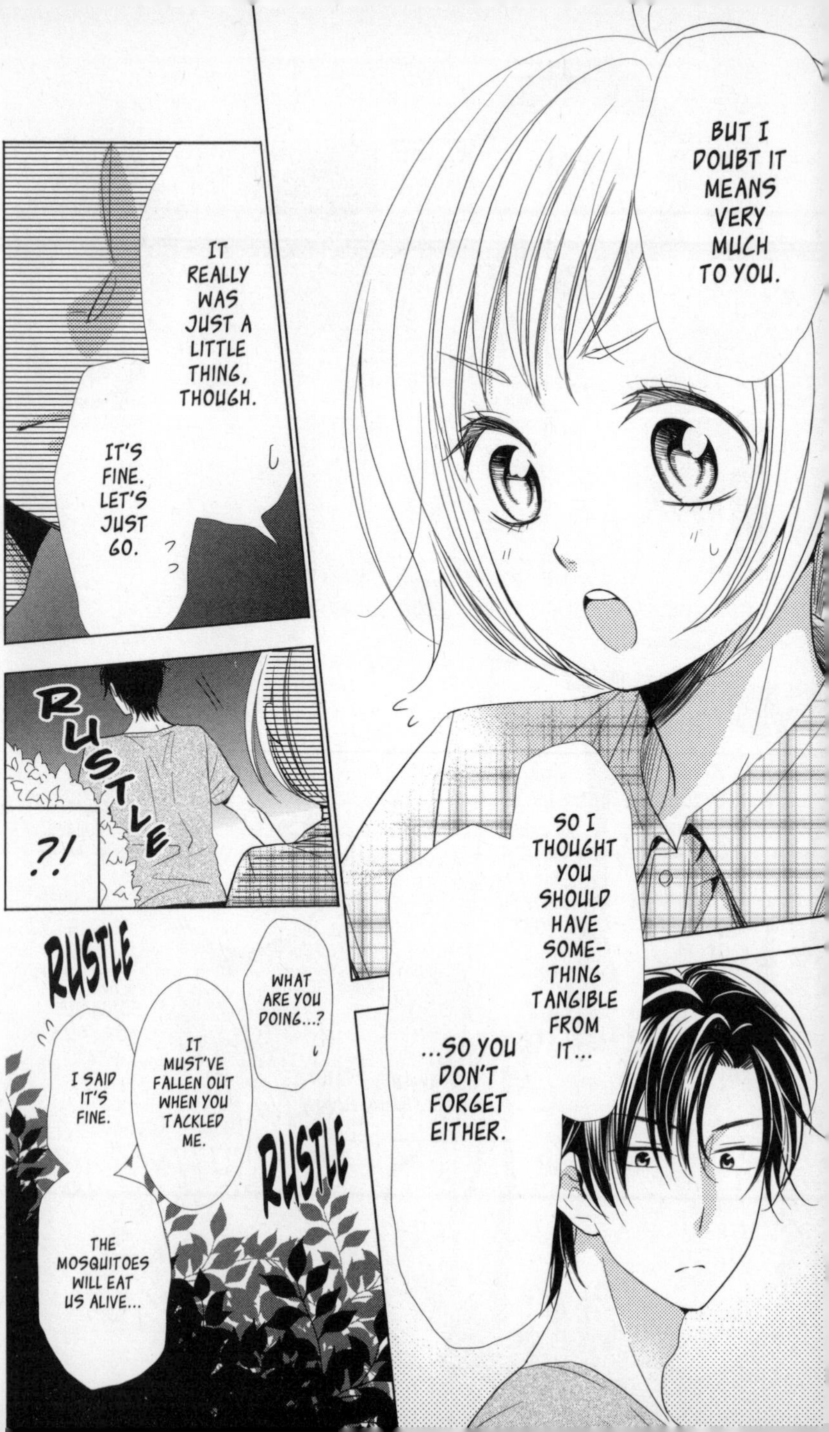
BUT I DOUBT IT MEANS VERY MUCH TO YOU.
SO I THOUGHT YOU SHOULD HAVE SOME-THING TANGIBLE FROM IT...
...SO YOU DON'T FORGET EITHER.
IT REALLY WAS JUST A LITTLE THING, THOUGH.
IT'S FINE. LET'S JUST GO.
RUSTLE
?!
RUSTLE
WHAT ARE YOU DOING...?
IT MUST'VE FALLEN OUT WHEN YOU TACKLED ME.
RUSTLE
I SAID IT'S FINE.
THE MOSQUITOES WILL EAT US ALIVE...

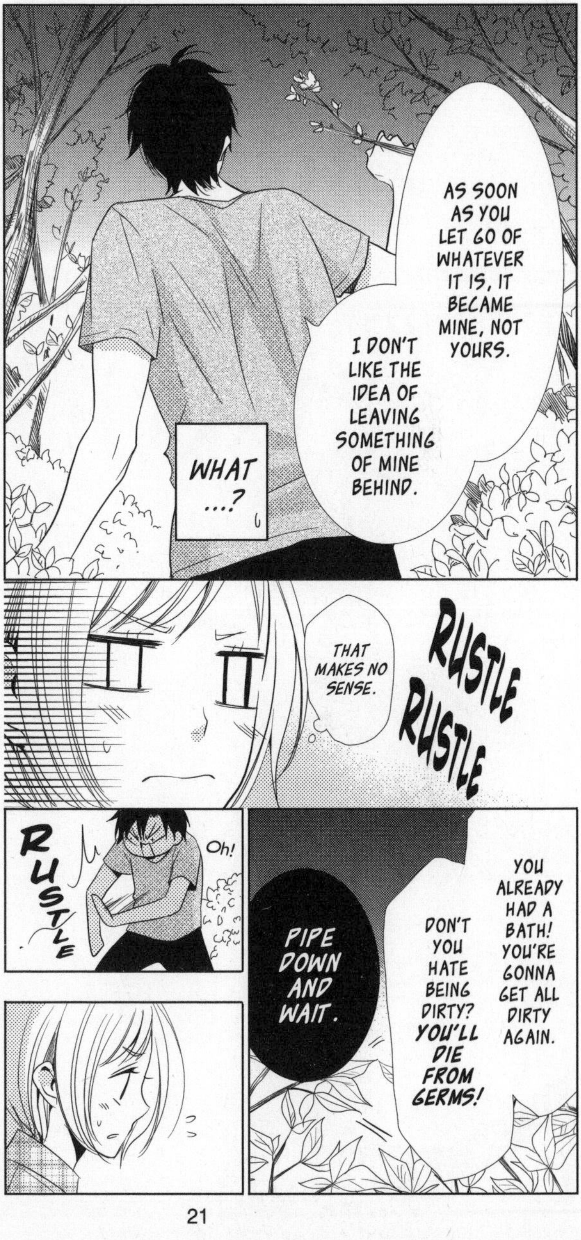
AS SOON AS YOU LET GO OF WHATEVER IT IS, IT BECAME MINE, NOT YOURS.
I DON'T LIKE THE IDEA OF LEAVING SOMETHING OF MINE BEHIND.
WHAT ...?
RUSTLE RUSTLE
THAT MAKES NO SENSE.
YOU ALREADY HAD A BATH! YOU'RE GONNA GET ALL DIRTY AGAIN.
DON'T YOU HATE BEING DIRTY? YOU'LL DIE FROM GERMS!
PIPE DOWN AND WAIT.
Oh!
RUSTLE

• Drama CD Bonus Track •

Fans who buy this series in compiled volumes may not know that the September 2015 issue of *Hana to Yume* came with a free drama CD bonus track! The CD included the first-ever audio track of *Takane & Hana*!

~ Cast ~
Hana: Yurika Kubo
Takane: Kazuyuki Okitsu

The wonderful cast, sound director and other staff members created a fun, powerful track that's definitely worth a listen. I attended the recording session, and I was blown away by the talent these professionals brought to the table.

The drama CD highlights the second chapter of the series. But in addition to that, there was a bonus track that used a dummy head mic. The concept behind the bonus track was "Takane whispering in your ear." The color frontispiece of chapter 17 was drawn with that in mind.

The idea is that you, the listener, are sleeping in the passenger seat and Takane's whispering in your ear.

"Come on, just say, 'You're so cool, Takane!' Say that and I'll buy you all the sukiyaki you can eat."

So...he's trying to brainwash you.

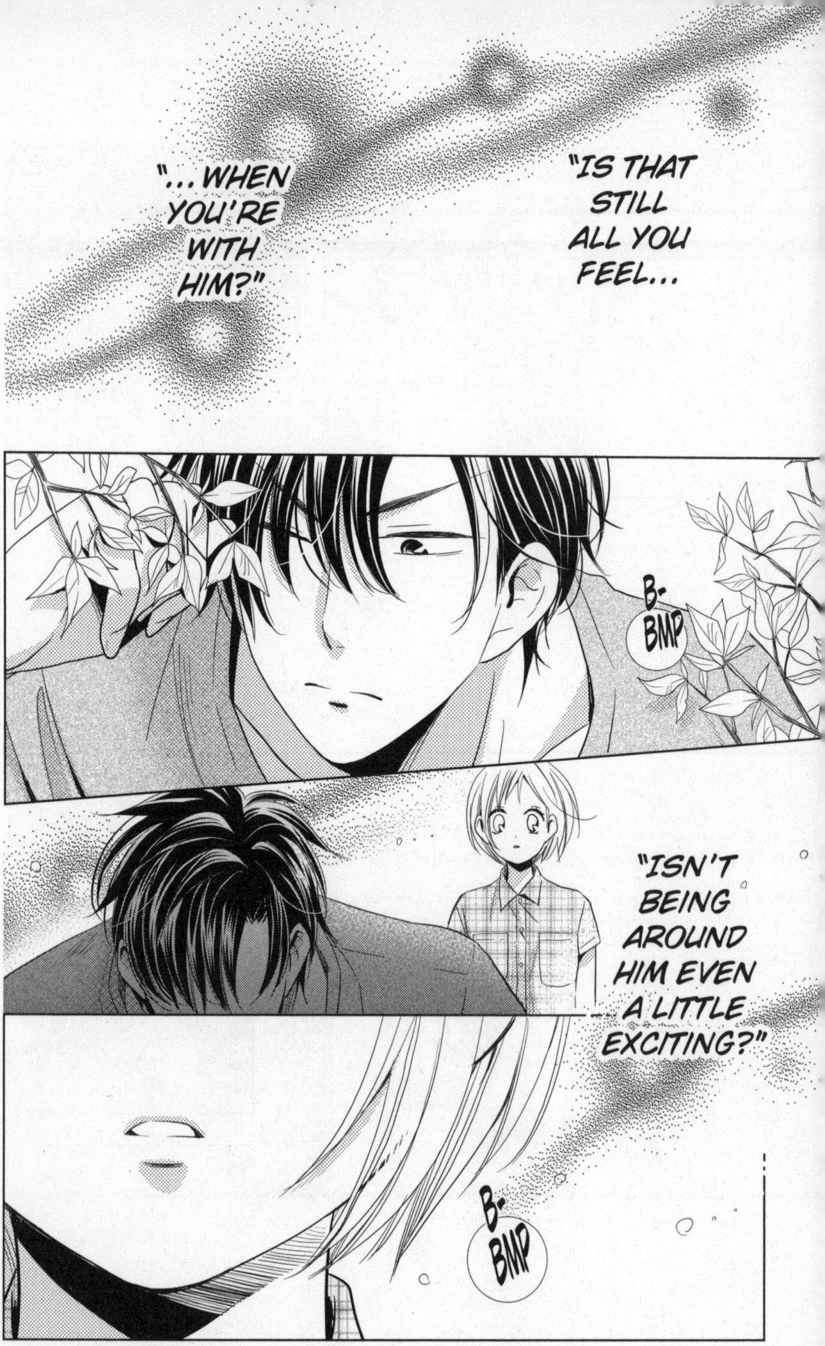
"IS THAT STILL ALL YOU FEEL...
"...WHEN YOU'RE WITH HIM?"
B-BMP
"ISN'T BEING AROUND HIM EVEN A LITTLE EXCITING?"
B-BMP

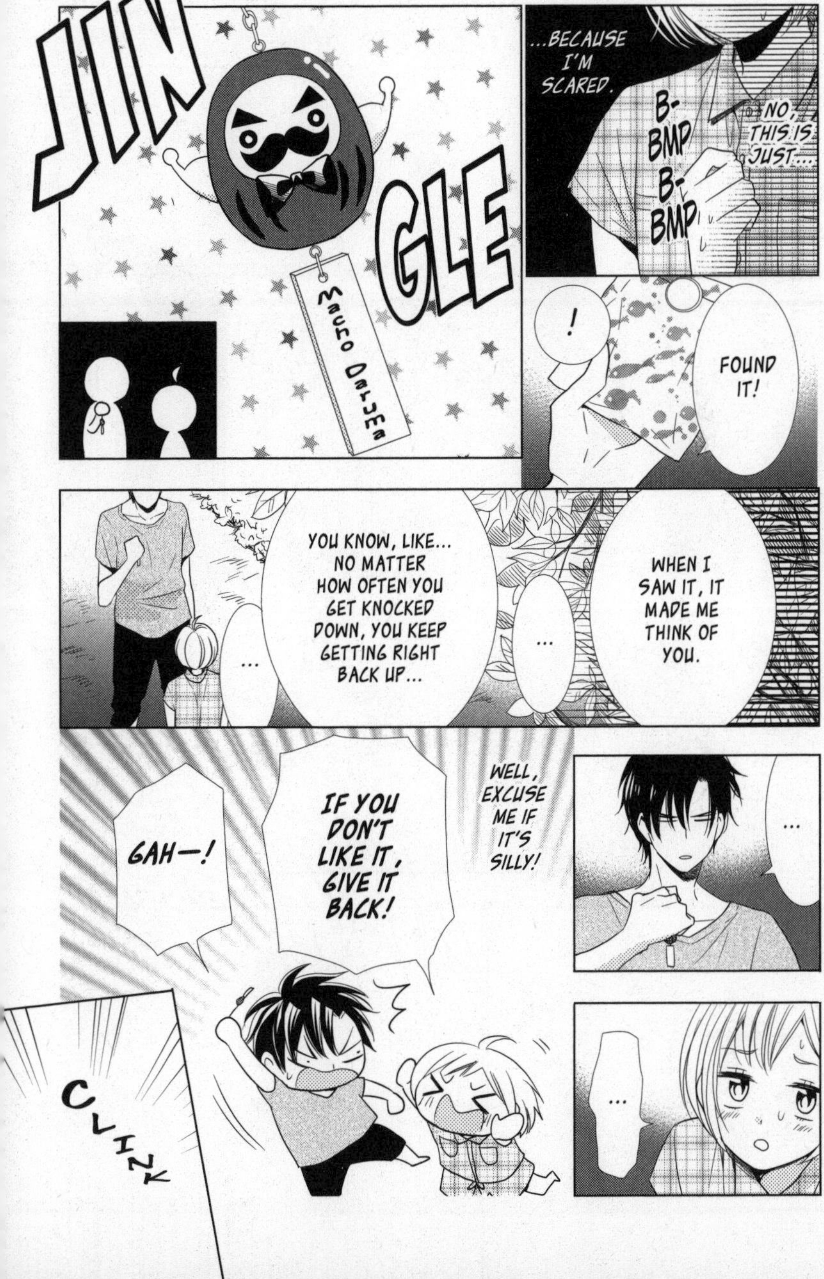
...BECAUSE I'M SCARED.
B-BMP B-BMP
NO, THIS IS JUST...
!
FOUND IT!
JINGLE
Macho Daruma
WHEN I SAW IT, IT MADE ME THINK OF YOU.
...
YOU KNOW, LIKE... NO MATTER HOW OFTEN YOU GET KNOCKED DOWN, YOU KEEP GETTING RIGHT BACK UP...
...
...
WELL, EXCUSE ME IF IT'S SILLY!
...
IF YOU DON'T LIKE IT, GIVE IT BACK!
GAH—!
CLINK

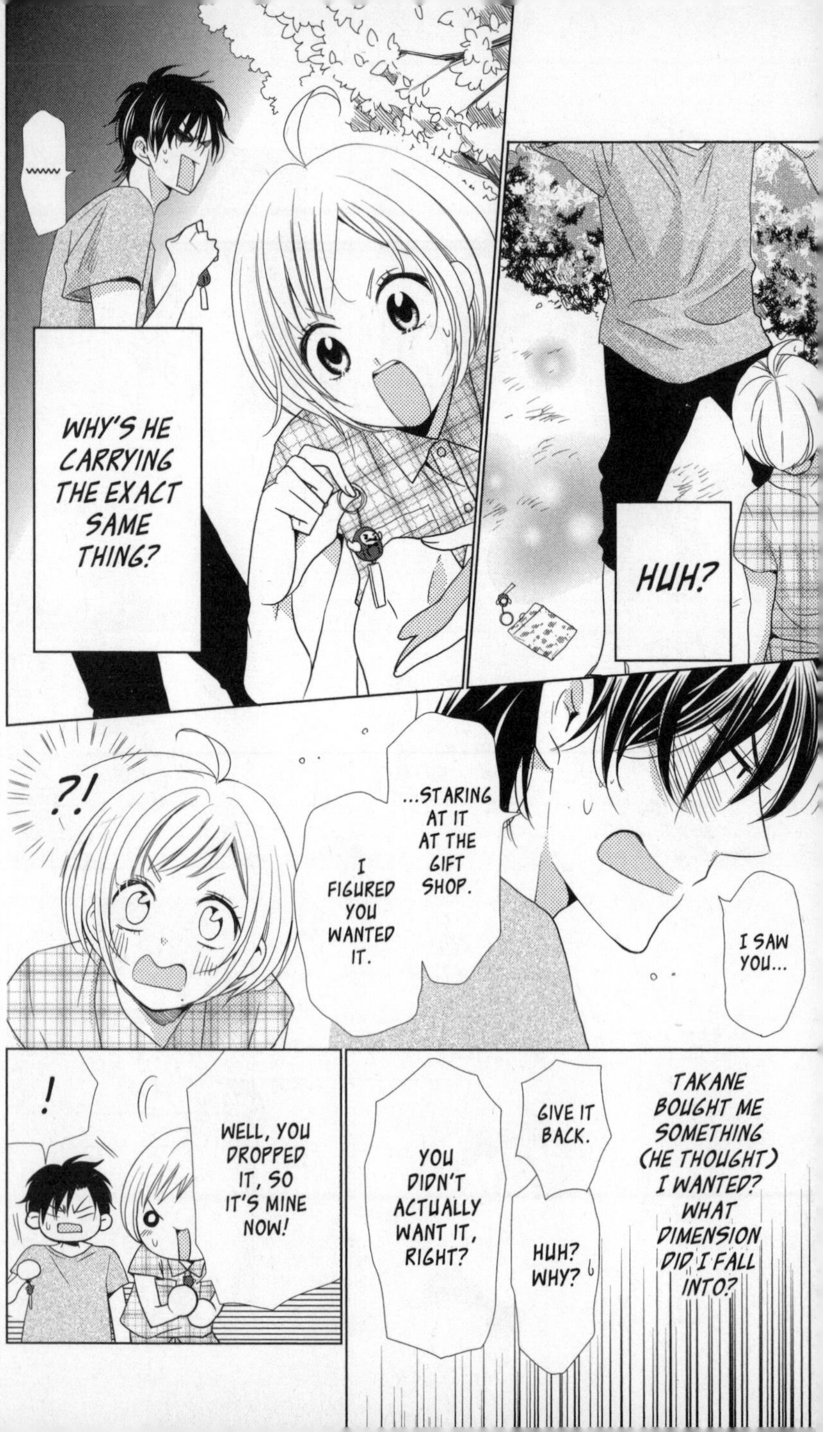
HUH?
WHY'S HE CARRYING THE EXACT SAME THING?
I SAW YOU...
...STARING AT IT AT THE GIFT SHOP.
I FIGURED YOU WANTED IT.
?!
TAKANE BOUGHT ME SOMETHING (HE THOUGHT) I WANTED? WHAT DIMENSION DID I FALL INTO?
GIVE IT BACK.
HUH? WHY?
YOU DIDN'T ACTUALLY WANT IT, RIGHT?
WELL, YOU DROPPED IT, SO IT'S MINE NOW!
!

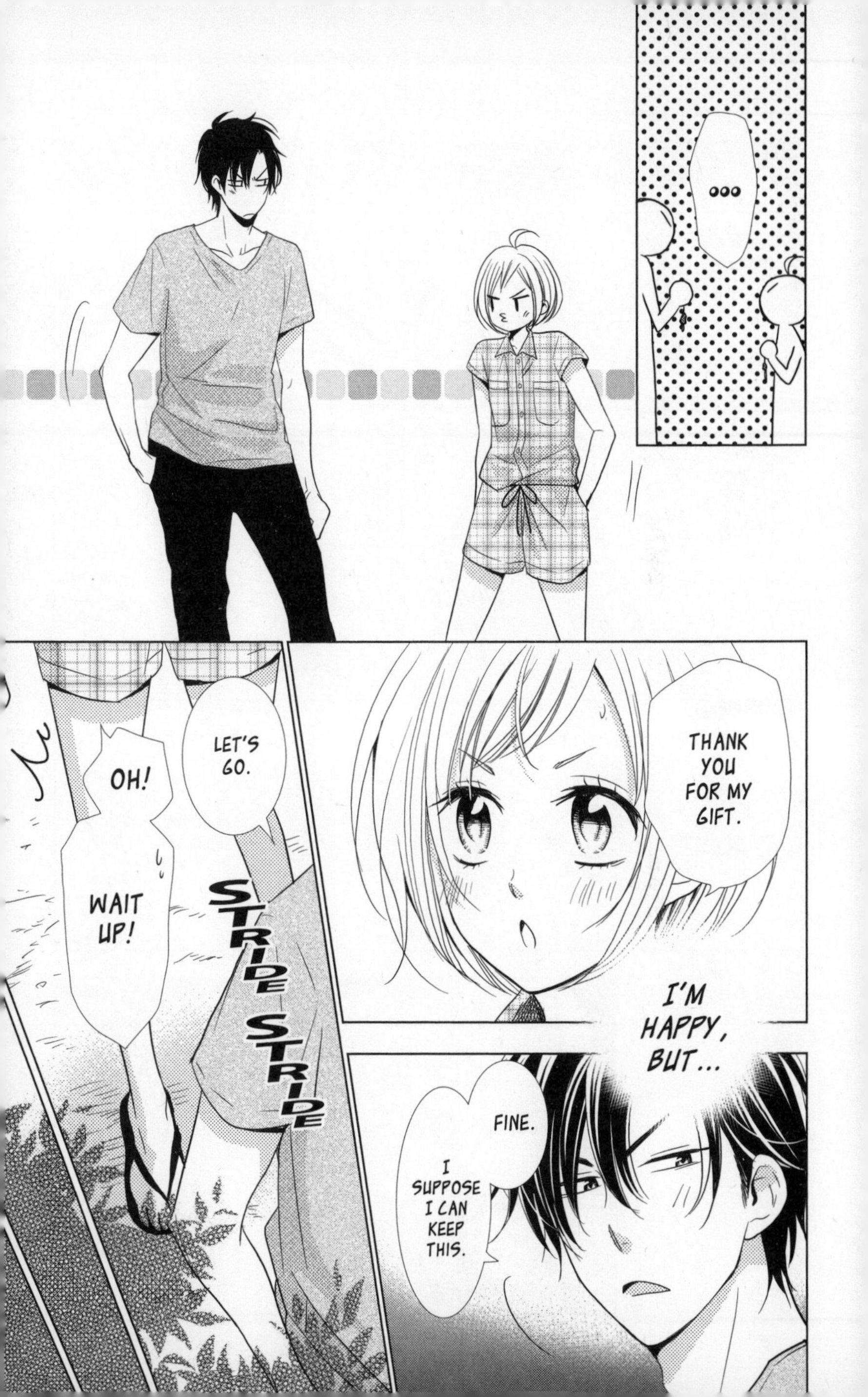
...
THANK YOU FOR MY GIFT.
I'M HAPPY, BUT...
FINE.
I SUPPOSE I CAN KEEP THIS.
LET'S GO.
OH!
WAIT UP!
STRIDE STRIDE

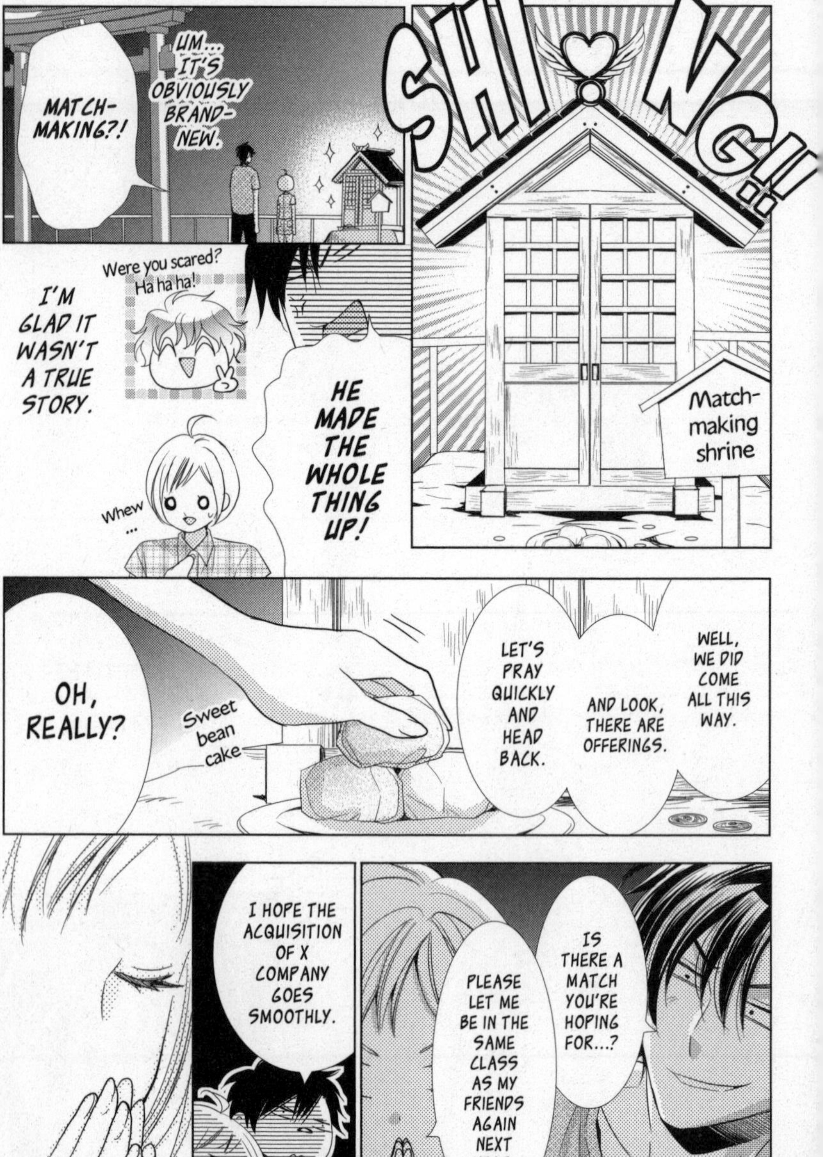
SHI♥NG!!
Match-making shrine
UM... IT'S OBVIOUSLY BRAND-NEW.
MATCH-MAKING?!
HE MADE THE WHOLE THING UP!
Were you scared? Ha ha ha!
I'M GLAD IT WASN'T A TRUE STORY.
Whew ...
WELL, WE DID COME ALL THIS WAY.
AND LOOK, THERE ARE OFFERINGS.
LET'S PRAY QUICKLY AND HEAD BACK.
Sweet bean cake
OH, REALLY?
IS THERE A MATCH YOU'RE HOPING FOR...?
PLEASE LET ME BE IN THE SAME CLASS AS MY FRIENDS AGAIN NEXT YEAR.
I HOPE THE ACQUISITION OF X COMPANY GOES SMOOTHLY.

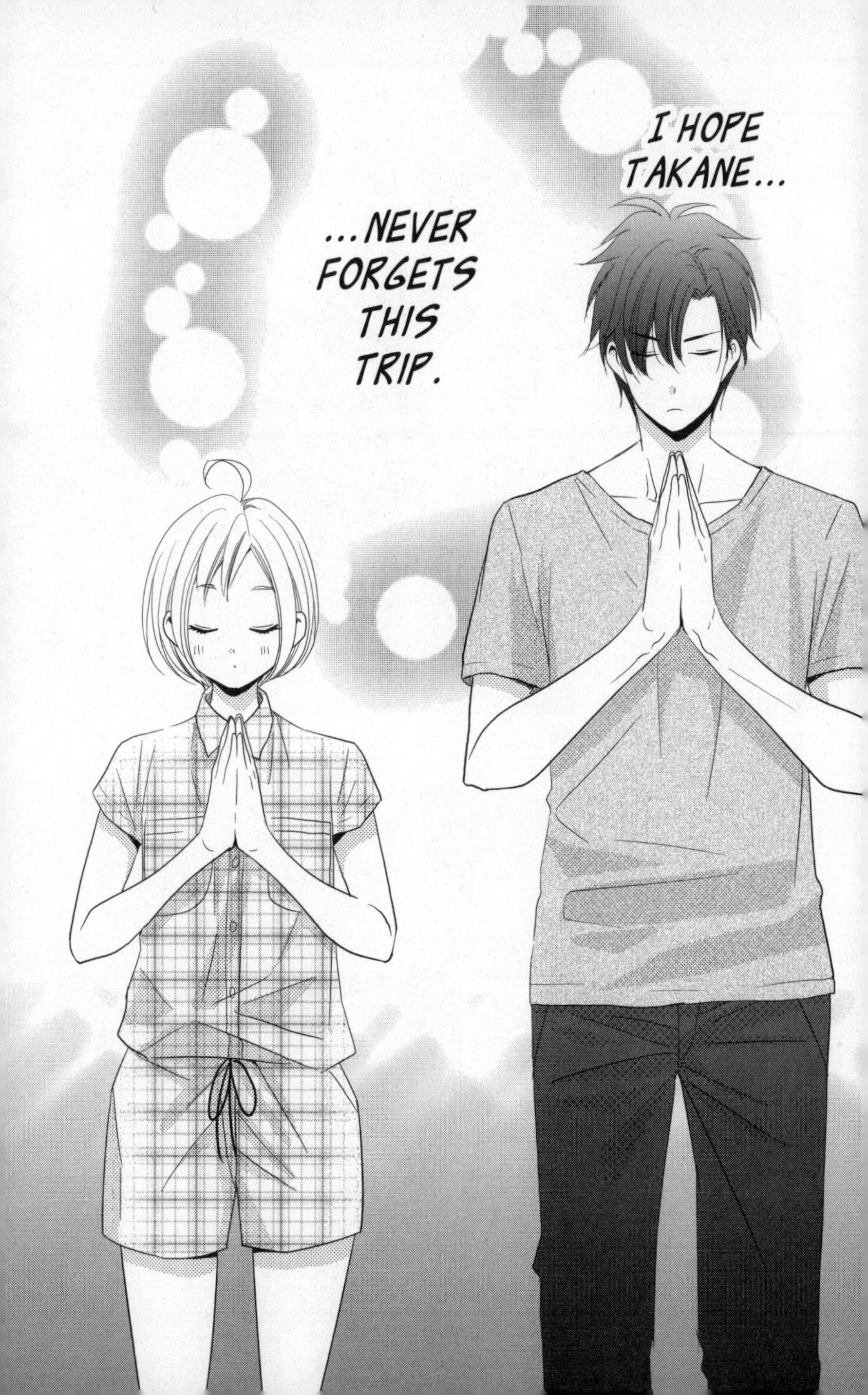
I HOPE TAKANE...
...NEVER FORGETS THIS TRIP.

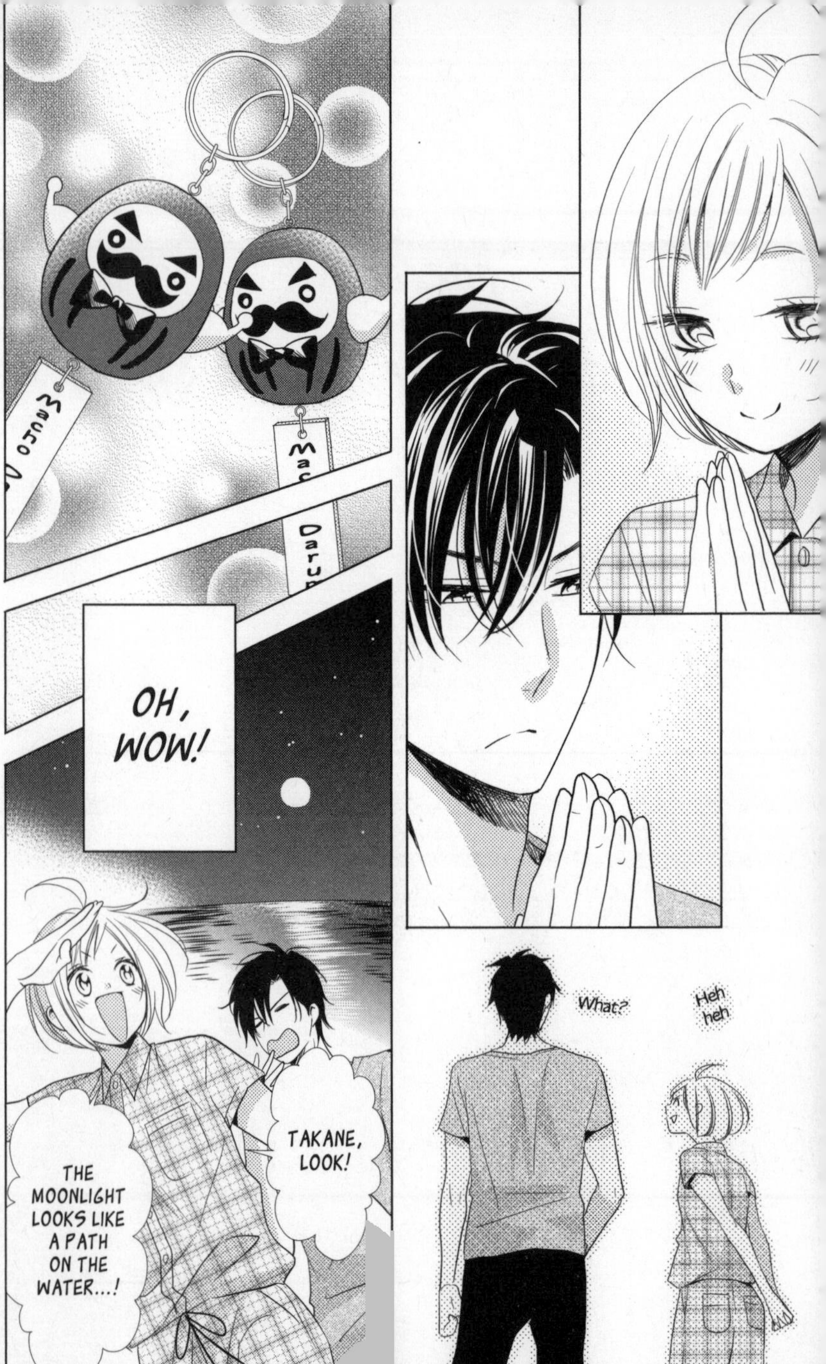
OH, WOW!
TAKANE, LOOK!
THE MOONLIGHT LOOKS LIKE A PATH ON THE WATER...!
What?
Heh heh

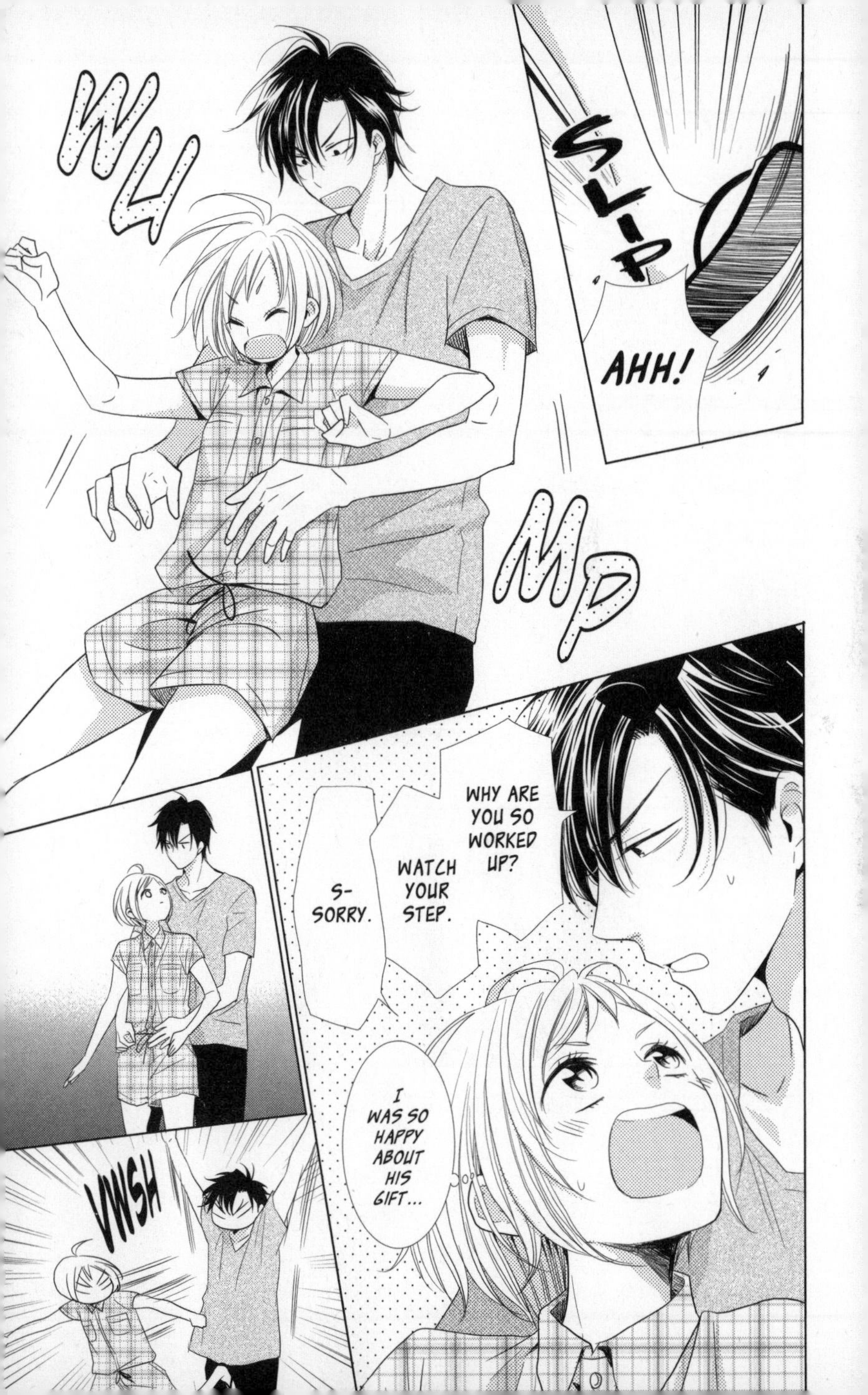
SLIP
AHH!
WU
MP
WHY ARE YOU SO WORKED UP?
WATCH YOUR STEP.
S-SORRY.
I WAS SO HAPPY ABOUT HIS GIFT...
VWSH

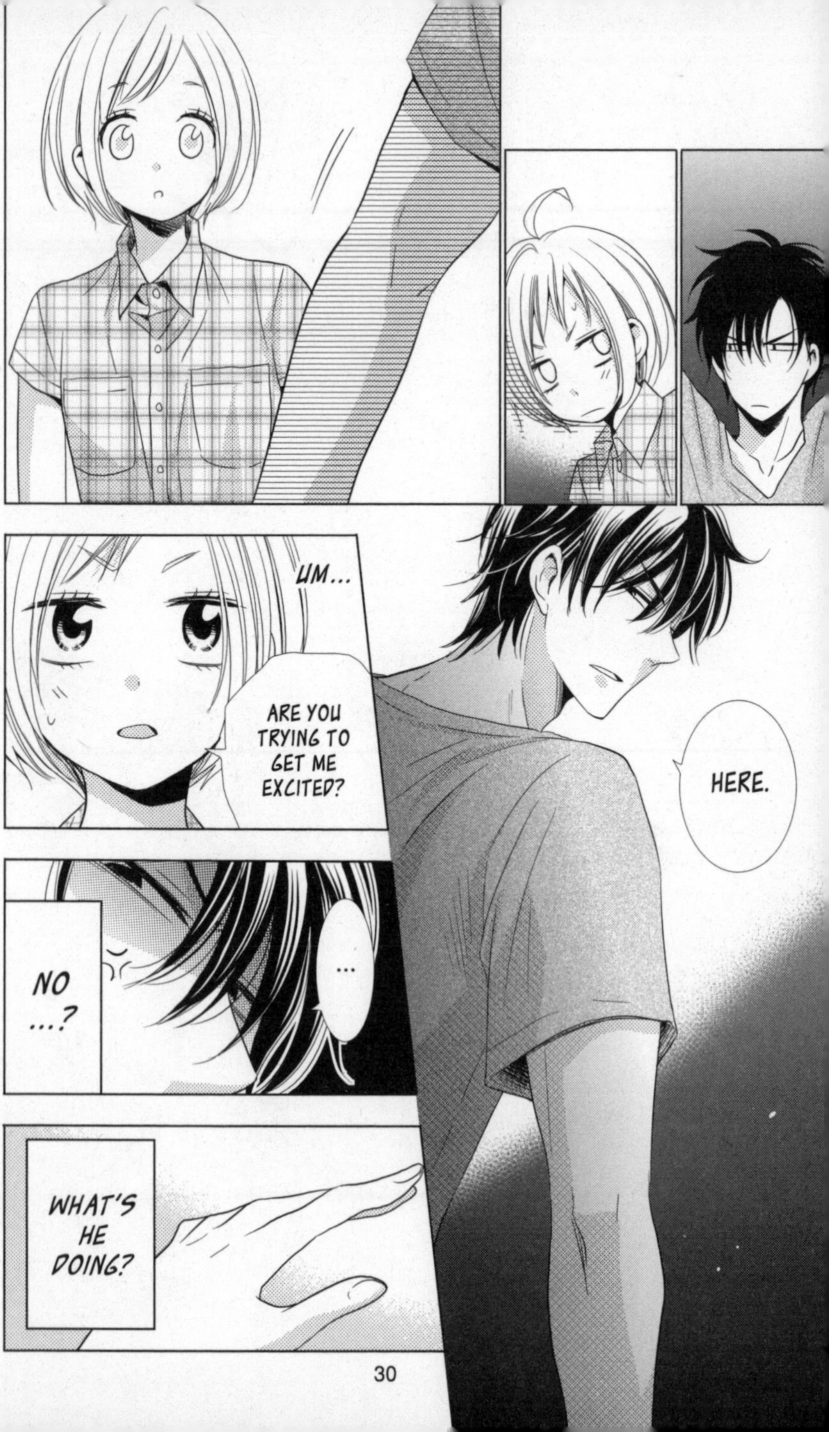
HERE.
UM...
ARE YOU TRYING TO GET ME EXCITED?
...
NO ...?
WHAT'S HE DOING?

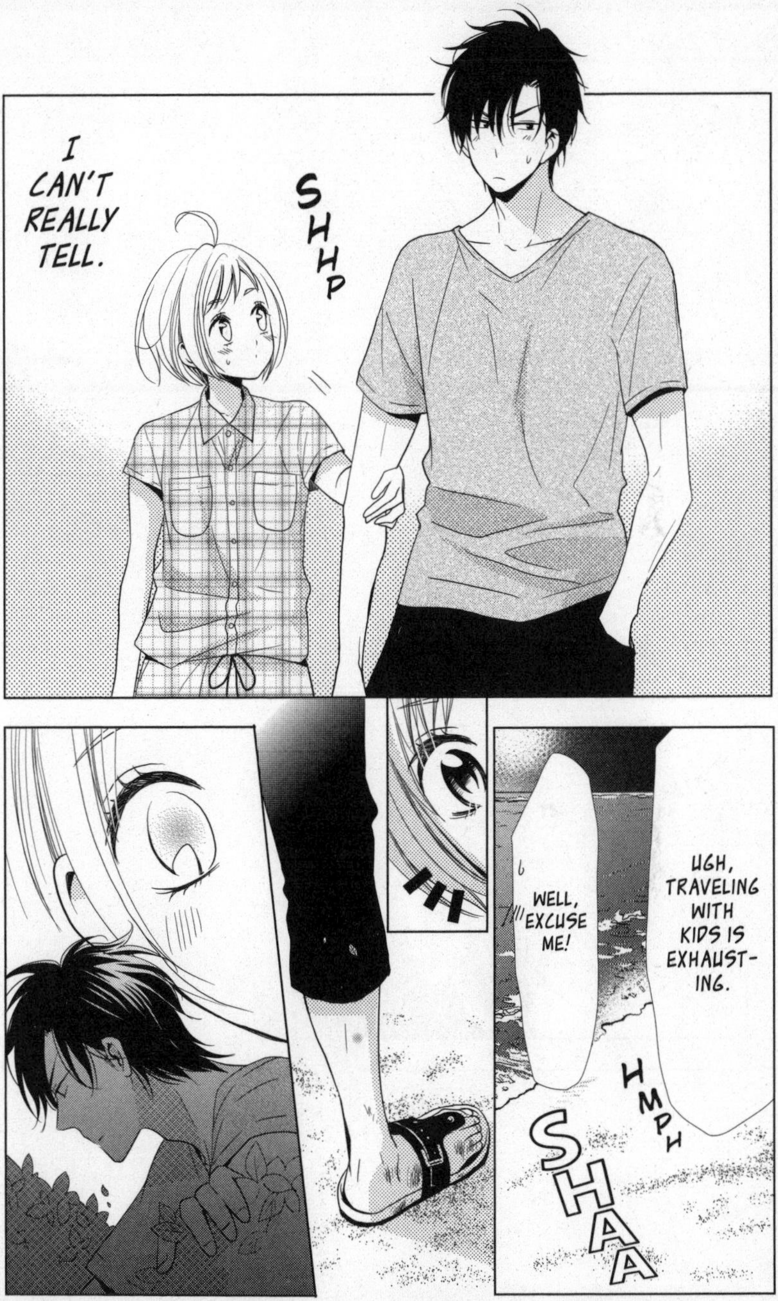
SHHP
I CAN'T REALLY TELL.
UGH, TRAVELING WITH KIDS IS EXHAUST-ING.
WELL, EXCUSE ME!
HMPH
SHAA

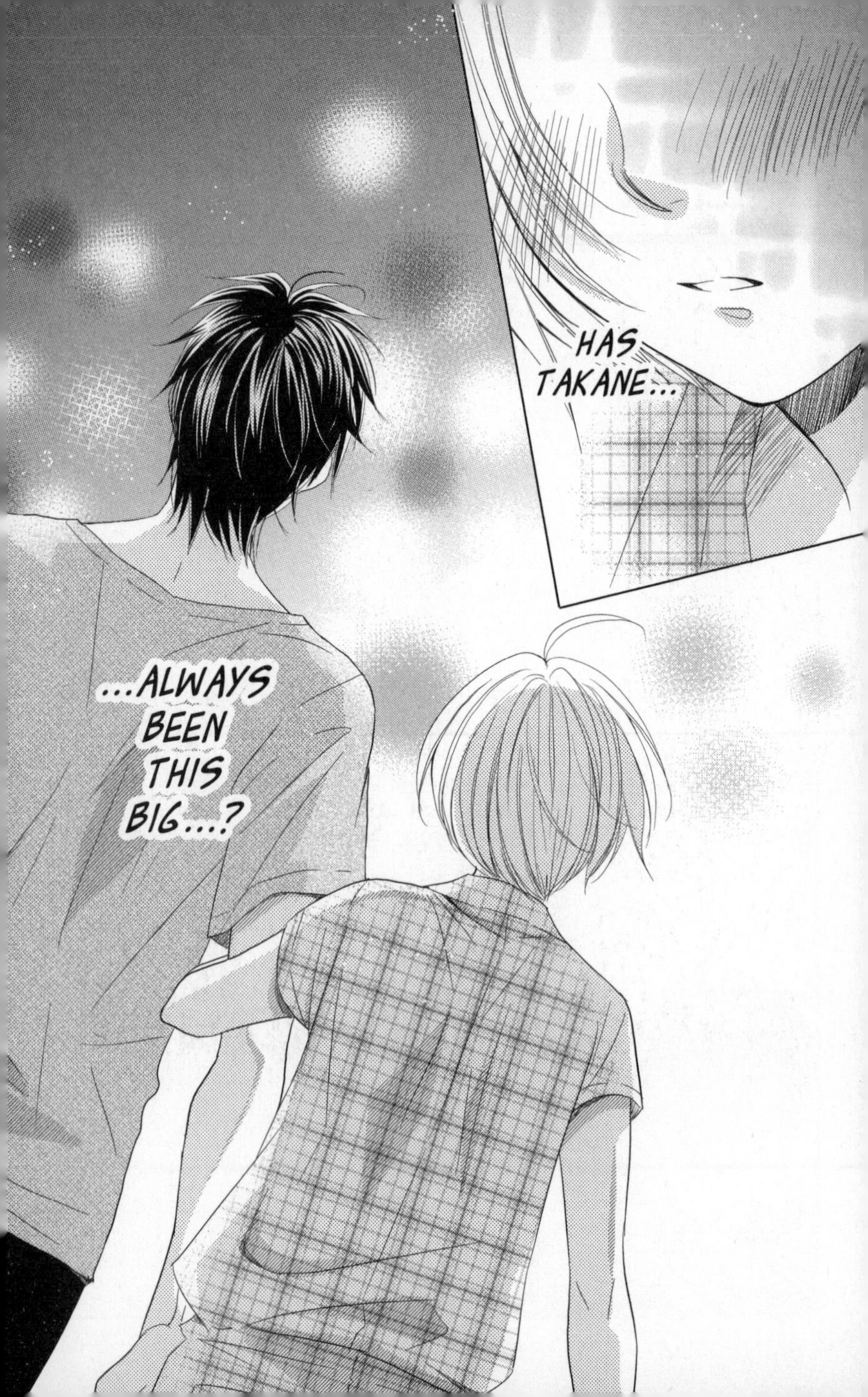
HAS TAKANE...
...ALWAYS BEEN THIS BIG...?

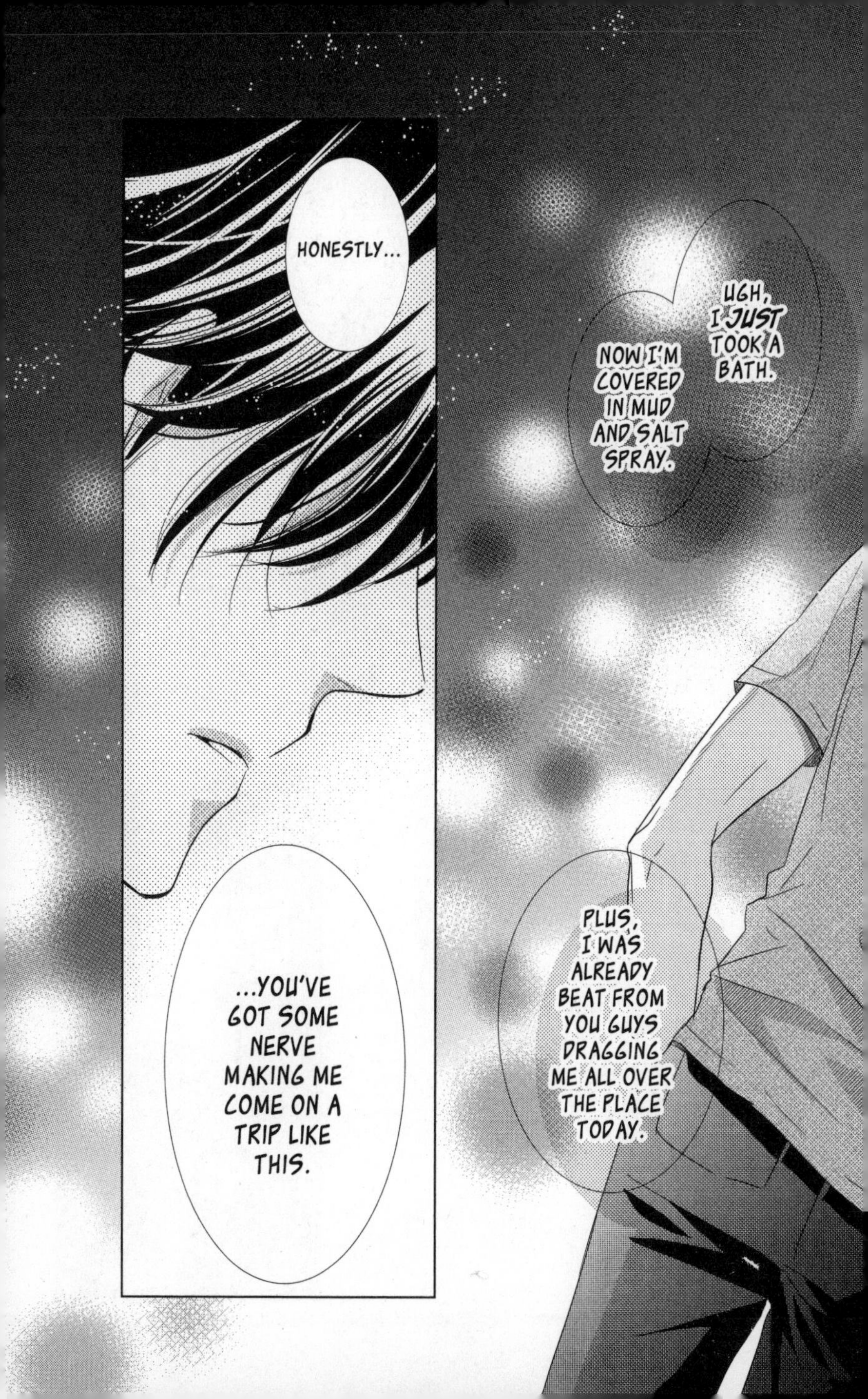
UGH, I JUST TOOK A BATH.
NOW I'M COVERED IN MUD AND SALT SPRAY.
PLUS, I WAS ALREADY BEAT FROM YOU GUYS DRAGGING ME ALL OVER THE PLACE TODAY.
HONESTLY...
...YOU'VE GOT SOME NERVE MAKING ME COME ON A TRIP LIKE THIS.

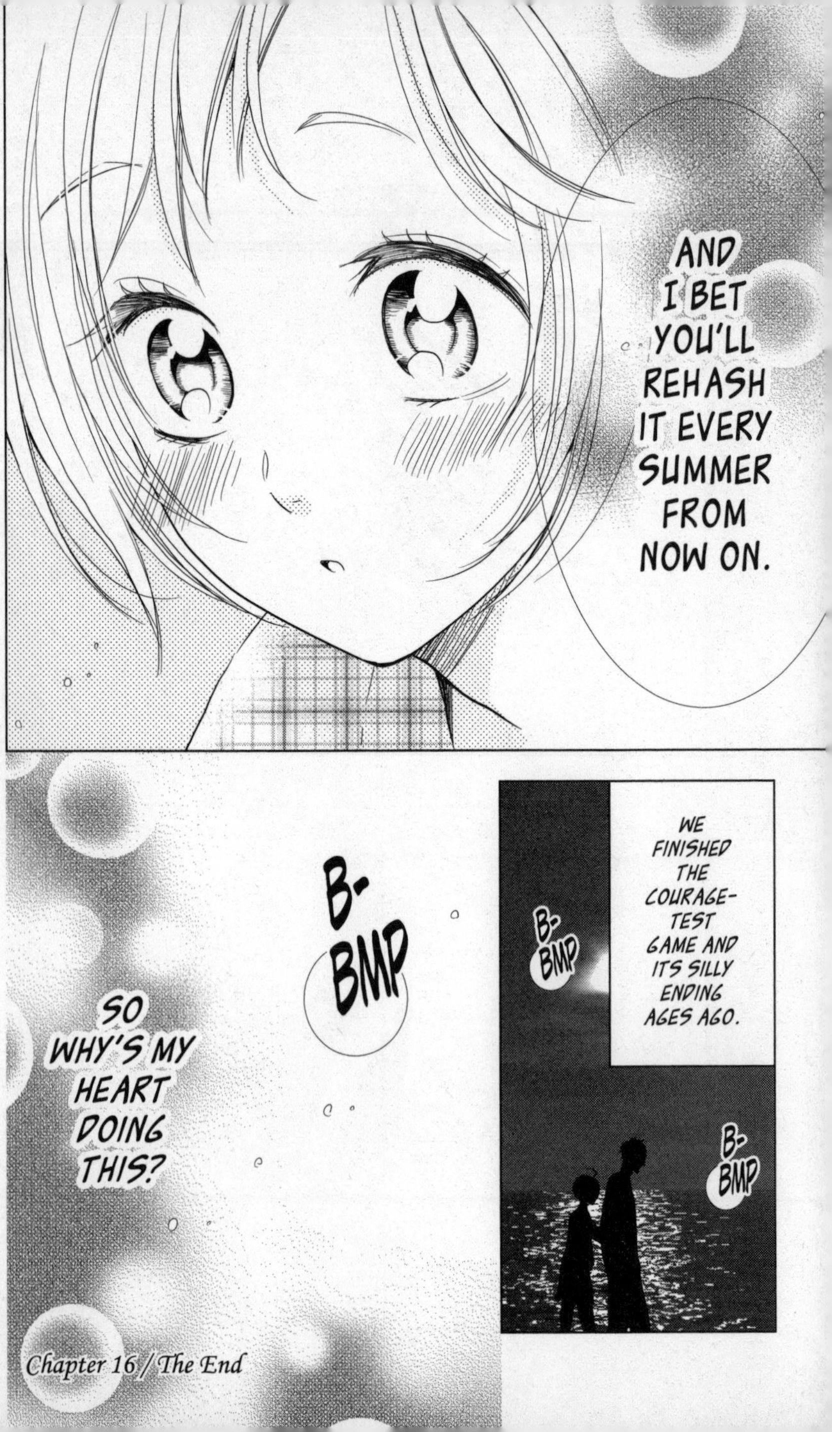
AND I BET YOU'LL REHASH IT EVERY SUMMER FROM NOW ON.
WE FINISHED THE COURAGE-TEST GAME AND ITS SILLY ENDING AGES AGO.
B-BMP
B-BMP
B-BMP
SO WHY'S MY HEART DOING THIS?

Chapter 16 / The End

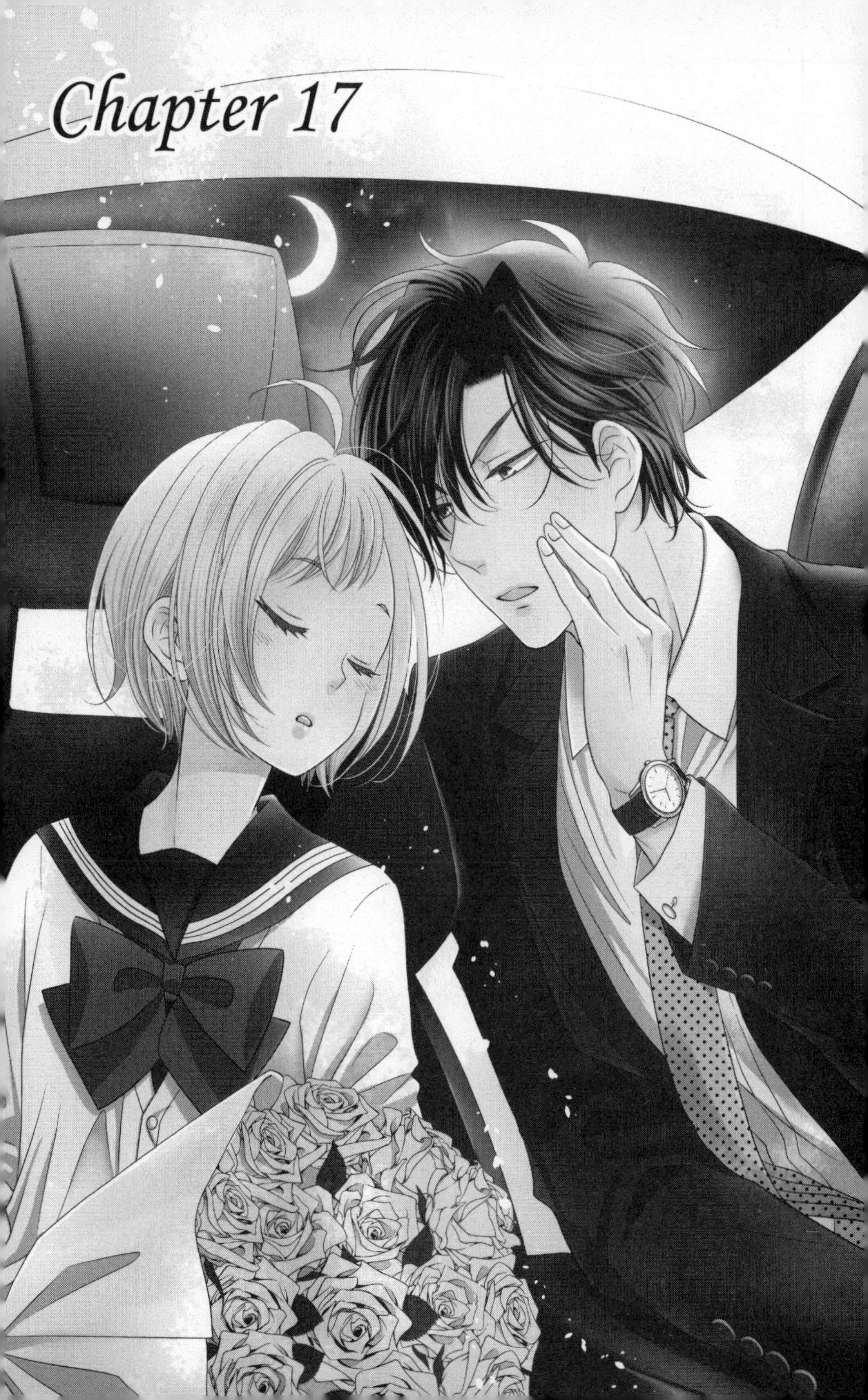
Chapter 17

Barrage

SCRUB SCRUB
SCRUB SCRUB
SCRUB SCRUB
WHAM
AAAAAHH!!
HAS TAKANE...
...ALWAYS BEEN THIS BIG?
THROB
UGH.
ZZZZT ZZZZT
MY BACK...

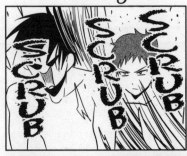

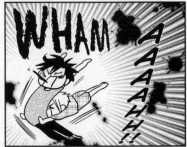

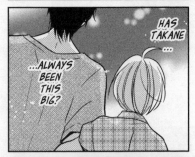

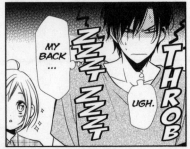

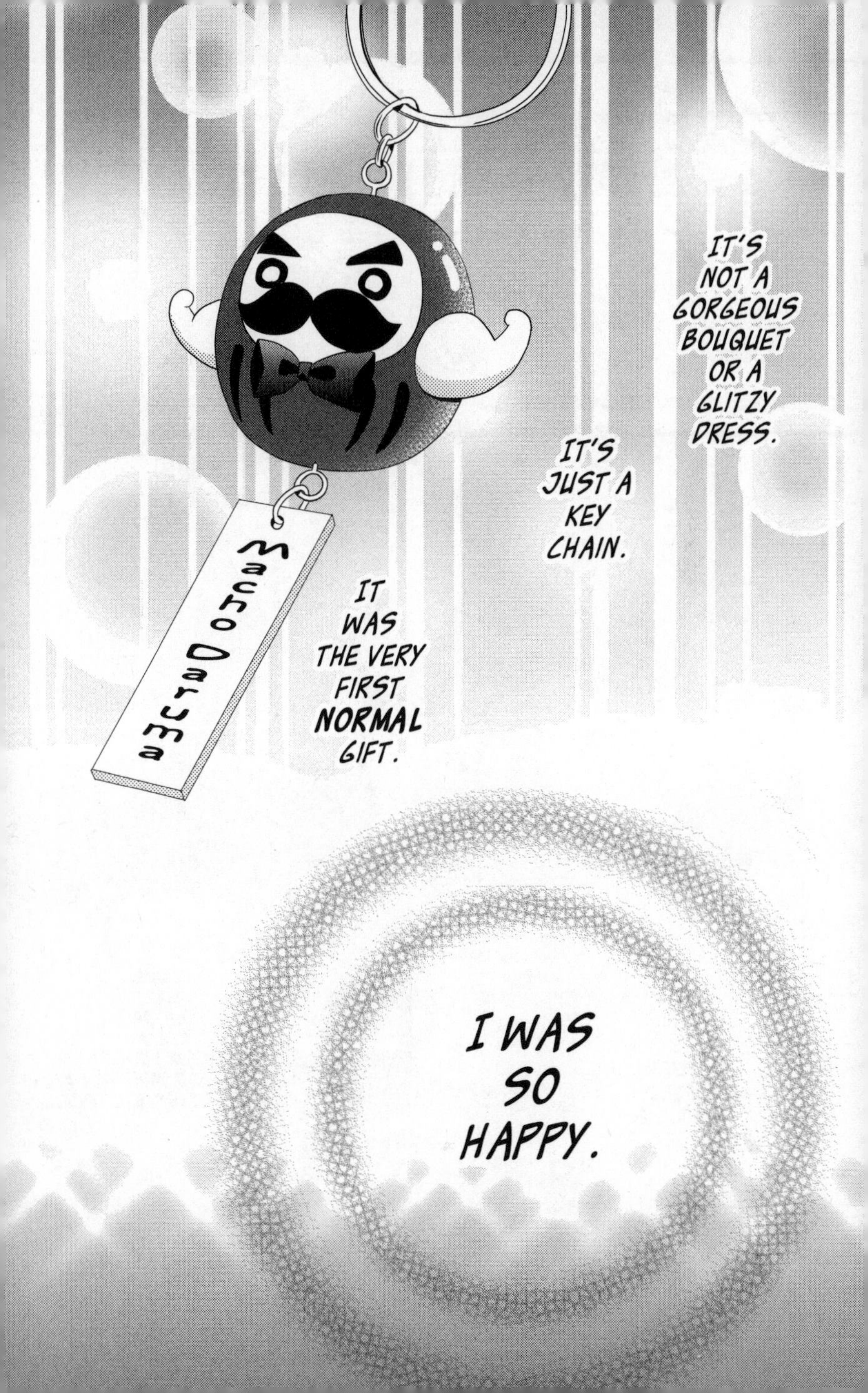
IT'S NOT A GORGEOUS BOUQUET OR A GLITZY DRESS.
IT'S JUST A KEY CHAIN.
Macho Daruma
IT WAS THE VERY FIRST **NORMAL** GIFT.
I WAS SO HAPPY.

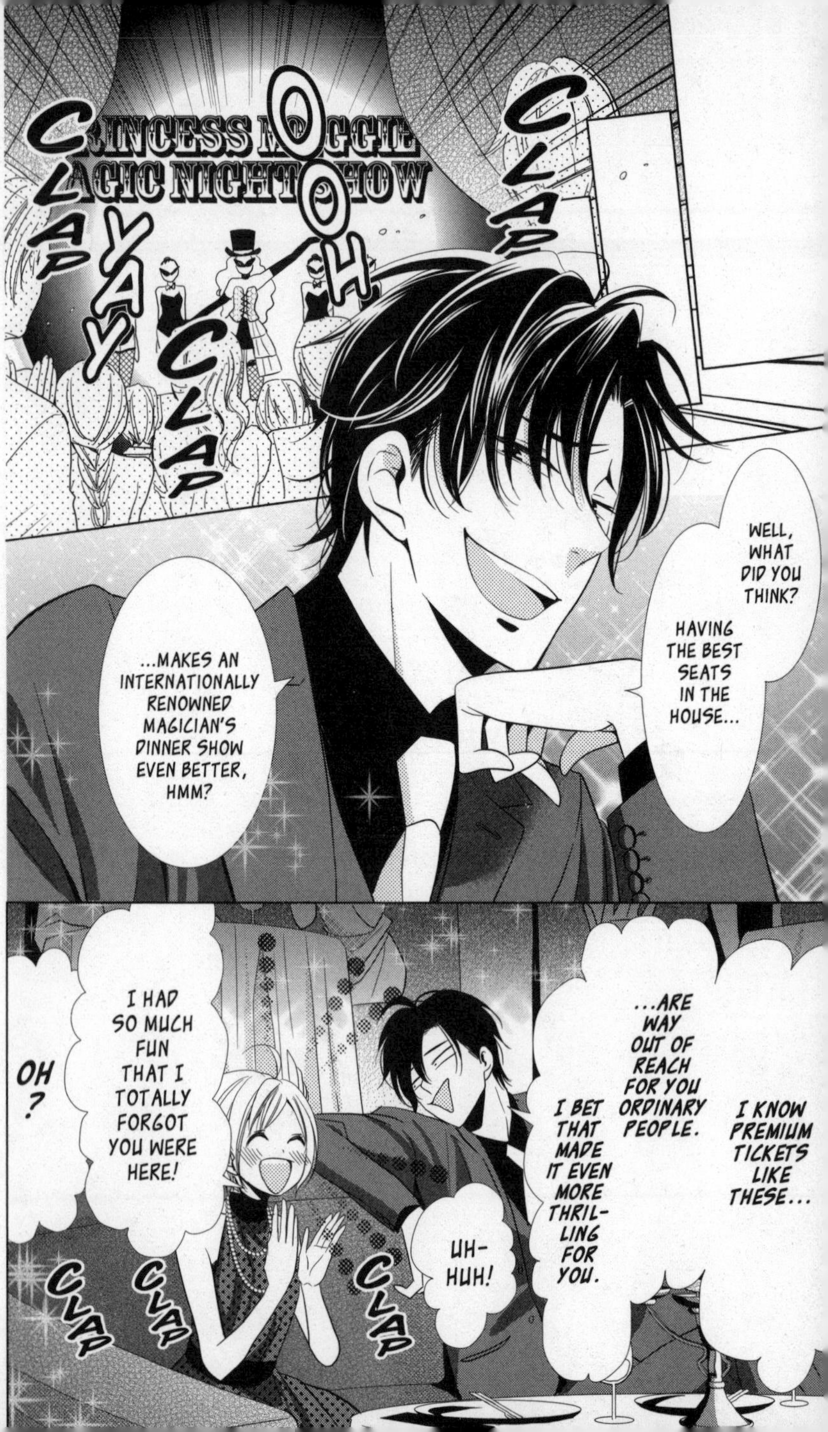
CLAP
OOOH
INCESS M GGIE
AGIC NIGHT HOW
CLAP
YAY
CLAP
CLAP
WELL, WHAT DID YOU THINK?
HAVING THE BEST SEATS IN THE HOUSE...
...MAKES AN INTERNATIONALLY RENOWNED MAGICIAN'S DINNER SHOW EVEN BETTER, HMM?
I KNOW PREMIUM TICKETS LIKE THESE...
...ARE WAY OUT OF REACH FOR YOU ORDINARY PEOPLE.
I BET THAT MADE IT EVEN MORE THRILLING FOR YOU.
UH-HUH!
I HAD SO MUCH FUN THAT I TOTALLY FORGOT YOU WERE HERE!
OH?
CLAP
CLAP
CLAP

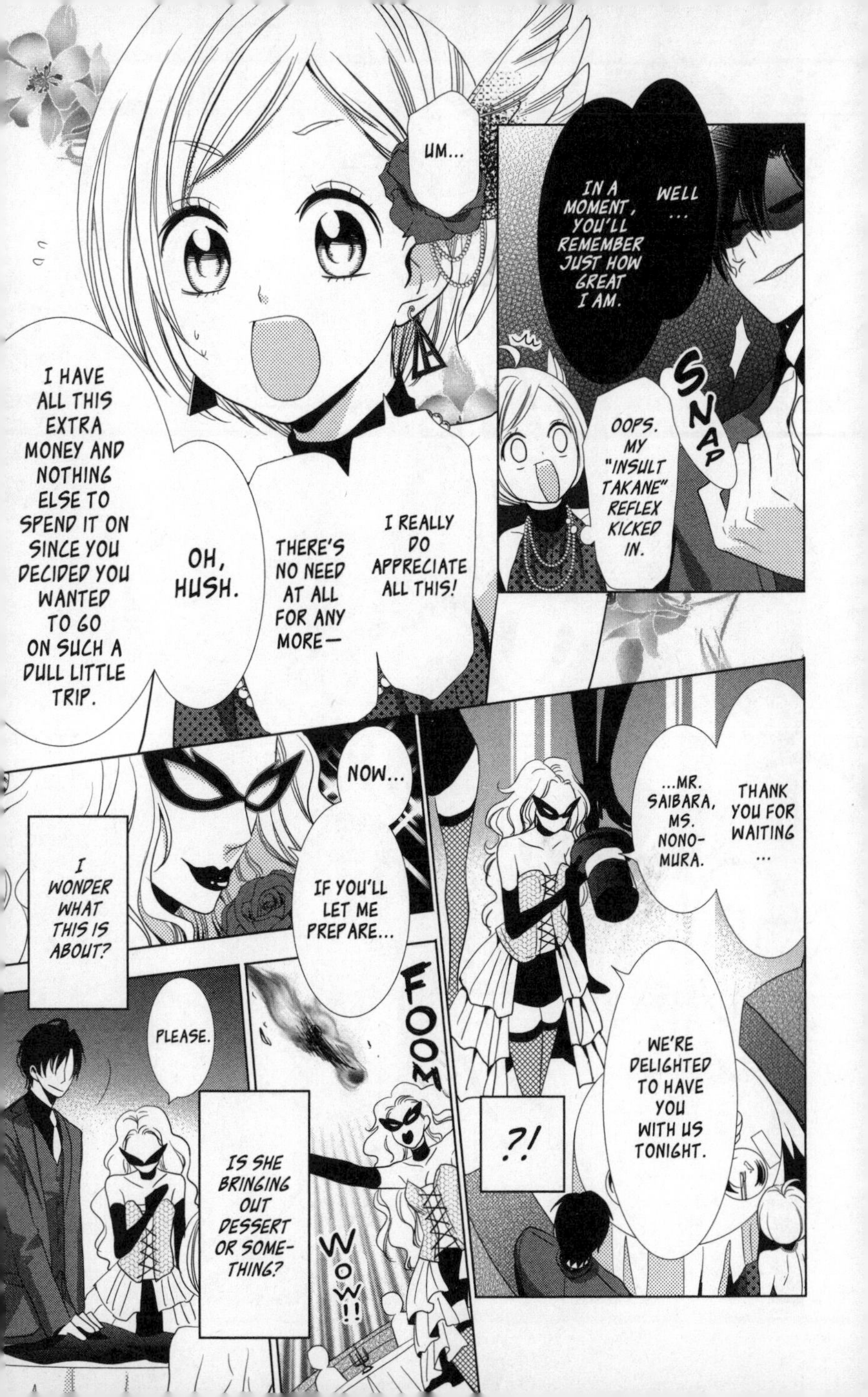
UM...
I REALLY DO APPRECIATE ALL THIS!
THERE'S NO NEED AT ALL FOR ANY MORE—
OH, HUSH.
I HAVE ALL THIS EXTRA MONEY AND NOTHING ELSE TO SPEND IT ON SINCE YOU DECIDED YOU WANTED TO GO ON SUCH A DULL LITTLE TRIP.
WELL...
IN A MOMENT, YOU'LL REMEMBER JUST HOW GREAT I AM.
SNAP
OOPS. MY "INSULT TAKANE" REFLEX KICKED IN.
THANK YOU FOR WAITING...
...MR. SAIBARA, MS. NONOMURA.
WE'RE DELIGHTED TO HAVE YOU WITH US TONIGHT.
?!
NOW...
IF YOU'LL LET ME PREPARE...
I WONDER WHAT THIS IS ABOUT?
FOOM
IS SHE BRINGING OUT DESSERT OR SOMETHING?
WOW!!
PLEASE.

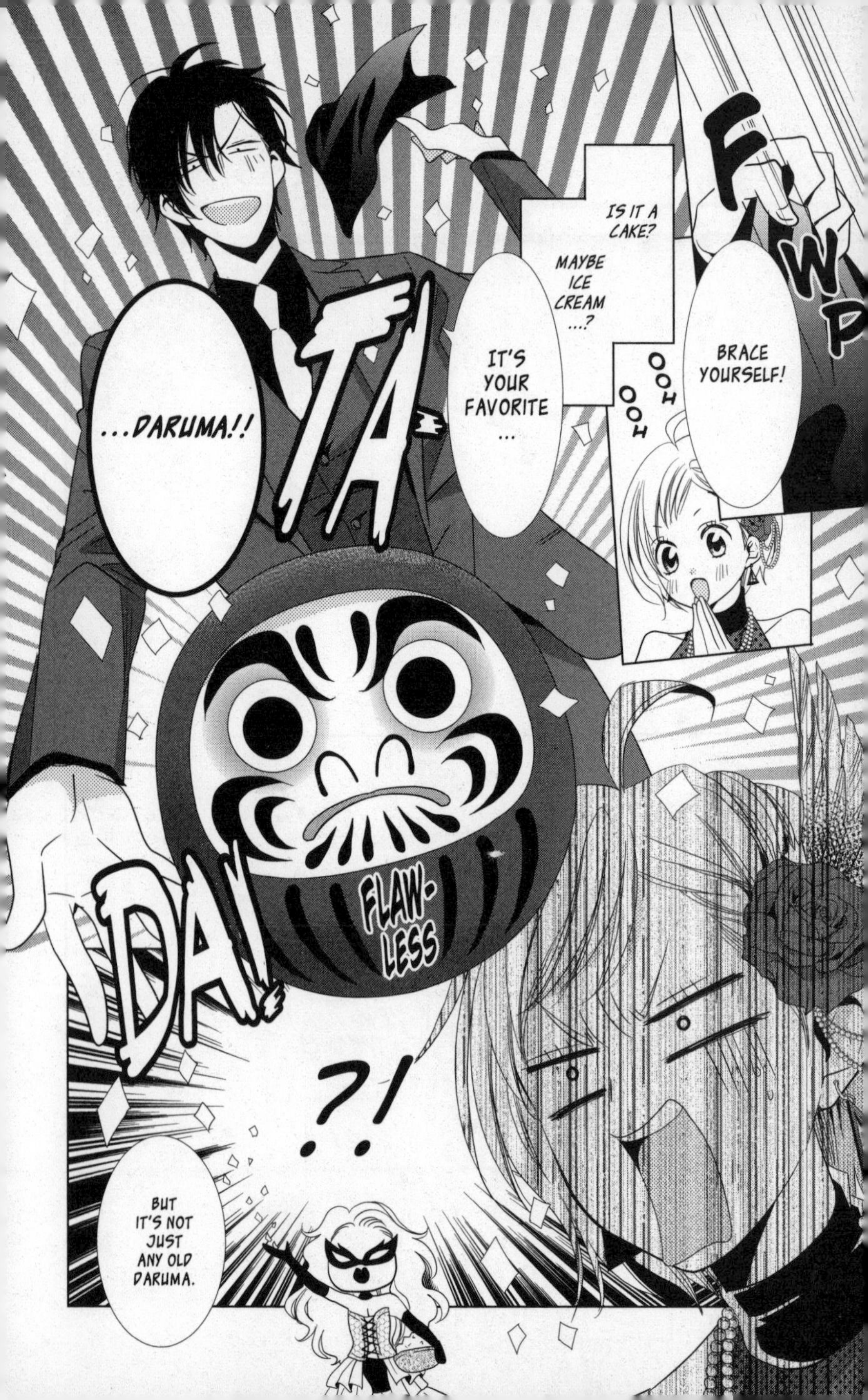
FWP
BRACE YOURSELF!
OOH OOH
IS IT A CAKE? MAYBE ICE CREAM ...?
IT'S YOUR FAVORITE ...
TA
...DARUMA!!
DA
FLAW-LESS
?!
BUT IT'S NOT JUST ANY OLD DARUMA.

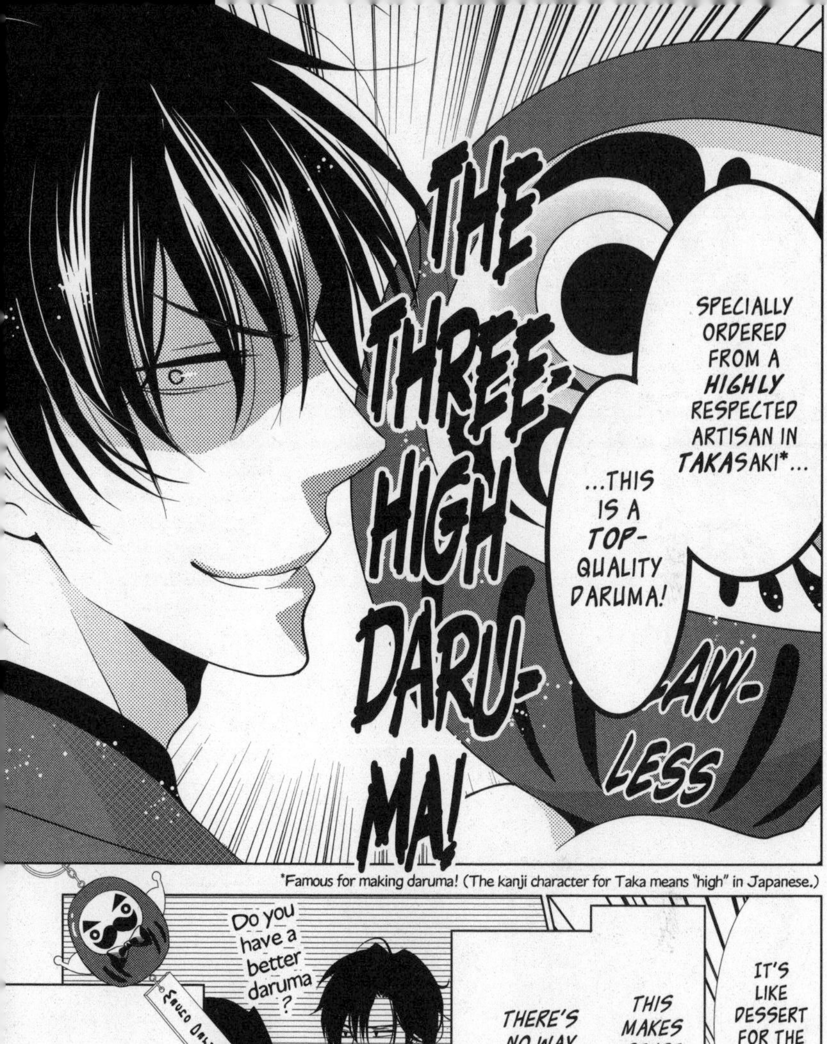
SPECIALLY ORDERED FROM A HIGHLY RESPECTED ARTISAN IN TAKASAKI*...
...THIS IS A TOP-QUALITY DARUMA!
THE THREE-HIGH DARUMA!
AW-LESS

*Famous for making daruma! (The kanji character for Taka means "high" in Japanese.)

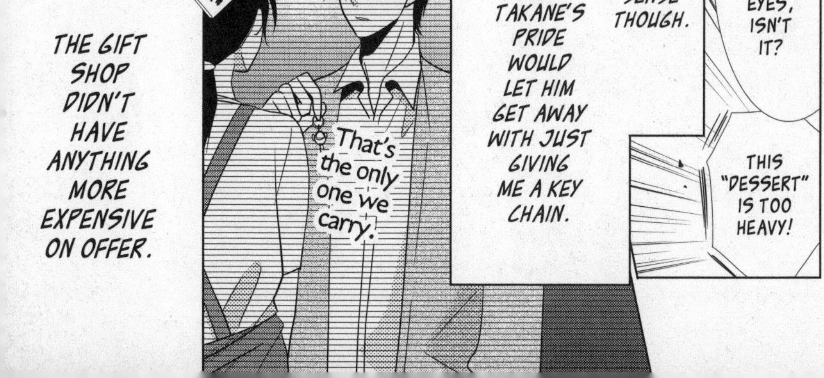
IT'S LIKE DESSERT FOR THE EYES, ISN'T IT?
THIS "DESSERT" IS TOO HEAVY!
THIS MAKES SENSE THOUGH.
THERE'S NO WAY TAKANE'S PRIDE WOULD LET HIM GET AWAY WITH JUST GIVING ME A KEY CHAIN.
Do you have a better daruma?
That's the only one we carry.
THE GIFT SHOP DIDN'T HAVE ANYTHING MORE EXPENSIVE ON OFFER.

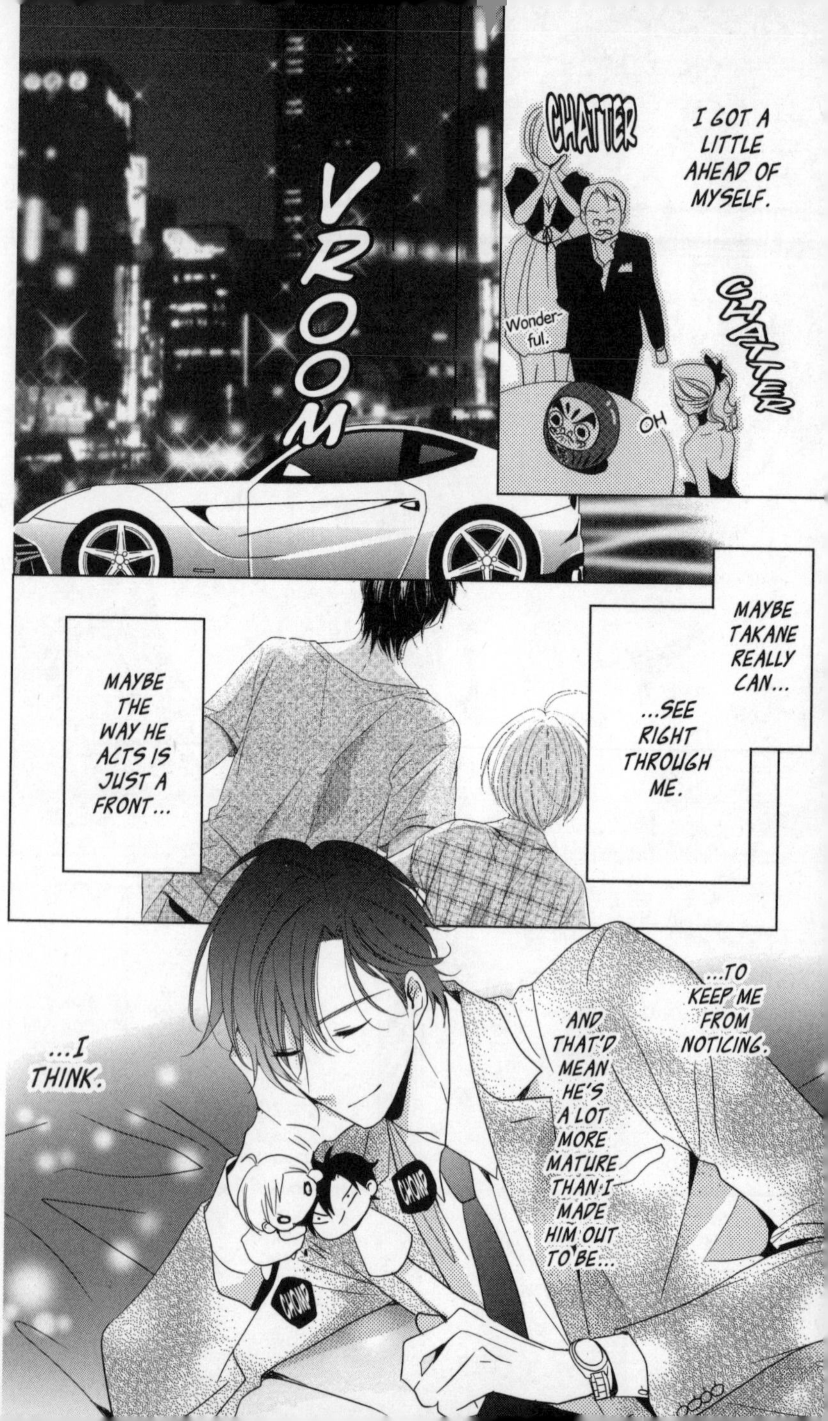
I GOT A LITTLE AHEAD OF MYSELF.
CHATTER
CHATTER
Wonder-ful.
OH
VROOM
MAYBE TAKANE REALLY CAN...
...SEE RIGHT THROUGH ME.
MAYBE THE WAY HE ACTS IS JUST A FRONT...
...TO KEEP ME FROM NOTICING.
AND THAT'D MEAN HE'S A LOT MORE MATURE THAN I MADE HIM OUT TO BE...
CHOMP
CHOMP
...I THINK.

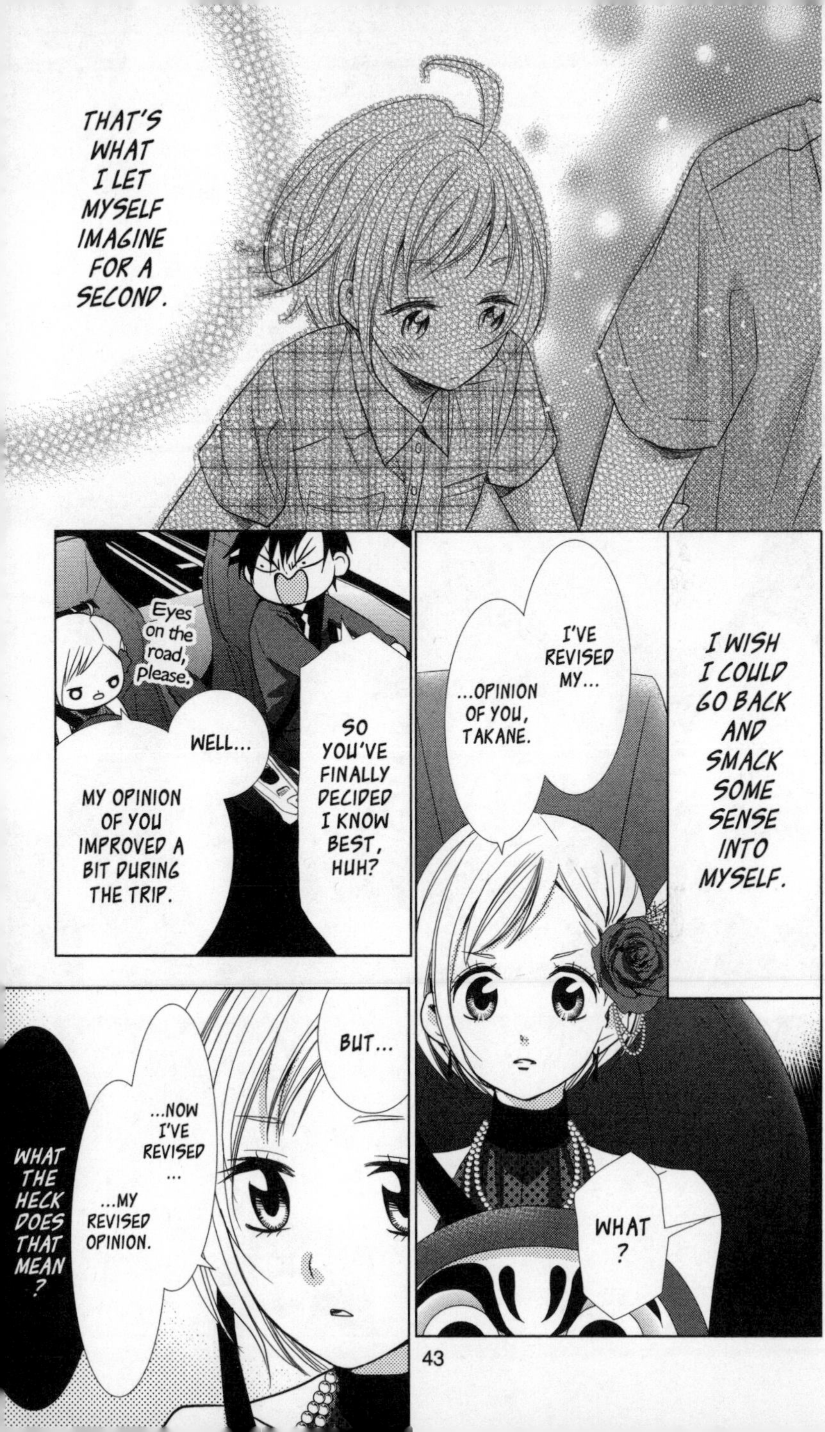
THAT'S WHAT I LET MYSELF IMAGINE FOR A SECOND.
I WISH I COULD GO BACK AND SMACK SOME SENSE INTO MYSELF.
SO YOU'VE FINALLY DECIDED I KNOW BEST, HUH?
WELL...
MY OPINION OF YOU IMPROVED A BIT DURING THE TRIP.
Eyes on the road, please.
I'VE REVISED MY...
...OPINION OF YOU, TAKANE.
BUT...
...NOW I'VE REVISED...
...MY REVISED OPINION.
WHAT?
WHAT THE HECK DOES THAT MEAN?

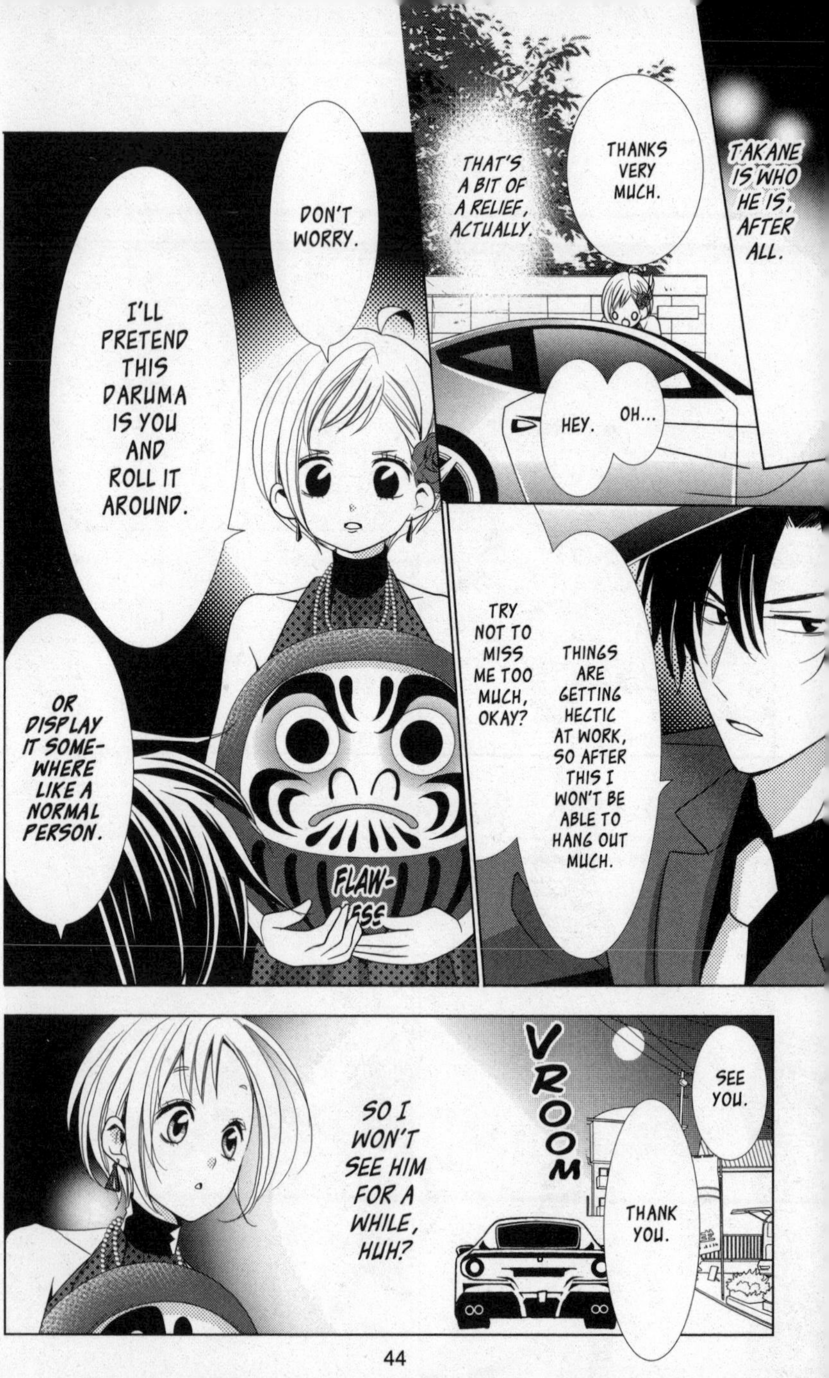

TAKANE IS WHO HE IS, AFTER ALL.
THANKS VERY MUCH.
THAT'S A BIT OF A RELIEF, ACTUALLY.
OH...
HEY.
THINGS ARE GETTING HECTIC AT WORK, SO AFTER THIS I WON'T BE ABLE TO HANG OUT MUCH.
TRY NOT TO MISS ME TOO MUCH, OKAY?
DON'T WORRY.
I'LL PRETEND THIS DARUMA IS YOU AND ROLL IT AROUND.
OR DISPLAY IT SOME-WHERE LIKE A NORMAL PERSON.
FLAW-LESS
SEE YOU.
THANK YOU.
VROOM
SO I WON'T SEE HIM FOR A WHILE, HUH?

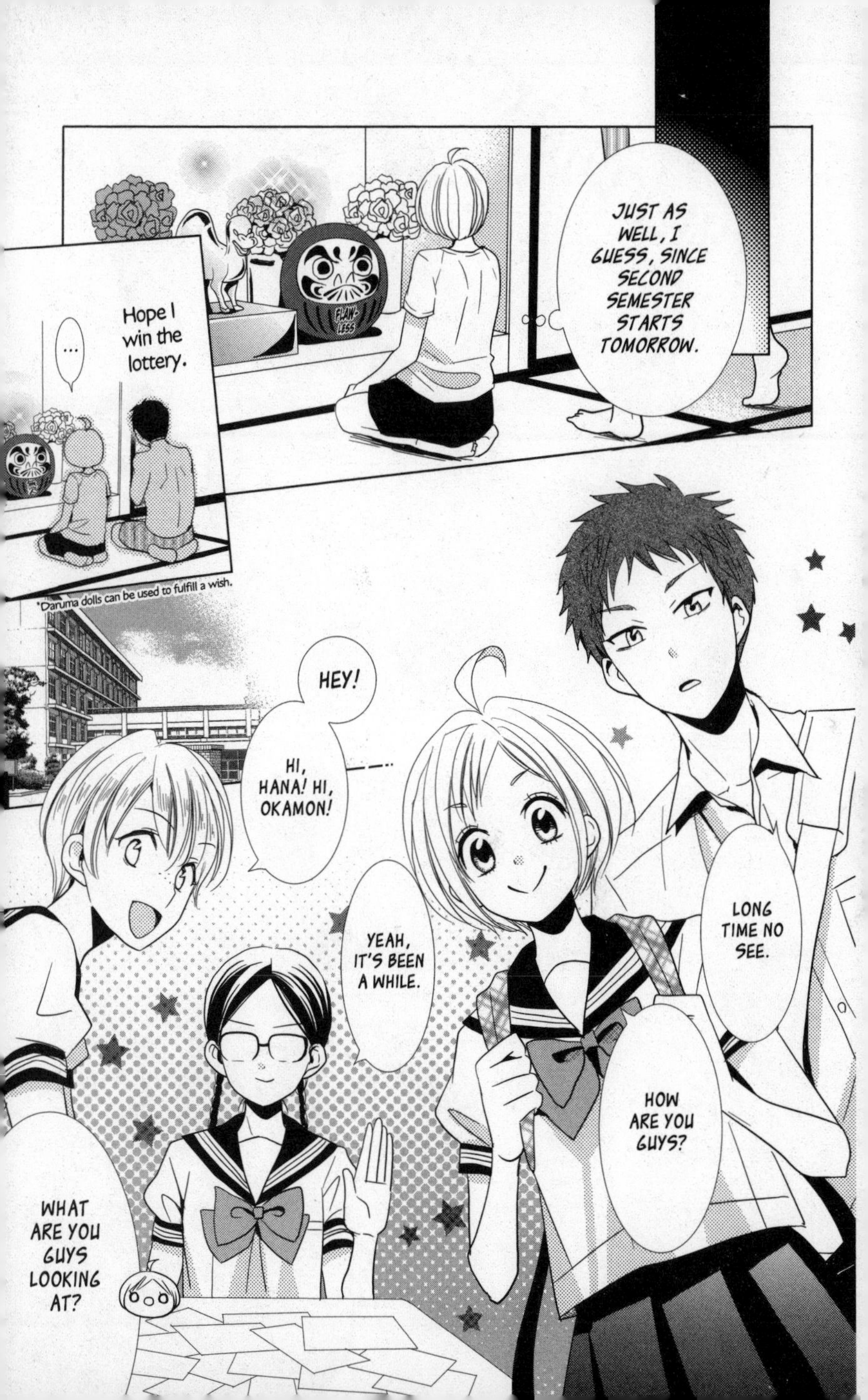
JUST AS WELL, I GUESS, SINCE SECOND SEMESTER STARTS TOMORROW.
FLAW-LESS
Hope I win the lottery.
...
HEY!
HI, HANA! HI, OKAMON!
LONG TIME NO SEE.
YEAH, IT'S BEEN A WHILE.
HOW ARE YOU GUYS?
WHAT ARE YOU GUYS LOOKING AT?
*Daruma dolls can be used to fulfill a wish.

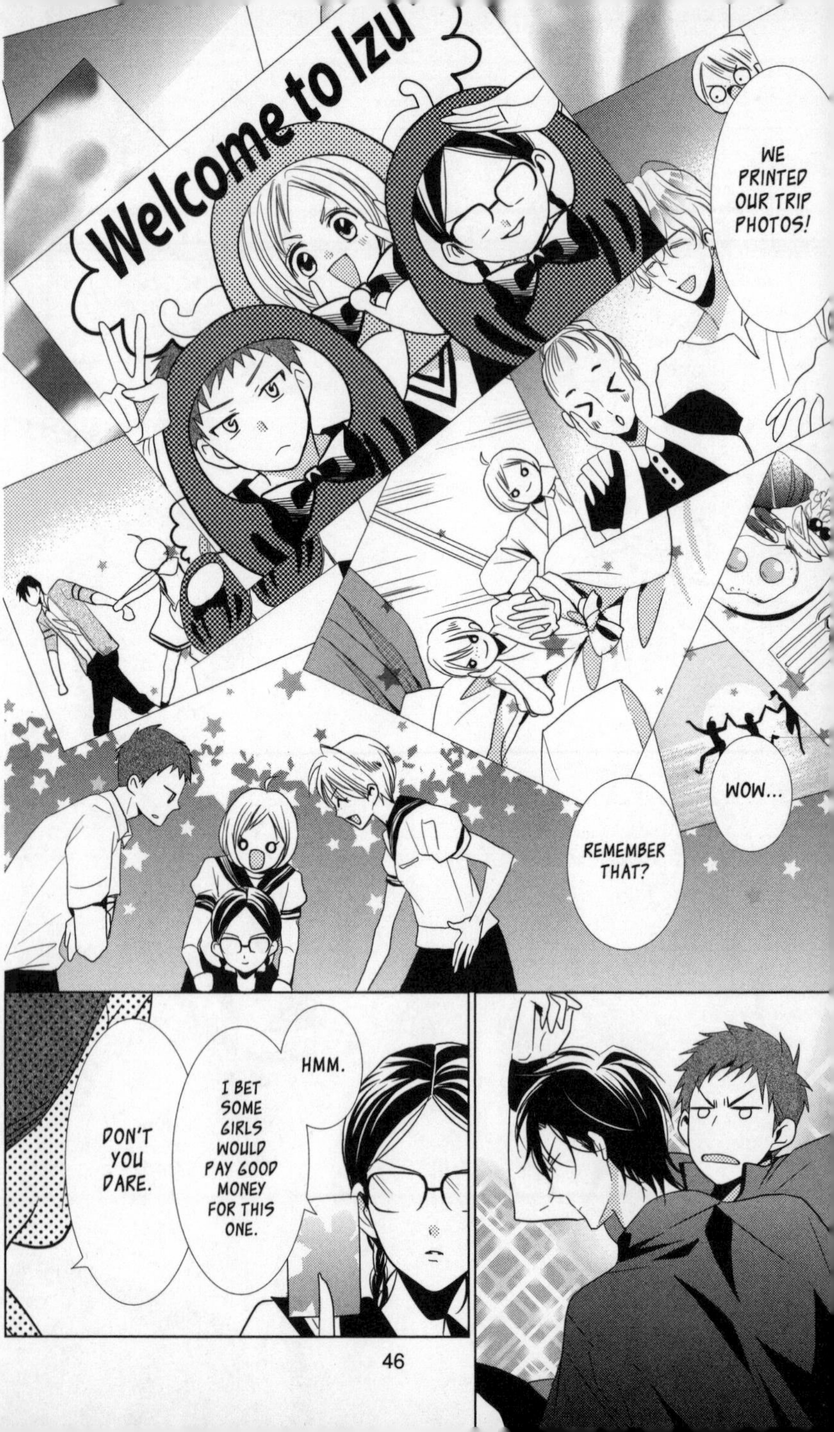
WE PRINTED OUR TRIP PHOTOS!
Welcome to Izu
WOW...
REMEMBER THAT?
HMM.
I BET SOME GIRLS WOULD PAY GOOD MONEY FOR THIS ONE.
DON'T YOU DARE.

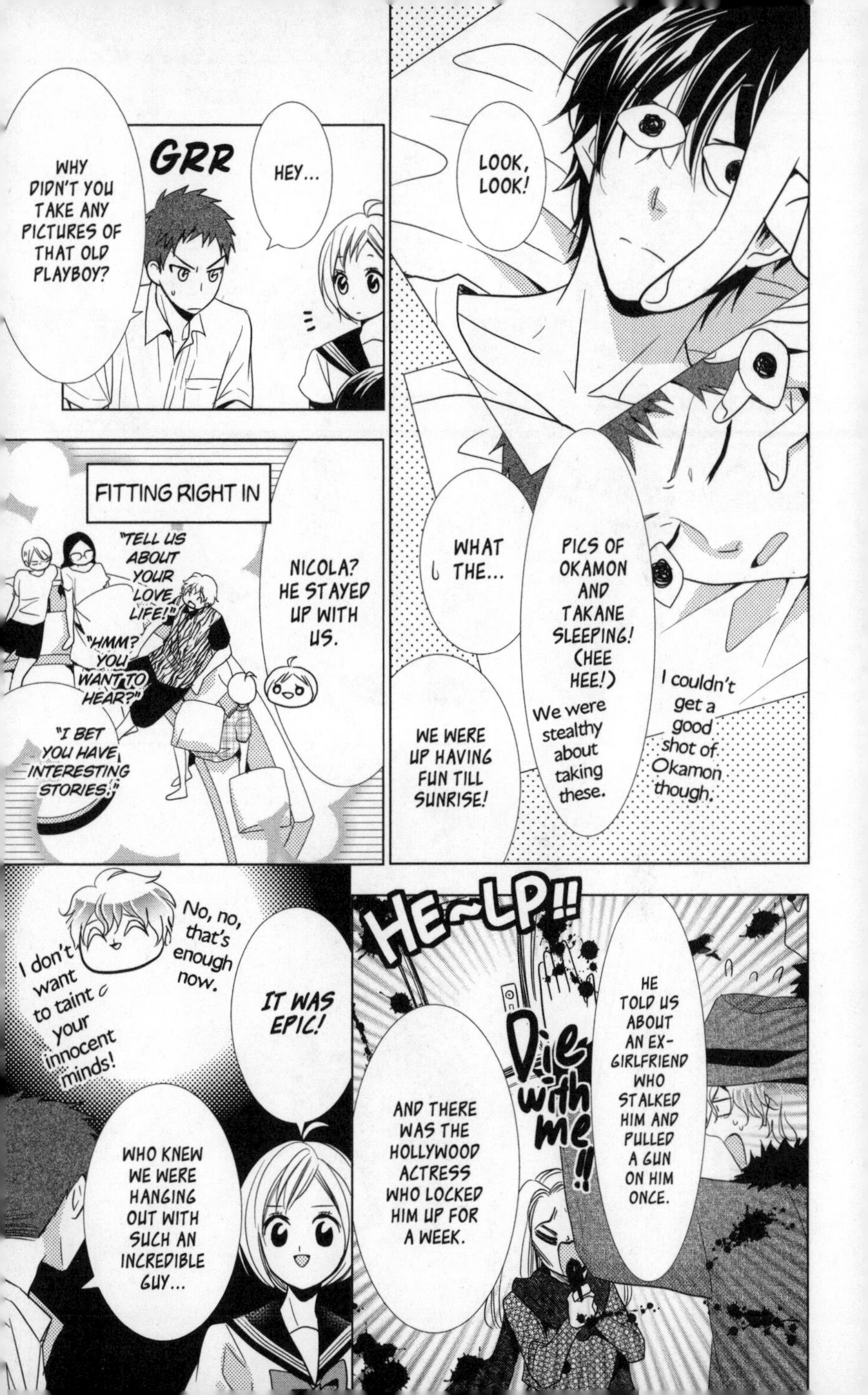
LOOK, LOOK!
PICS OF OKAMON AND TAKANE SLEEPING! (HEE HEE!)
I couldn't get a good shot of Okamon though.
WHAT THE...
We were stealthy about taking these.
WE WERE UP HAVING FUN TILL SUNRISE!
HEY...
GRR
WHY DIDN'T YOU TAKE ANY PICTURES OF THAT OLD PLAYBOY?
FITTING RIGHT IN
NICOLA? HE STAYED UP WITH US.
"TELL US ABOUT YOUR LOVE LIFE!"
"HMM? YOU WANT TO HEAR?"
"I BET YOU HAVE INTERESTING STORIES."
HE~LP!!
HE TOLD US ABOUT AN EX-GIRLFRIEND WHO STALKED HIM AND PULLED A GUN ON HIM ONCE.
Die with me!!
AND THERE WAS THE HOLLYWOOD ACTRESS WHO LOCKED HIM UP FOR A WEEK.
IT WAS EPIC!
No, no, that's enough now.
I don't want to taint your innocent minds!
WHO KNEW WE WERE HANGING OUT WITH SUCH AN INCREDIBLE GUY...

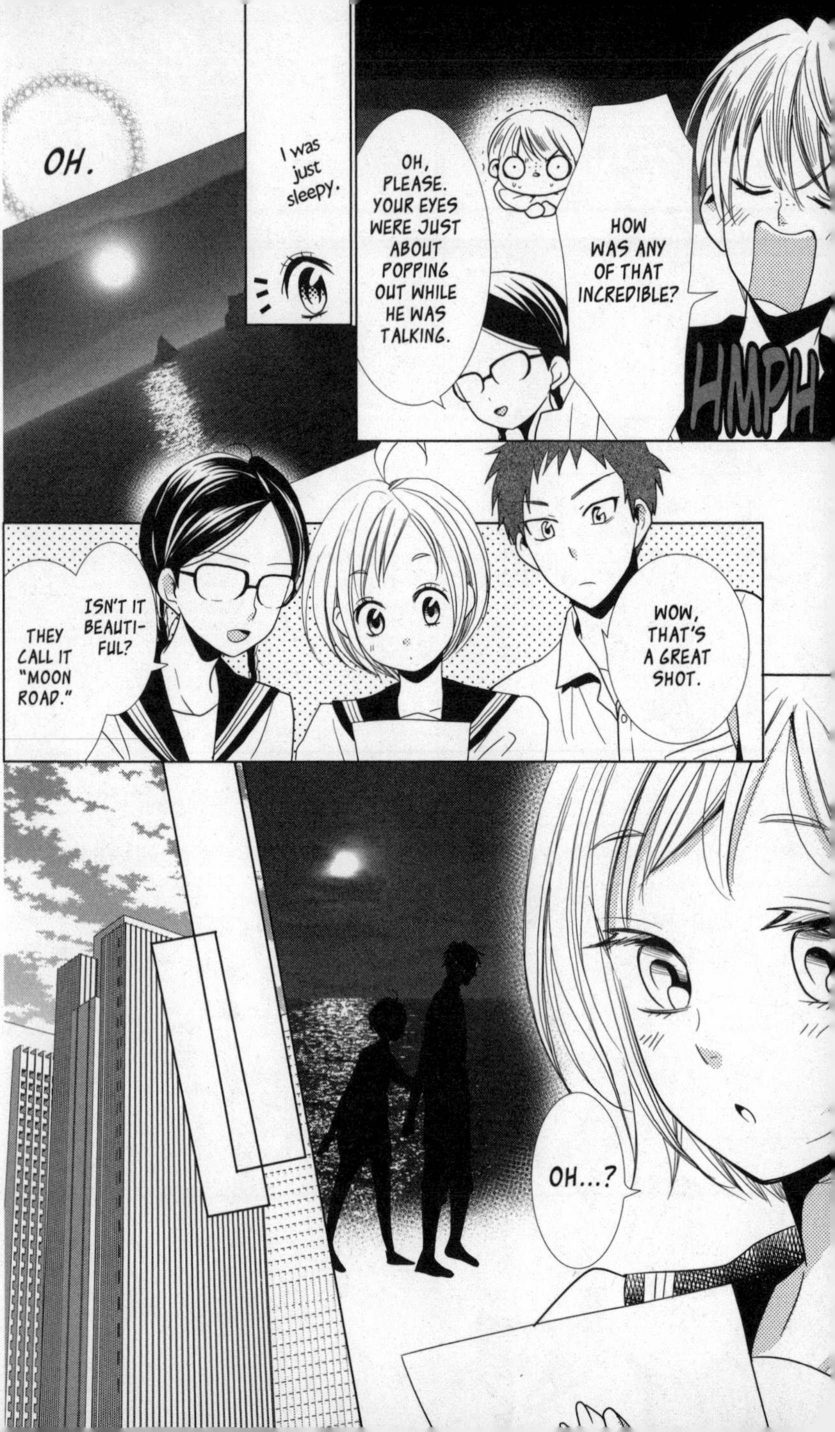
HOW WAS ANY OF THAT INCREDIBLE?
HMPH
OH, PLEASE. YOUR EYES WERE JUST ABOUT POPPING OUT WHILE HE WAS TALKING.
I was just sleepy.
OH.
WOW, THAT'S A GREAT SHOT.
ISN'T IT BEAUTI-FUL?
THEY CALL IT "MOON ROAD."
OH...?

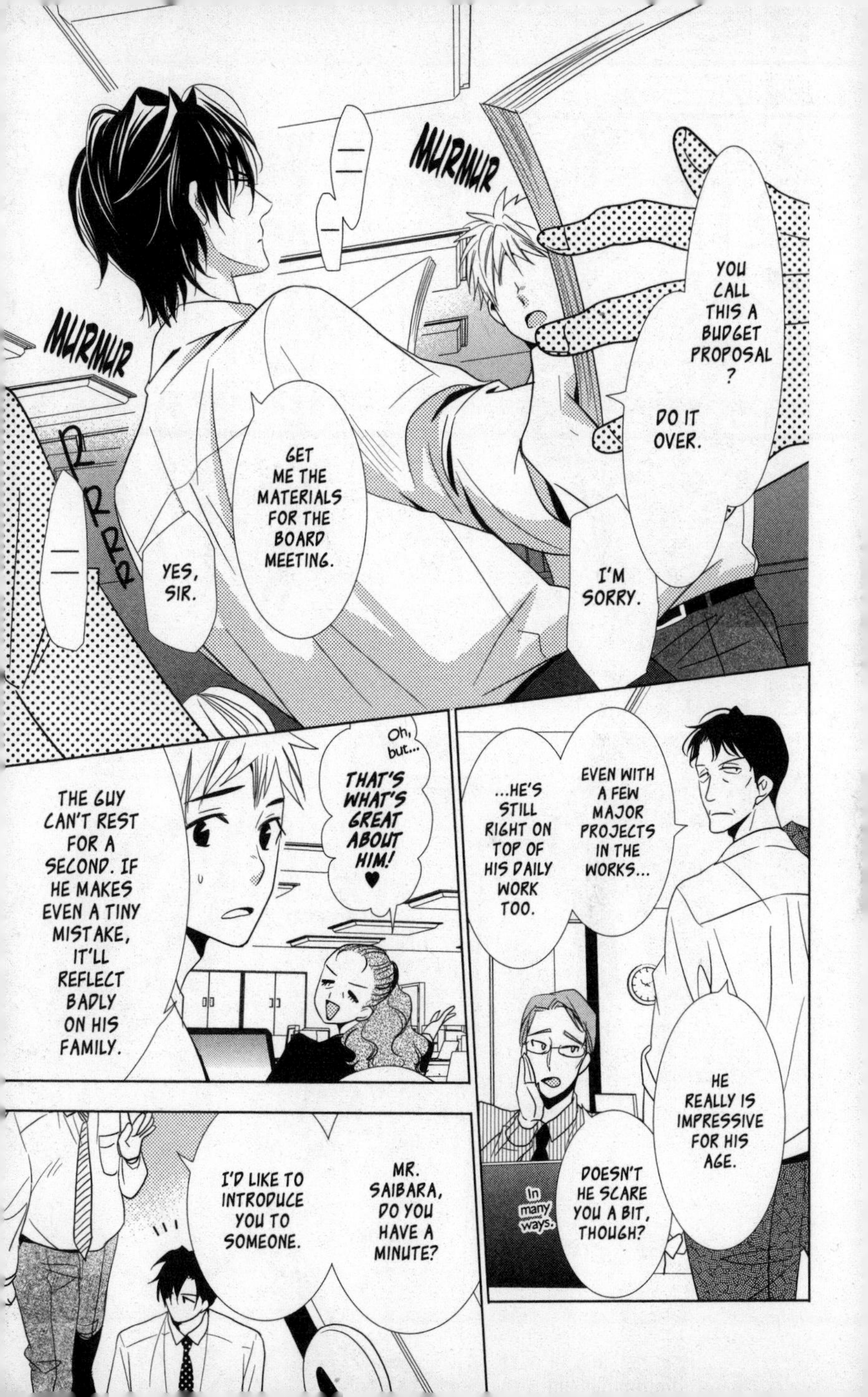
YOU CALL THIS A BUDGET PROPOSAL?
DO IT OVER.
I'M SORRY.
MURMUR
—
GET ME THE MATERIALS FOR THE BOARD MEETING.
MURMUR
YES, SIR.
RRRR
——
EVEN WITH A FEW MAJOR PROJECTS IN THE WORKS...
...HE'S STILL RIGHT ON TOP OF HIS DAILY WORK TOO.
HE REALLY IS IMPRESSIVE FOR HIS AGE.
DOESN'T HE SCARE YOU A BIT, THOUGH?
In many ways.
Oh, but...
THAT'S WHAT'S GREAT ABOUT HIM! ♥
THE GUY CAN'T REST FOR A SECOND. IF HE MAKES EVEN A TINY MISTAKE, IT'LL REFLECT BADLY ON HIS FAMILY.
MR. SAIBARA, DO YOU HAVE A MINUTE?
I'D LIKE TO INTRODUCE YOU TO SOMEONE.

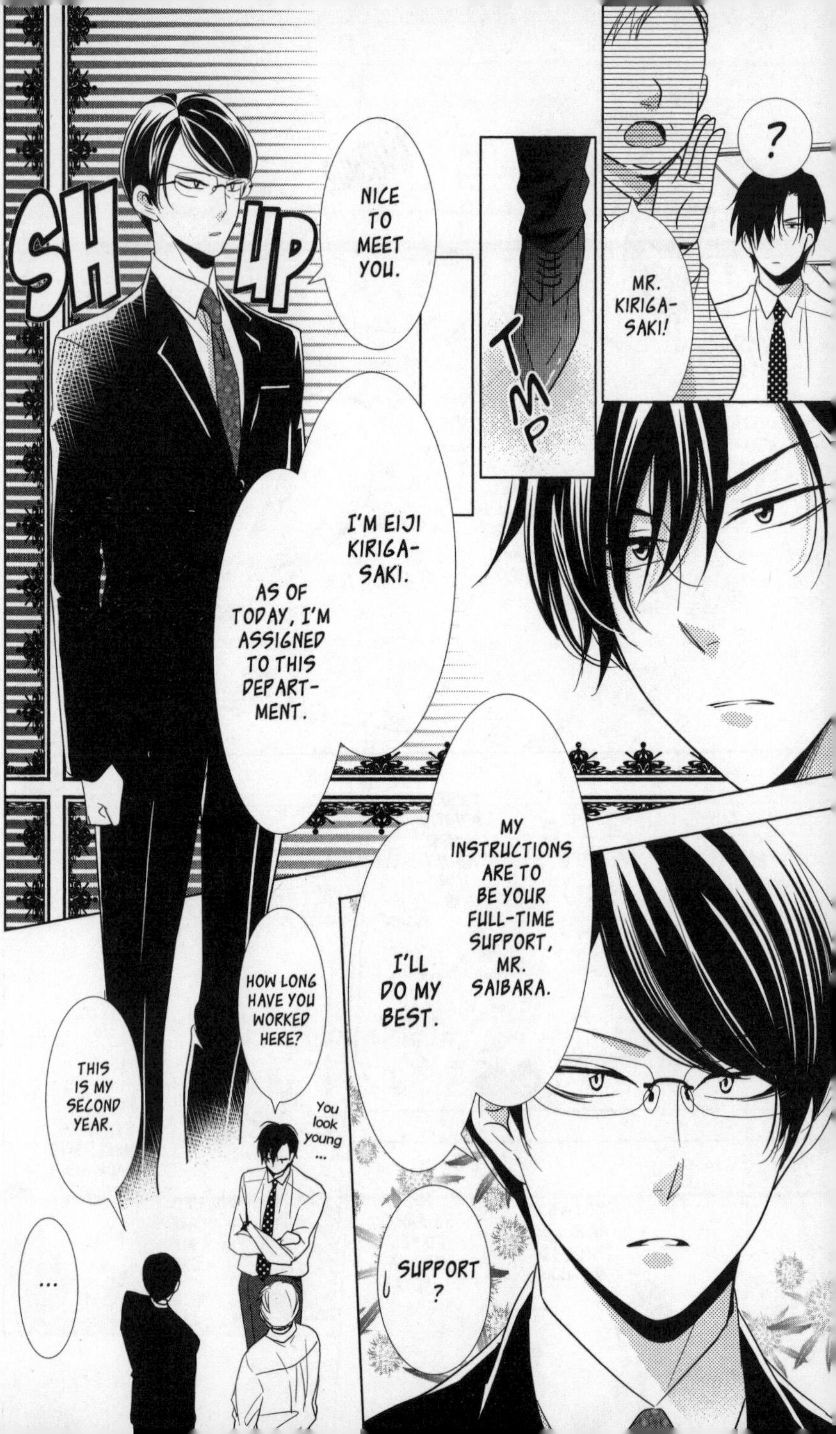
?
MR. KIRIGA-SAKI!
TMP
SHUP
NICE TO MEET YOU.
I'M EIJI KIRIGA-SAKI.
AS OF TODAY, I'M ASSIGNED TO THIS DEPART-MENT.
MY INSTRUCTIONS ARE TO BE YOUR FULL-TIME SUPPORT, MR. SAIBARA.
I'LL DO MY BEST.
SUPPORT?
HOW LONG HAVE YOU WORKED HERE?
THIS IS MY SECOND YEAR.
You look young...
...

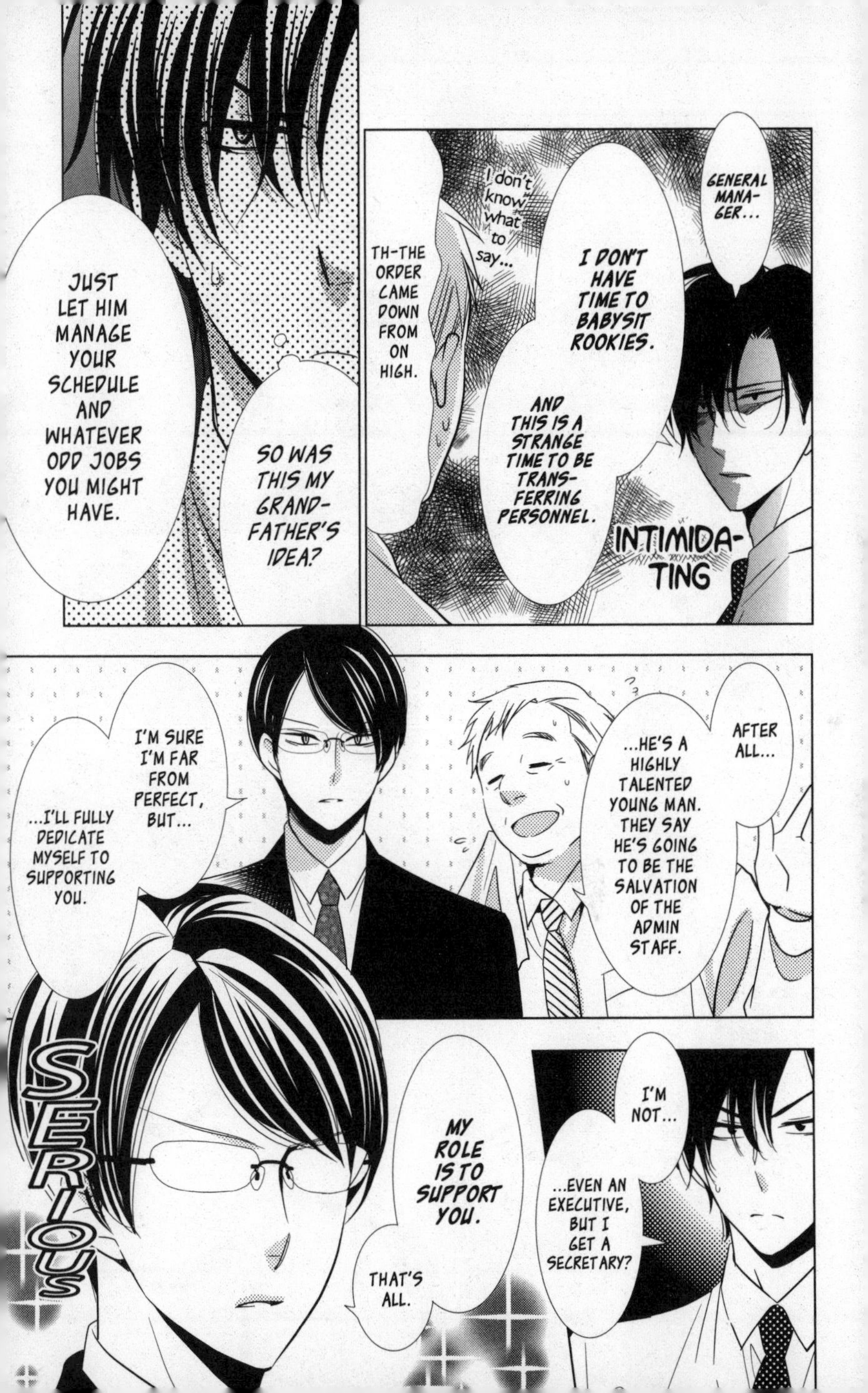
GENERAL MANA-GER...
I DON'T HAVE TIME TO BABYSIT ROOKIES.
AND THIS IS A STRANGE TIME TO BE TRANS-FERRING PERSONNEL.
INTIMIDA-TING
I don't know what to say...
TH-THE ORDER CAME DOWN FROM ON HIGH.
SO WAS THIS MY GRAND-FATHER'S IDEA?
JUST LET HIM MANAGE YOUR SCHEDULE AND WHATEVER ODD JOBS YOU MIGHT HAVE.
AFTER ALL...
...HE'S A HIGHLY TALENTED YOUNG MAN. THEY SAY HE'S GOING TO BE THE SALVATION OF THE ADMIN STAFF.
I'M SURE I'M FAR FROM PERFECT, BUT...
...I'LL FULLY DEDICATE MYSELF TO SUPPORTING YOU.
I'M NOT...
...EVEN AN EXECUTIVE, BUT I GET A SECRETARY?
MY ROLE IS TO SUPPORT YOU.
THAT'S ALL.
SERIOUS

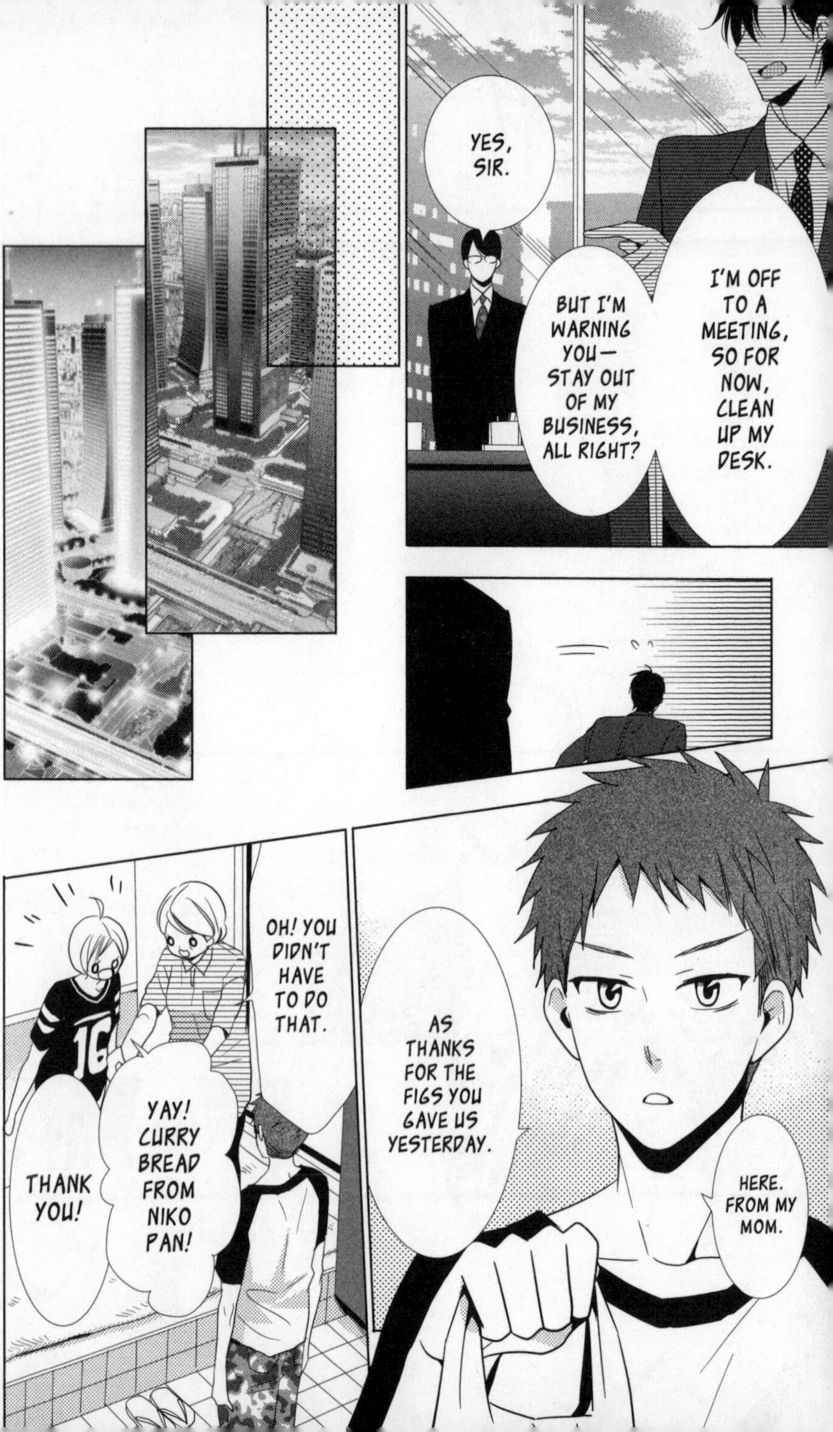
I'M OFF TO A MEETING, SO FOR NOW, CLEAN UP MY DESK.
BUT I'M WARNING YOU— STAY OUT OF MY BUSINESS, ALL RIGHT?
YES, SIR.
HERE. FROM MY MOM.
AS THANKS FOR THE FIGS YOU GAVE US YESTERDAY.
OH! YOU DIDN'T HAVE TO DO THAT.
YAY! CURRY BREAD FROM NIKO PAN!
THANK YOU!

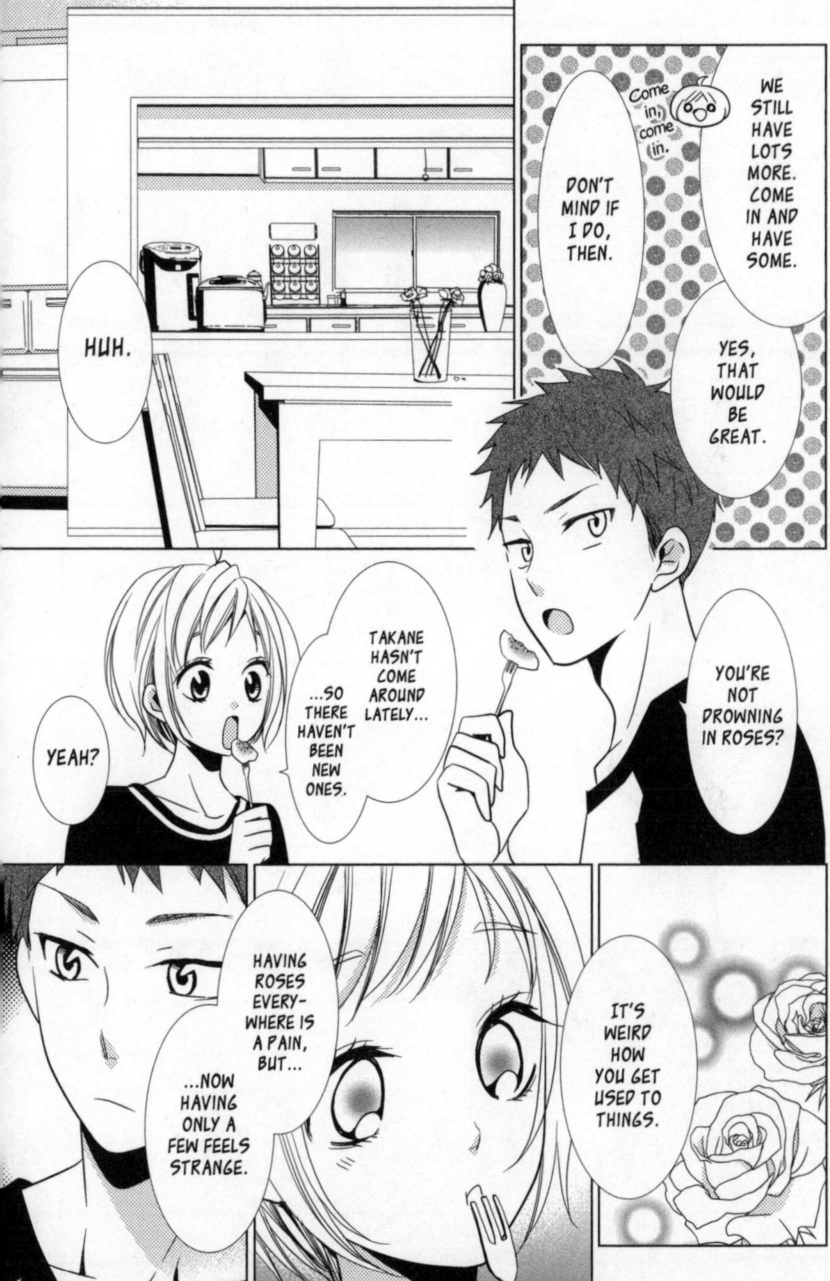
WE STILL HAVE LOTS MORE. COME IN AND HAVE SOME.
Come in, come in.
DON'T MIND IF I DO, THEN.
YES, THAT WOULD BE GREAT.
HUH.
YOU'RE NOT DROWNING IN ROSES?
TAKANE HASN'T COME AROUND LATELY...
...SO THERE HAVEN'T BEEN NEW ONES.
YEAH?
IT'S WEIRD HOW YOU GET USED TO THINGS.
HAVING ROSES EVERY-WHERE IS A PAIN, BUT...
...NOW HAVING ONLY A FEW FEELS STRANGE.

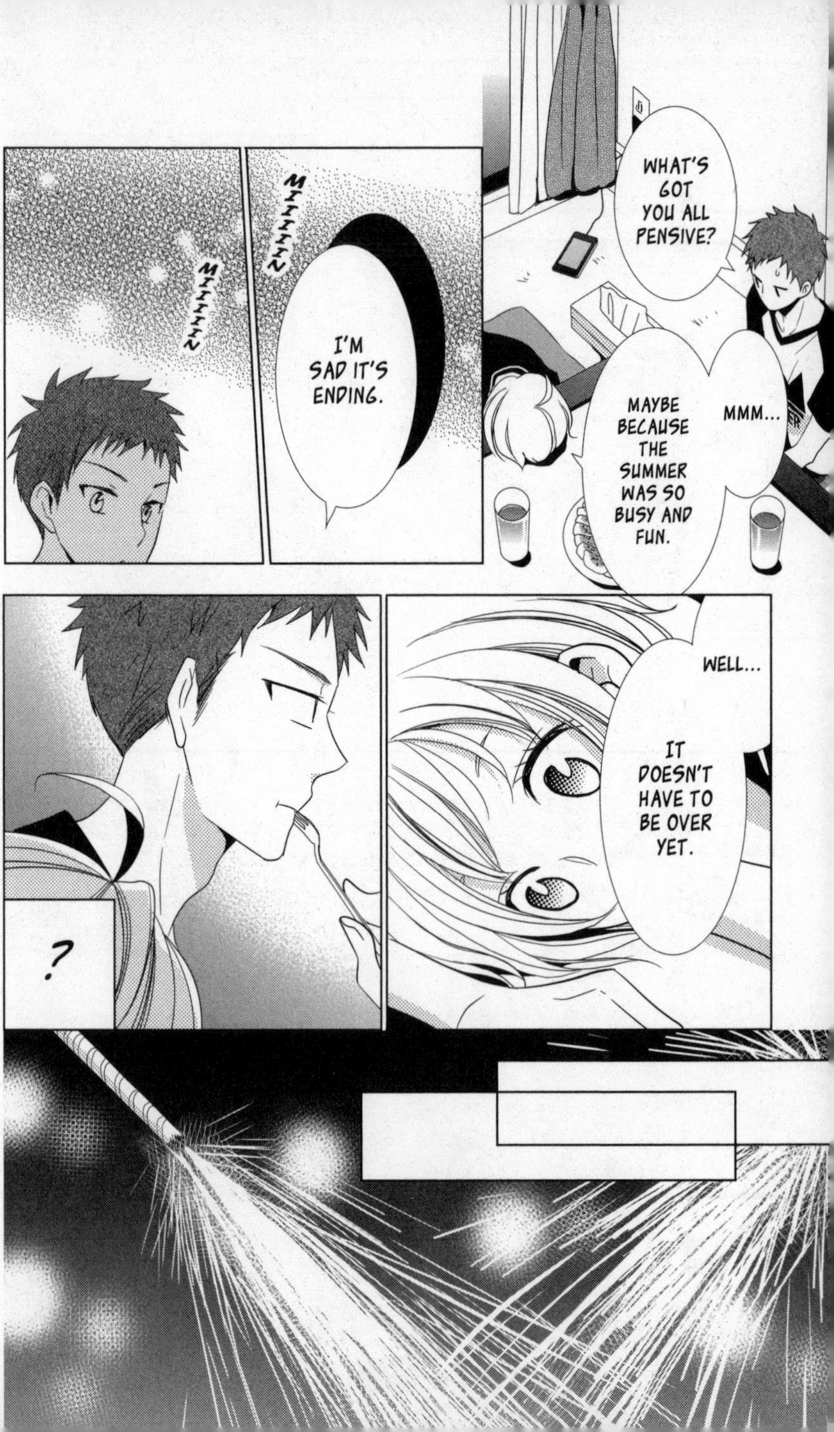
WHAT'S GOT YOU ALL PENSIVE?
MMM...
MAYBE BECAUSE THE SUMMER WAS SO BUSY AND FUN.
MIIIIIN
I'M SAD IT'S ENDING.
MIIIIIN
WELL...
IT DOESN'T HAVE TO BE OVER YET.
?

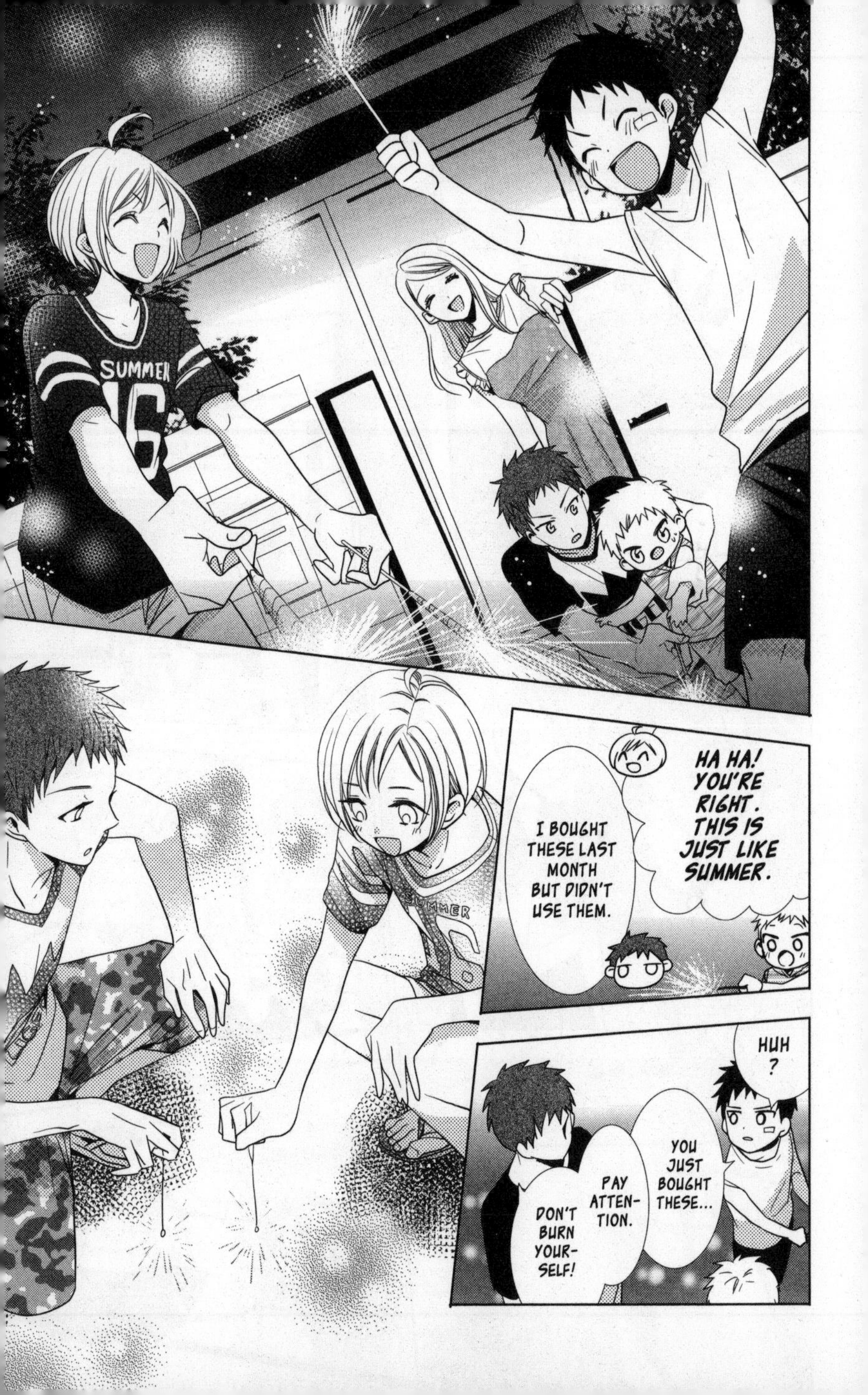
SUMMER 16
HA HA! YOU'RE RIGHT. THIS IS JUST LIKE SUMMER.
I BOUGHT THESE LAST MONTH BUT DIDN'T USE THEM.
SUMMER
HUH?
YOU JUST BOUGHT THESE...
PAY ATTENTION.
DON'T BURN YOURSELF!

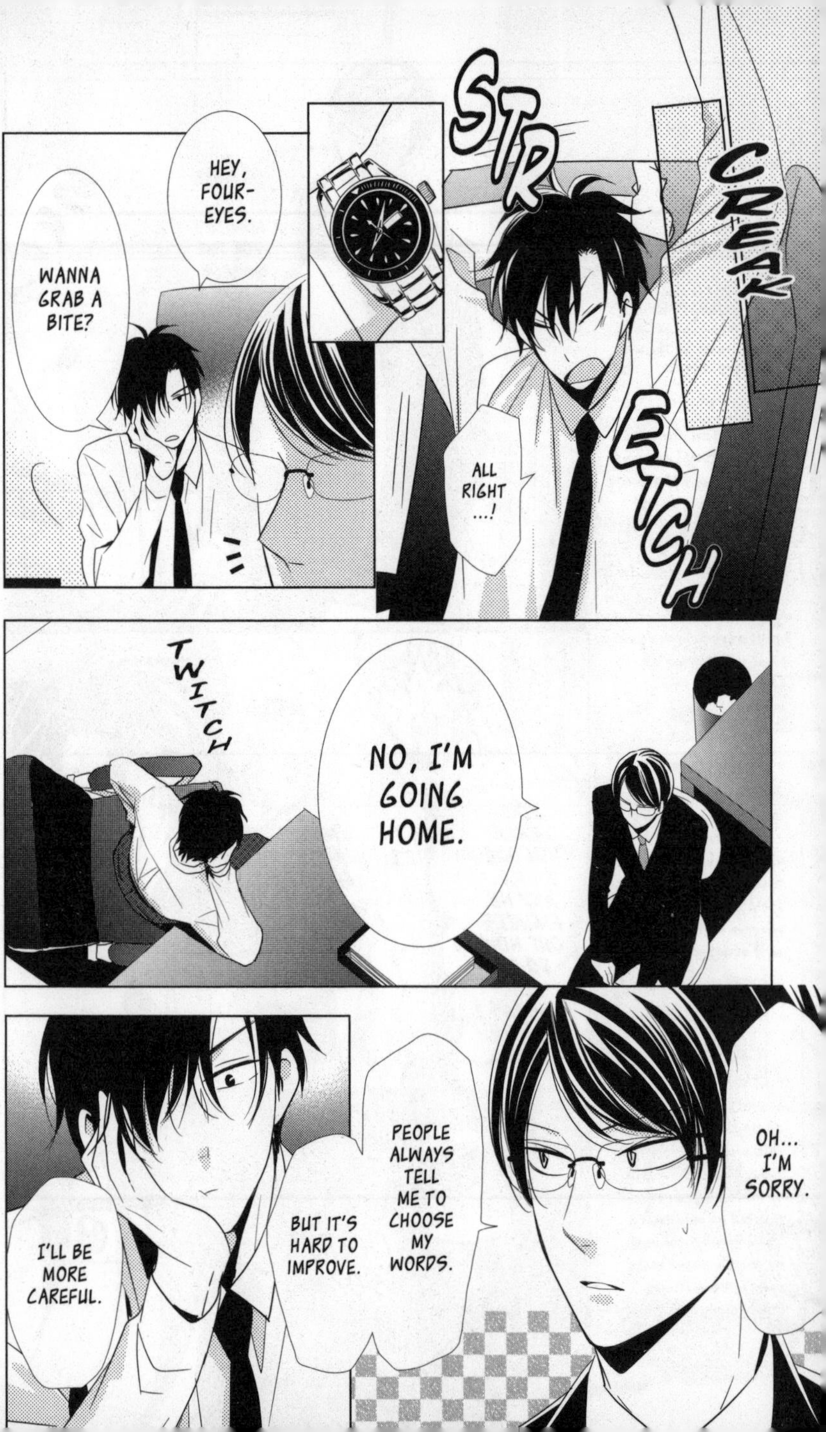
STRETCH
CREAK
ALL RIGHT...!
HEY, FOUR-EYES.
WANNA GRAB A BITE?
NO, I'M GOING HOME.
TWITCH
OH... I'M SORRY.
PEOPLE ALWAYS TELL ME TO CHOOSE MY WORDS.
BUT IT'S HARD TO IMPROVE.
I'LL BE MORE CAREFUL.

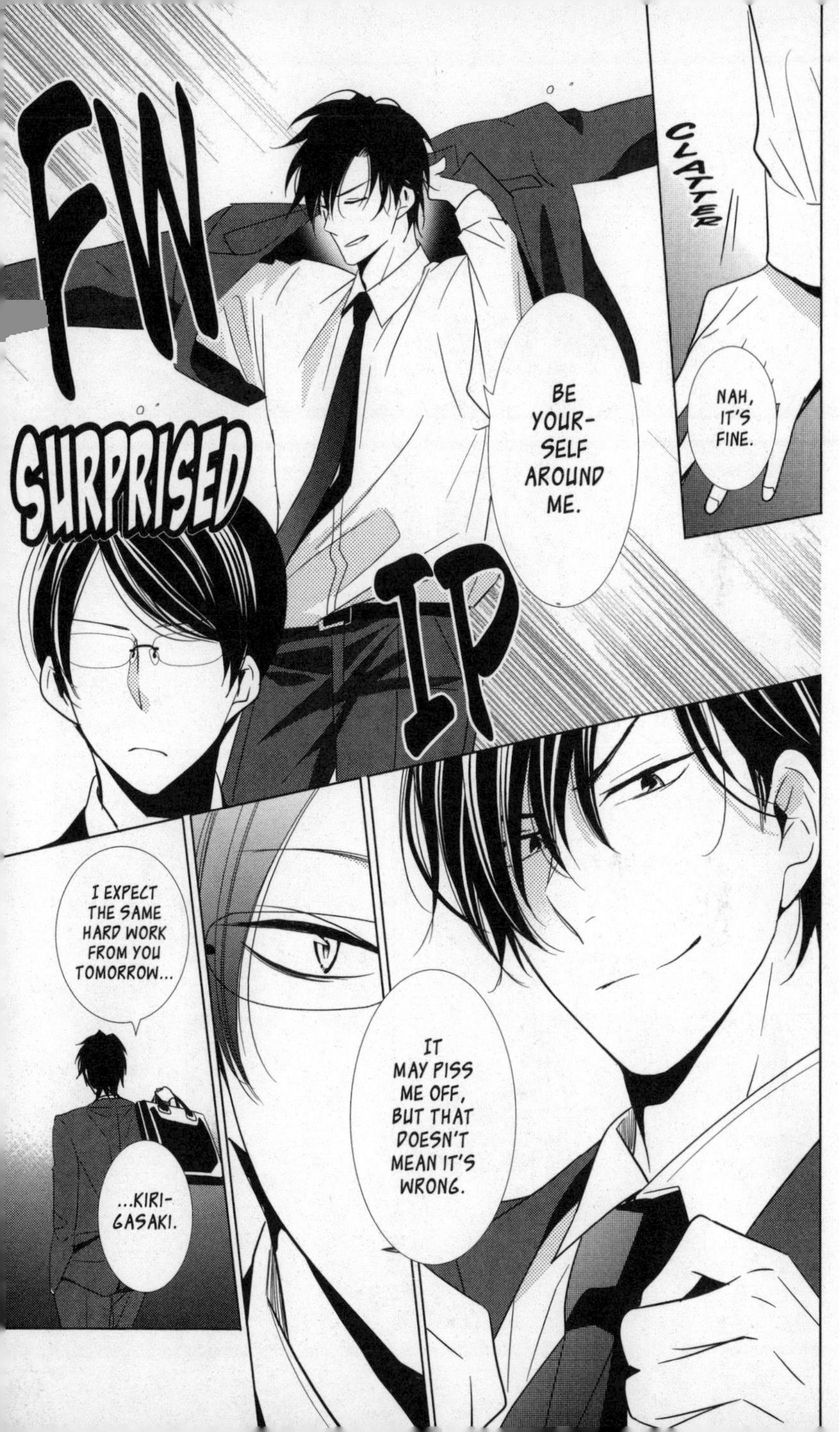
CLATTER
NAH, IT'S FINE.
BE YOURSELF AROUND ME.
FW
SURPRISED
IP
IT MAY PISS ME OFF, BUT THAT DOESN'T MEAN IT'S WRONG.
I EXPECT THE SAME HARD WORK FROM YOU TOMORROW...
...KIRI-GASAKI.

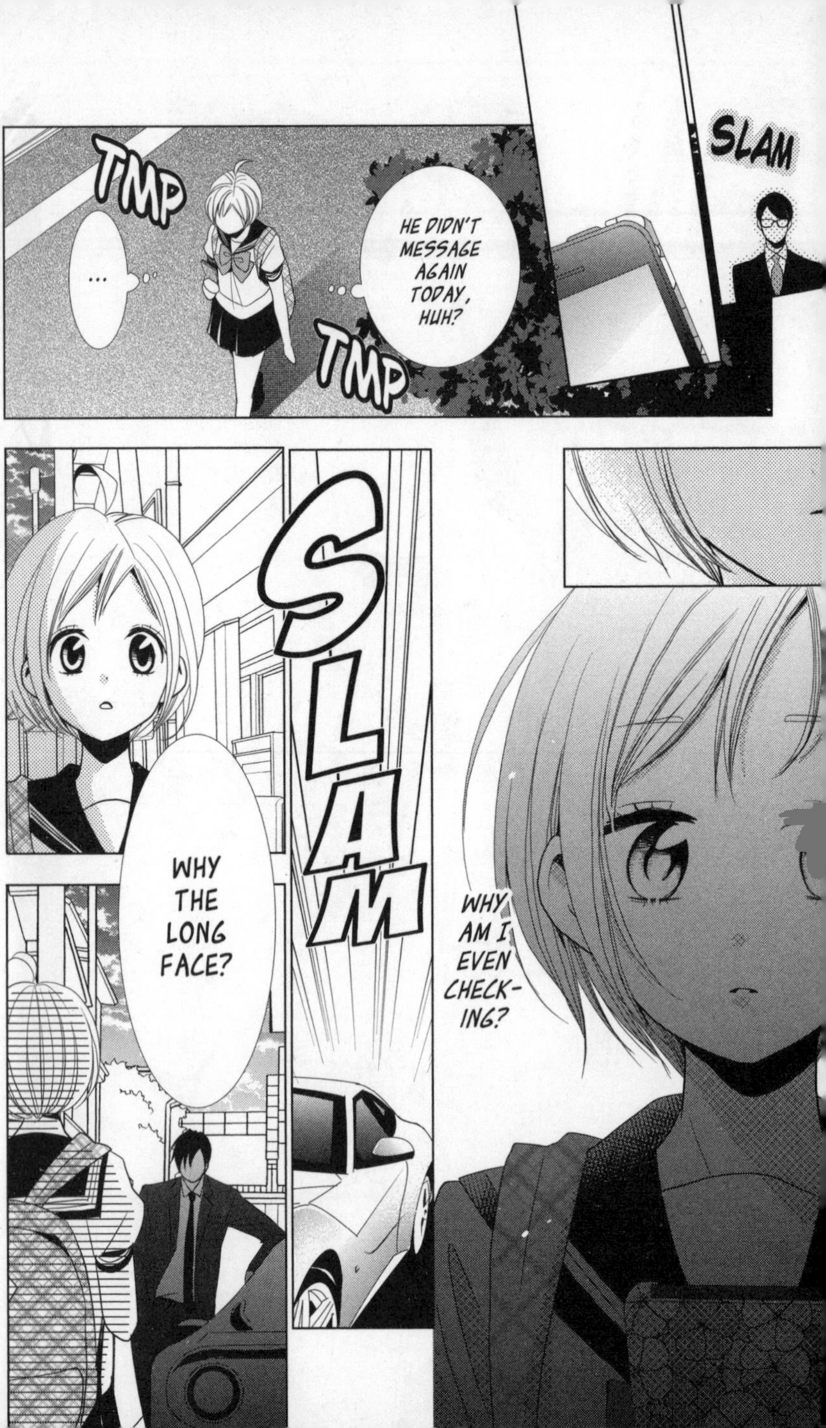
SLAM
HE DIDN'T MESSAGE AGAIN TODAY, HUH?
TMP
...
TMP
WHY AM I EVEN CHECKING?
SLAM
WHY THE LONG FACE?

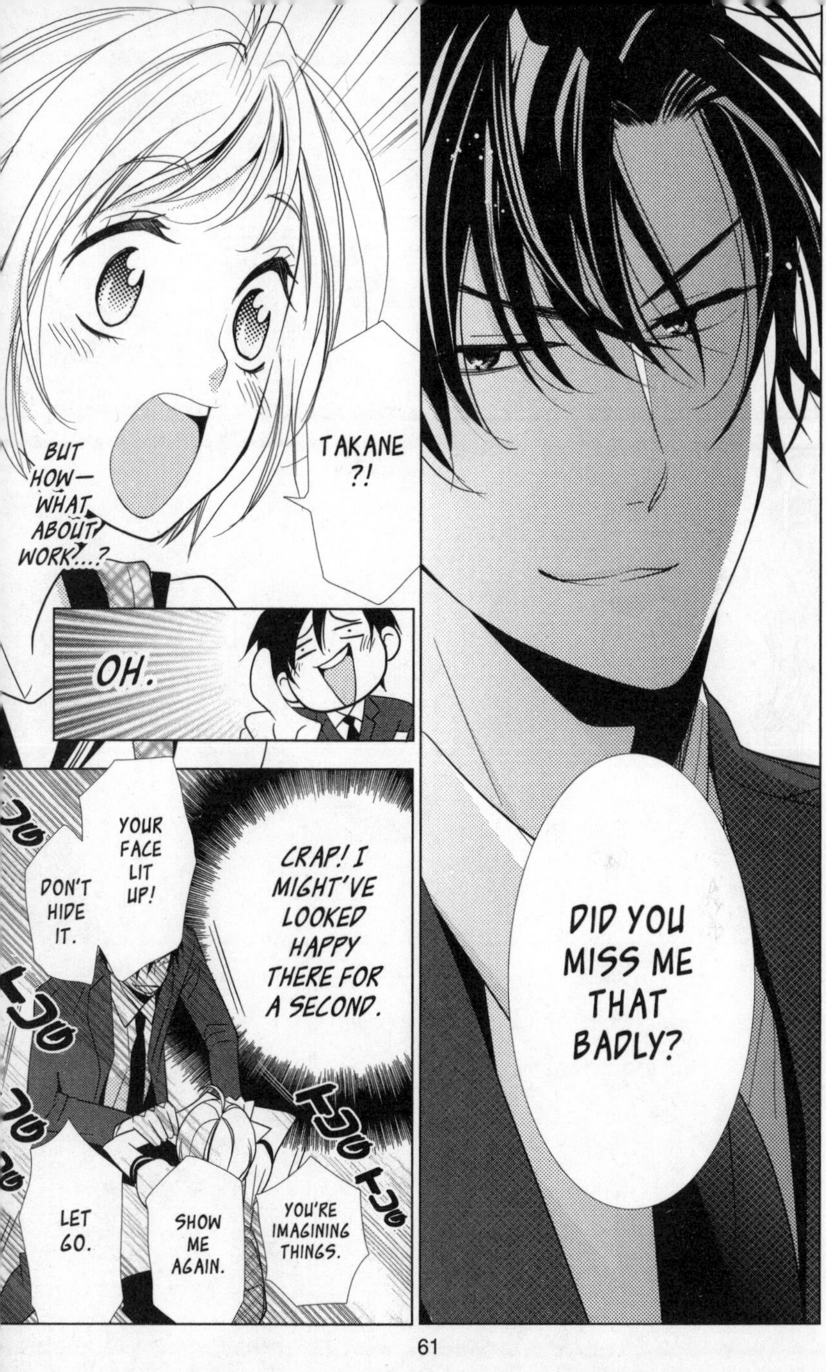
DID YOU MISS ME THAT BADLY?
TAKANE ?!
BUT HOW— WHAT ABOUT WORK...?
OH.
CRAP! I MIGHT'VE LOOKED HAPPY THERE FOR A SECOND.
YOUR FACE LIT UP!
DON'T HIDE IT.
YOU'RE IMAGINING THINGS.
SHOW ME AGAIN.
LET GO.

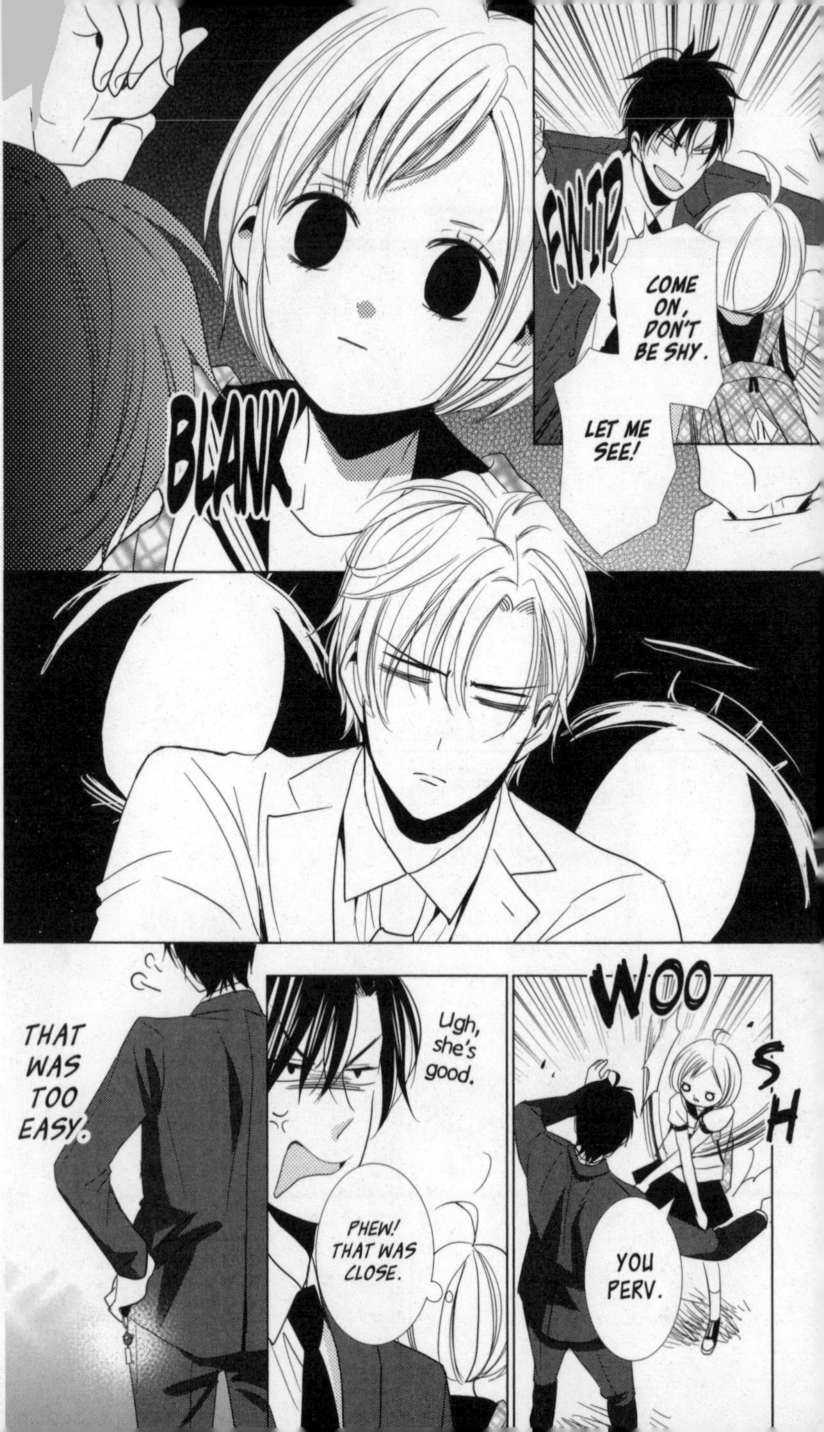
FWIP
COME ON, DON'T BE SHY.
LET ME SEE!
BLANK
WOOSH
YOU PERV.
Ugh, she's good.
PHEW! THAT WAS CLOSE.
THAT WAS TOO EASY.

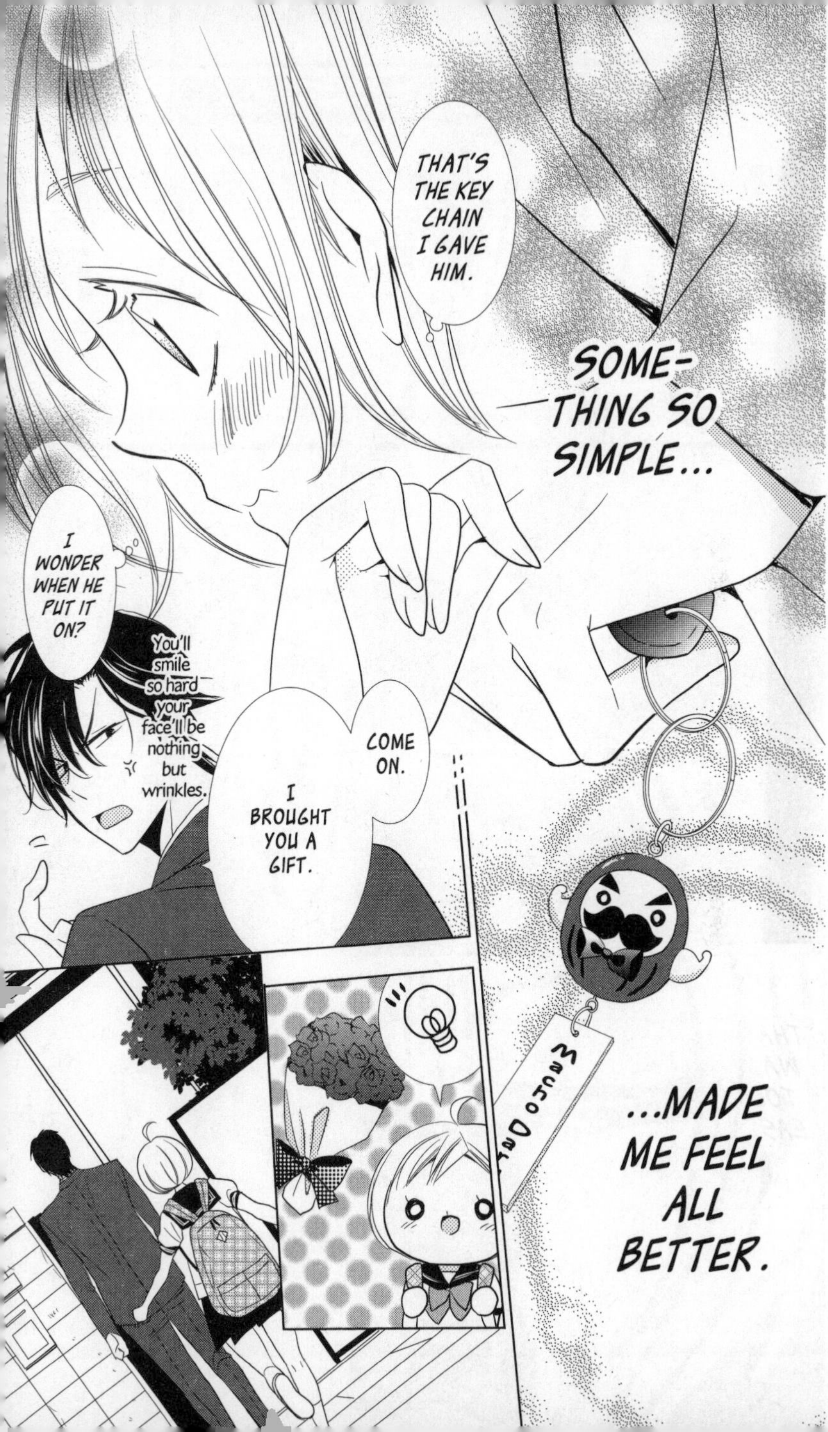
THAT'S THE KEY CHAIN I GAVE HIM.
SOME-THING SO SIMPLE...
I WONDER WHEN HE PUT IT ON?
COME ON.
I BROUGHT YOU A GIFT.
You'll smile so hard your face'll be nothing but wrinkles.
...MADE ME FEEL ALL BETTER.

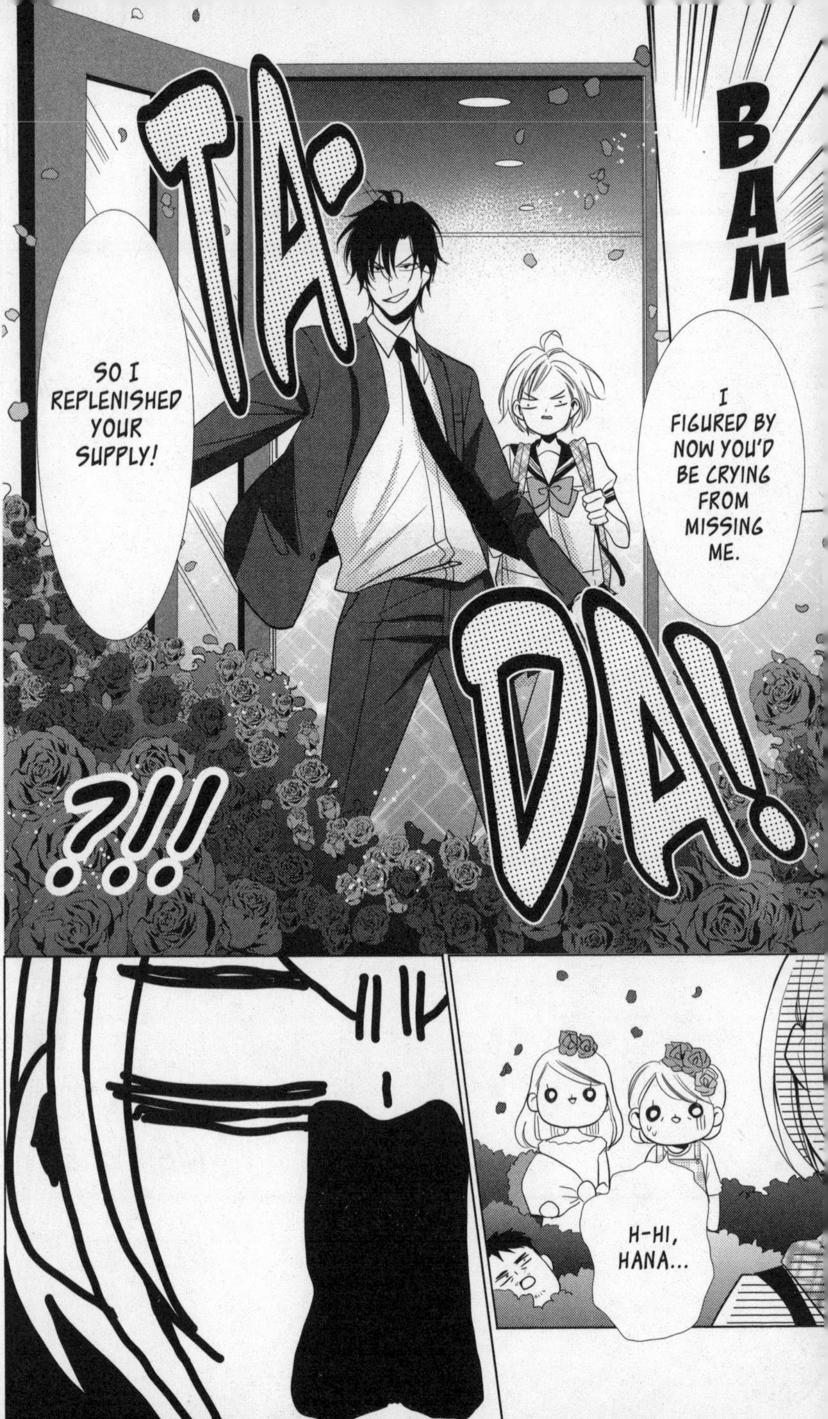
BAM
I FIGURED BY NOW YOU'D BE CRYING FROM MISSING ME.
TA-DA!
SO I REPLENISHED YOUR SUPPLY!
?!!
H-HI, HANA...

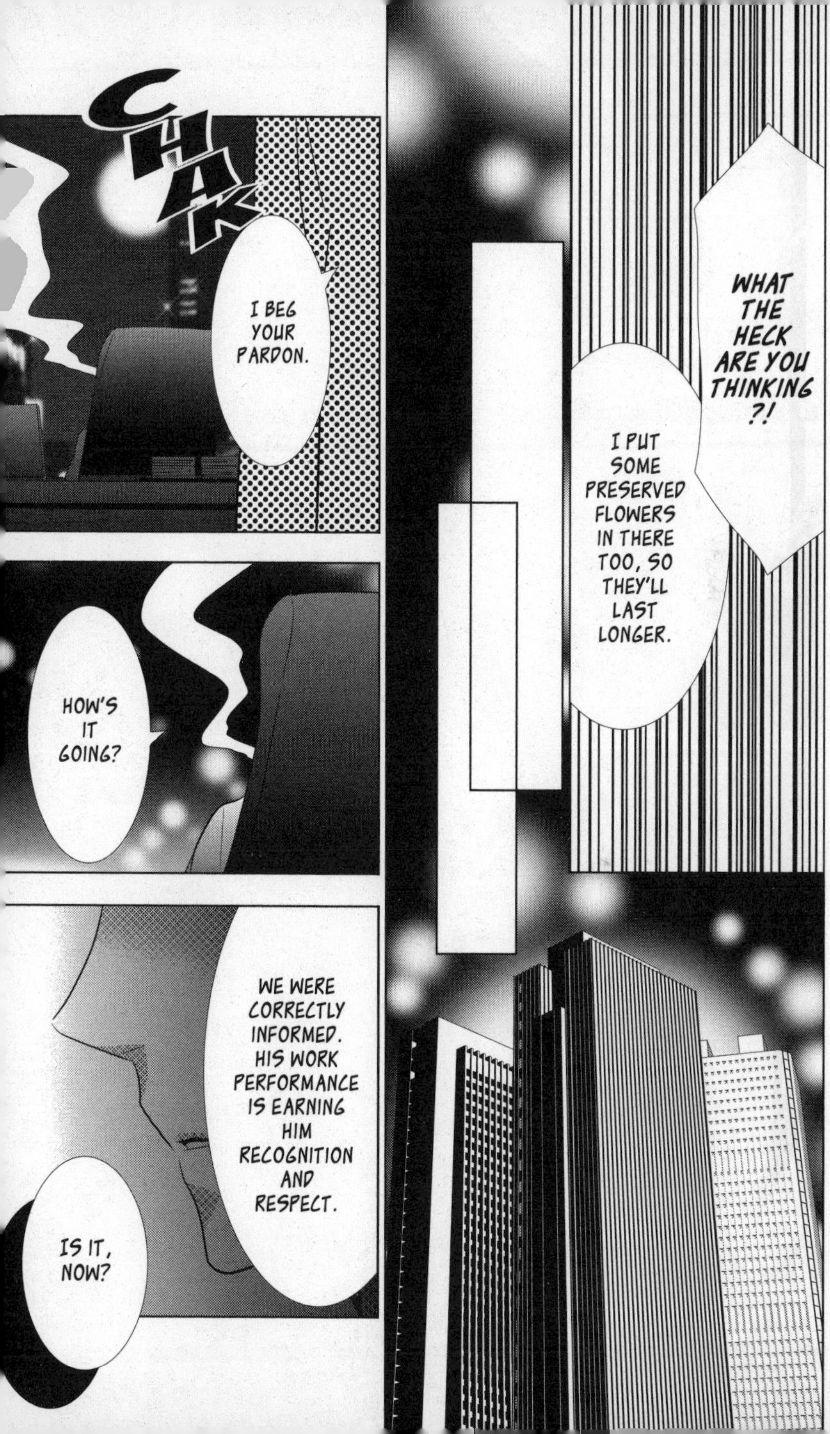
WHAT THE HECK ARE YOU THINKING?!
I PUT SOME PRESERVED FLOWERS IN THERE TOO, SO THEY'LL LAST LONGER.
CHAK
I BEG YOUR PARDON.
HOW'S IT GOING?
WE WERE CORRECTLY INFORMED. HIS WORK PERFORMANCE IS EARNING HIM RECOGNITION AND RESPECT.
IS IT, NOW?

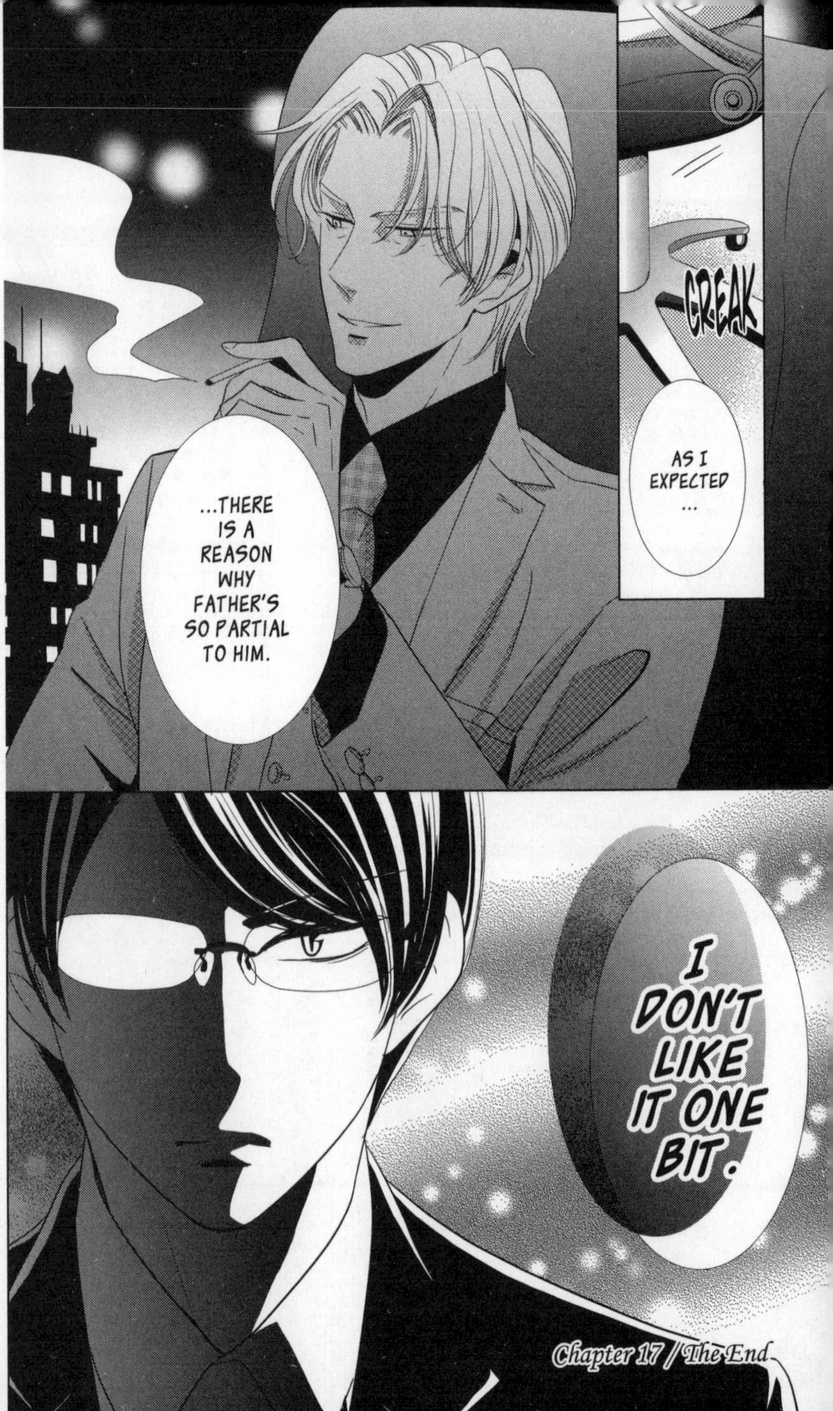
CREAK
AS I EXPECTED ...
...THERE IS A REASON WHY FATHER'S SO PARTIAL TO HIM.
I DON'T LIKE IT ONE BIT.
Chapter 17 / The End

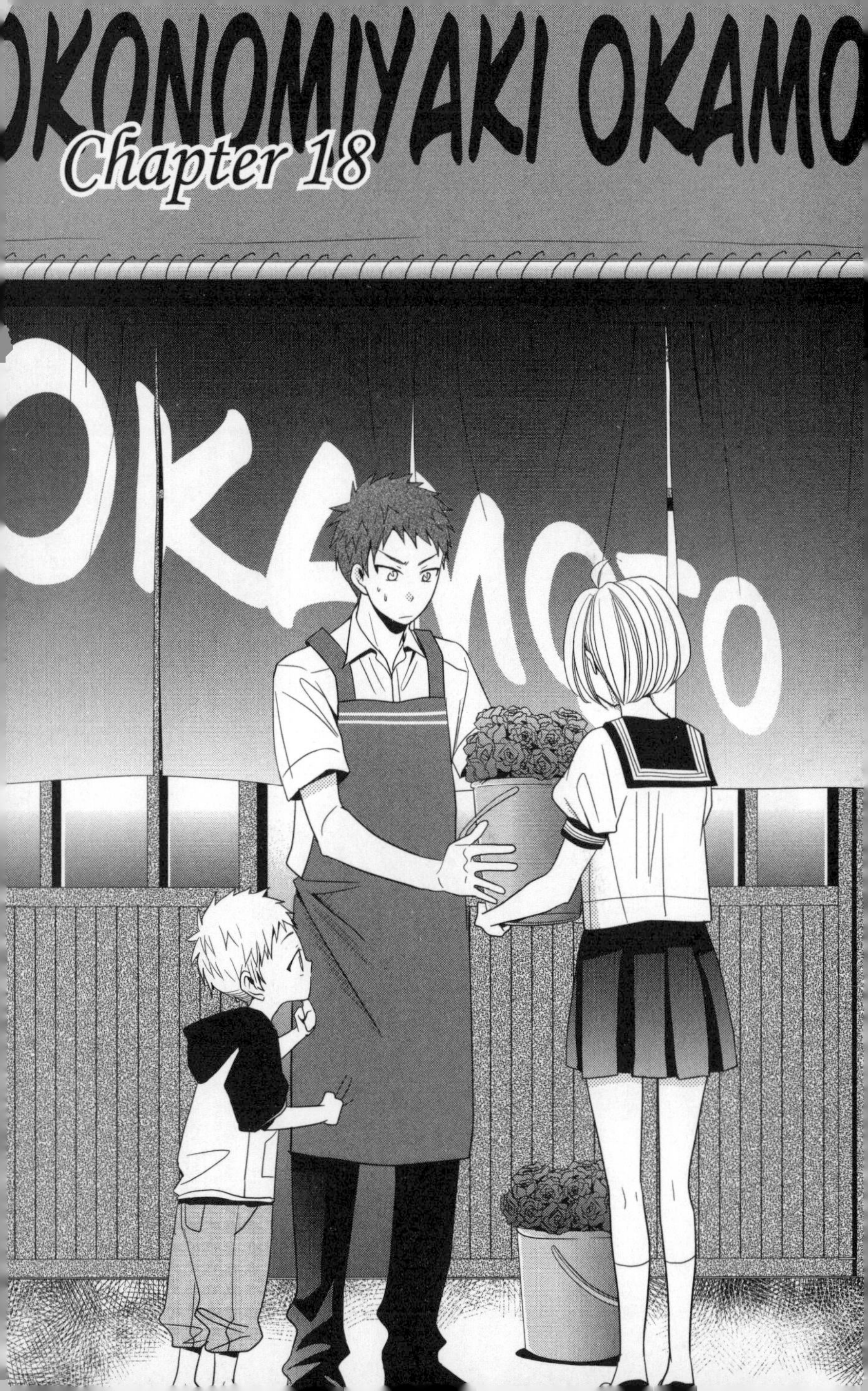
OKONOMIYAKI OKAMO
Chapter 18
OKAMOTO

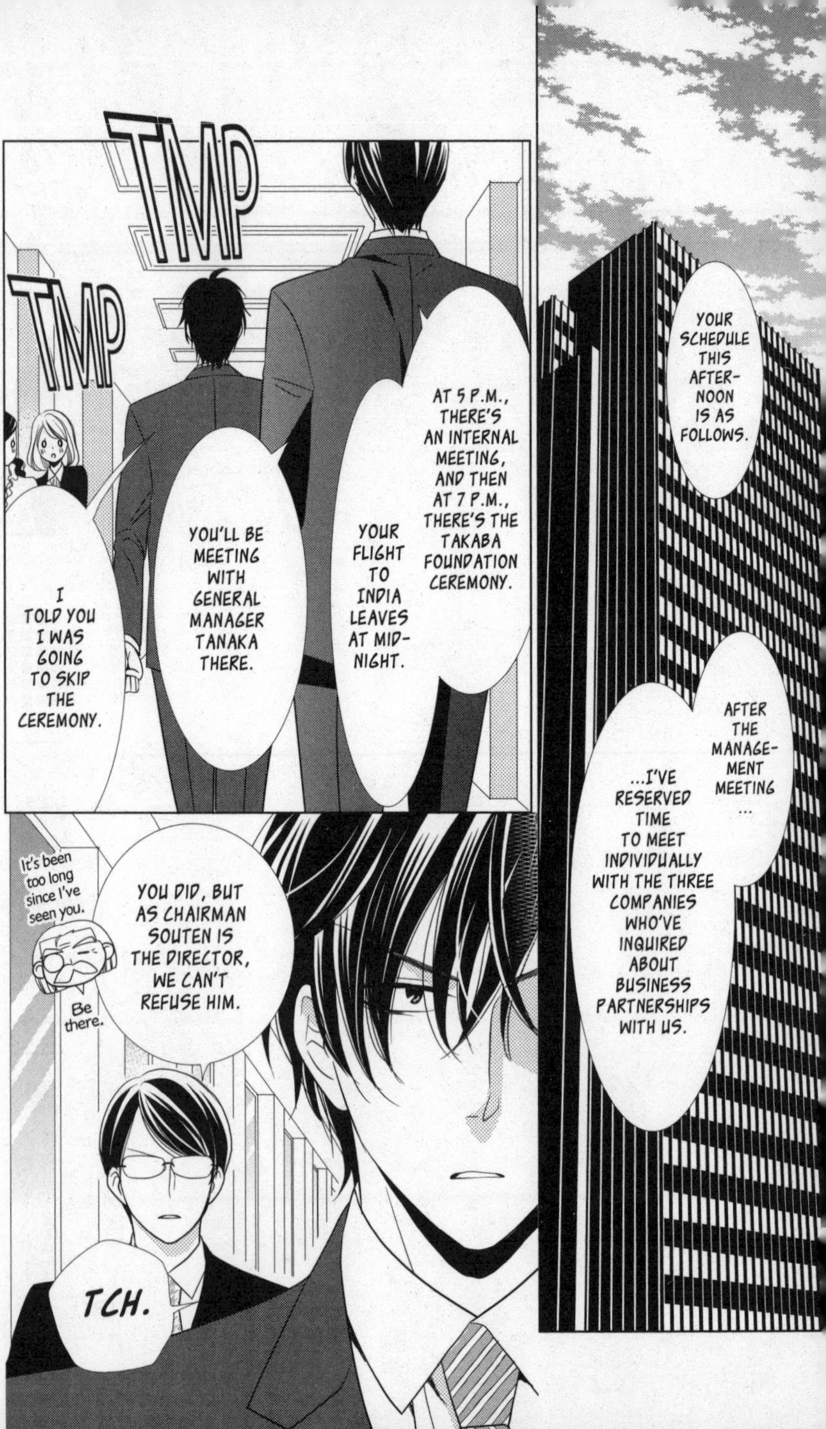
YOUR SCHEDULE THIS AFTERNOON IS AS FOLLOWS.
AFTER THE MANAGEMENT MEETING...
...I'VE RESERVED TIME TO MEET INDIVIDUALLY WITH THE THREE COMPANIES WHO'VE INQUIRED ABOUT BUSINESS PARTNERSHIPS WITH US.
TMP
TMP
AT 5 P.M., THERE'S AN INTERNAL MEETING, AND THEN AT 7 P.M., THERE'S THE TAKABA FOUNDATION CEREMONY.
YOUR FLIGHT TO INDIA LEAVES AT MIDNIGHT.
YOU'LL BE MEETING WITH GENERAL MANAGER TANAKA THERE.
I TOLD YOU I WAS GOING TO SKIP THE CEREMONY.
YOU DID, BUT AS CHAIRMAN SOUTEN IS THE DIRECTOR, WE CAN'T REFUSE HIM.
It's been too long since I've seen you.
Be there.
TCH.

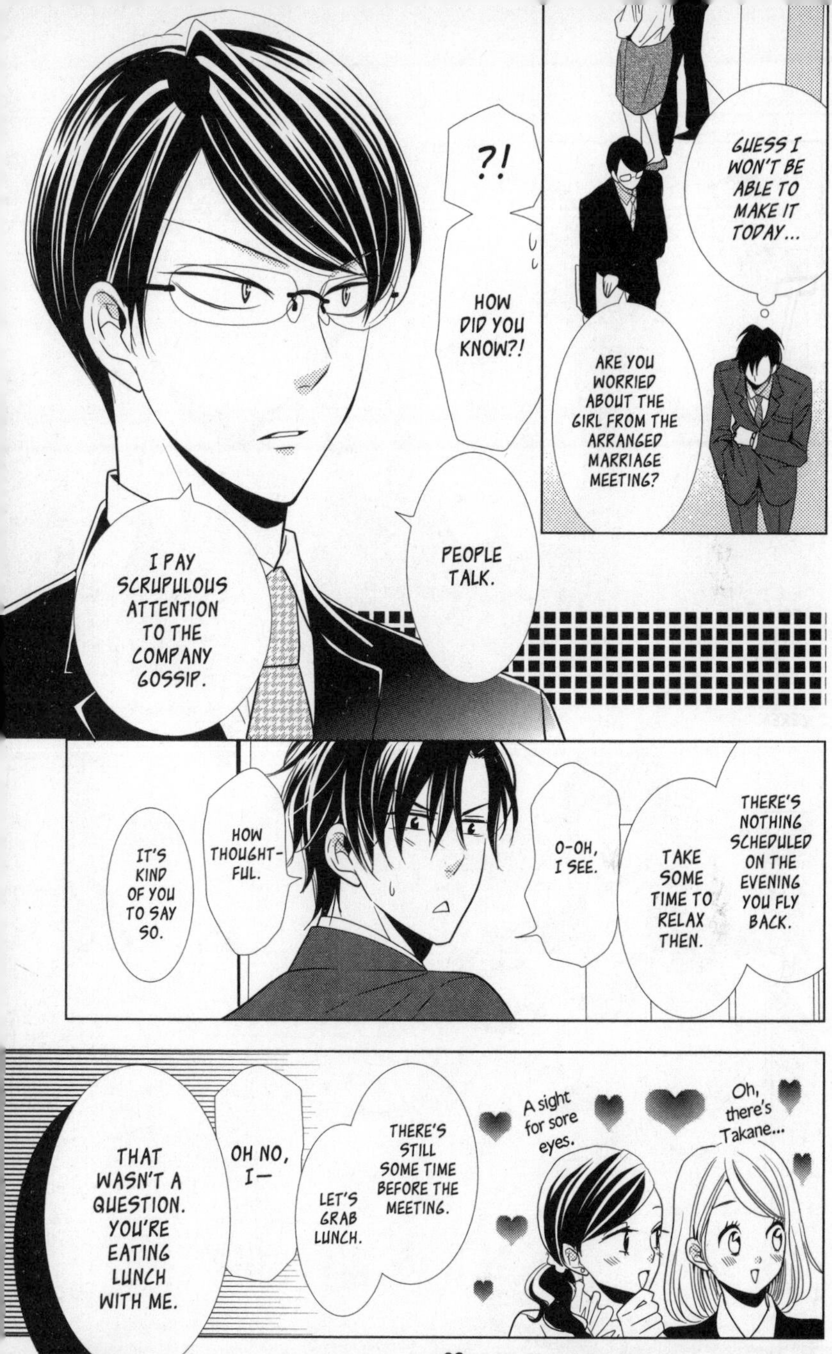
GUESS I WON'T BE ABLE TO MAKE IT TODAY...
ARE YOU WORRIED ABOUT THE GIRL FROM THE ARRANGED MARRIAGE MEETING?
?!
HOW DID YOU KNOW?!
PEOPLE TALK.
I PAY SCRUPULOUS ATTENTION TO THE COMPANY GOSSIP.
THERE'S NOTHING SCHEDULED ON THE EVENING YOU FLY BACK.
TAKE SOME TIME TO RELAX THEN.
O-OH, I SEE.
HOW THOUGHTFUL.
IT'S KIND OF YOU TO SAY SO.
Oh, there's Takane...
A sight for sore eyes.
THERE'S STILL SOME TIME BEFORE THE MEETING.
LET'S GRAB LUNCH.
OH NO, I—
THAT WASN'T A QUESTION. YOU'RE EATING LUNCH WITH ME.

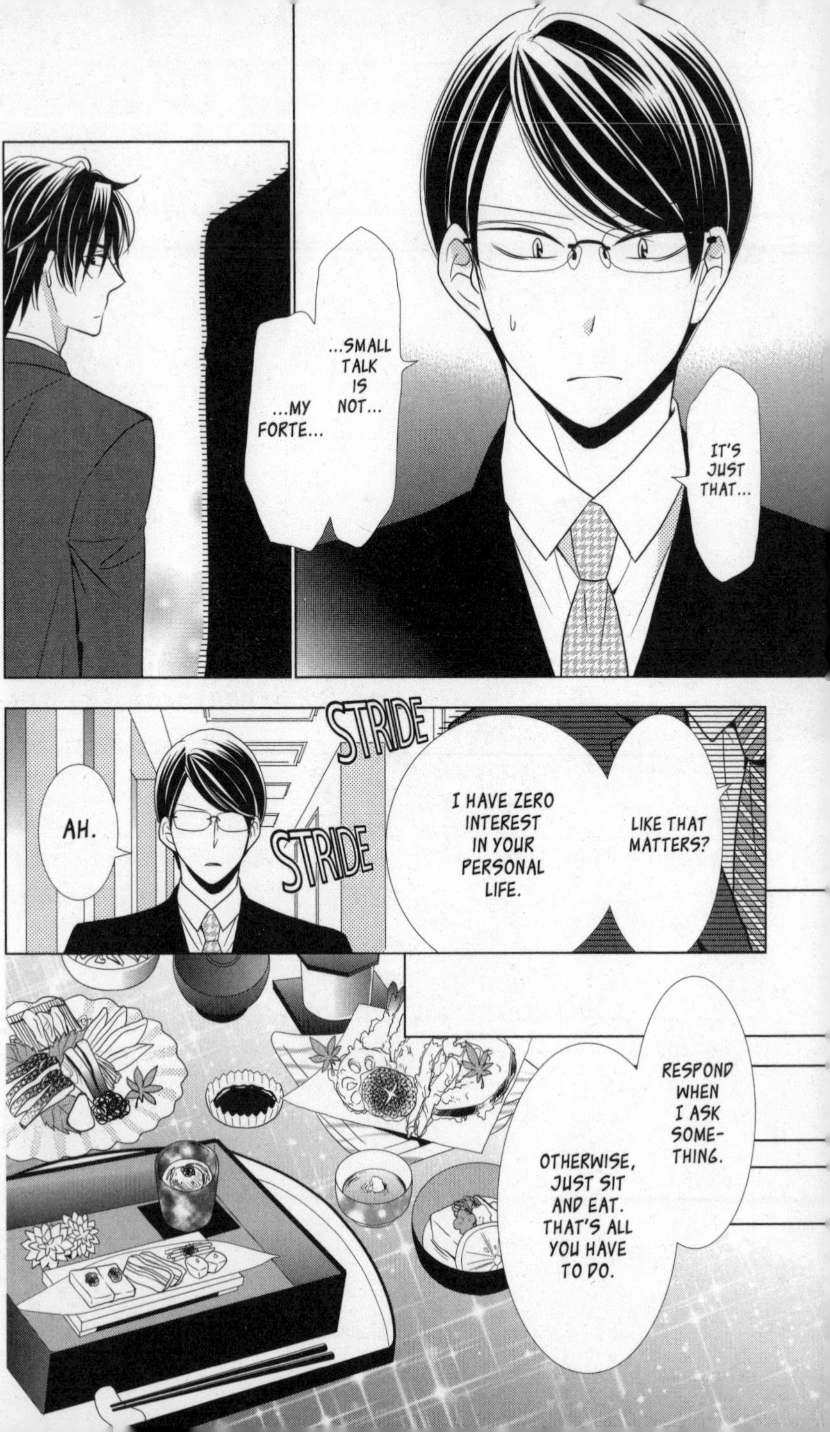
IT'S JUST THAT...
...SMALL TALK IS NOT...
...MY FORTE...
LIKE THAT MATTERS?
I HAVE ZERO INTEREST IN YOUR PERSONAL LIFE.
STRIDE
STRIDE
AH.
RESPOND WHEN I ASK SOME-THING.
OTHERWISE, JUST SIT AND EAT. THAT'S ALL YOU HAVE TO DO.

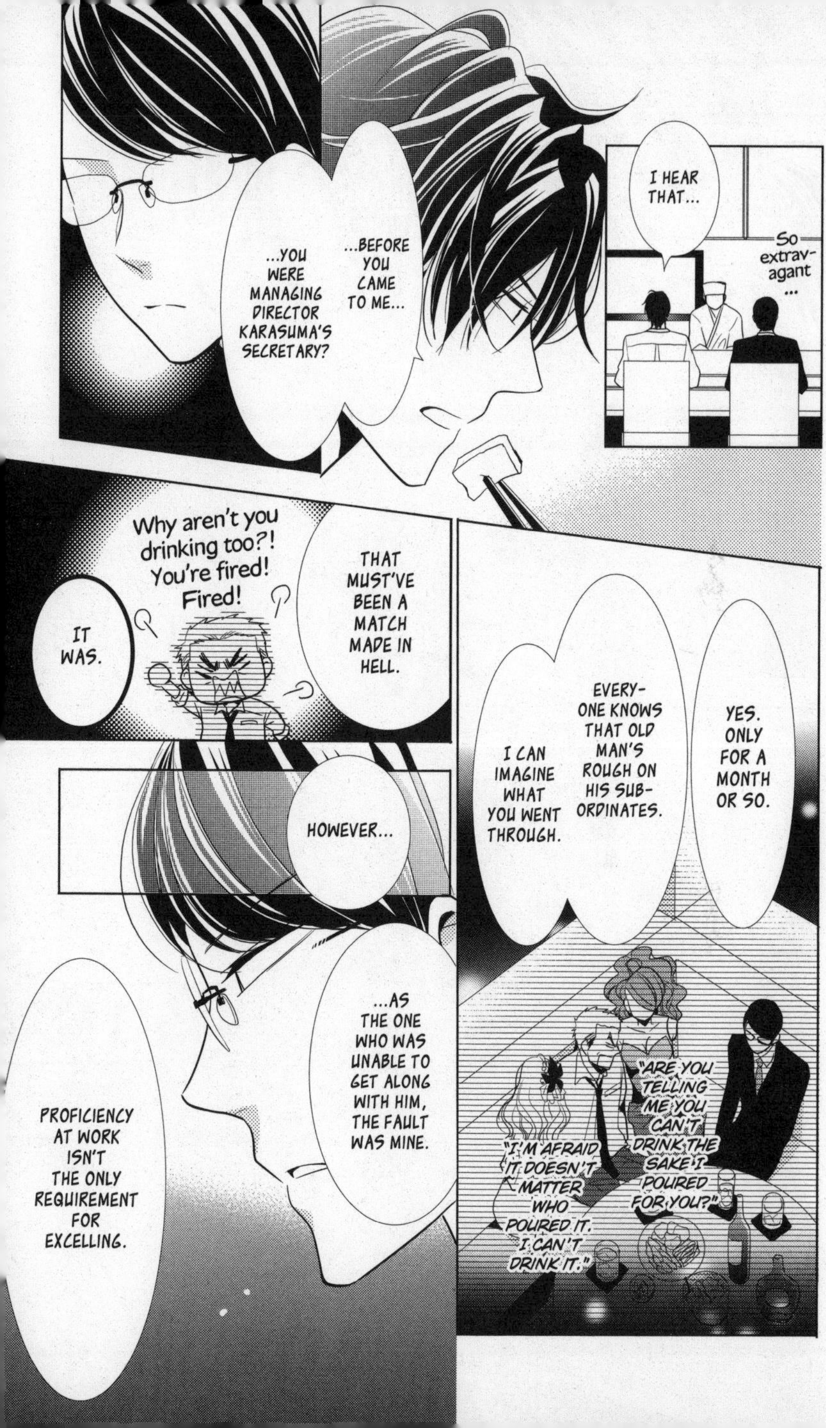
I HEAR THAT...
So extravagant...
...BEFORE YOU CAME TO ME...
...YOU WERE MANAGING DIRECTOR KARASUMA'S SECRETARY?
YES. ONLY FOR A MONTH OR SO.
EVERYONE KNOWS THAT OLD MAN'S ROUGH ON HIS SUBORDINATES.
I CAN IMAGINE WHAT YOU WENT THROUGH.
"ARE YOU TELLING ME YOU CAN'T DRINK THE SAKE I POURED FOR YOU?"
"I'M AFRAID IT DOESN'T MATTER WHO POURED IT. I CAN'T DRINK IT."
THAT MUST'VE BEEN A MATCH MADE IN HELL.
Why aren't you drinking too?! You're fired! Fired!
IT WAS.
HOWEVER...
...AS THE ONE WHO WAS UNABLE TO GET ALONG WITH HIM, THE FAULT WAS MINE.
PROFICIENCY AT WORK ISN'T THE ONLY REQUIREMENT FOR EXCELLING.

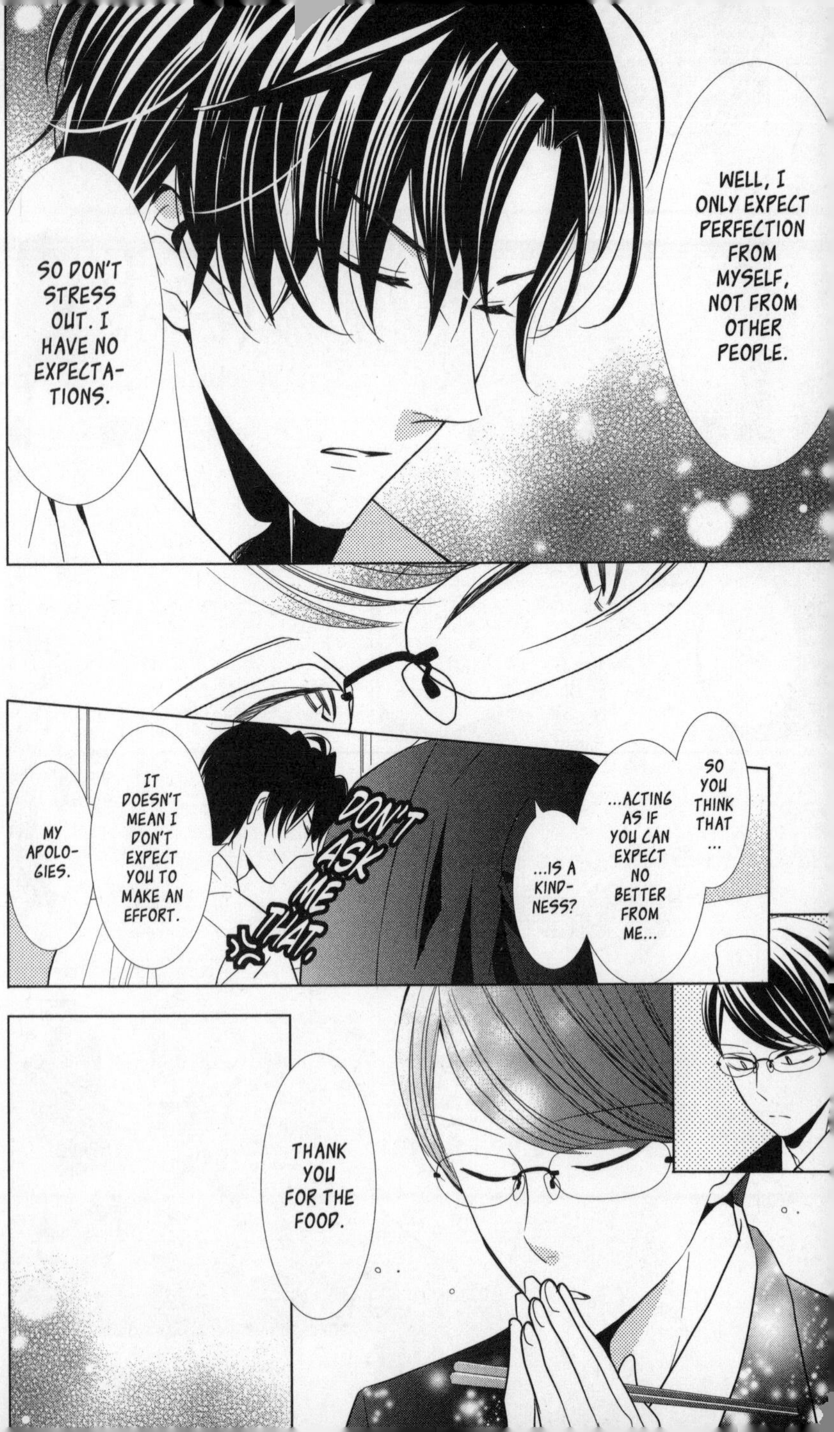
WELL, I ONLY EXPECT PERFECTION FROM MYSELF, NOT FROM OTHER PEOPLE.
SO DON'T STRESS OUT. I HAVE NO EXPECTATIONS.
SO YOU THINK THAT...
...ACTING AS IF YOU CAN EXPECT NO BETTER FROM ME...
...IS A KINDNESS?
DON'T ASK ME THAT.
IT DOESN'T MEAN I DON'T EXPECT YOU TO MAKE AN EFFORT.
MY APOLOGIES.
THANK YOU FOR THE FOOD.

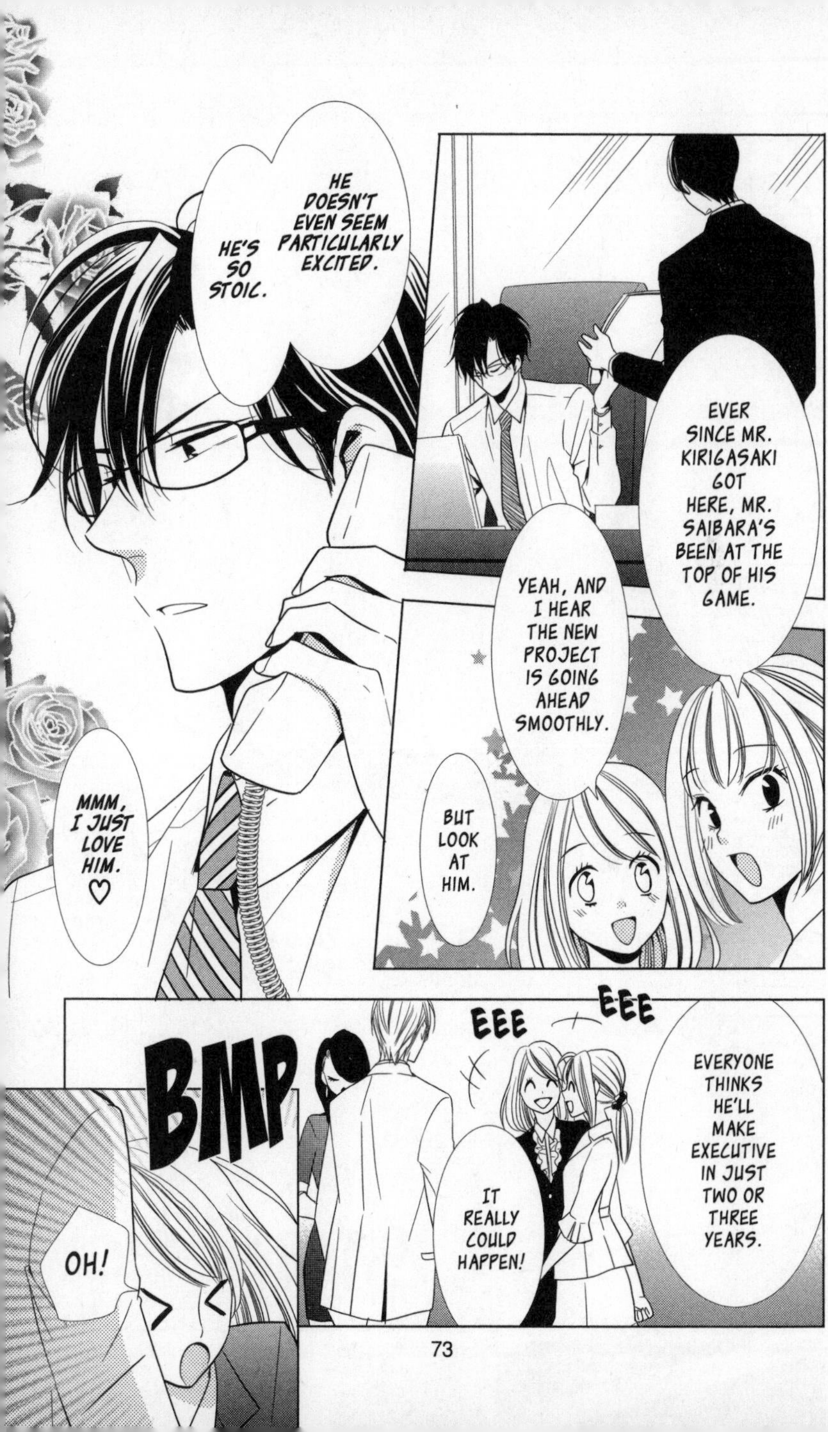
EVER SINCE MR. KIRIGASAKI GOT HERE, MR. SAIBARA'S BEEN AT THE TOP OF HIS GAME.
YEAH, AND I HEAR THE NEW PROJECT IS GOING AHEAD SMOOTHLY.
BUT LOOK AT HIM.
HE DOESN'T EVEN SEEM PARTICULARLY EXCITED.
HE'S SO STOIC.
MMM, I JUST LOVE HIM. ♡
EVERYONE THINKS HE'LL MAKE EXECUTIVE IN JUST TWO OR THREE YEARS.
EEE
EEE
IT REALLY COULD HAPPEN!
BMP
OH!

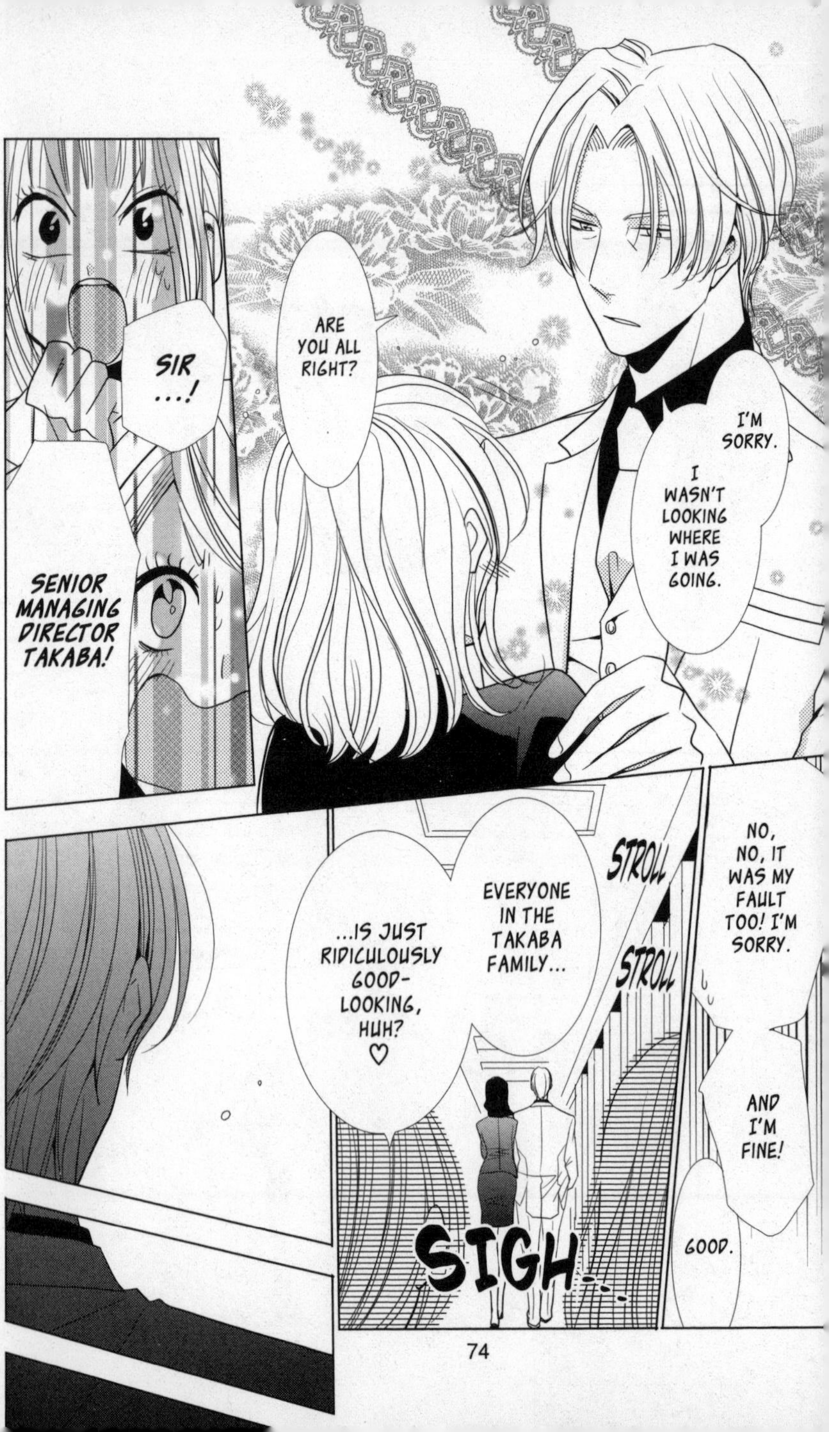
ARE YOU ALL RIGHT?
I'M SORRY.
I WASN'T LOOKING WHERE I WAS GOING.
SIR ...!
SENIOR MANAGING DIRECTOR TAKABA!
NO, NO, IT WAS MY FAULT TOO! I'M SORRY.
AND I'M FINE!
GOOD.
STROLL
STROLL
EVERYONE IN THE TAKABA FAMILY...
...IS JUST RIDICULOUSLY GOOD-LOOKING, HUH? ♡
SIGH...

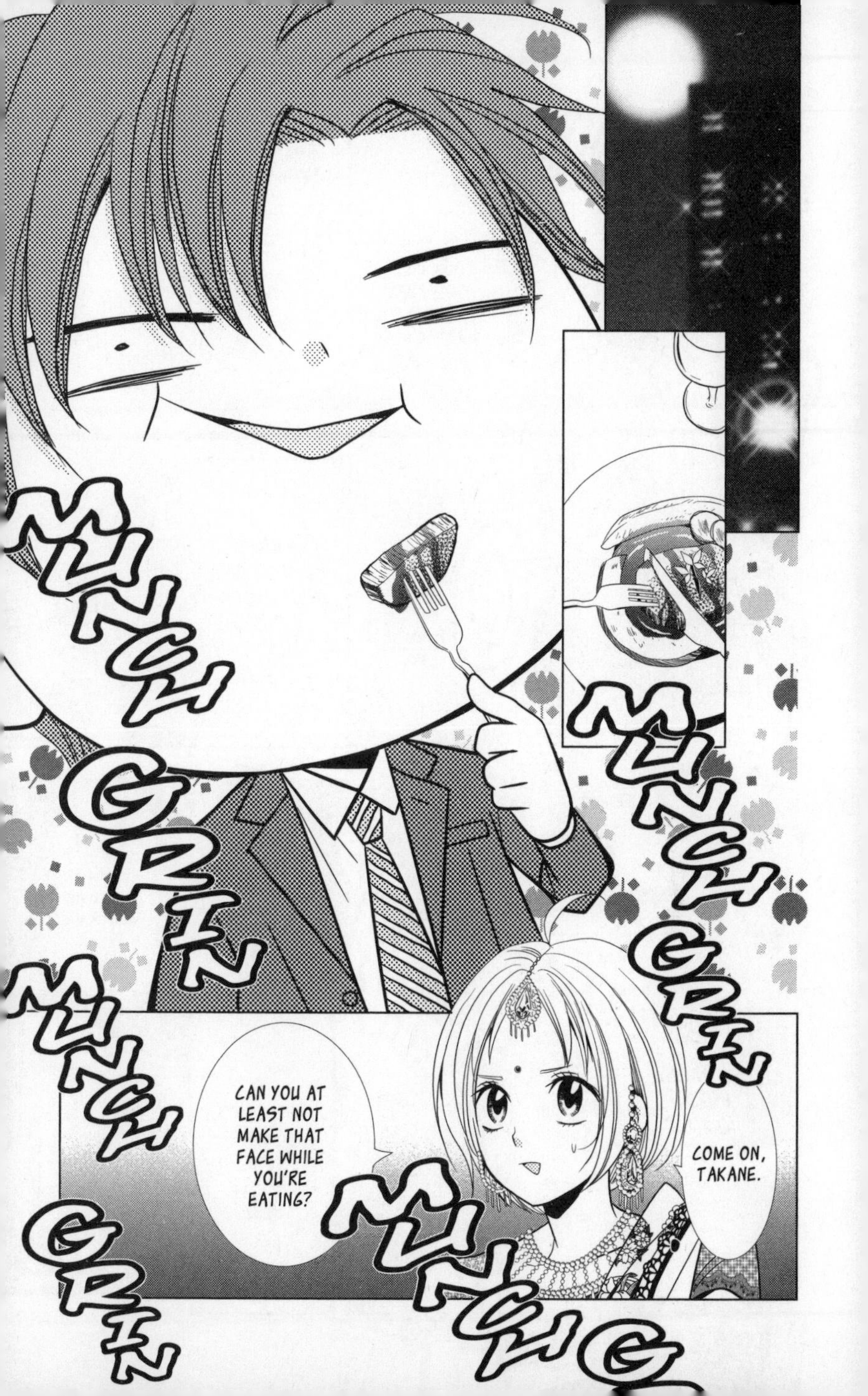
MUNCH
GRIN
MUNCH
GRIN
COME ON, TAKANE.
CAN YOU AT LEAST NOT MAKE THAT FACE WHILE YOU'RE EATING?
MUNCH
MUNCH
GRIN

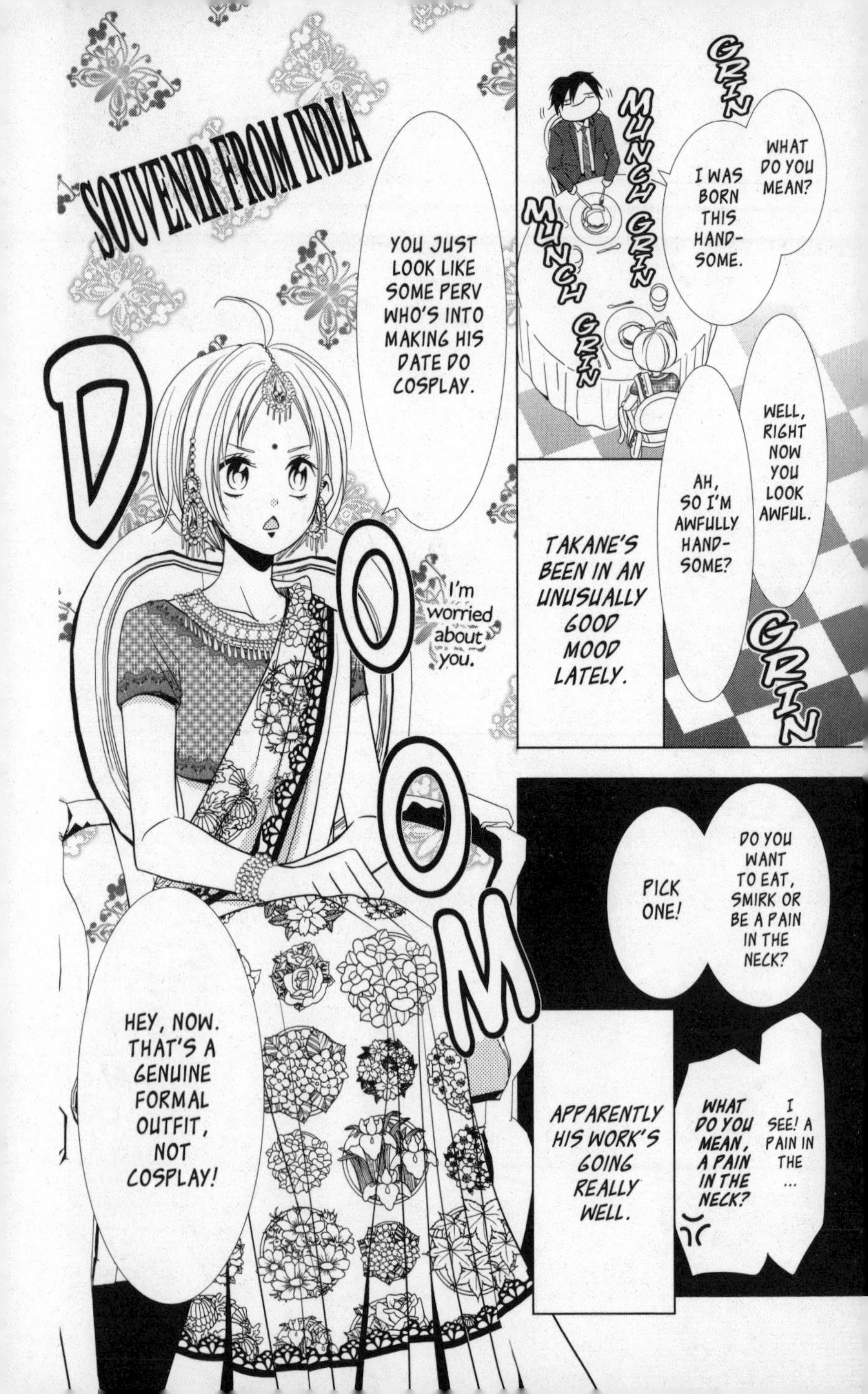
GRIN
WHAT DO YOU MEAN?
I WAS BORN THIS HAND-SOME.
MUNCH GRIN
MUNCH GRIN
WELL, RIGHT NOW YOU LOOK AWFUL.
AH, SO I'M AWFULLY HAND-SOME?
GRIN
TAKANE'S BEEN IN AN UNUSUALLY GOOD MOOD LATELY.
DO YOU WANT TO EAT, SMIRK OR BE A PAIN IN THE NECK?
PICK ONE!
I SEE! A PAIN IN THE ...
WHAT DO YOU MEAN, A PAIN IN THE NECK?
APPARENTLY HIS WORK'S GOING REALLY WELL.
SOUVENR FROM INDIA
YOU JUST LOOK LIKE SOME PERV WHO'S INTO MAKING HIS DATE DO COSPLAY.
I'm worried about you.
DOOOM
HEY, NOW. THAT'S A GENUINE FORMAL OUTFIT, NOT COSPLAY!

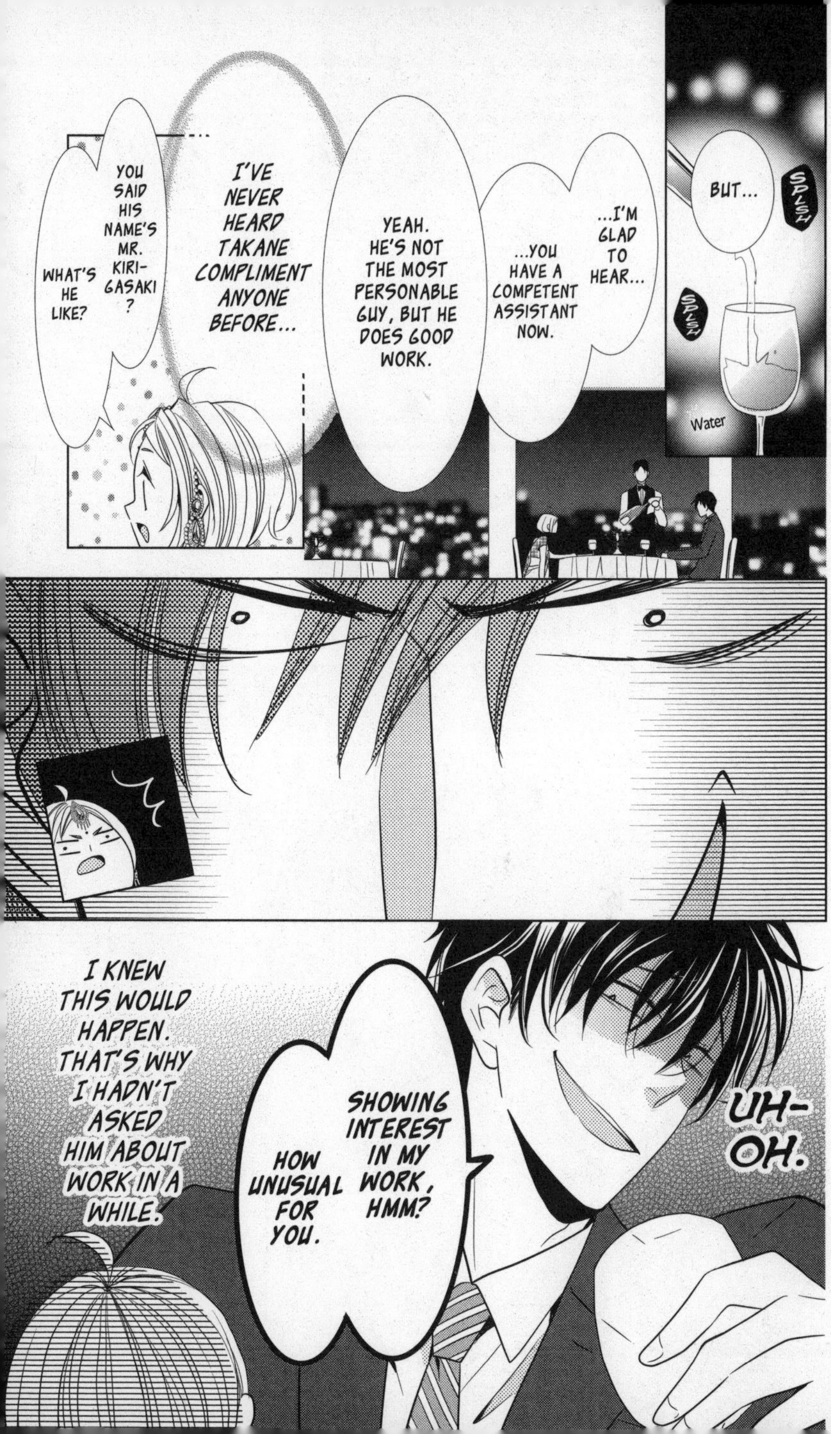
SPLSH
BUT...
SPLSH
Water
...I'M GLAD TO HEAR...
...YOU HAVE A COMPETENT ASSISTANT NOW.
YEAH. HE'S NOT THE MOST PERSONABLE GUY, BUT HE DOES GOOD WORK.
I'VE NEVER HEARD TAKANE COMPLIMENT ANYONE BEFORE...
YOU SAID HIS NAME'S MR. KIRI-GASAKI?
WHAT'S HE LIKE?
UH-OH.
SHOWING INTEREST IN MY WORK, HMM?
HOW UNUSUAL FOR YOU.
I KNEW THIS WOULD HAPPEN. THAT'S WHY I HADN'T ASKED HIM ABOUT WORK IN A WHILE.

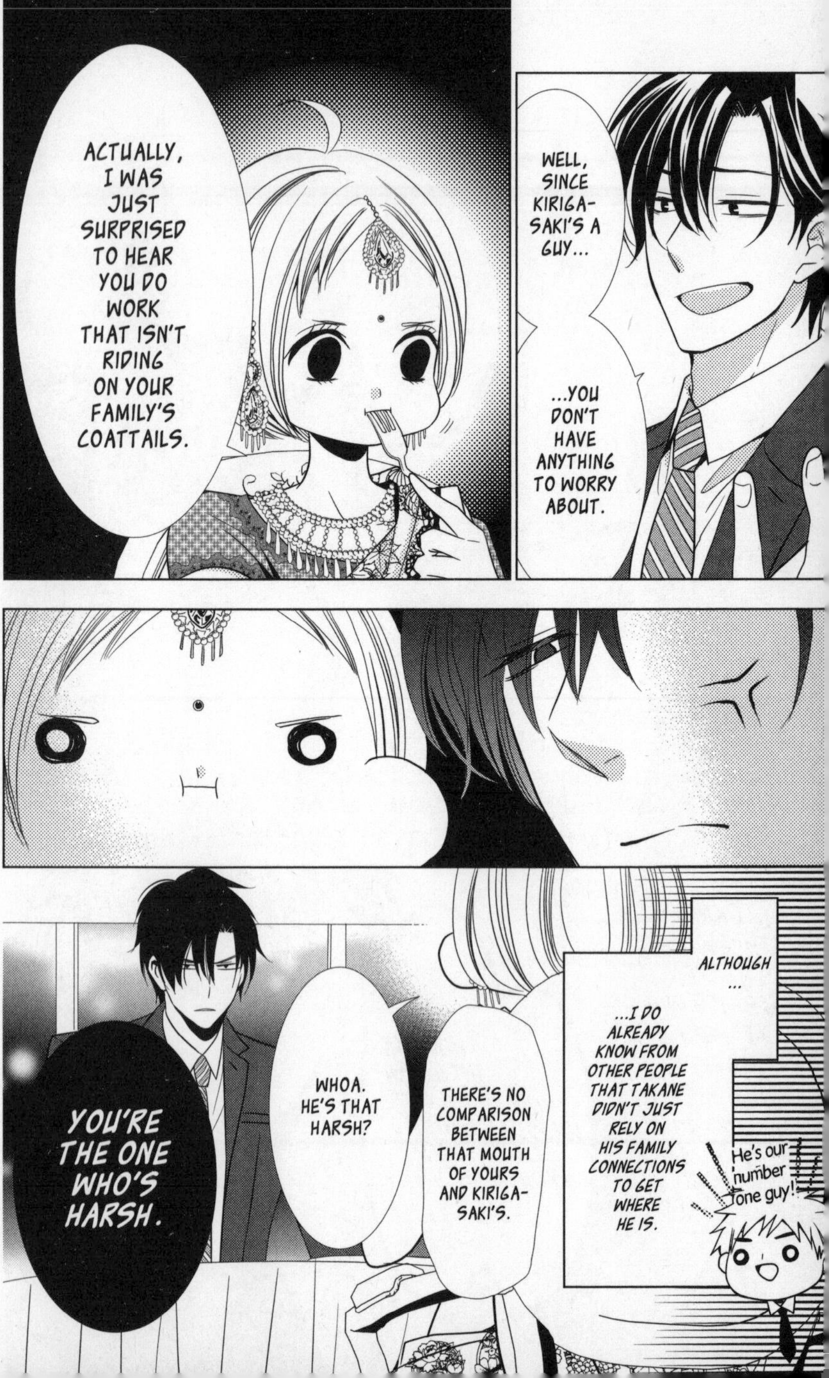
WELL, SINCE KIRIGA-SAKI'S A GUY...
...YOU DON'T HAVE ANYTHING TO WORRY ABOUT.
ACTUALLY, I WAS JUST SURPRISED TO HEAR YOU DO WORK THAT ISN'T RIDING ON YOUR FAMILY'S COATTAILS.
ALTHOUGH ...
...I DO ALREADY KNOW FROM OTHER PEOPLE THAT TAKANE DIDN'T JUST RELY ON HIS FAMILY CONNECTIONS TO GET WHERE HE IS.
He's our number one guy!
THERE'S NO COMPARISON BETWEEN THAT MOUTH OF YOURS AND KIRIGA-SAKI'S.
WHOA. HE'S THAT HARSH?
YOU'RE THE ONE WHO'S HARSH.

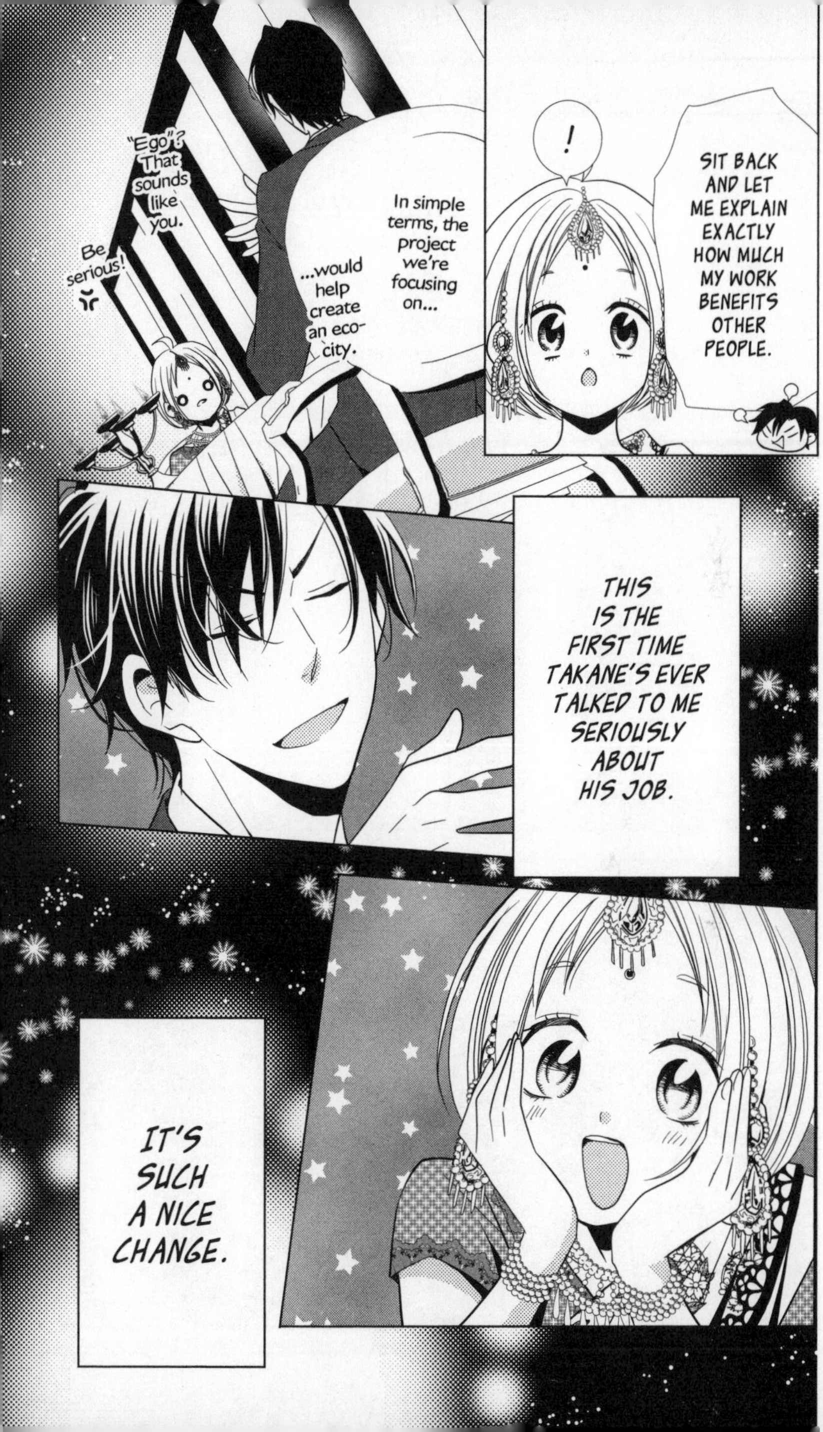
!
SIT BACK AND LET ME EXPLAIN EXACTLY HOW MUCH MY WORK BENEFITS OTHER PEOPLE.
In simple terms, the project we're focusing on...
...would help create an eco-city.
"Ego"? That sounds like you.
Be serious!
THIS IS THE FIRST TIME TAKANE'S EVER TALKED TO ME SERIOUSLY ABOUT HIS JOB.
IT'S SUCH A NICE CHANGE.

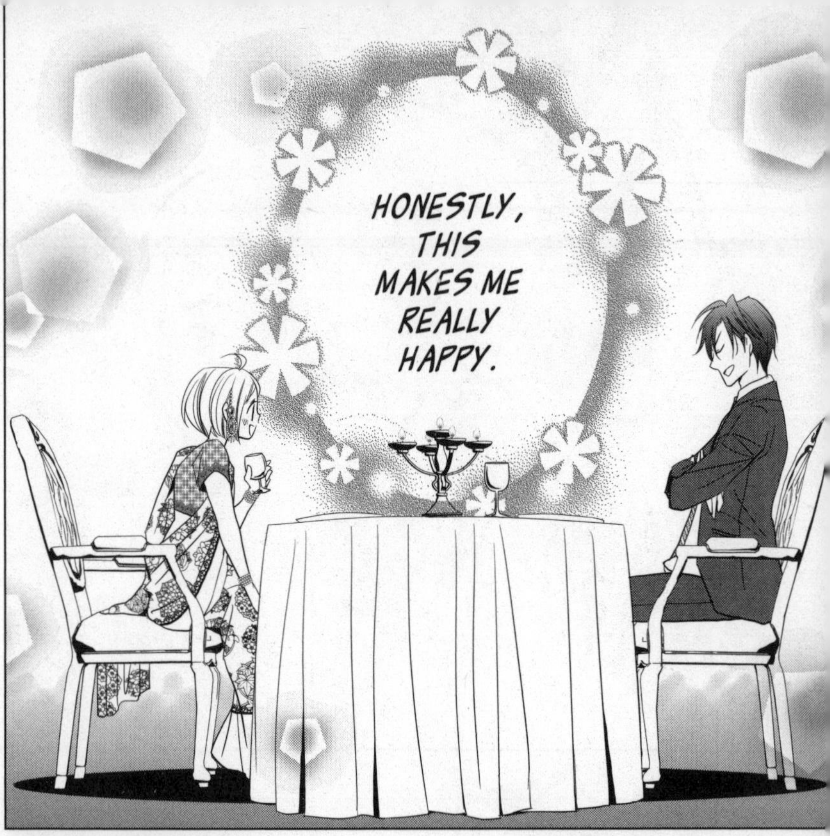
HONESTLY, THIS MAKES ME REALLY HAPPY.

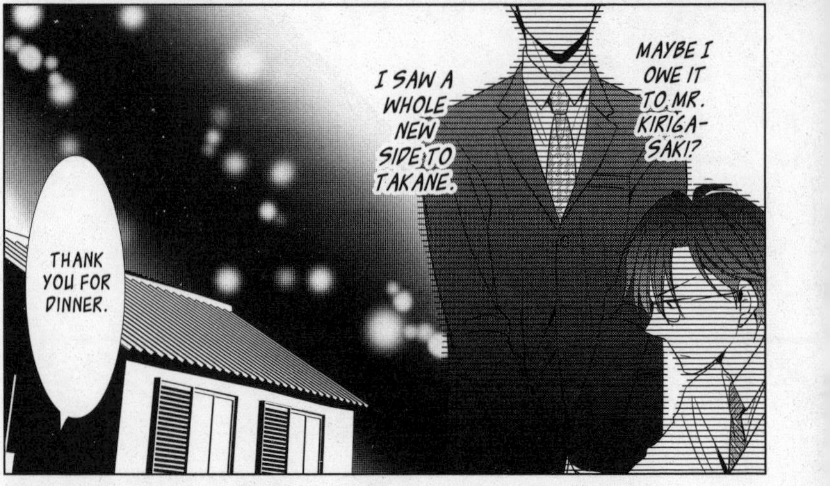
MAYBE I OWE IT TO MR. KIRIGA-SAKI?
I SAW A WHOLE NEW SIDE TO TAKANE.
THANK YOU FOR DINNER.

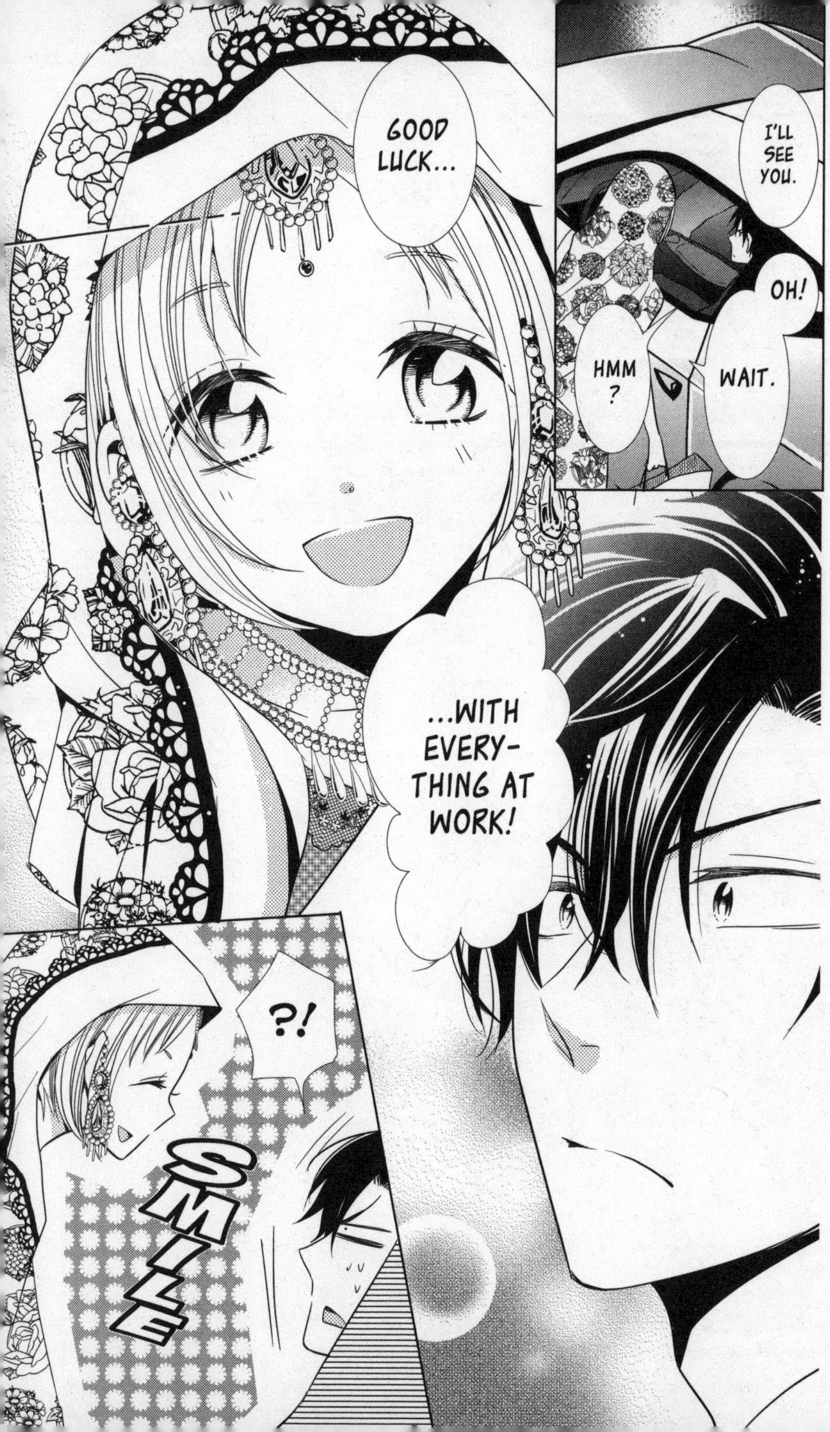
I'LL SEE YOU.
OH! WAIT.
HMM?
GOOD LUCK...
...WITH EVERY-THING AT WORK!
?!
SMILE

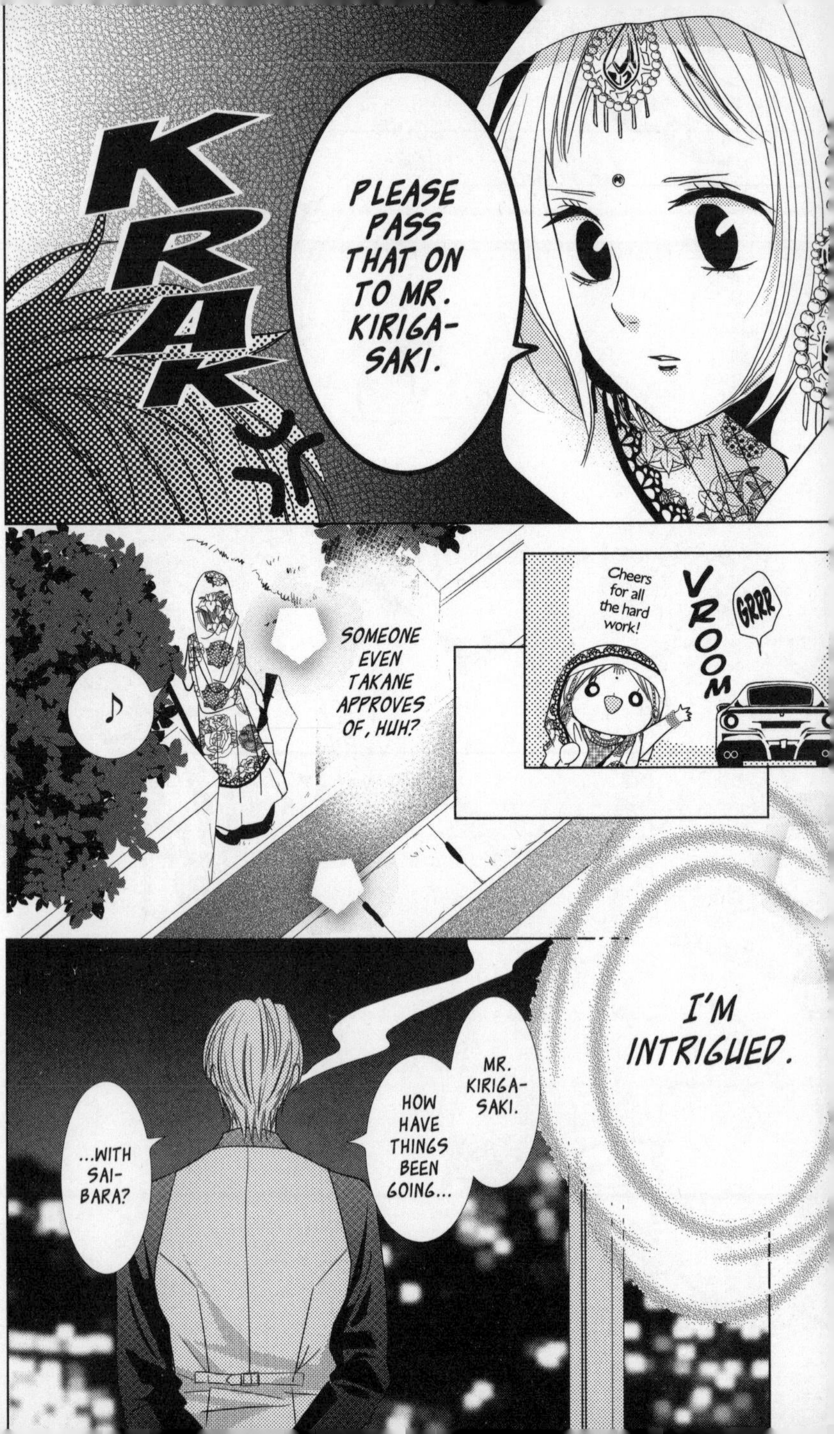
PLEASE PASS THAT ON TO MR. KIRIGA-SAKI.
KRAK
GRRR
VROOM
Cheers for all the hard work!
SOMEONE EVEN TAKANE APPROVES OF, HUH?
♪
I'M INTRIGUED.
MR. KIRIGA-SAKI.
HOW HAVE THINGS BEEN GOING...
...WITH SAI-BARA?

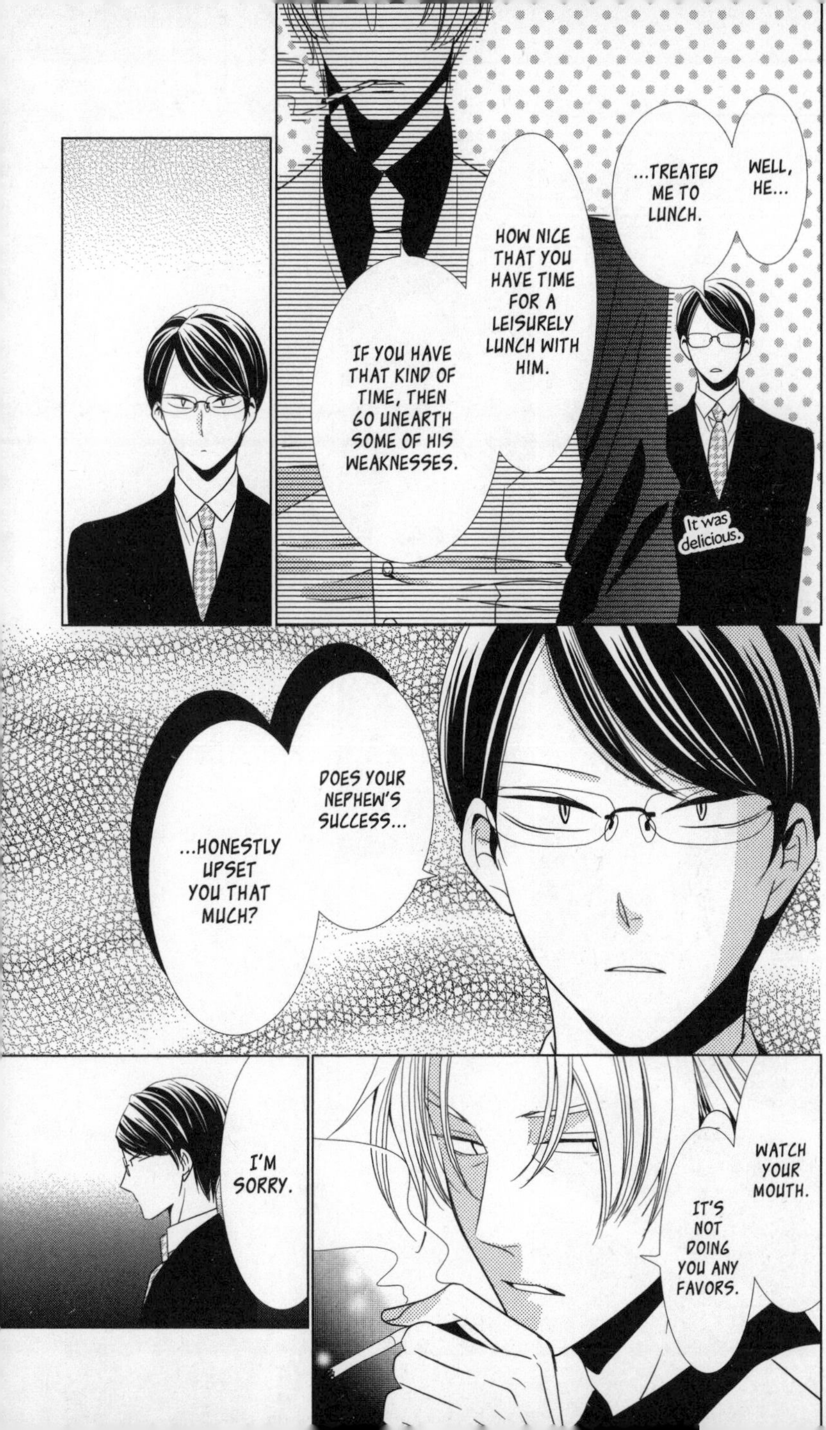
WELL, HE...
...TREATED ME TO LUNCH.
It was delicious.
HOW NICE THAT YOU HAVE TIME FOR A LEISURELY LUNCH WITH HIM.
IF YOU HAVE THAT KIND OF TIME, THEN GO UNEARTH SOME OF HIS WEAKNESSES.
DOES YOUR NEPHEW'S SUCCESS...
...HONESTLY UPSET YOU THAT MUCH?
WATCH YOUR MOUTH.
IT'S NOT DOING YOU ANY FAVORS.
I'M SORRY.

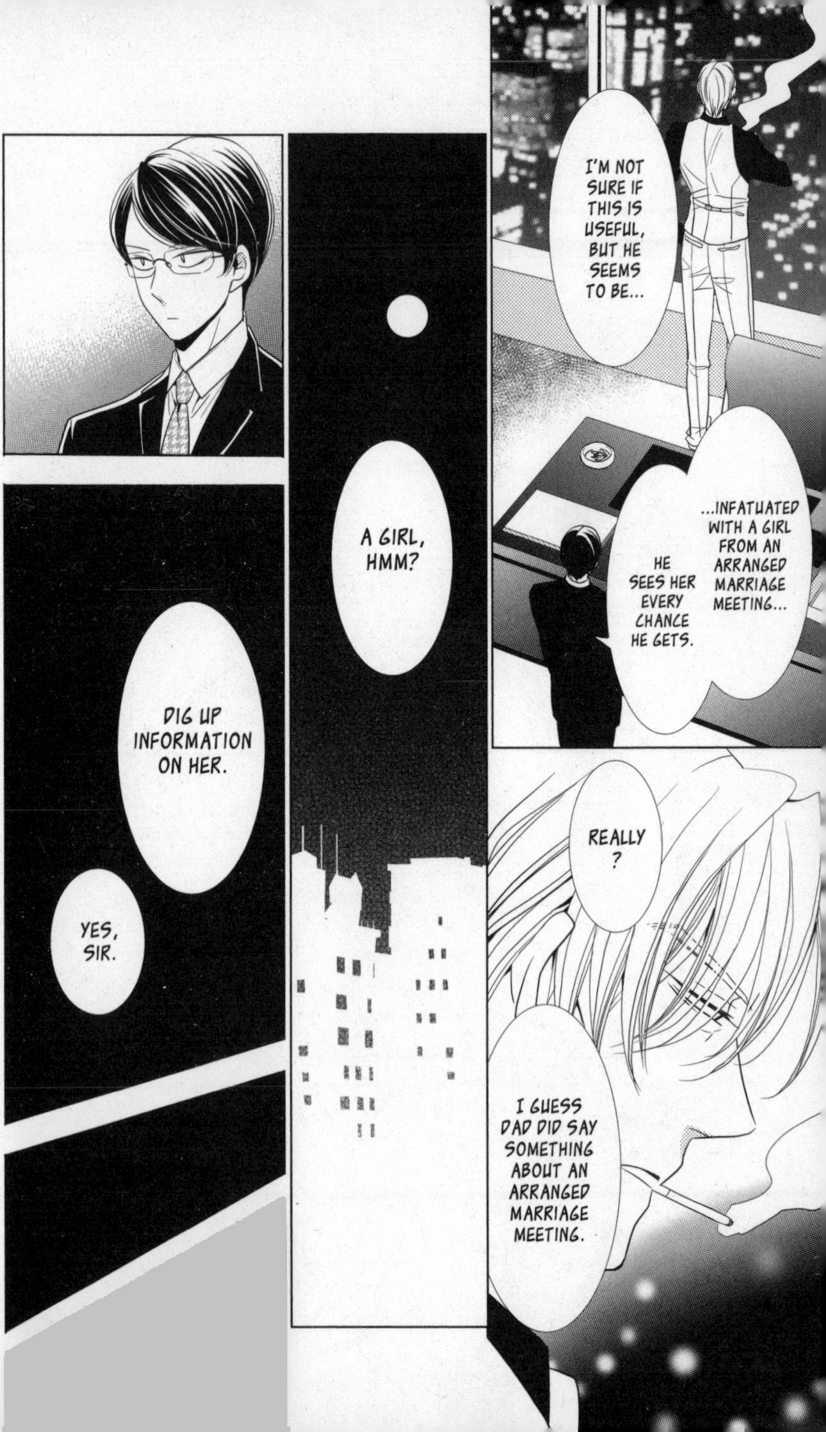
I'M NOT SURE IF THIS IS USEFUL, BUT HE SEEMS TO BE...
...INFATUATED WITH A GIRL FROM AN ARRANGED MARRIAGE MEETING...
HE SEES HER EVERY CHANCE HE GETS.
REALLY?
I GUESS DAD DID SAY SOMETHING ABOUT AN ARRANGED MARRIAGE MEETING.
A GIRL, HMM?
DIG UP INFORMATION ON HER.
YES, SIR.

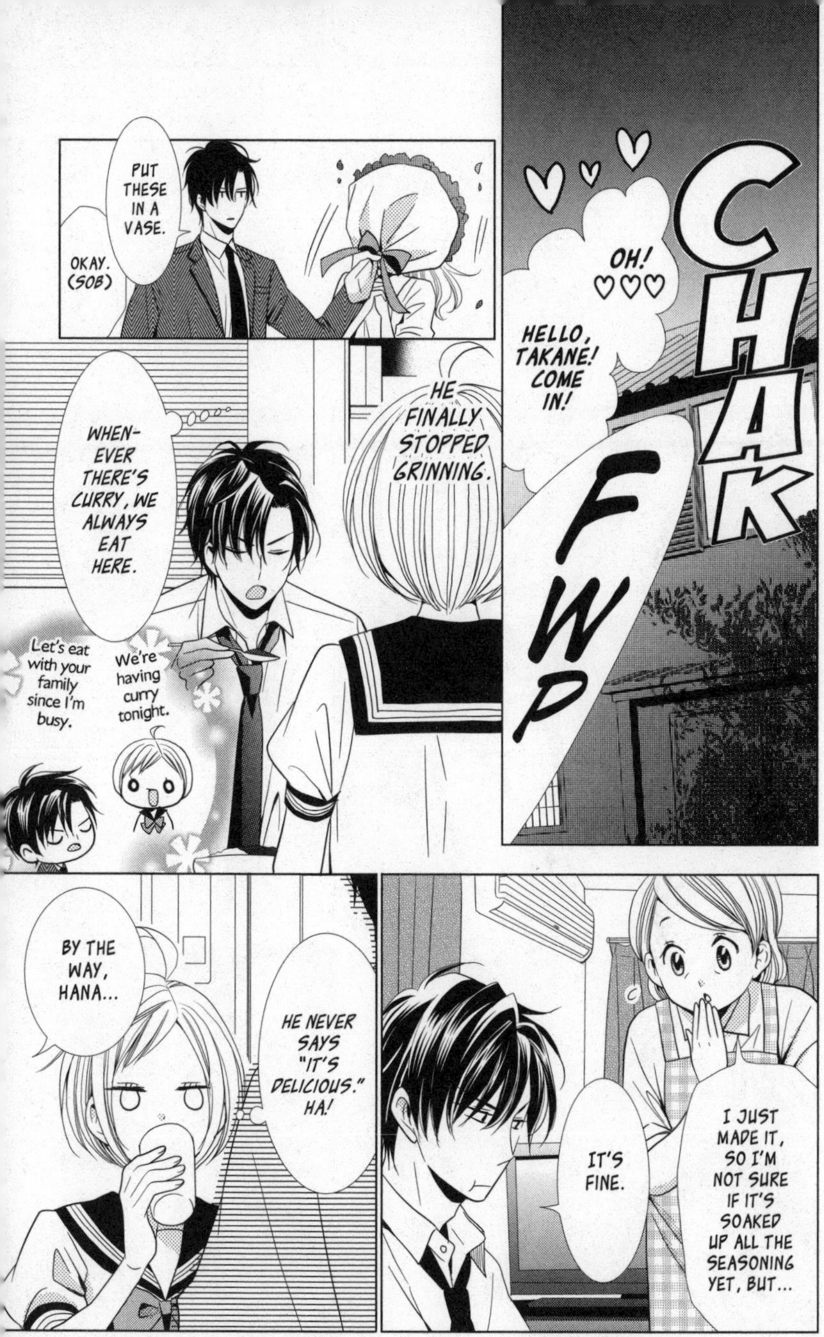
CHAK
OH! ♡♡♡
HELLO, TAKANE! COME IN!
FWP
PUT THESE IN A VASE.
OKAY. (SOB)
HE FINALLY STOPPED GRINNING.
WHEN-EVER THERE'S CURRY, WE ALWAYS EAT HERE.
We're having curry tonight.
Let's eat with your family since I'm busy.
I JUST MADE IT, SO I'M NOT SURE IF IT'S SOAKED UP ALL THE SEASONING YET, BUT...
IT'S FINE.
HE NEVER SAYS "IT'S DELICIOUS." HA!
BY THE WAY, HANA...

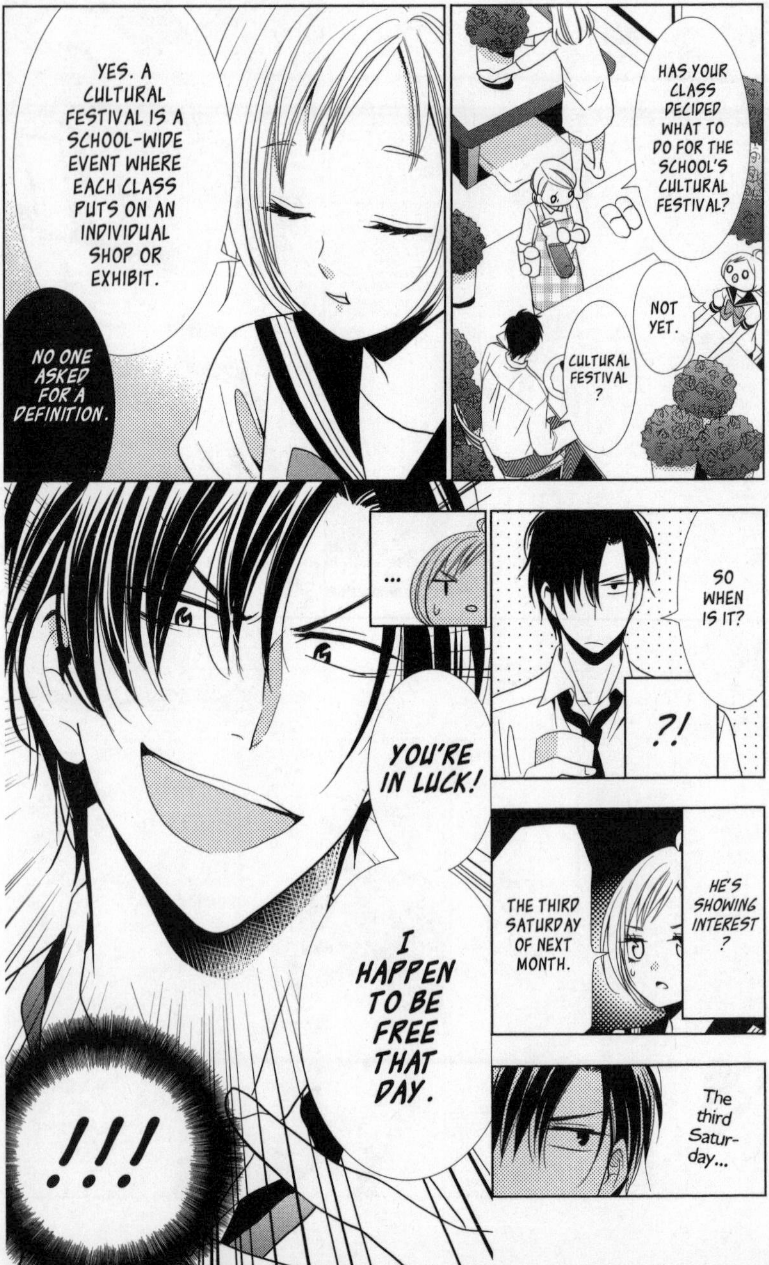
HAS YOUR CLASS DECIDED WHAT TO DO FOR THE SCHOOL'S CULTURAL FESTIVAL?
NOT YET.
CULTURAL FESTIVAL?
YES. A CULTURAL FESTIVAL IS A SCHOOL-WIDE EVENT WHERE EACH CLASS PUTS ON AN INDIVIDUAL SHOP OR EXHIBIT.
NO ONE ASKED FOR A DEFINITION.
SO WHEN IS IT?
?!
HE'S SHOWING INTEREST?
THE THIRD SATURDAY OF NEXT MONTH.
The third Satur-day...
...
YOU'RE IN LUCK!
I HAPPEN TO BE FREE THAT DAY.
!!!

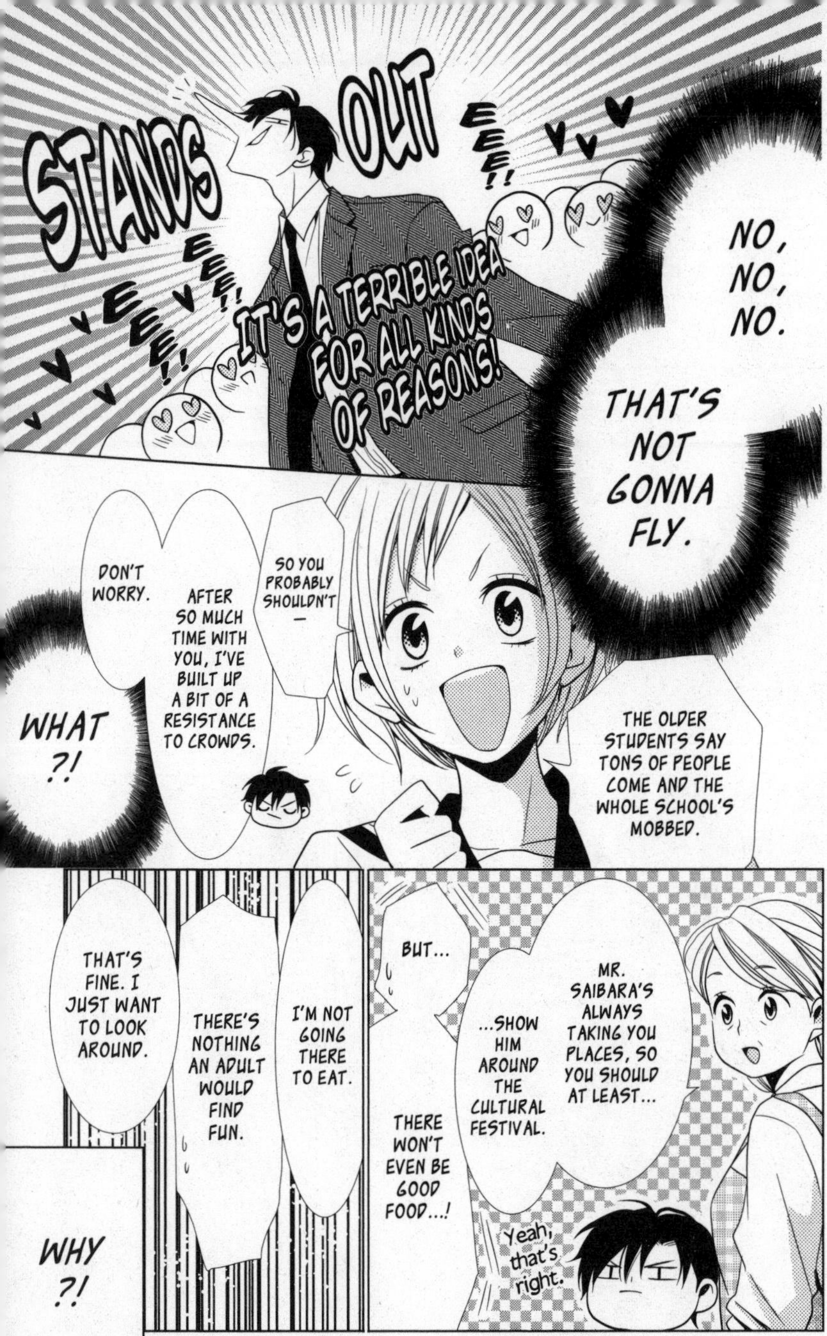
NO, NO, NO.
THAT'S NOT GONNA FLY.
EEEE!!
OUT
STANDS
IT'S A TERRIBLE IDEA FOR ALL KINDS OF REASONS!
EEEE!!
EEEE!!
THE OLDER STUDENTS SAY TONS OF PEOPLE COME AND THE WHOLE SCHOOL'S MOBBED.
SO YOU PROBABLY SHOULDN'T—
DON'T WORRY.
AFTER SO MUCH TIME WITH YOU, I'VE BUILT UP A BIT OF A RESISTANCE TO CROWDS.
WHAT?!
MR. SAIBARA'S ALWAYS TAKING YOU PLACES, SO YOU SHOULD AT LEAST...
...SHOW HIM AROUND THE CULTURAL FESTIVAL.
Yeah, that's right.
BUT...
THERE WON'T EVEN BE GOOD FOOD...!
I'M NOT GOING THERE TO EAT.
THERE'S NOTHING AN ADULT WOULD FIND FUN.
THAT'S FINE. I JUST WANT TO LOOK AROUND.
WHY?!

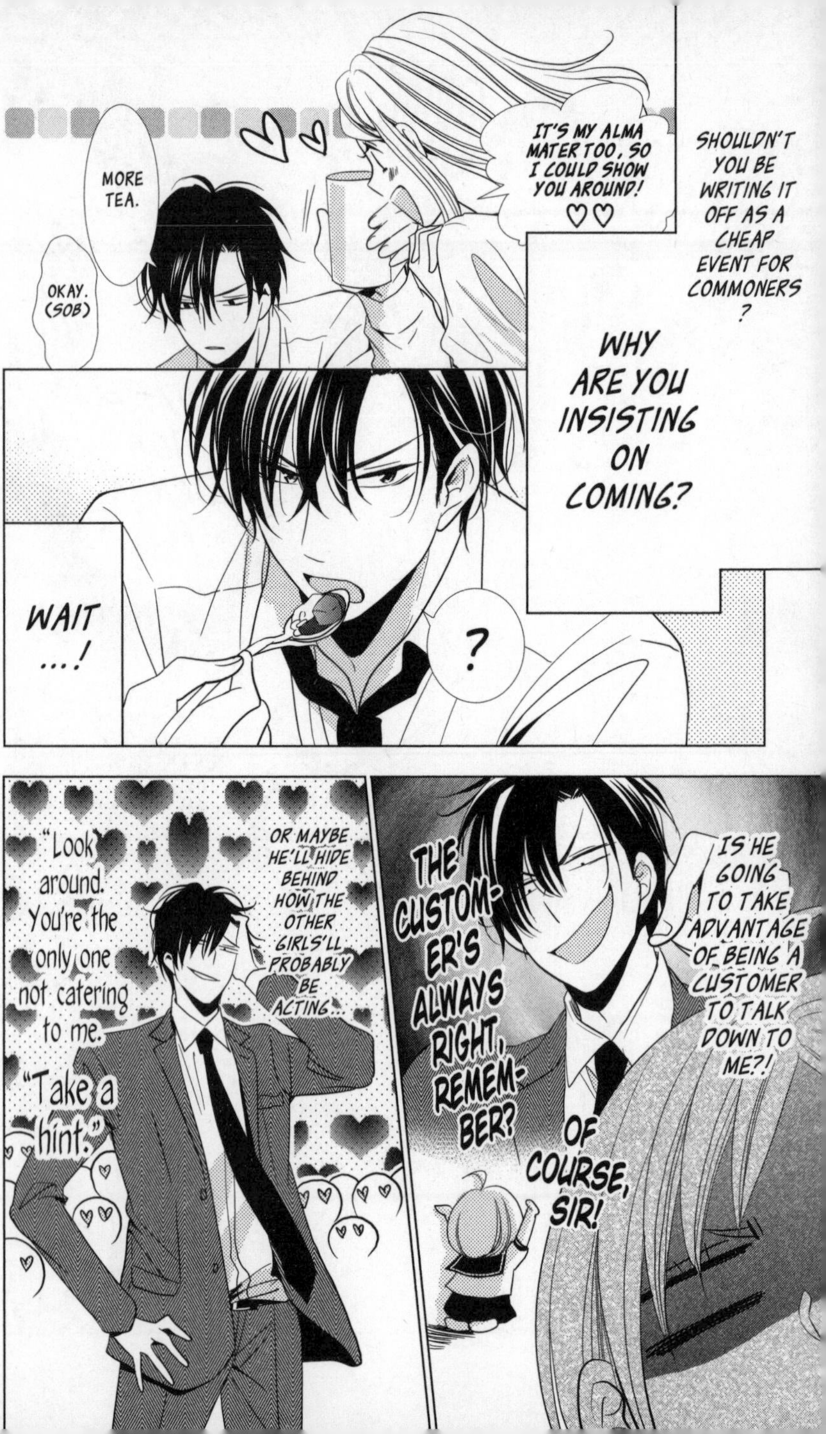
IT'S MY ALMA MATER TOO, SO I COULD SHOW YOU AROUND! ♡♡
MORE TEA.
OKAY. (SOB)
SHOULDN'T YOU BE WRITING IT OFF AS A CHEAP EVENT FOR COMMONERS?
WHY ARE YOU INSISTING ON COMING?
?
WAIT...!
IS HE GOING TO TAKE ADVANTAGE OF BEING A CUSTOMER TO TALK DOWN TO ME?!
THE CUSTOMER'S ALWAYS RIGHT, REMEMBER?
OF COURSE, SIR!
OR MAYBE HE'LL HIDE BEHIND HOW THE OTHER GIRLS'LL PROBABLY BE ACTING...
"Look around. You're the only one not catering to me.
"Take a hint."

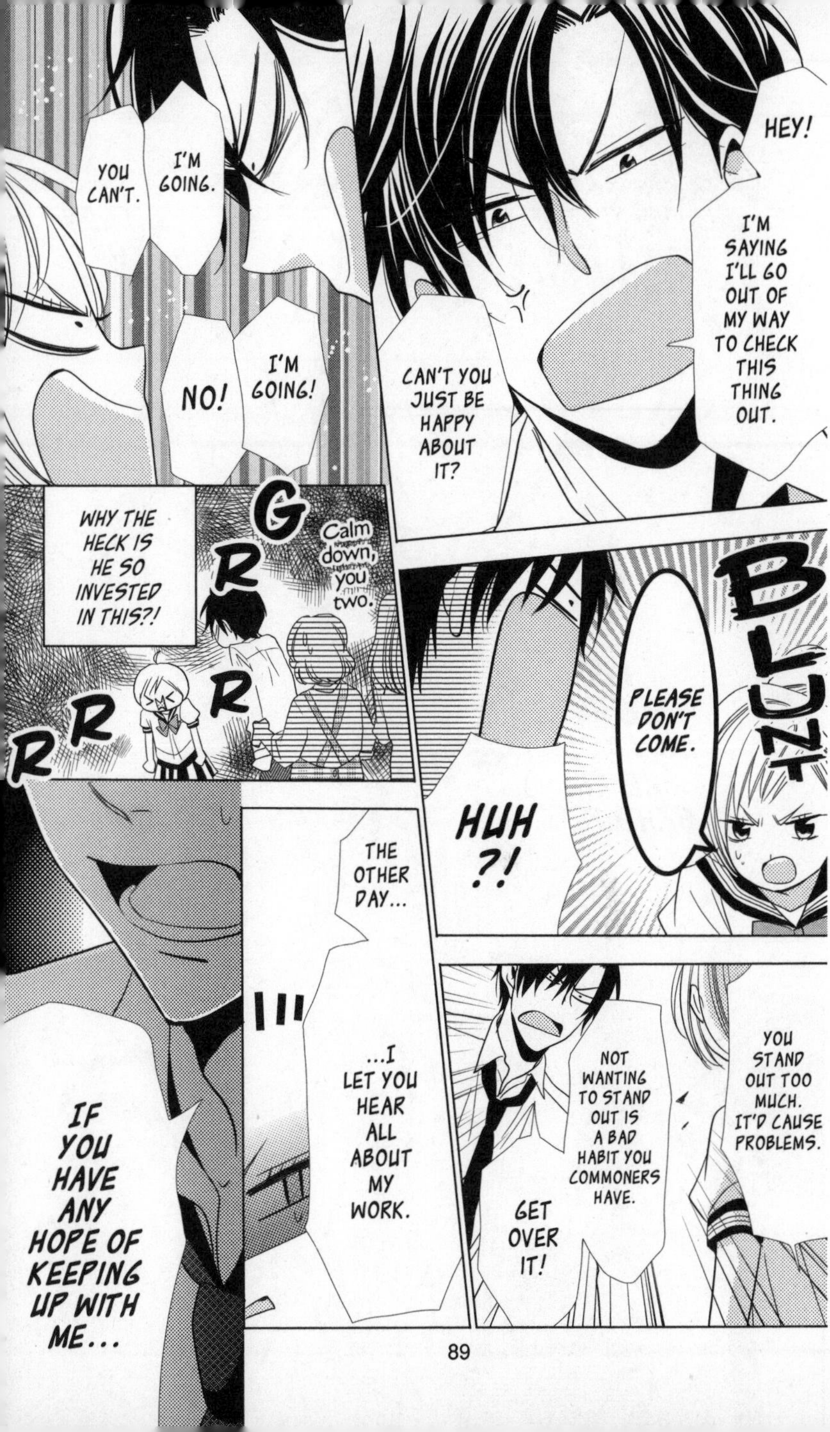
HEY!
I'M SAYING I'LL GO OUT OF MY WAY TO CHECK THIS THING OUT.
CAN'T YOU JUST BE HAPPY ABOUT IT?
I'M GOING.
YOU CAN'T.
I'M GOING!
NO!
BLUNT
PLEASE DON'T COME.
HUH?!
WHY THE HECK IS HE SO INVESTED IN THIS?!
GRRRRR
Calm down, you two.
YOU STAND OUT TOO MUCH. IT'D CAUSE PROBLEMS.
NOT WANTING TO STAND OUT IS A BAD HABIT YOU COMMONERS HAVE.
GET OVER IT!
THE OTHER DAY...
...I LET YOU HEAR ALL ABOUT MY WORK.
IF YOU HAVE ANY HOPE OF KEEPING UP WITH ME...

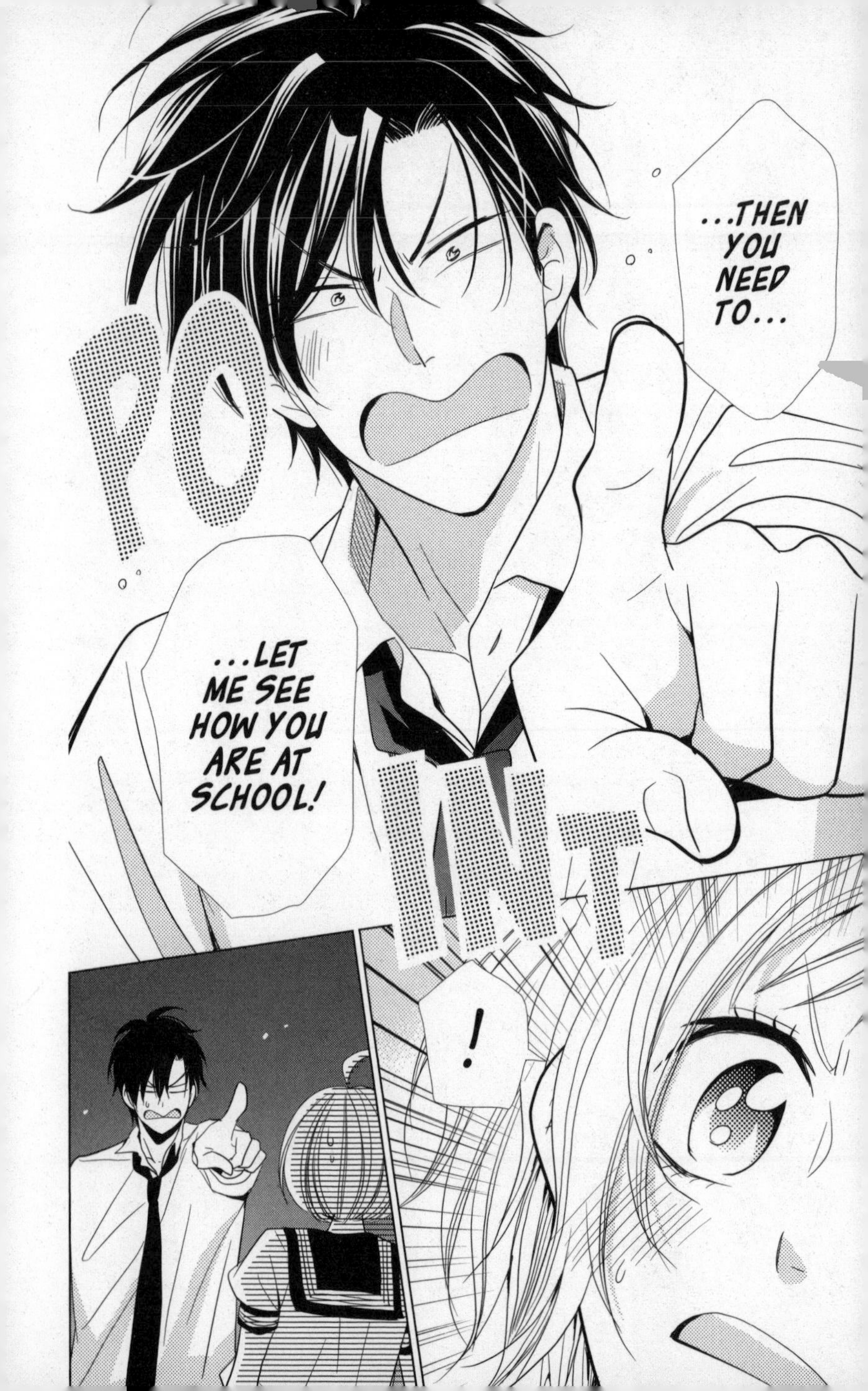
...THEN YOU NEED TO...
PO
...LET ME SEE HOW YOU ARE AT SCHOOL!
INT
!

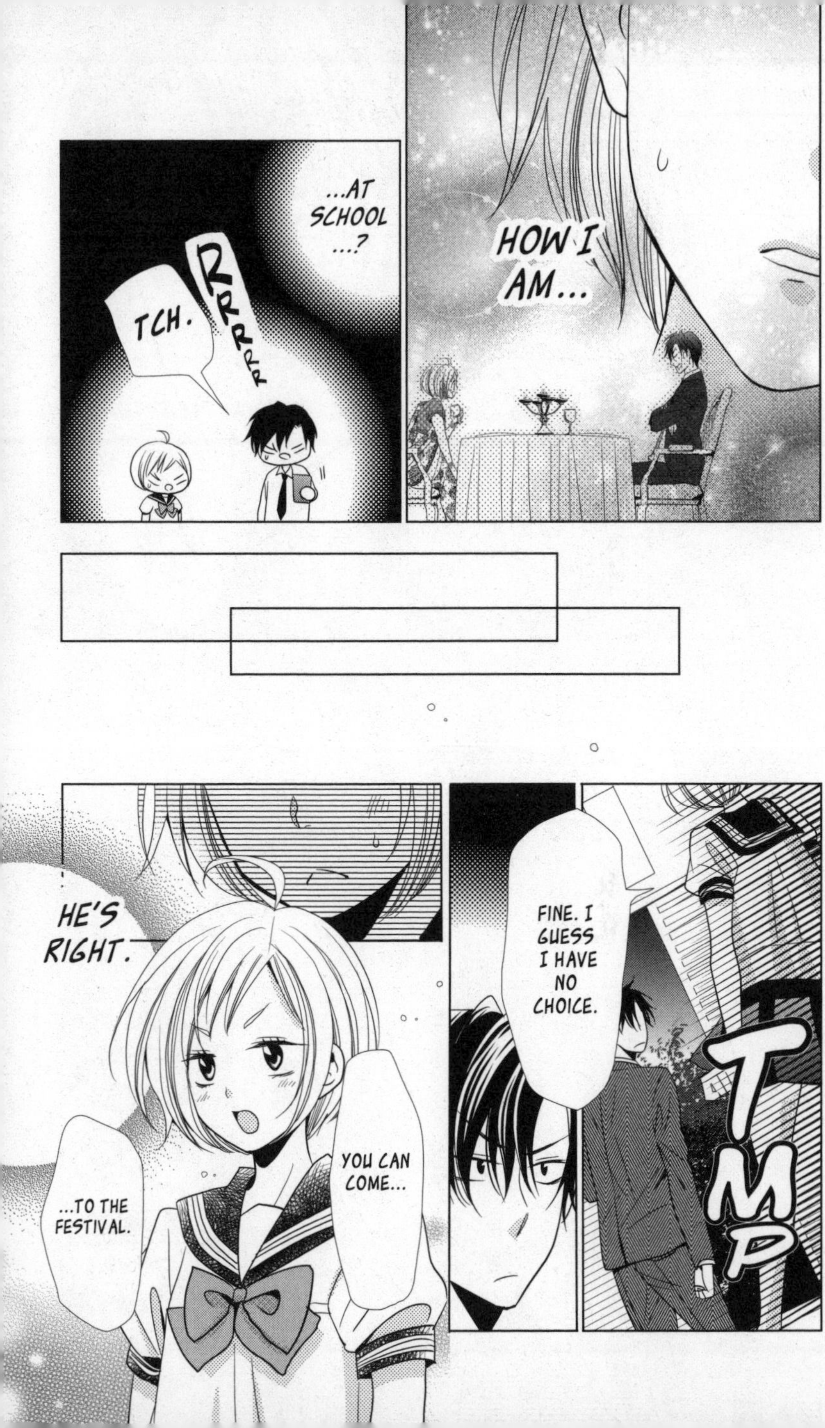
HOW I AM...
...AT SCHOOL ...?
RRRRRR
TCH.
FINE. I GUESS I HAVE NO CHOICE.
TMP
HE'S RIGHT.
YOU CAN COME...
...TO THE FESTIVAL.

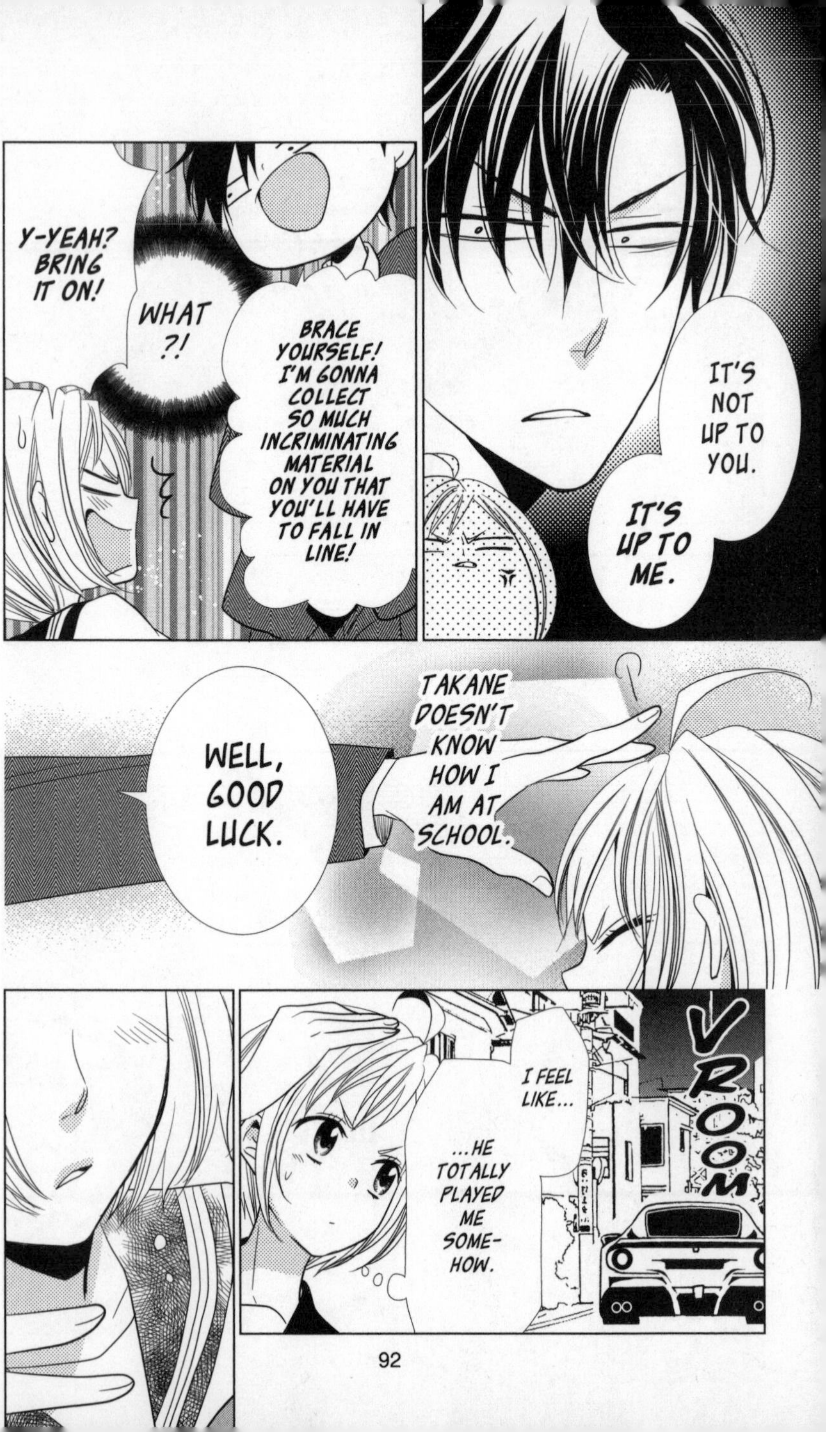
IT'S NOT UP TO YOU.
IT'S UP TO ME.
Y-YEAH? BRING IT ON!
WHAT?!
BRACE YOURSELF! I'M GONNA COLLECT SO MUCH INCRIMINATING MATERIAL ON YOU THAT YOU'LL HAVE TO FALL IN LINE!
TAKANE DOESN'T KNOW HOW I AM AT SCHOOL.
WELL, GOOD LUCK.
VROOM
I FEEL LIKE...
...HE TOTALLY PLAYED ME SOME-HOW.

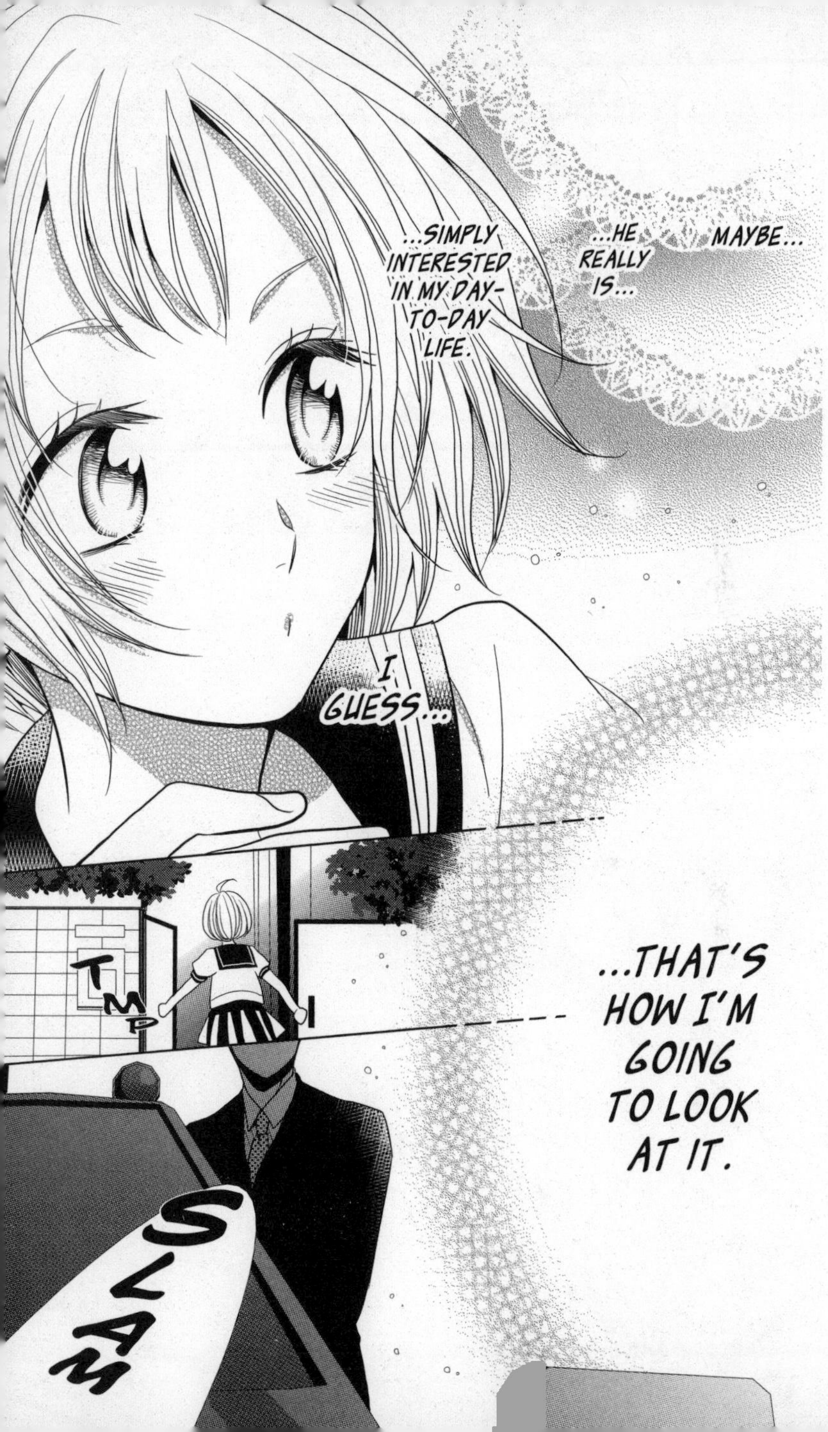
MAYBE...
...HE REALLY IS...
...SIMPLY INTERESTED IN MY DAY-TO-DAY LIFE.
I GUESS...
...THAT'S HOW I'M GOING TO LOOK AT IT.
TMP
SLAM

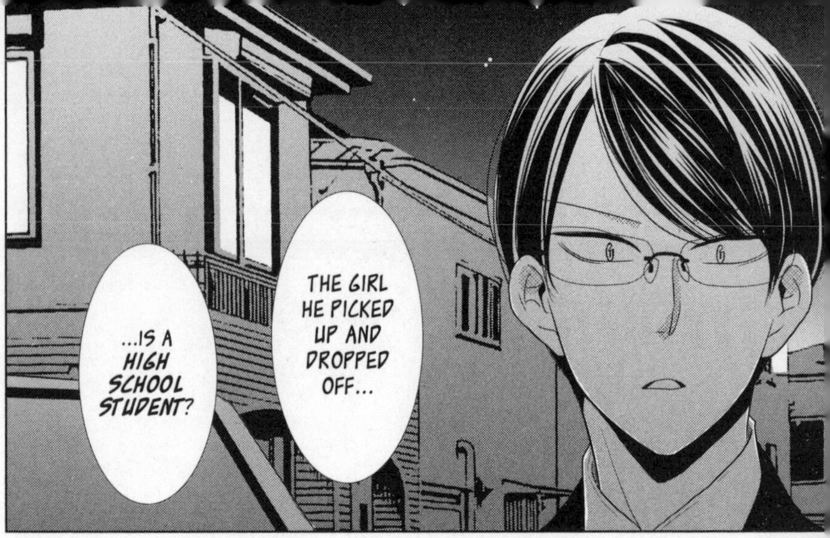
THE GIRL HE PICKED UP AND DROPPED OFF...
...IS A HIGH SCHOOL STUDENT?

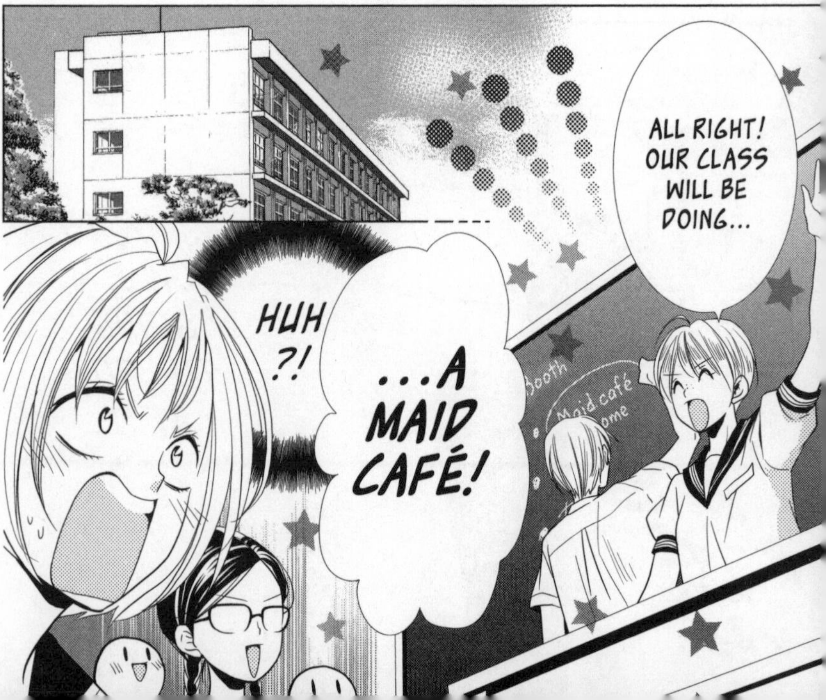
ALL RIGHT! OUR CLASS WILL BE DOING...
...A MAID CAFÉ!
HUH ?!
Maid café

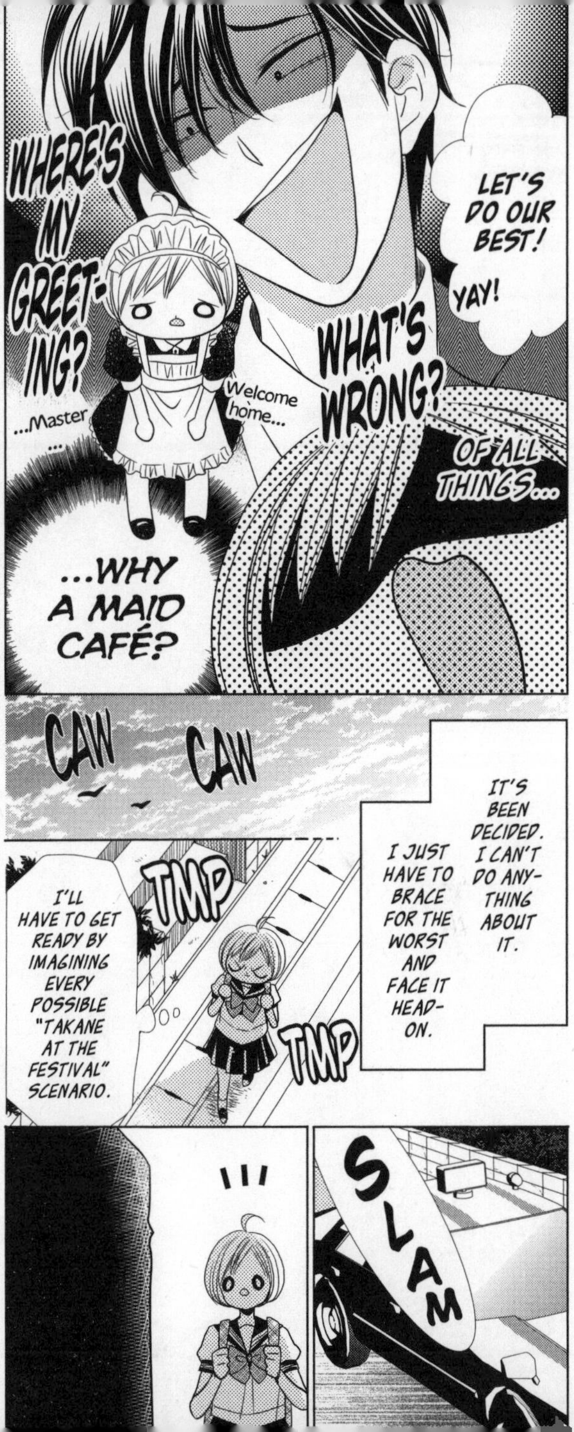
LET'S DO OUR BEST!
YAY!
WHAT'S WRONG?
OF ALL THINGS...
WHERE'S MY GREETING?
Welcome home...
...Master...
...WHY A MAID CAFÉ?
CAW
CAW
IT'S BEEN DECIDED. I CAN'T DO ANYTHING ABOUT IT.
I JUST HAVE TO BRACE FOR THE WORST AND FACE IT HEAD-ON.
TMP
I'LL HAVE TO GET READY BY IMAGINING EVERY POSSIBLE "TAKANE AT THE FESTIVAL" SCENARIO.
TMP
SLAM
!!!

•Drawing Manga, Part 2•

~ Storyboard (cont.) ~

Specific dialogue and character interactions are developed during this stage. When the plot's coming together, I usually get reined in if I go off on a tangent. But at this point, I'm given more room to play around. While sticking to the plot, I work in as many little punch lines as I can.

This may be the hardest part for me, since what may have looked good as sentences (plot) may not work or might be boring when it becomes a manga (storyboard).

~ Preliminary Sketches ~

My personal process is to do a rough panel layout and composition during the storyboard stage and then clean it up during the preliminary sketches. I also rework some of the dialogue at this point, so it can be pretty time consuming. Preliminary sketches can take about four days or sometimes even longer...

I fold a B4 size copy paper in half and draw on it.

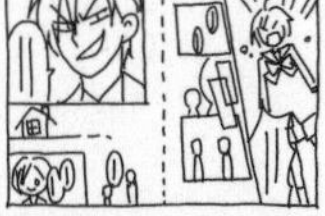

Once I'm done with the preliminary sketches, I fax it all to my editor. After it's approved, the next step is to ink the pencil sketches.

~ Inking the Pencil Sketches ~

I scan the preliminary sketches and use the computer to ink them. The software I use is Comic Studio. (Comic Studio has been discontinued, so I'd really like to switch over to something newer...)

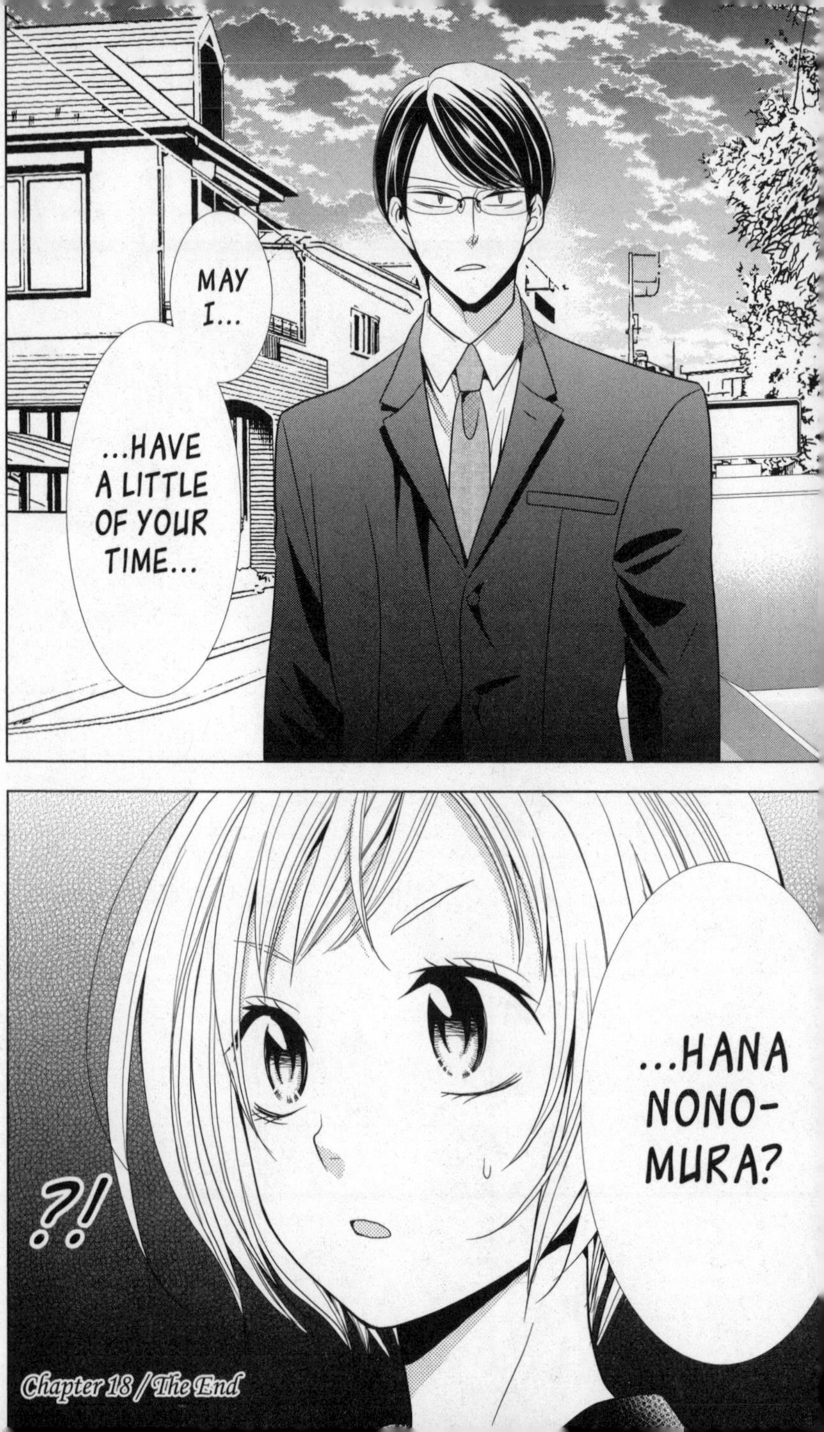
MAY I...
...HAVE A LITTLE OF YOUR TIME...
...HANA NONO-MURA?
?!
Chapter 18 / The End

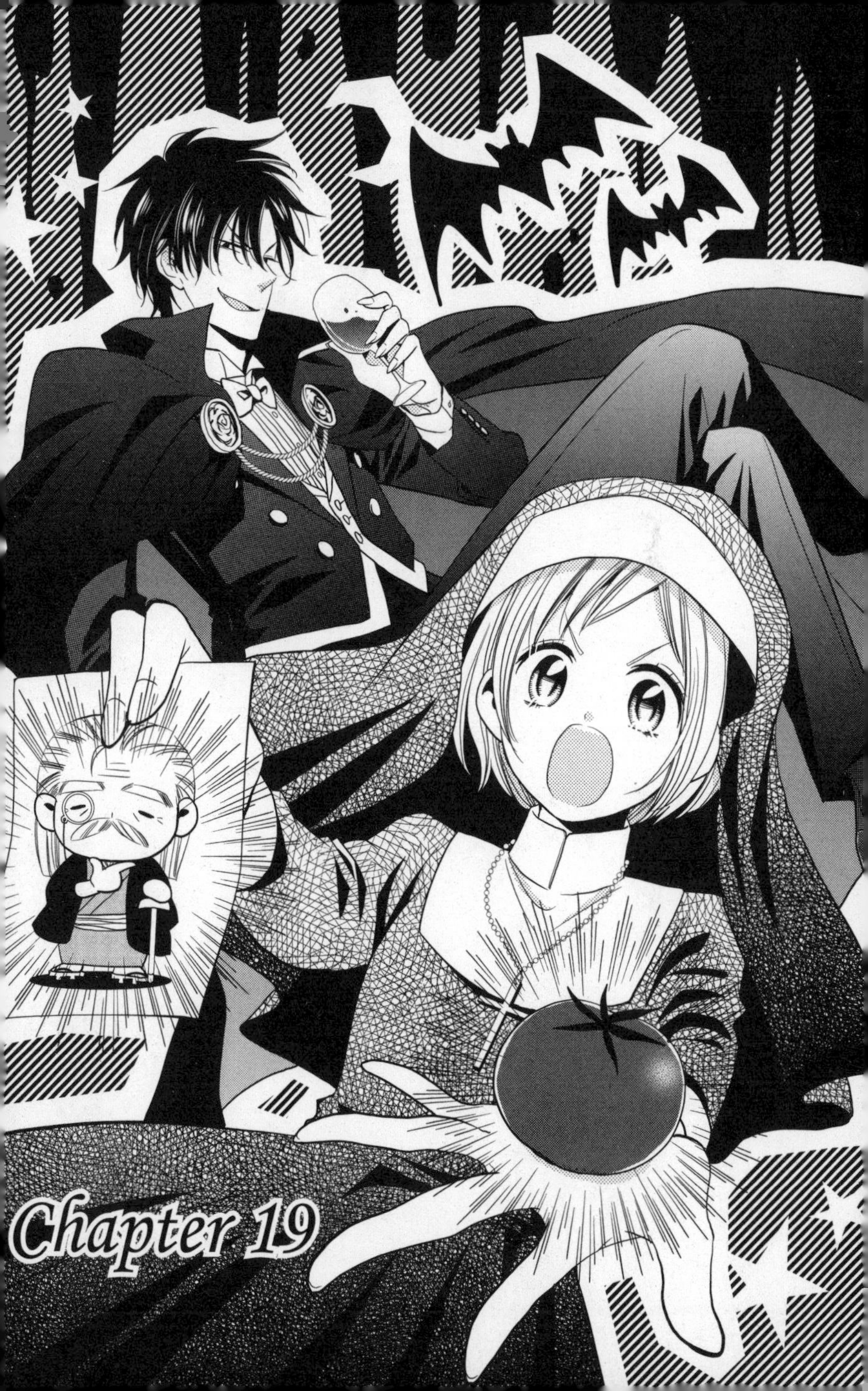
Chapter 19

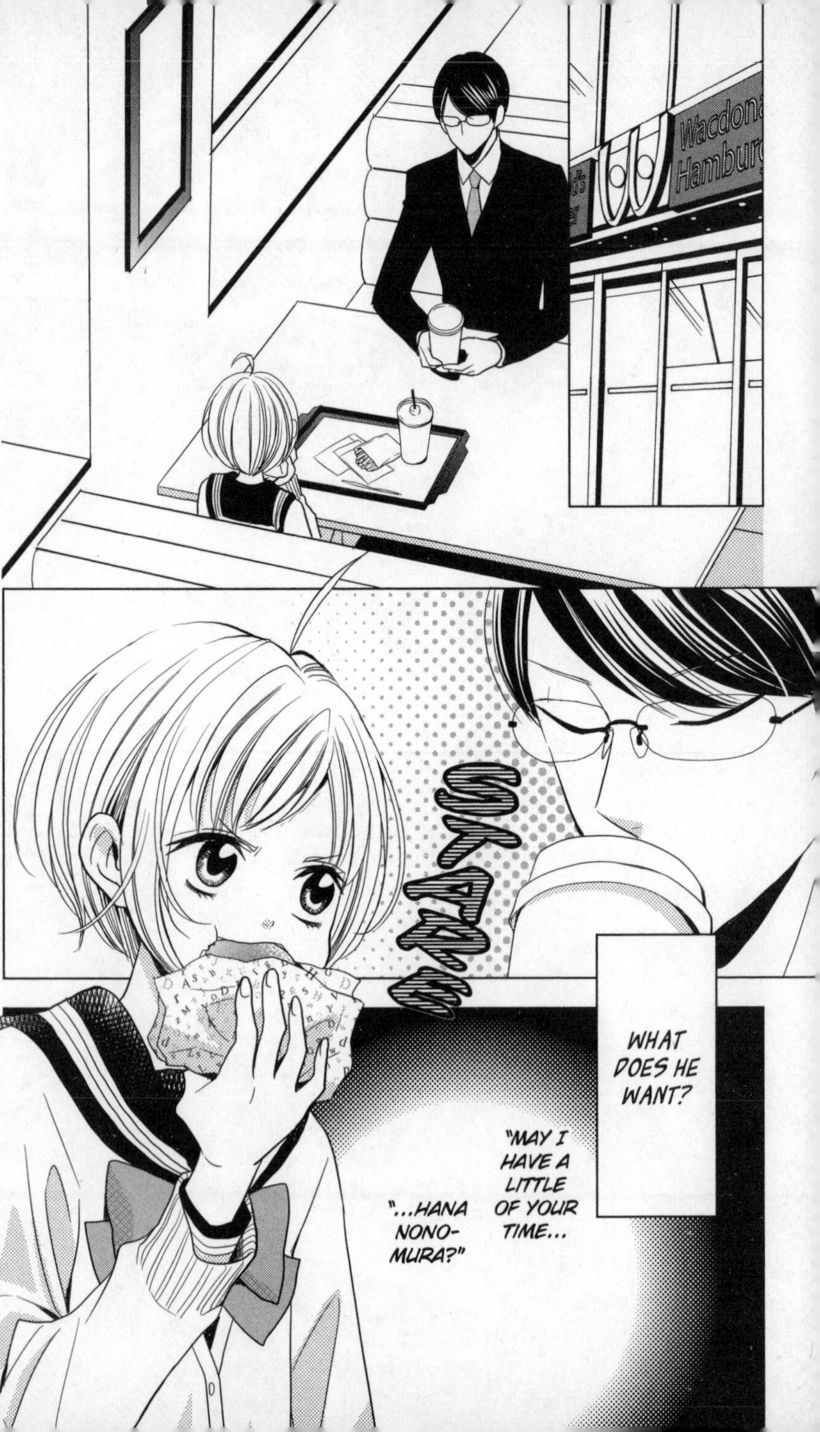
STARE
WHAT DOES HE WANT?
"MAY I HAVE A LITTLE OF YOUR TIME...
"...HANA NONO-MURA?"

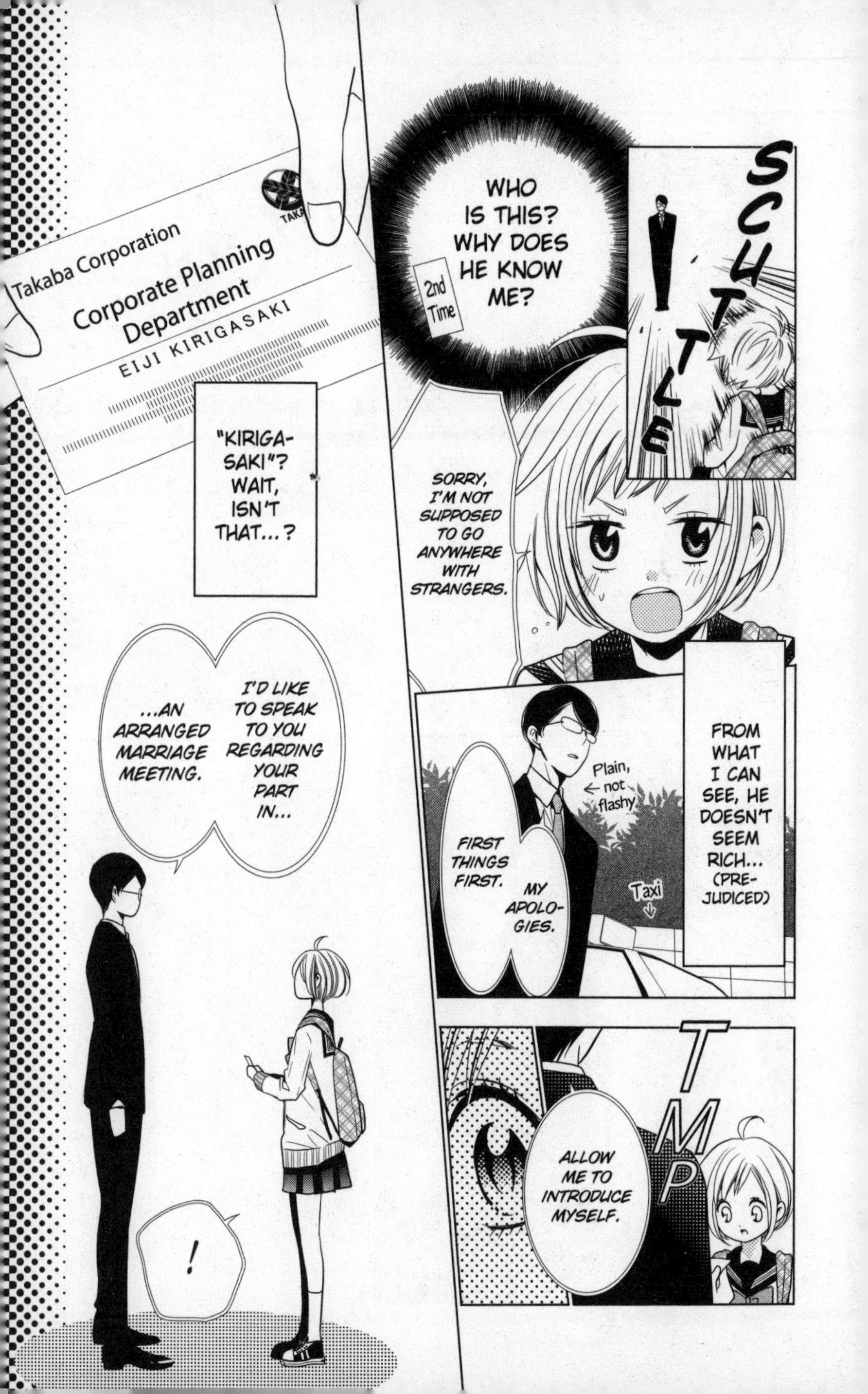
SCUTTLE
2nd Time
WHO IS THIS? WHY DOES HE KNOW ME?
SORRY, I'M NOT SUPPOSED TO GO ANYWHERE WITH STRANGERS.
FROM WHAT I CAN SEE, HE DOESN'T SEEM RICH... (PREJUDICED)
Plain, not flashy
Taxi
FIRST THINGS FIRST.
MY APOLOGIES.
TMP
ALLOW ME TO INTRODUCE MYSELF.
Takaba Corporation
Corporate Planning Department
EIJI KIRIGASAKI
TAKA
"KIRIGASAKI"? WAIT, ISN'T THAT...?
I'D LIKE TO SPEAK TO YOU REGARDING YOUR PART IN...
...AN ARRANGED MARRIAGE MEETING.
!

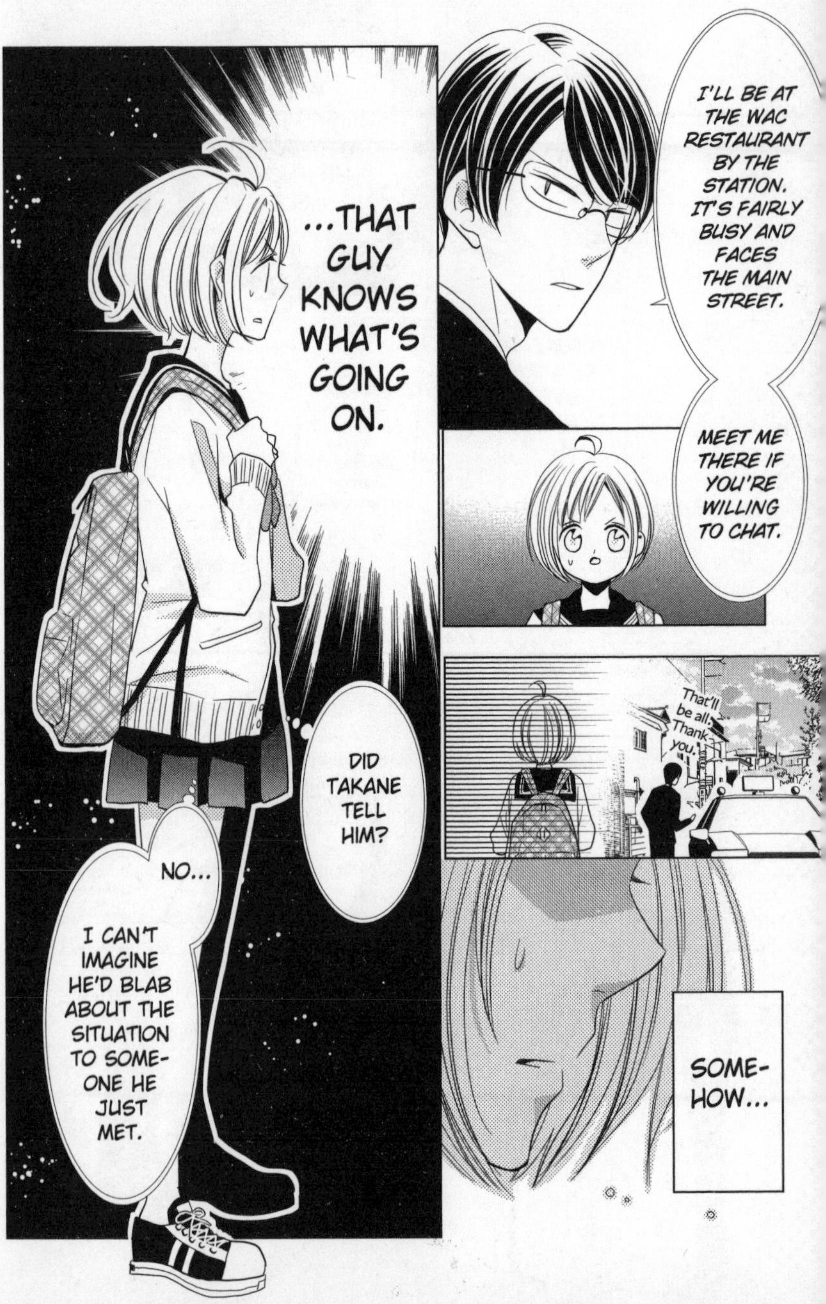
I'LL BE AT THE WAC RESTAURANT BY THE STATION. IT'S FAIRLY BUSY AND FACES THE MAIN STREET.
MEET ME THERE IF YOU'RE WILLING TO CHAT.
That'll be all. Thank you.
SOME-HOW...
...THAT GUY KNOWS WHAT'S GOING ON.
DID TAKANE TELL HIM?
NO...
I CAN'T IMAGINE HE'D BLAB ABOUT THE SITUATION TO SOME-ONE HE JUST MET.

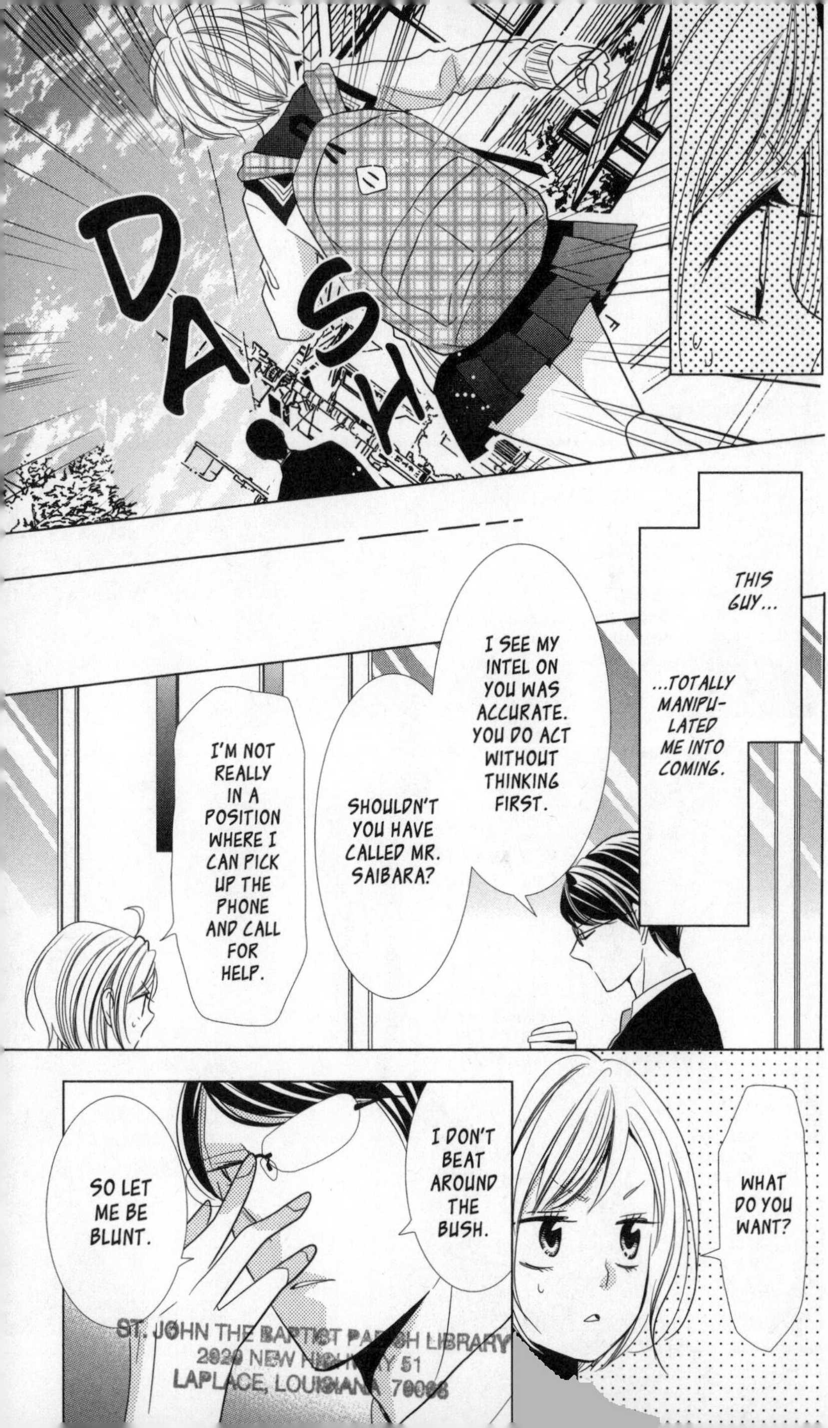
DASH
THIS GUY...
...TOTALLY MANIPU-LATED ME INTO COMING.
I SEE MY INTEL ON YOU WAS ACCURATE. YOU DO ACT WITHOUT THINKING FIRST.
SHOULDN'T YOU HAVE CALLED MR. SAIBARA?
I'M NOT REALLY IN A POSITION WHERE I CAN PICK UP THE PHONE AND CALL FOR HELP.
WHAT DO YOU WANT?
I DON'T BEAT AROUND THE BUSH.
SO LET ME BE BLUNT.

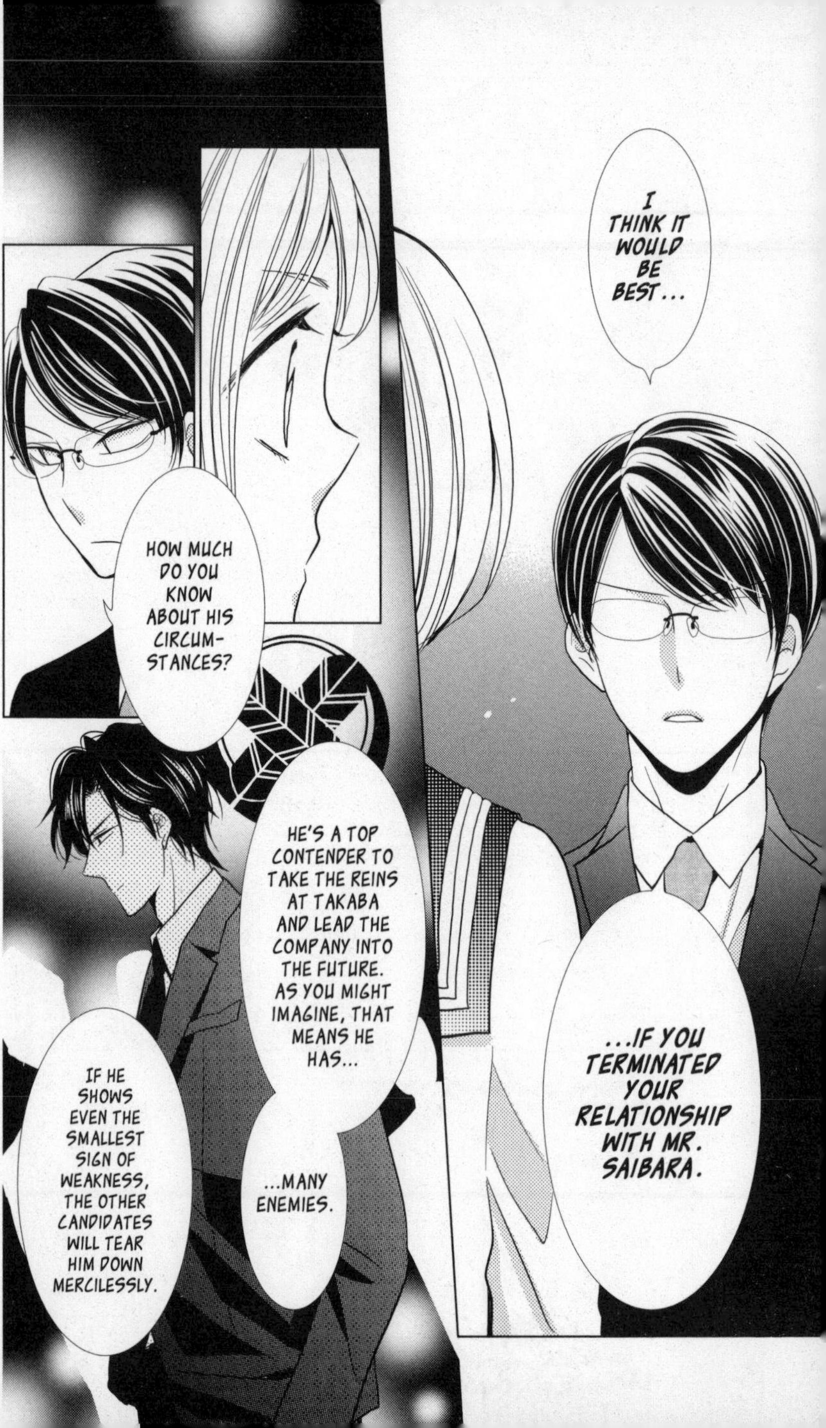
I THINK IT WOULD BE BEST...
...IF YOU TERMINATED YOUR RELATIONSHIP WITH MR. SAIBARA.
HOW MUCH DO YOU KNOW ABOUT HIS CIRCUM-STANCES?
HE'S A TOP CONTENDER TO TAKE THE REINS AT TAKABA AND LEAD THE COMPANY INTO THE FUTURE. AS YOU MIGHT IMAGINE, THAT MEANS HE HAS...
...MANY ENEMIES.
IF HE SHOWS EVEN THE SMALLEST SIGN OF WEAKNESS, THE OTHER CANDIDATES WILL TEAR HIM DOWN MERCILESSLY.

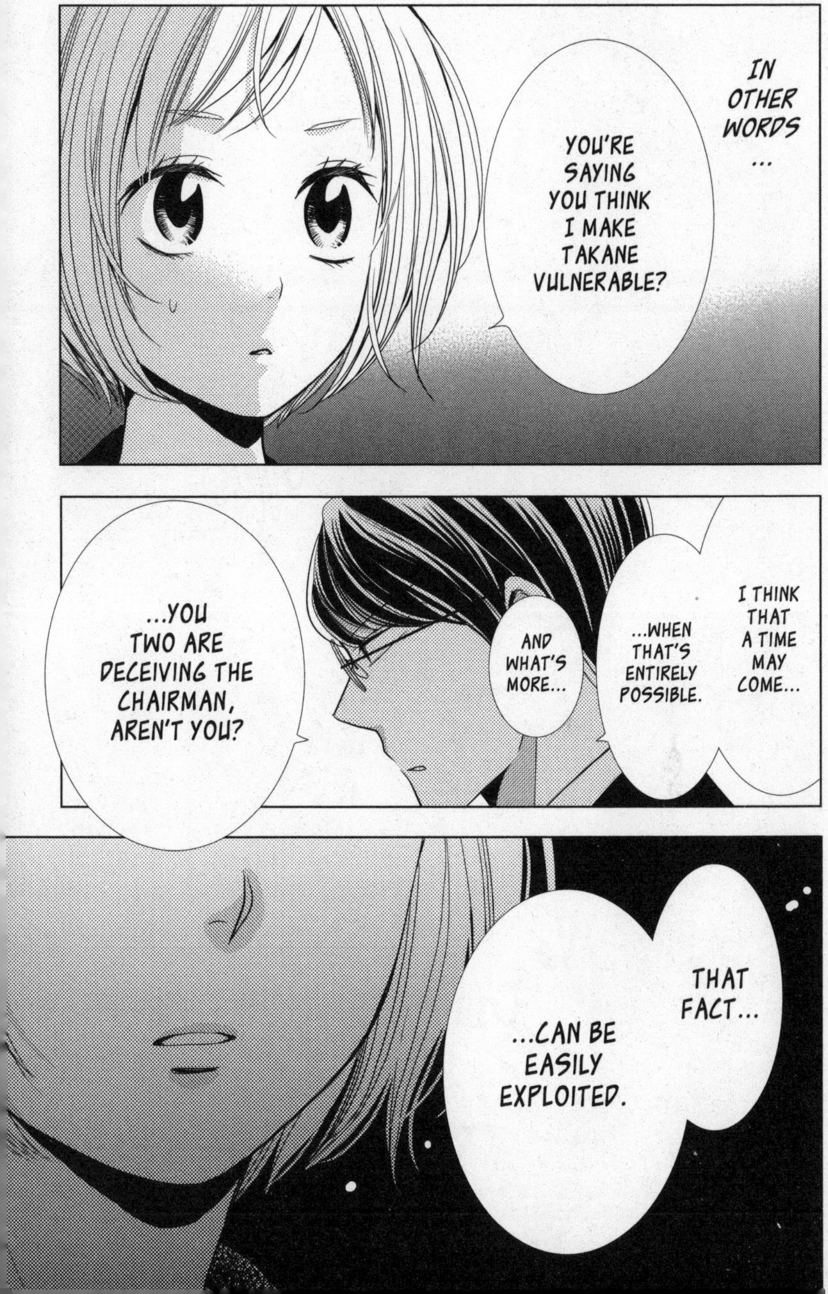
IN OTHER WORDS...
YOU'RE SAYING YOU THINK I MAKE TAKANE VULNERABLE?
I THINK THAT A TIME MAY COME...
...WHEN THAT'S ENTIRELY POSSIBLE.
AND WHAT'S MORE...
...YOU TWO ARE DECEIVING THE CHAIRMAN, AREN'T YOU?
THAT FACT...
...CAN BE EASILY EXPLOITED.

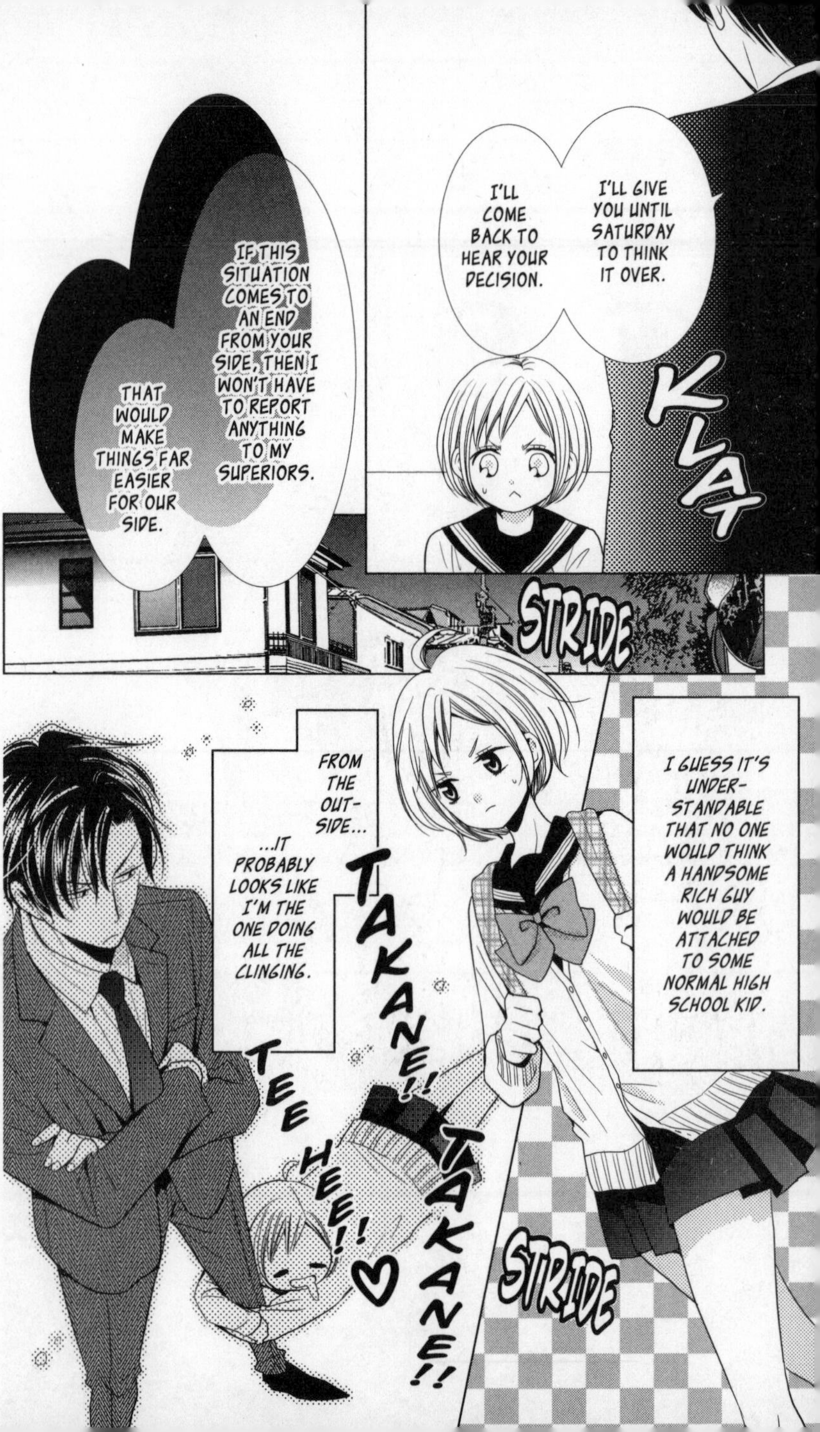
I'LL GIVE YOU UNTIL SATURDAY TO THINK IT OVER.
I'LL COME BACK TO HEAR YOUR DECISION.
KLAK
IF THIS SITUATION COMES TO AN END FROM YOUR SIDE, THEN I WON'T HAVE TO REPORT ANYTHING TO MY SUPERIORS.
THAT WOULD MAKE THINGS FAR EASIER FOR OUR SIDE.
STRIDE
I GUESS IT'S UNDER-STANDABLE THAT NO ONE WOULD THINK A HANDSOME RICH GUY WOULD BE ATTACHED TO SOME NORMAL HIGH SCHOOL KID.
FROM THE OUT-SIDE...
...IT PROBABLY LOOKS LIKE I'M THE ONE DOING ALL THE CLINGING.
TAKANE!! TAKANE!!
TAKANE!!
TEE HEE!! ♥
STRIDE

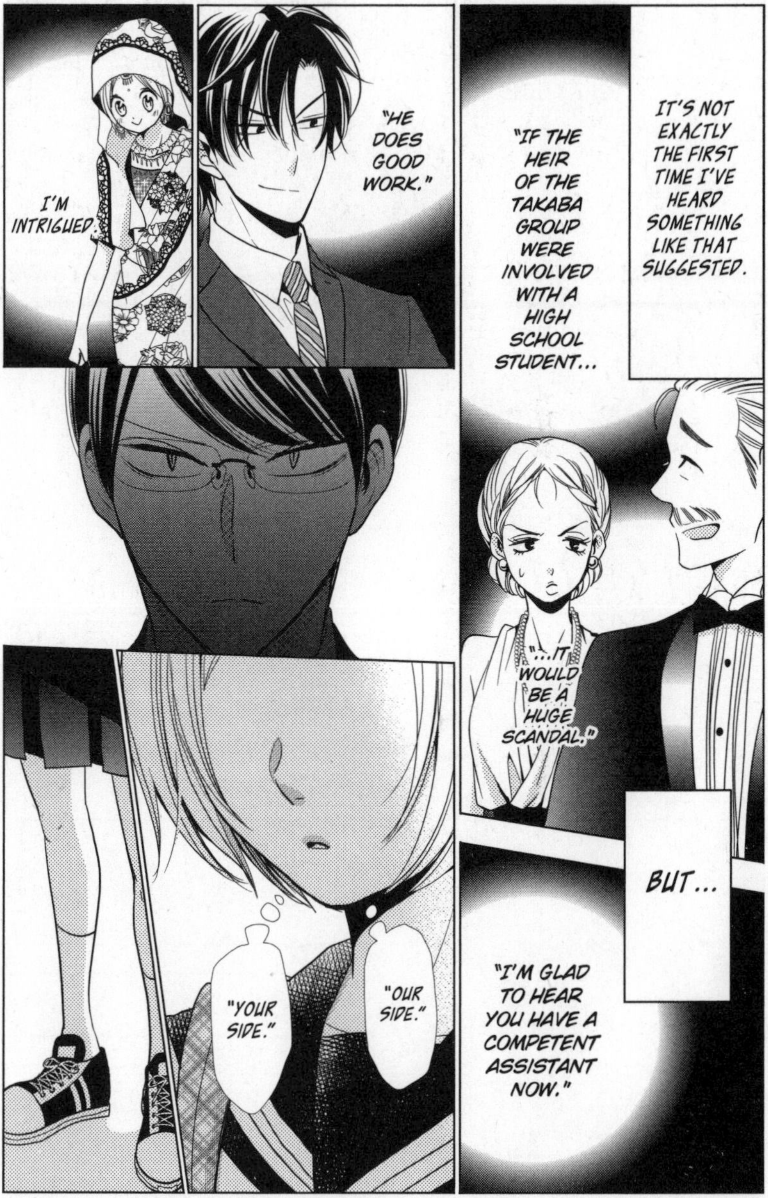
IT'S NOT EXACTLY THE FIRST TIME I'VE HEARD SOMETHING LIKE THAT SUGGESTED.
"IF THE HEIR OF THE TAKABA GROUP WERE INVOLVED WITH A HIGH SCHOOL STUDENT...
"...IT WOULD BE A HUGE SCANDAL."
"HE DOES GOOD WORK."
I'M INTRIGUED.
BUT...
"I'M GLAD TO HEAR YOU HAVE A COMPETENT ASSISTANT NOW."
"OUR SIDE."
"YOUR SIDE."

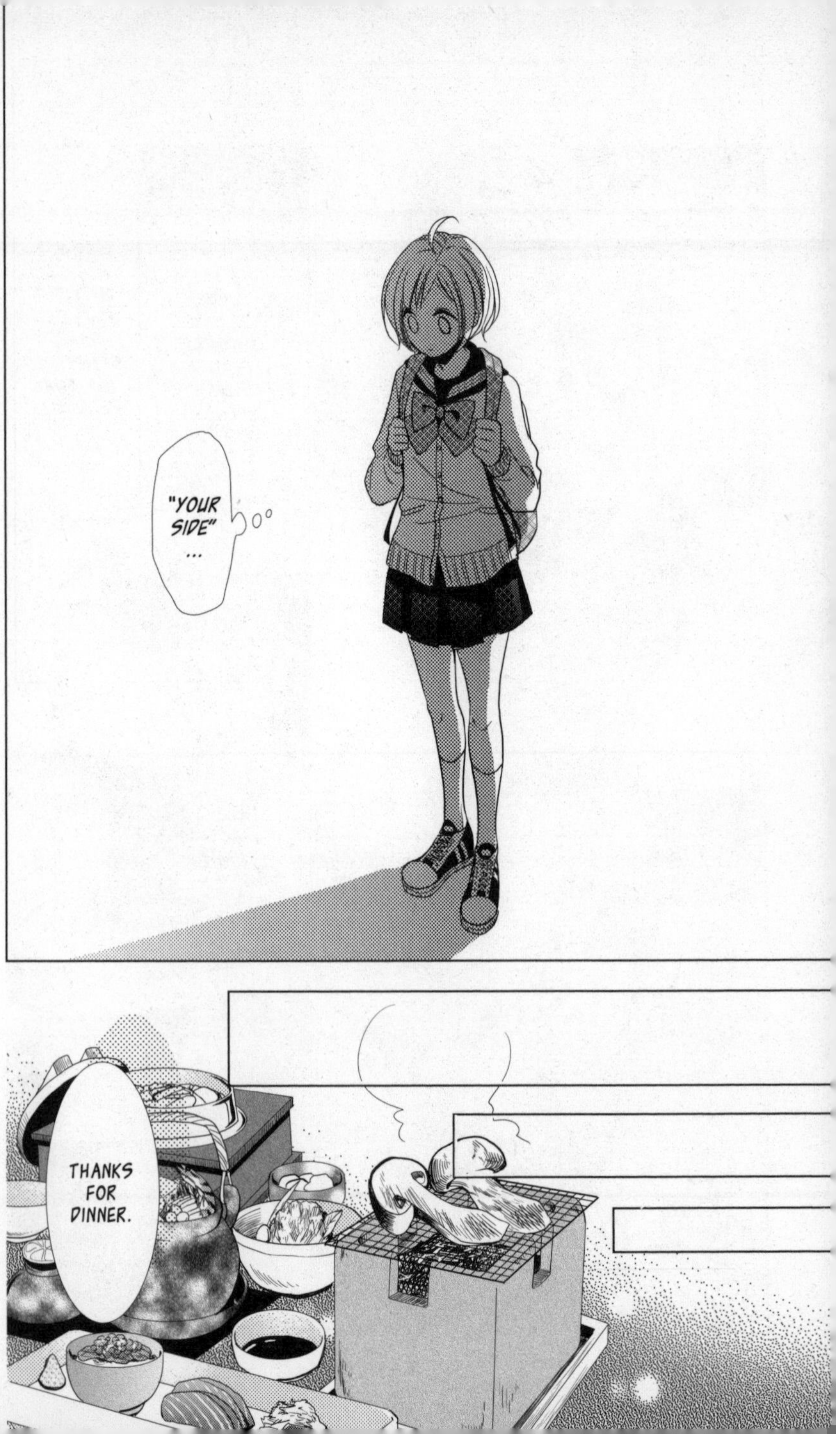
"YOUR SIDE"...
THANKS FOR DINNER.

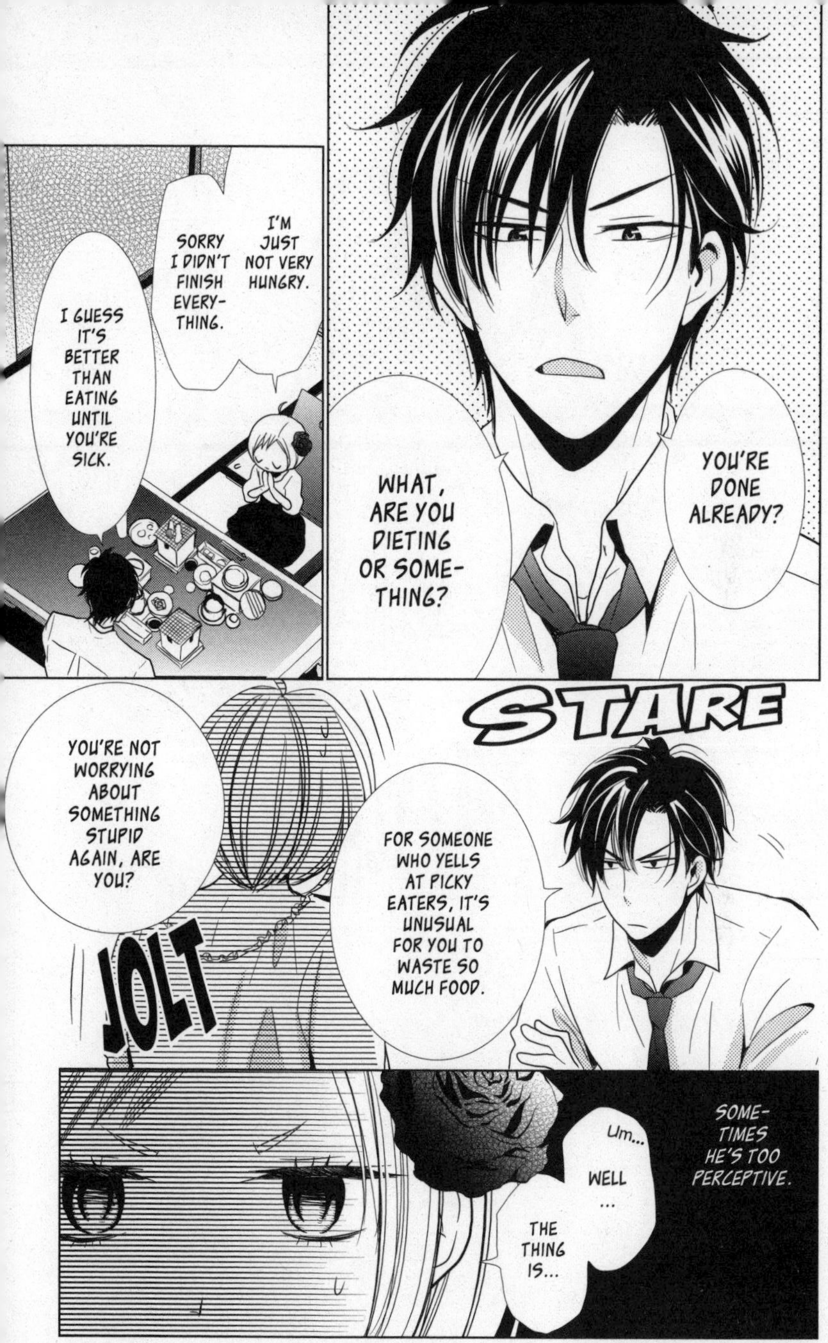
YOU'RE DONE ALREADY?
WHAT, ARE YOU DIETING OR SOMETHING?
I'M JUST NOT VERY HUNGRY.
SORRY I DIDN'T FINISH EVERYTHING.
I GUESS IT'S BETTER THAN EATING UNTIL YOU'RE SICK.
STARE
FOR SOMEONE WHO YELLS AT PICKY EATERS, IT'S UNUSUAL FOR YOU TO WASTE SO MUCH FOOD.
YOU'RE NOT WORRYING ABOUT SOMETHING STUPID AGAIN, ARE YOU?
JOLT
SOMETIMES HE'S TOO PERCEPTIVE.
Um... WELL ... THE THING IS...

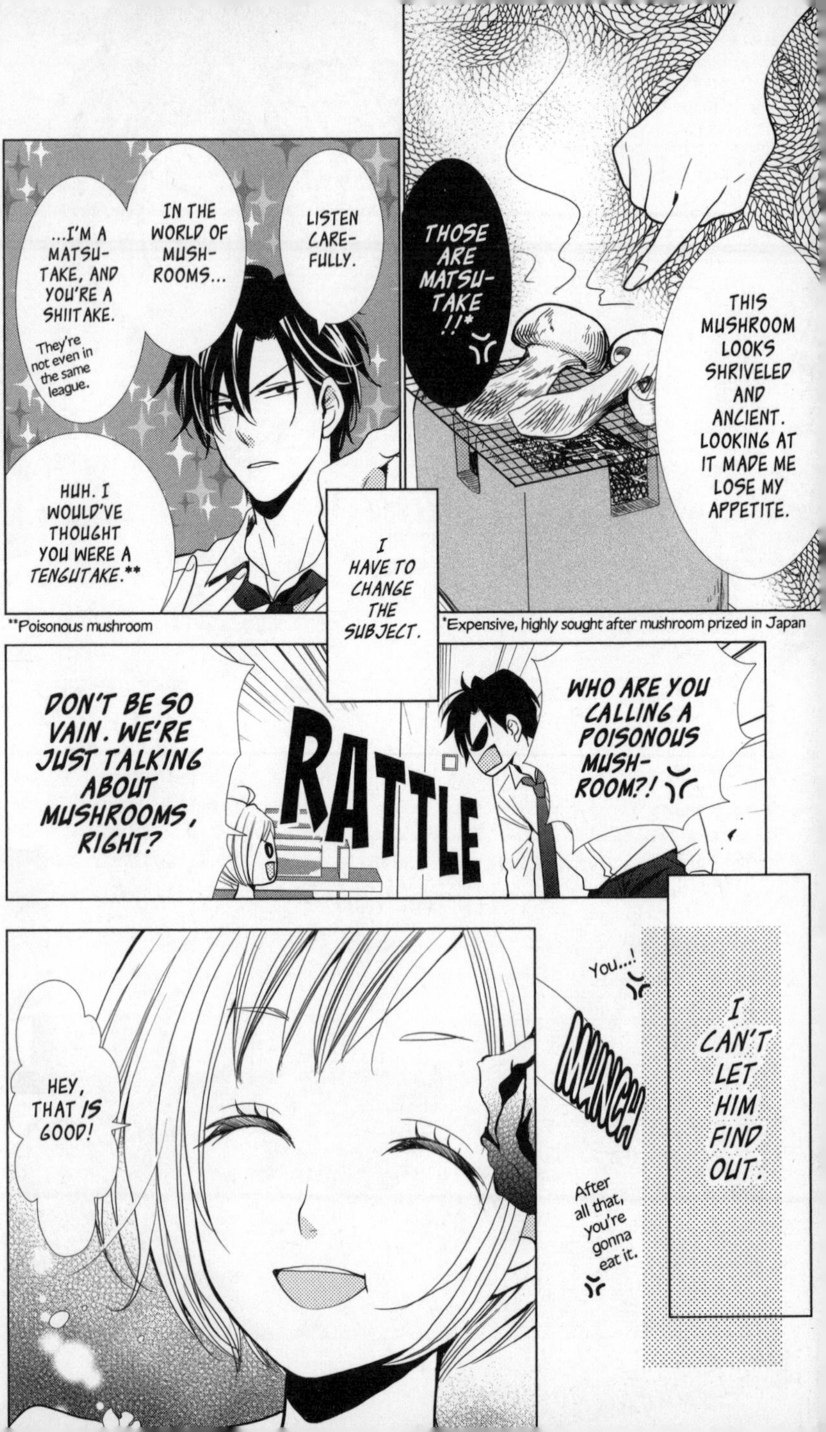
THIS MUSHROOM LOOKS SHRIVELED AND ANCIENT. LOOKING AT IT MADE ME LOSE MY APPETITE.
THOSE ARE MATSUTAKE!!*
LISTEN CAREFULLY.
IN THE WORLD OF MUSHROOMS...
...I'M A MATSUTAKE, AND YOU'RE A SHIITAKE.
They're not even in the same league.
HUH. I WOULD'VE THOUGHT YOU WERE A TENGUTAKE.**
I HAVE TO CHANGE THE SUBJECT.
WHO ARE YOU CALLING A POISONOUS MUSHROOM?!
RATTLE
DON'T BE SO VAIN. WE'RE JUST TALKING ABOUT MUSHROOMS, RIGHT?
I CAN'T LET HIM FIND OUT.
You...!
MUNCH
After all that, you're gonna eat it.
HEY, THAT IS GOOD!
*Expensive, highly sought after mushroom prized in Japan
**Poisonous mushroom

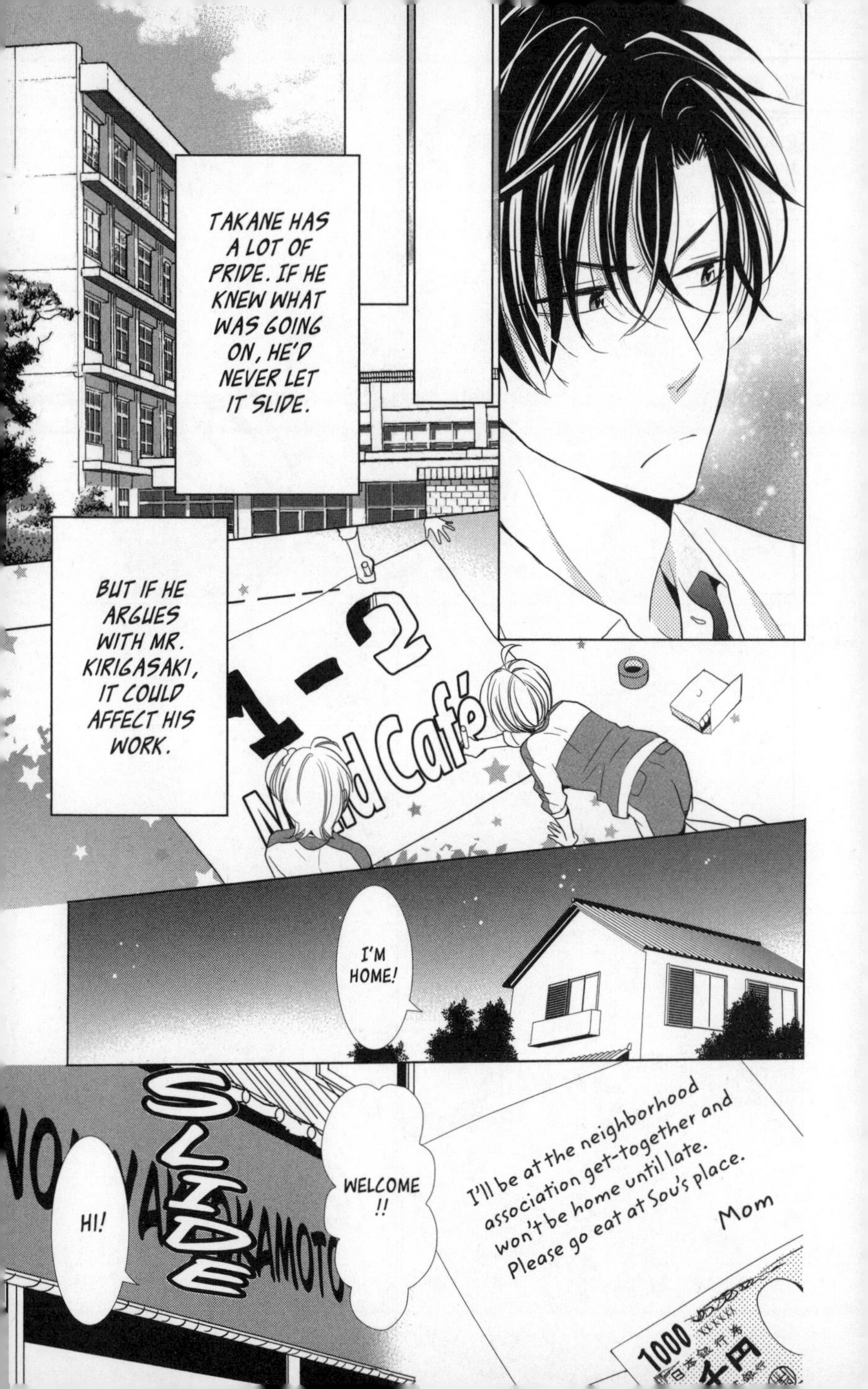
TAKANE HAS A LOT OF PRIDE. IF HE KNEW WHAT WAS GOING ON, HE'D NEVER LET IT SLIDE.
BUT IF HE ARGUES WITH MR. KIRIGASAKI, IT COULD AFFECT HIS WORK.
I'M HOME!
I'll be at the neighborhood association get-together and won't be home until late. Please go eat at Sou's place.
Mom
WELCOME !!
SLIDE
HI!

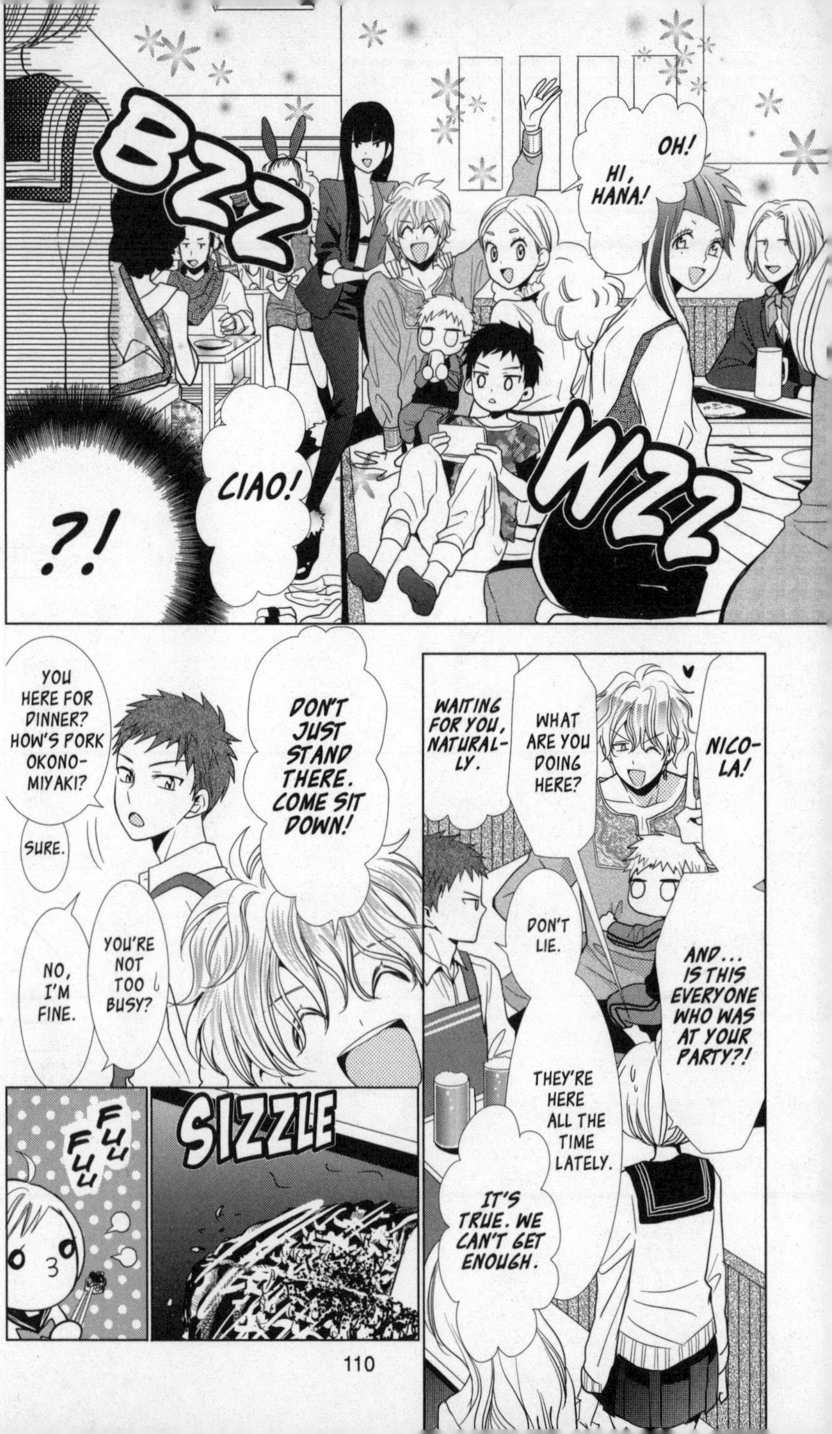
OH!
HI, HANA!
BZZ
WZZ
CIAO!
?!
NICO-LA!
WHAT ARE YOU DOING HERE?
WAITING FOR YOU, NATURAL-LY.
AND... IS THIS EVERYONE WHO WAS AT YOUR PARTY?!
DON'T LIE.
THEY'RE HERE ALL THE TIME LATELY.
IT'S TRUE. WE CAN'T GET ENOUGH.
DON'T JUST STAND THERE. COME SIT DOWN!
YOU HERE FOR DINNER? HOW'S PORK OKONO-MIYAKI?
SURE.
YOU'RE NOT TOO BUSY?
NO, I'M FINE.
SIZZLE
FUU FUU

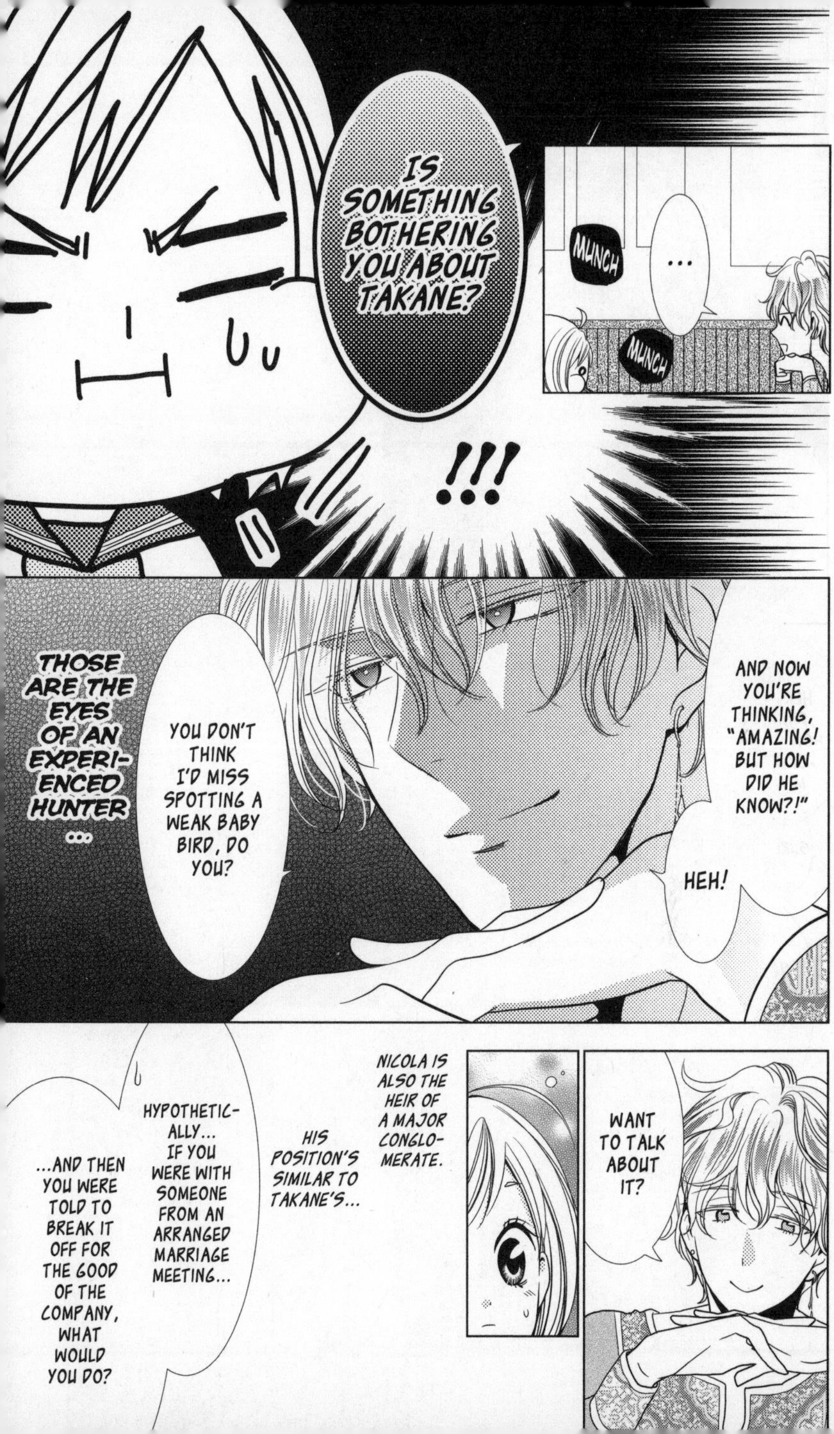
MUNCH
...
MUNCH
IS SOMETHING BOTHERING YOU ABOUT TAKANE?
!!!
AND NOW YOU'RE THINKING, "AMAZING! BUT HOW DID HE KNOW?!"
HEH!
YOU DON'T THINK I'D MISS SPOTTING A WEAK BABY BIRD, DO YOU?
THOSE ARE THE EYES OF AN EXPERIENCED HUNTER...
WANT TO TALK ABOUT IT?
NICOLA IS ALSO THE HEIR OF A MAJOR CONGLOMERATE.
HIS POSITION'S SIMILAR TO TAKANE'S...
HYPOTHETICALLY... IF YOU WERE WITH SOMEONE FROM AN ARRANGED MARRIAGE MEETING...
...AND THEN YOU WERE TOLD TO BREAK IT OFF FOR THE GOOD OF THE COMPANY, WHAT WOULD YOU DO?

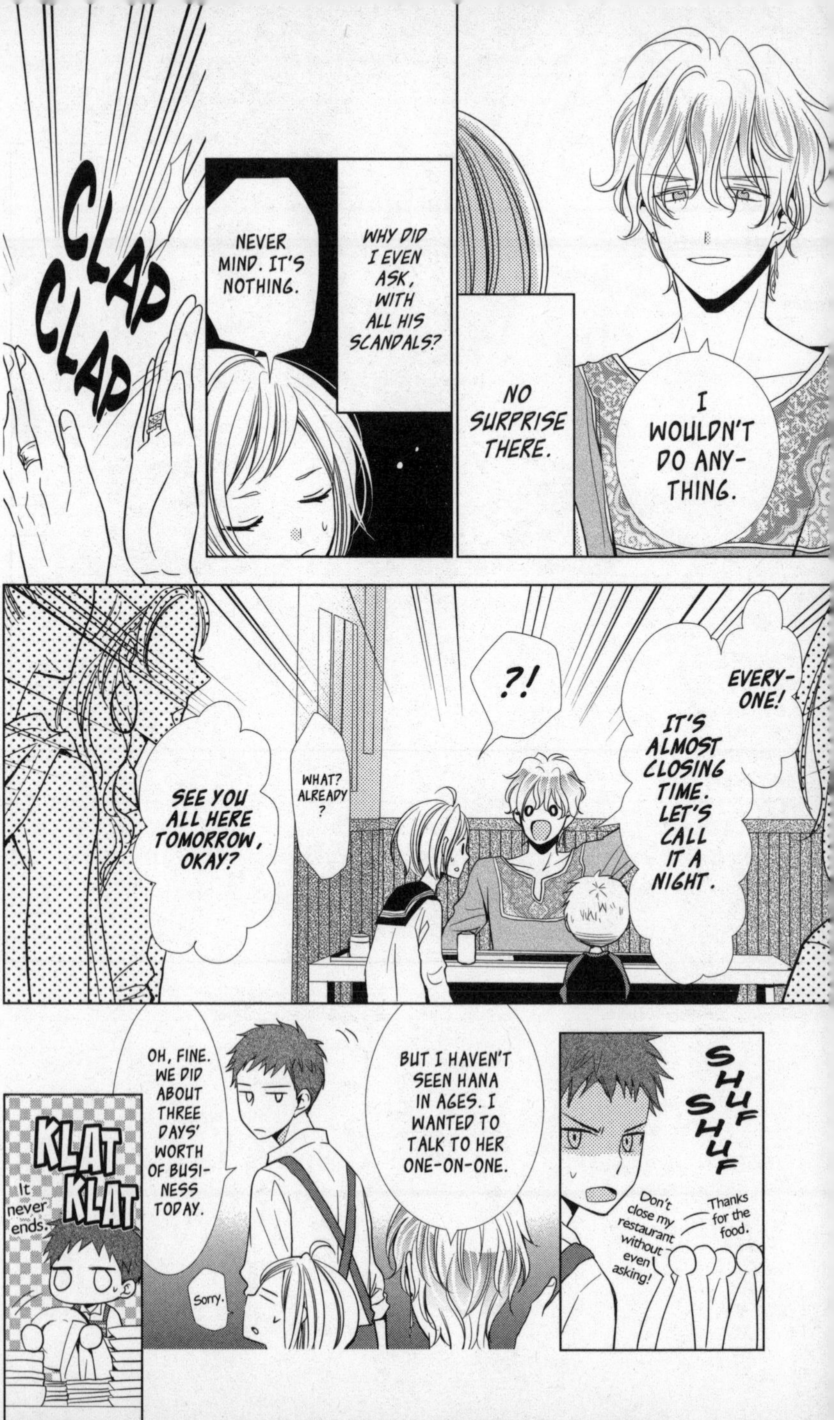
I WOULDN'T DO ANYTHING.
NO SURPRISE THERE.
WHY DID I EVEN ASK, WITH ALL HIS SCANDALS?
NEVER MIND. IT'S NOTHING.
CLAP CLAP
EVERYONE!
IT'S ALMOST CLOSING TIME. LET'S CALL IT A NIGHT.
?!
WHAT? ALREADY?
SEE YOU ALL HERE TOMORROW, OKAY?
SHUF SHUF
Thanks for the food.
Don't close my restaurant without even asking!
BUT I HAVEN'T SEEN HANA IN AGES. I WANTED TO TALK TO HER ONE-ON-ONE.
OH, FINE. WE DID ABOUT THREE DAYS' WORTH OF BUSINESS TODAY.
Sorry.
KLAT KLAT
It never ends.

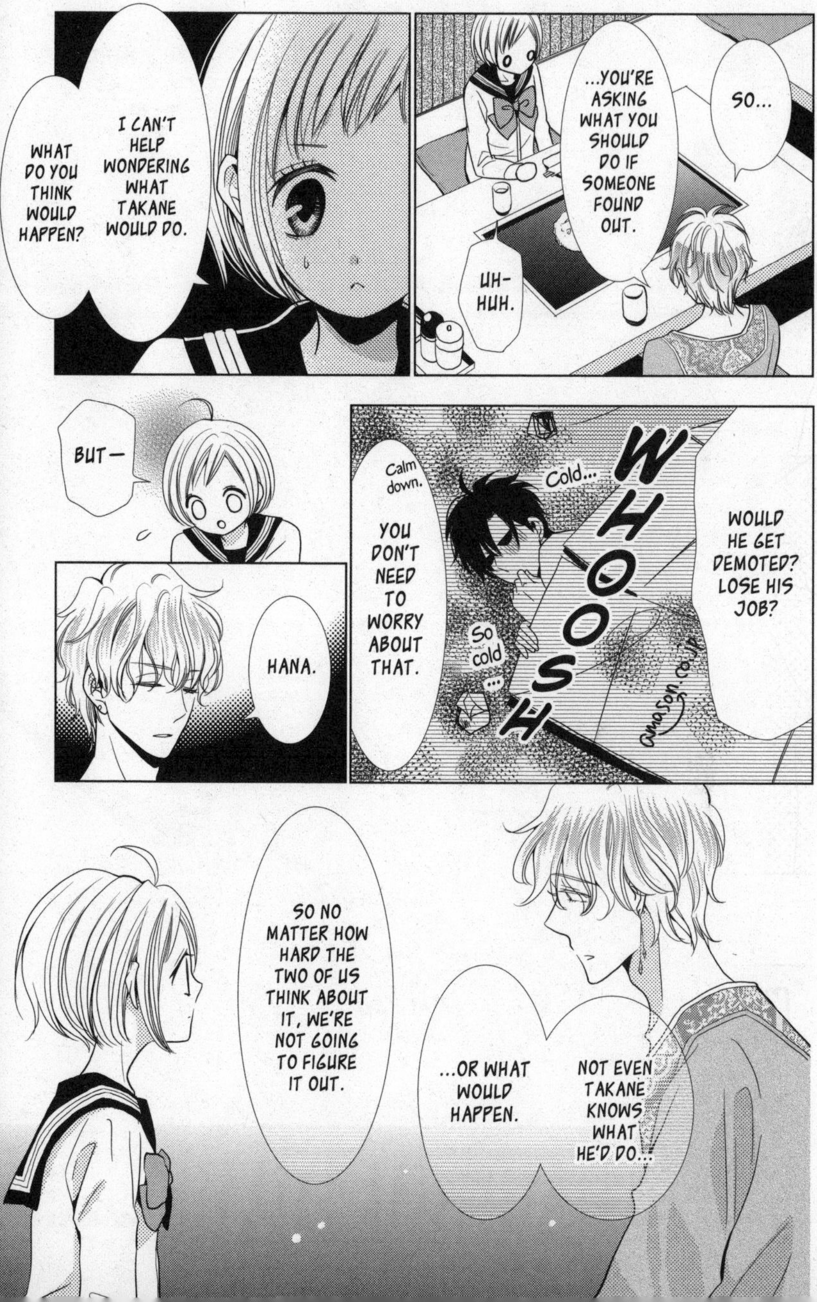
SO...
...YOU'RE ASKING WHAT YOU SHOULD DO IF SOMEONE FOUND OUT.
UH-HUH.
I CAN'T HELP WONDERING WHAT TAKANE WOULD DO.
WHAT DO YOU THINK WOULD HAPPEN?
WOULD HE GET DEMOTED? LOSE HIS JOB?
WHOOOSH
Cold...
So cold...
amason.co.jp
Calm down.
YOU DON'T NEED TO WORRY ABOUT THAT.
BUT—
HANA.
NOT EVEN TAKANE KNOWS WHAT HE'D DO...
...OR WHAT WOULD HAPPEN.
SO NO MATTER HOW HARD THE TWO OF US THINK ABOUT IT, WE'RE NOT GOING TO FIGURE IT OUT.

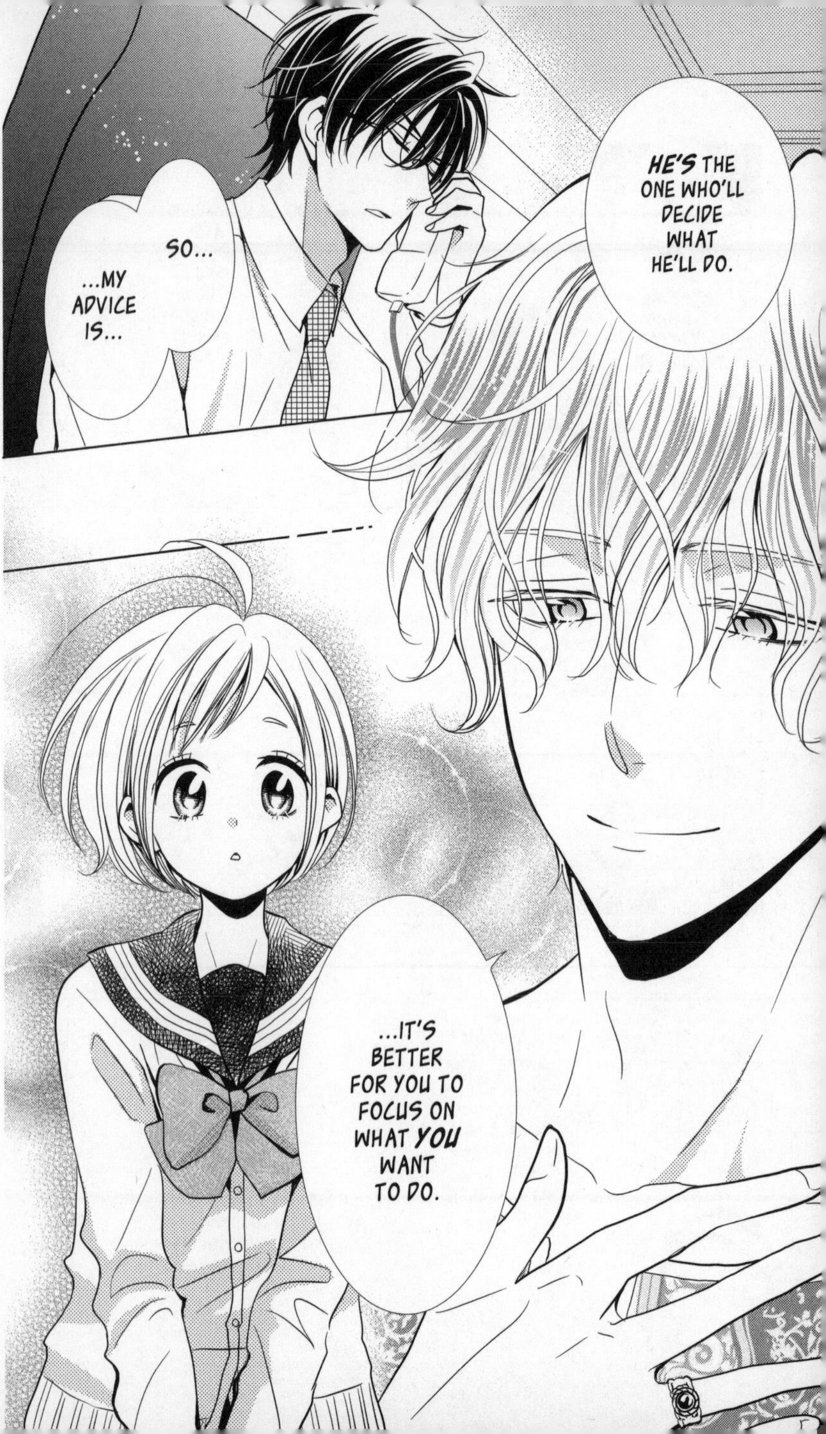
HE'S THE ONE WHO'LL DECIDE WHAT HE'LL DO.
SO...
...MY ADVICE IS...
...IT'S BETTER FOR YOU TO FOCUS ON WHAT YOU WANT TO DO.

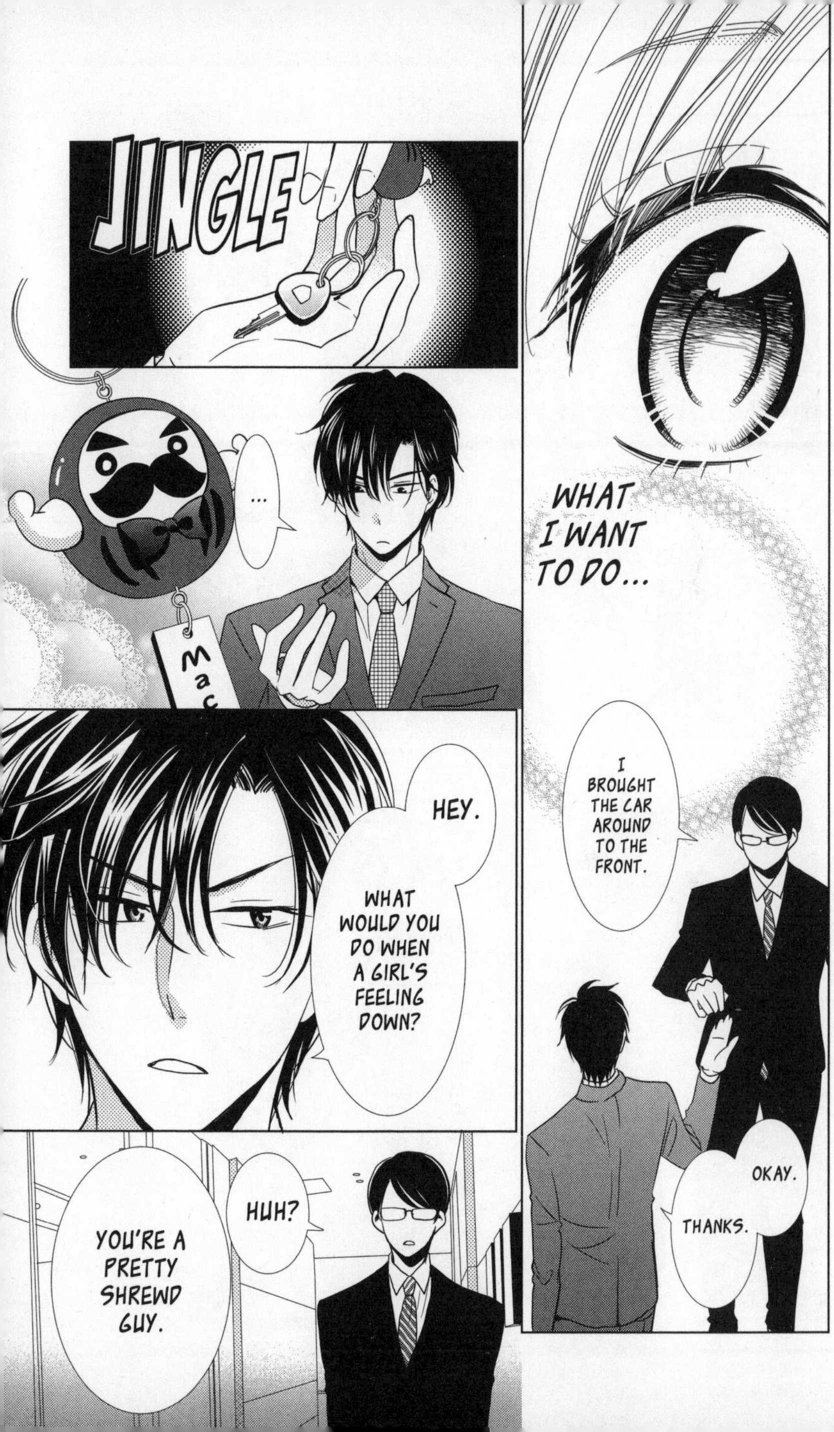

WHAT I WANT TO DO...
I BROUGHT THE CAR AROUND TO THE FRONT.
OKAY.
THANKS.
JINGLE
...
Mac
HEY.
WHAT WOULD YOU DO WHEN A GIRL'S FEELING DOWN?
HUH?
YOU'RE A PRETTY SHREWD GUY.

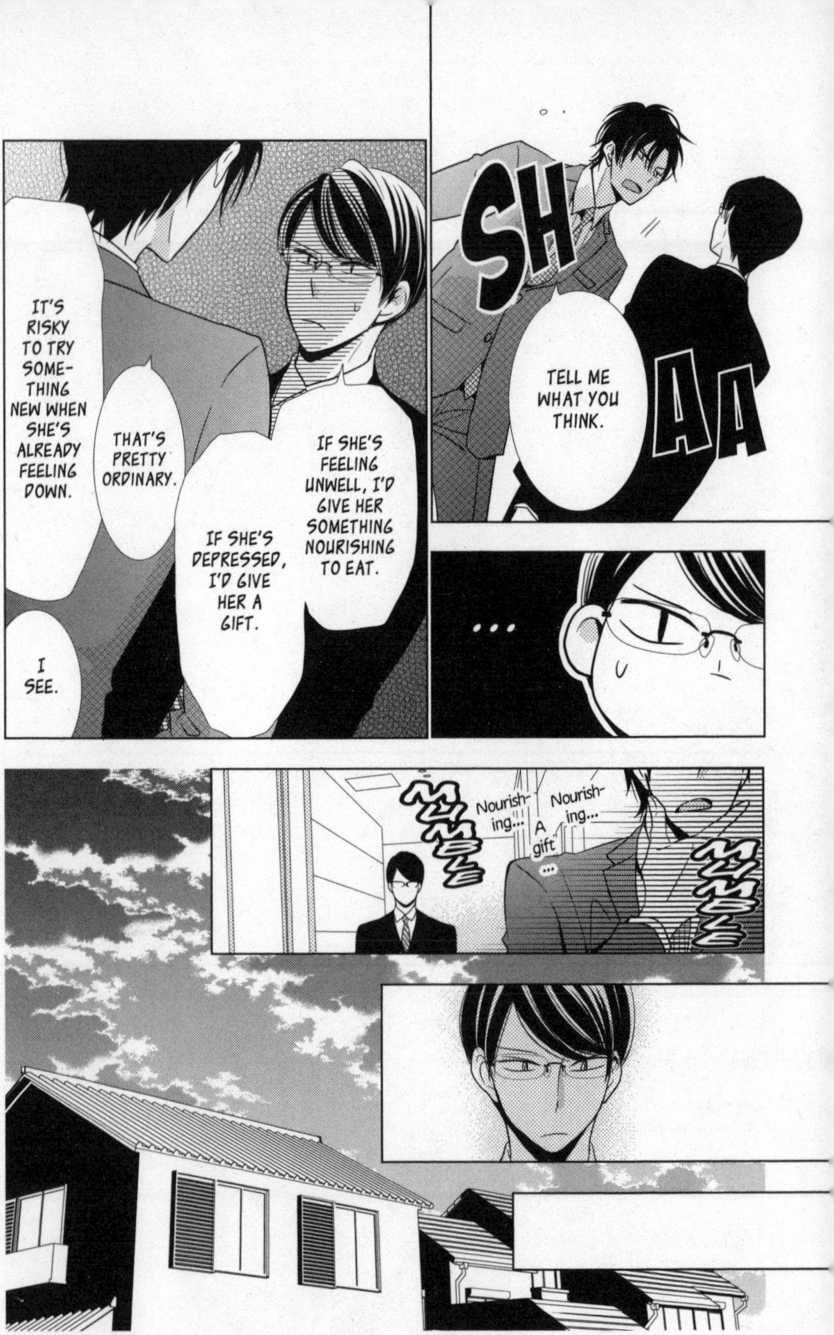
SH
AA
TELL ME WHAT YOU THINK.
...
IF SHE'S FEELING UNWELL, I'D GIVE HER SOMETHING NOURISHING TO EAT.
IF SHE'S DEPRESSED, I'D GIVE HER A GIFT.
THAT'S PRETTY ORDINARY.
IT'S RISKY TO TRY SOME-THING NEW WHEN SHE'S ALREADY FEELING DOWN.
I SEE.
MUMBLE
Nourish-ing...
A gift...
Nourish-ing...
MUMBLE

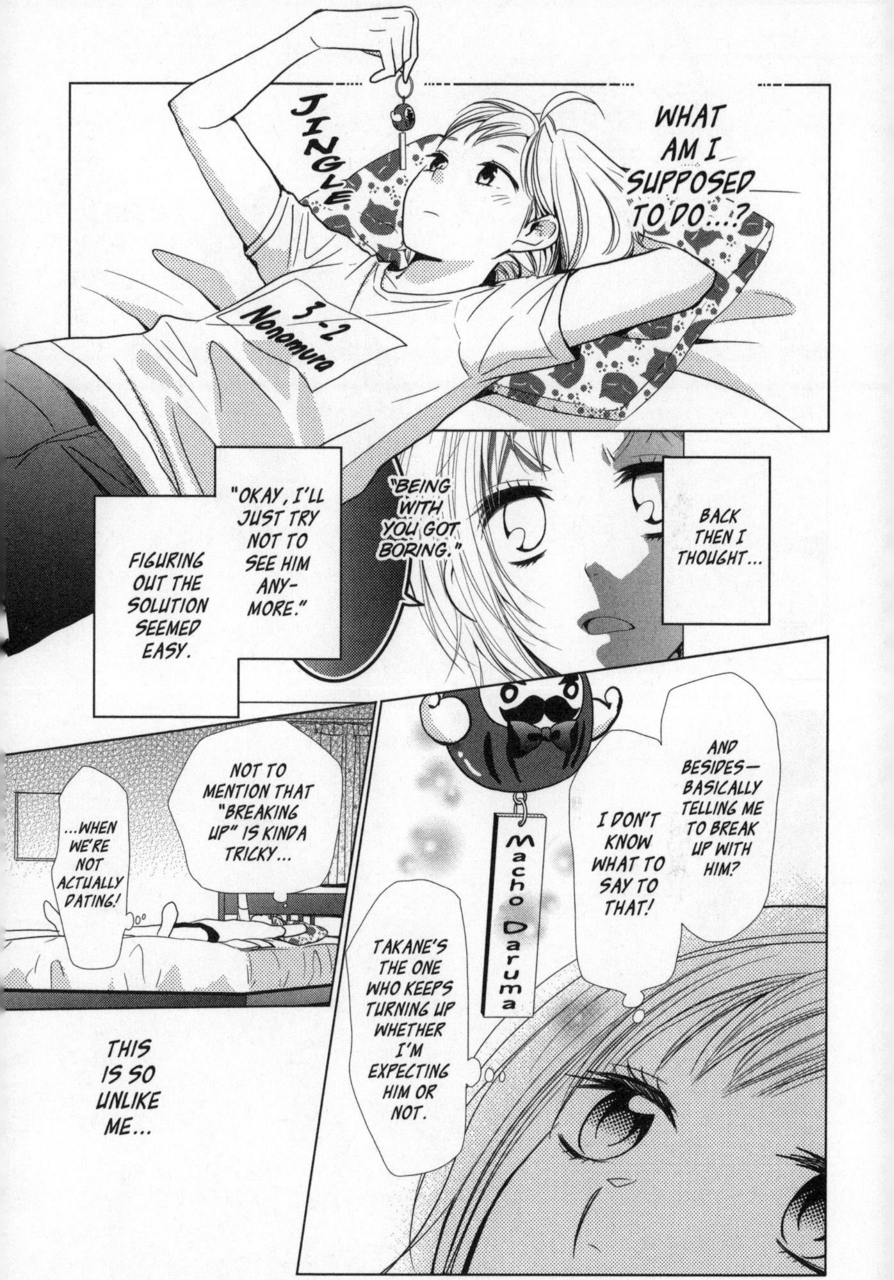
WHAT AM I SUPPOSED TO DO...?
JINGLE
3-2 Nonomura
BACK THEN I THOUGHT...
"BEING WITH YOU GOT BORING."
"OKAY, I'LL JUST TRY NOT TO SEE HIM ANYMORE."
FIGURING OUT THE SOLUTION SEEMED EASY.
AND BESIDES— BASICALLY TELLING ME TO BREAK UP WITH HIM?
I DON'T KNOW WHAT TO SAY TO THAT!
Macho Daruma
TAKANE'S THE ONE WHO KEEPS TURNING UP WHETHER I'M EXPECTING HIM OR NOT.
NOT TO MENTION THAT "BREAKING UP" IS KINDA TRICKY...
...WHEN WE'RE NOT ACTUALLY DATING!
THIS IS SO UNLIKE ME...

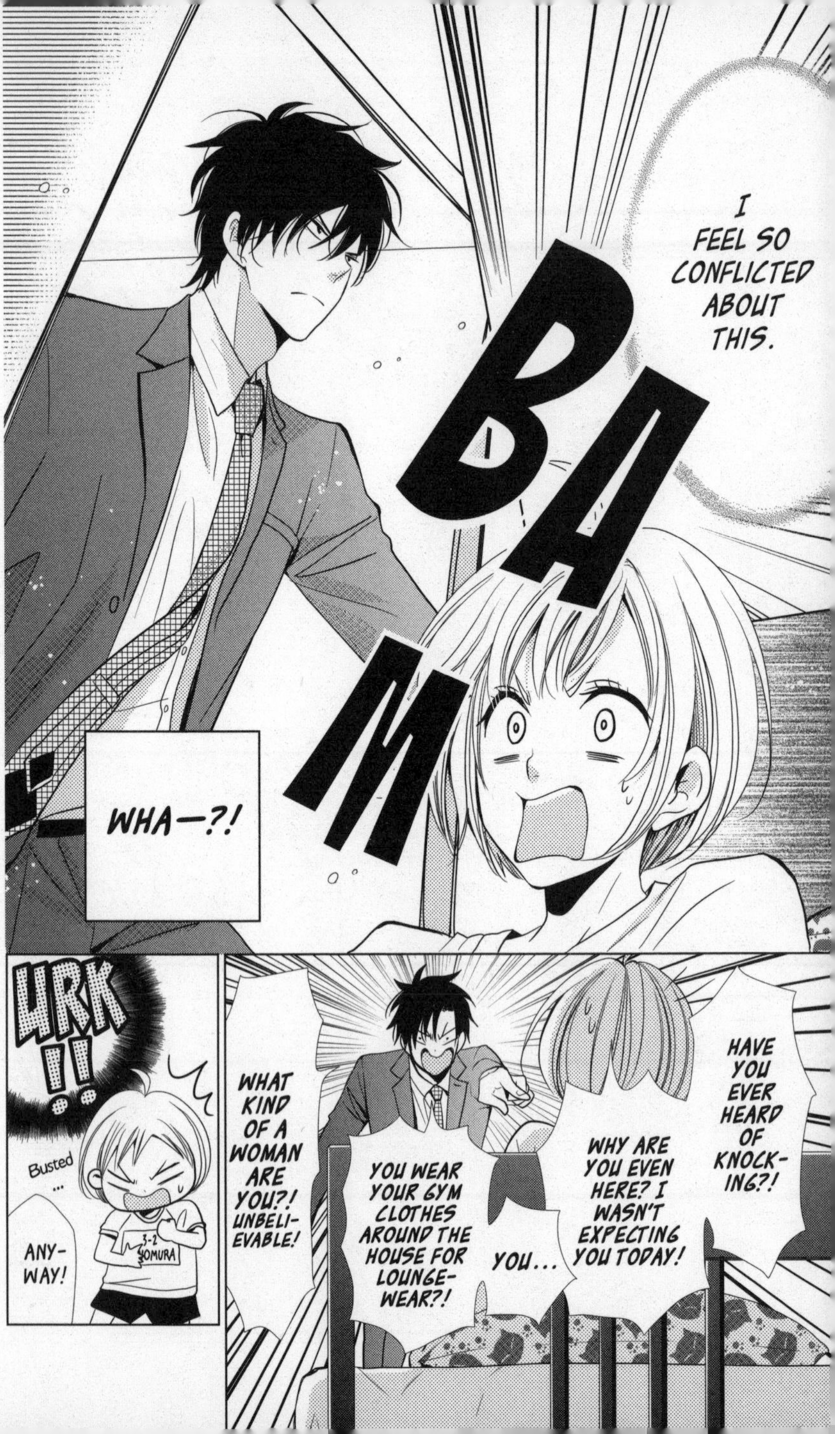
I FEEL SO CONFLICTED ABOUT THIS.
BAM
WHA—?!
HAVE YOU EVER HEARD OF KNOCKING?!
WHY ARE YOU EVEN HERE? I WASN'T EXPECTING YOU TODAY!
YOU...
YOU WEAR YOUR GYM CLOTHES AROUND THE HOUSE FOR LOUNGEWEAR?!
WHAT KIND OF A WOMAN ARE YOU?! UNBELIEVABLE!
URK!!
Busted...
3-2 YOMURA
ANYWAY!

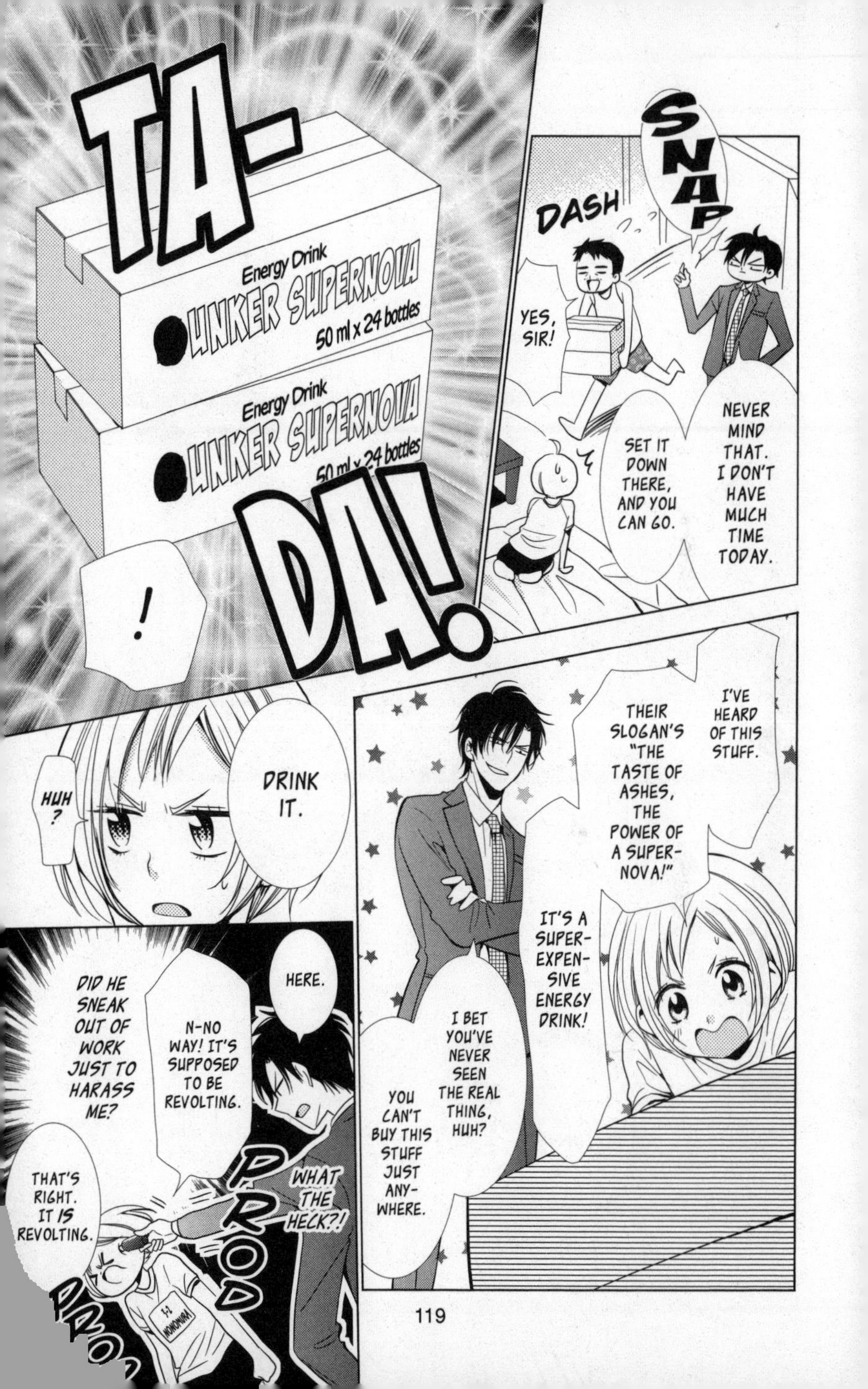
SNAP
DASH
YES, SIR!
NEVER MIND THAT. I DON'T HAVE MUCH TIME TODAY.
SET IT DOWN THERE, AND YOU CAN GO.
TA-
Energy Drink
UNKER SUPERNOVA
50 ml x 24 bottles
Energy Drink
UNKER SUPERNOVA
50 ml x 24 bottles
DA!
!
I'VE HEARD OF THIS STUFF.
THEIR SLOGAN'S "THE TASTE OF ASHES, THE POWER OF A SUPER-NOVA!"
IT'S A SUPER-EXPENSIVE ENERGY DRINK!
I BET YOU'VE NEVER SEEN THE REAL THING, HUH?
YOU CAN'T BUY THIS STUFF JUST ANY-WHERE.
DRINK IT.
HUH?
HERE.
N-NO WAY! IT'S SUPPOSED TO BE REVOLTING.
DID HE SNEAK OUT OF WORK JUST TO HARASS ME?
WHAT THE HECK?!
PROD
THAT'S RIGHT. IT IS REVOLTING.

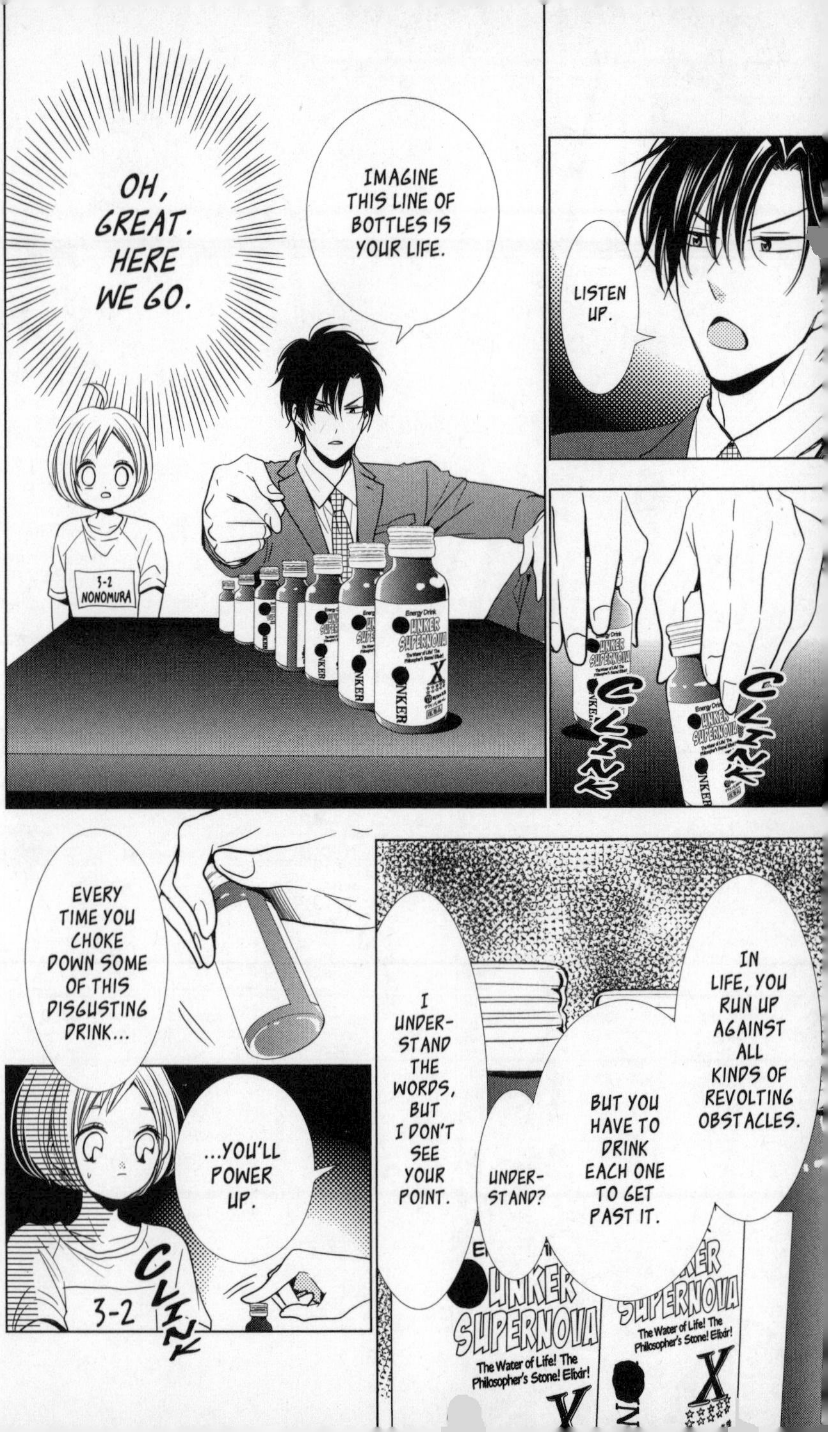
LISTEN UP.
CLINK
CLINK
IMAGINE THIS LINE OF BOTTLES IS YOUR LIFE.
OH, GREAT. HERE WE GO.
3-2 NONOMURA
Energy Drink
UNKER SUPERNOVA
IN LIFE, YOU RUN UP AGAINST ALL KINDS OF REVOLTING OBSTACLES.
BUT YOU HAVE TO DRINK EACH ONE TO GET PAST IT.
UNDERSTAND?
I UNDERSTAND THE WORDS, BUT I DON'T SEE YOUR POINT.
UNKER SUPERNOVA
The Water of Life! The Philosopher's Stone! Elixir!
SUPERNOVA
The Water of Life! The Philosopher's Stone! Elixir!
EVERY TIME YOU CHOKE DOWN SOME OF THIS DISGUSTING DRINK...
...YOU'LL POWER UP.
CLINK
3-2

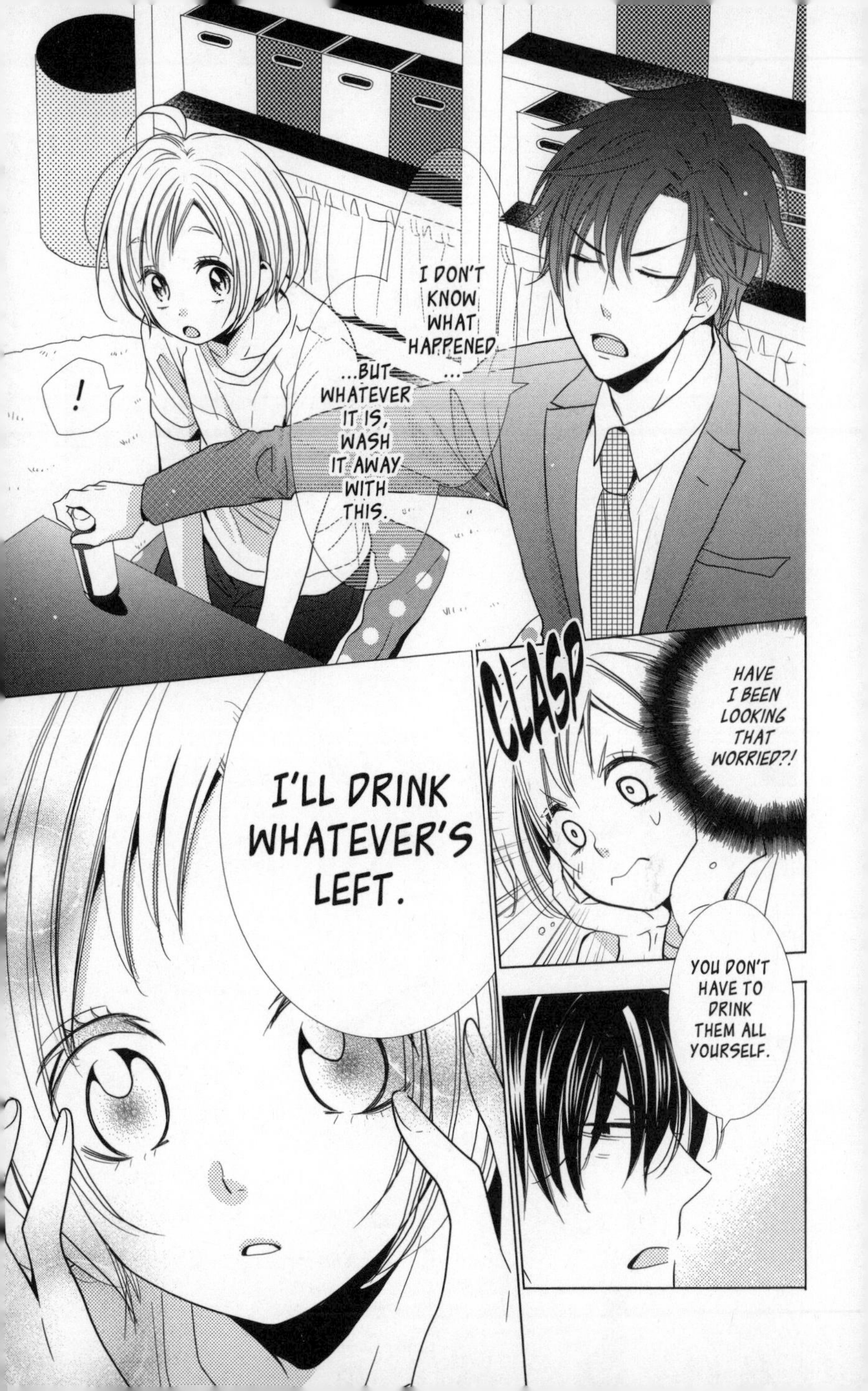
I DON'T KNOW WHAT HAPPENED...
...BUT WHATEVER IT IS, WASH IT AWAY WITH THIS.
!
CLASP
HAVE I BEEN LOOKING THAT WORRIED?!
YOU DON'T HAVE TO DRINK THEM ALL YOURSELF.
I'LL DRINK WHATEVER'S LEFT.

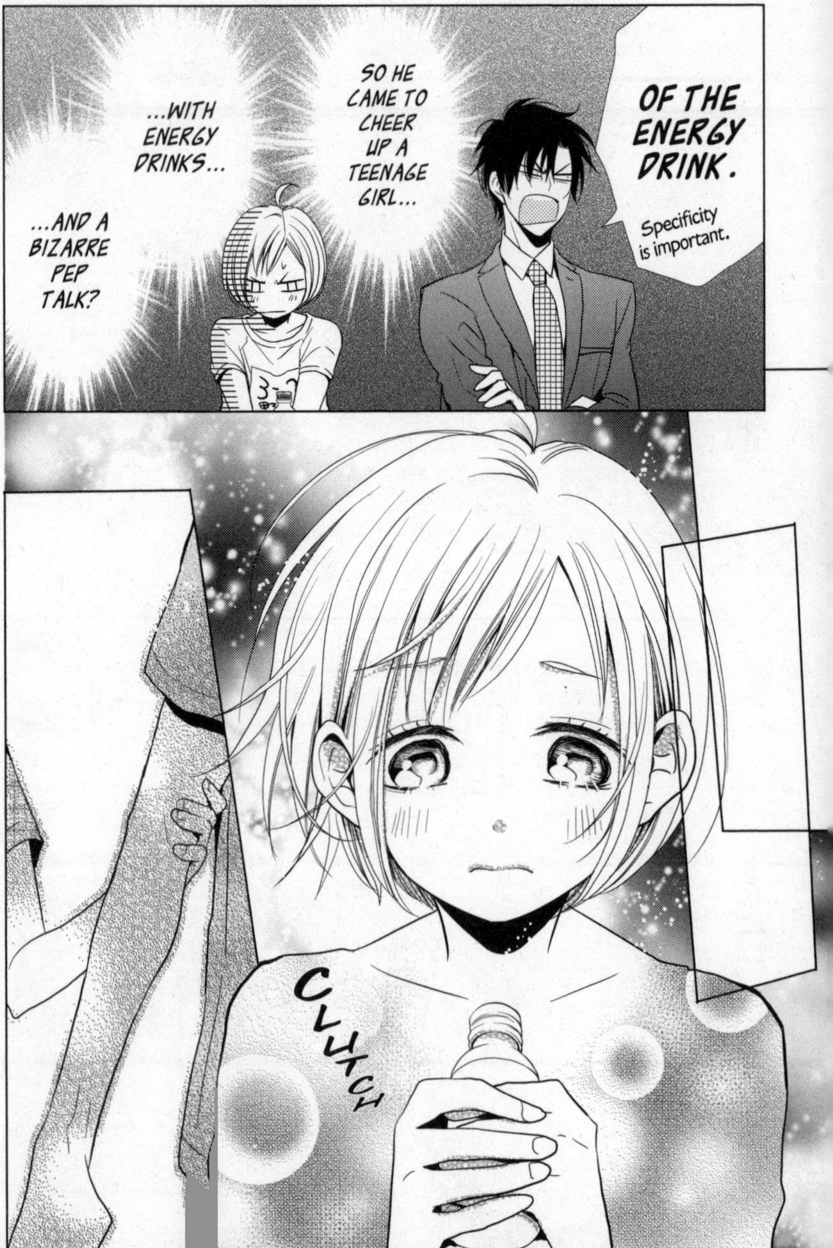
OF THE ENERGY DRINK.
Specificity is important.
SO HE CAME TO CHEER UP A TEENAGE GIRL...
...WITH ENERGY DRINKS...
...AND A BIZARRE PEP TALK?
CLUTCH

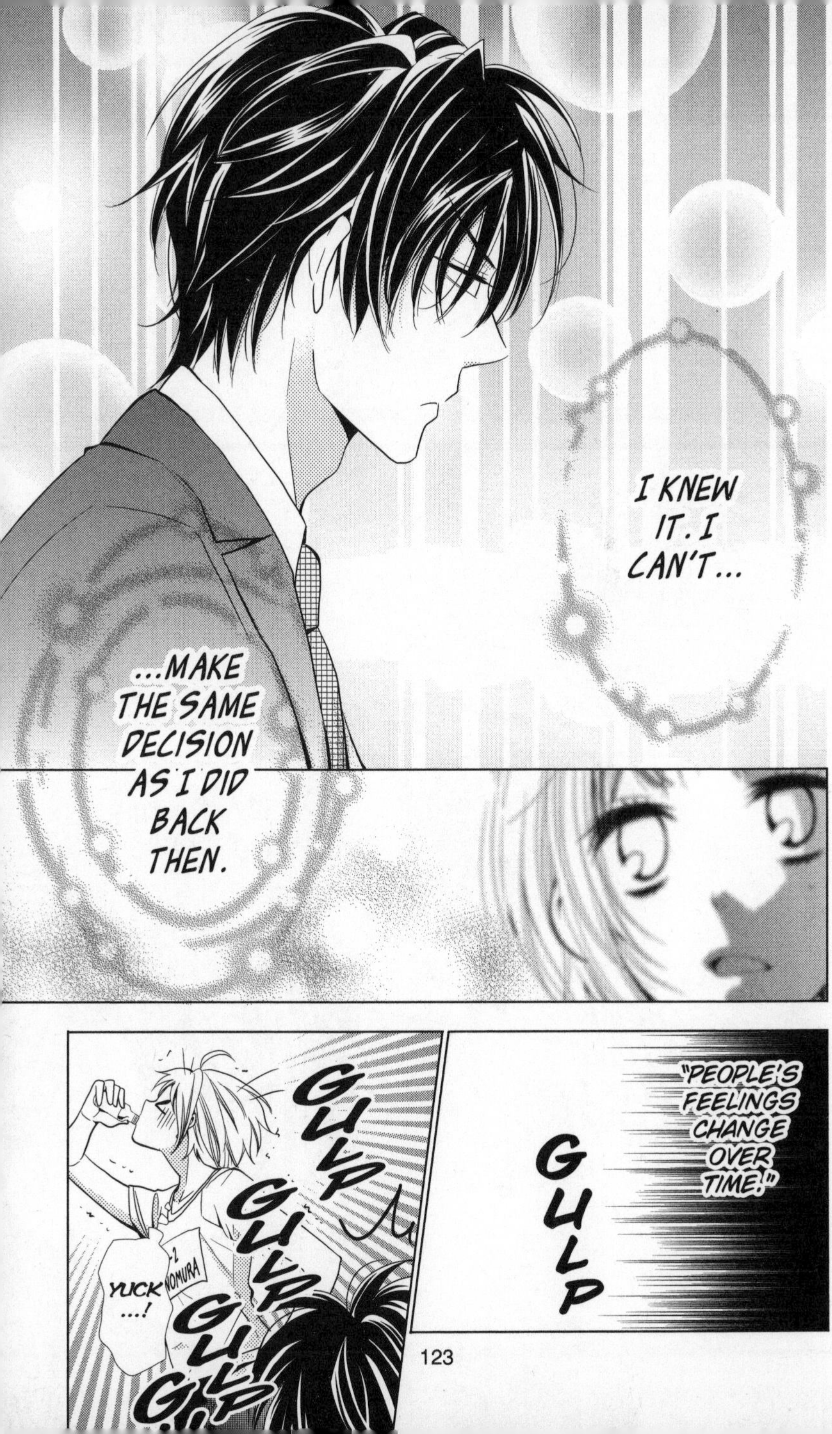
I KNEW IT. I CAN'T...
...MAKE THE SAME DECISION AS I DID BACK THEN.
"PEOPLE'S FEELINGS CHANGE OVER TIME."
GULP
GULP
GULP
GULP
G...
YUCK ...!
NOMURA

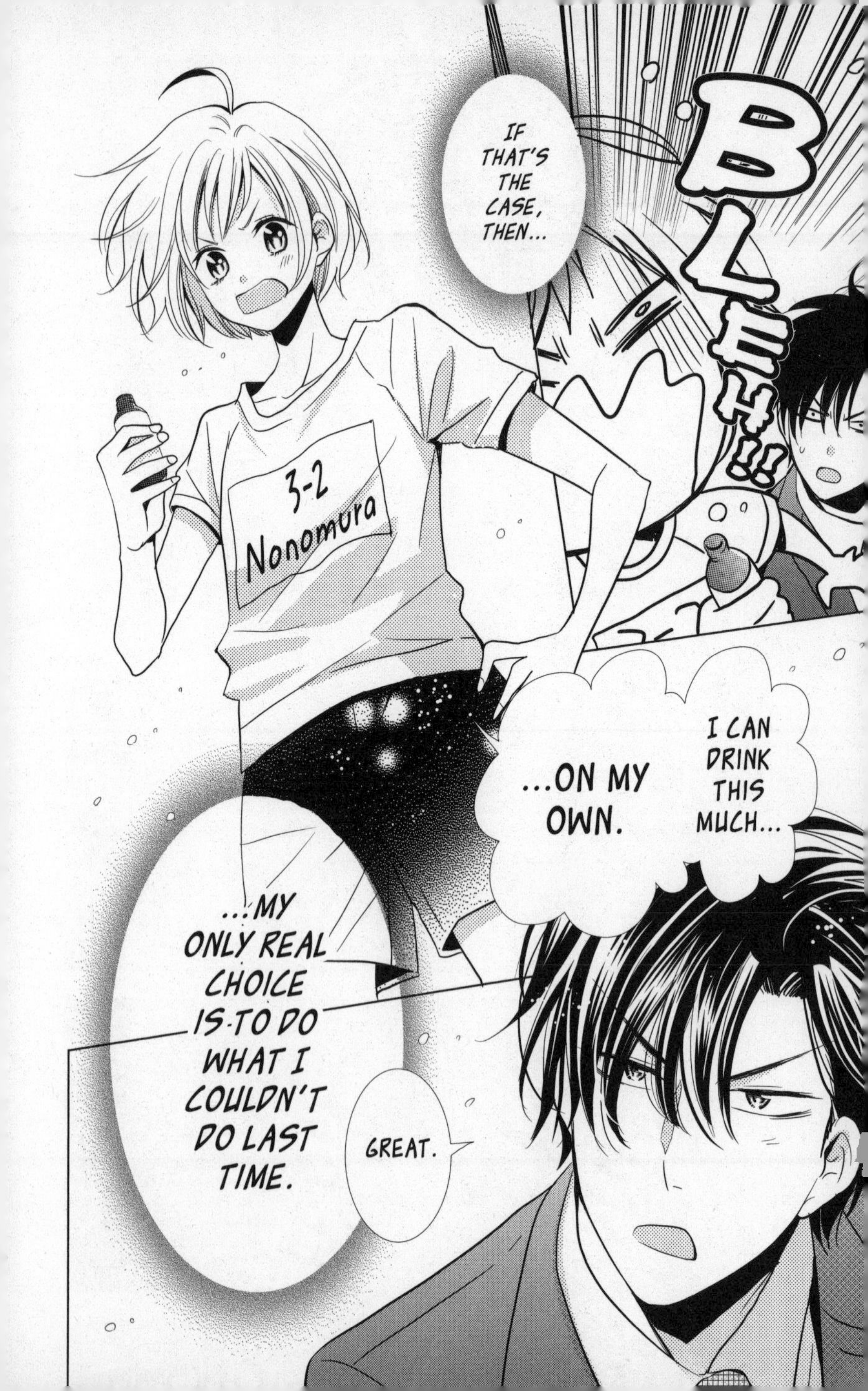
BLEH!!
IF THAT'S THE CASE, THEN...
3-2 Nonomura
I CAN DRINK THIS MUCH...
...ON MY OWN.
...MY ONLY REAL CHOICE IS TO DO WHAT I COULDN'T DO LAST TIME.
GREAT.

● Drawing Manga, Part 3 ●

~ Inking the Pencil Sketches (cont.) ~

Panel border → Speech bubble → Sound Effects → Background → People

That's the order in which I ink (although sometimes I change it up depending on my mood). I start with whatever page I'm in the mood for, in no particular order. It takes three or four days.

This part doesn't take much brainpower, so the biggest challenge is staying awake. For some reason, even when I get enough sleep, doing this makes me sleepy. I have to have the TV on or music playing constantly. Humming along helps me stay awake. I tend to keep the TV on news channels, since anime or dramas get me caught up in the story.

~ Adding Screentones ~

To finish up, the screentone (the grey areas) is applied. This takes about a day.

And that's the process of creating manga! At the moment, I draw the pictures myself. Everyone has their own way of drawing manga, so think of this as just one example. I often get letters from people interested in creating manga, so I hope this was helpful in some way!

"How do I get better at drawing?" I sometimes get questions like this. Basically, I think you need to look at a wide variety of things and try to draw them. I'm not sure I'm skilled enough to really be handing out advice, though.

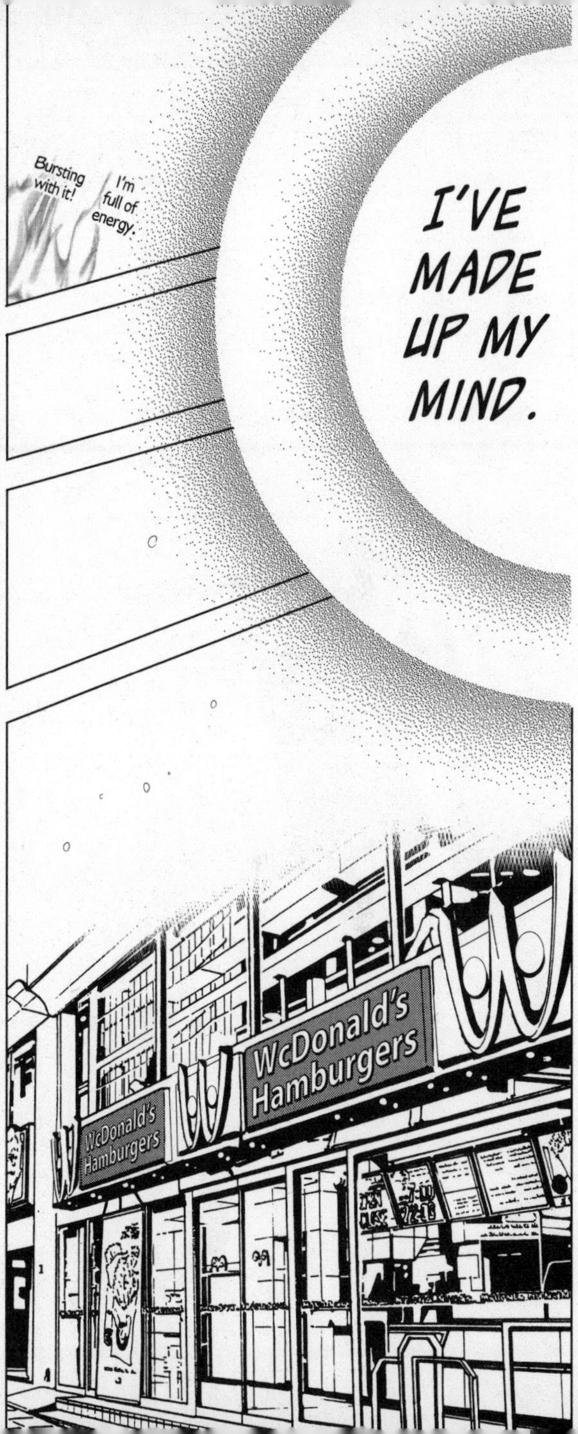
I'VE MADE UP MY MIND.
I'm full of energy.
Bursting with it!
WcDonald's Hamburgers
WcDonald's Hamburgers

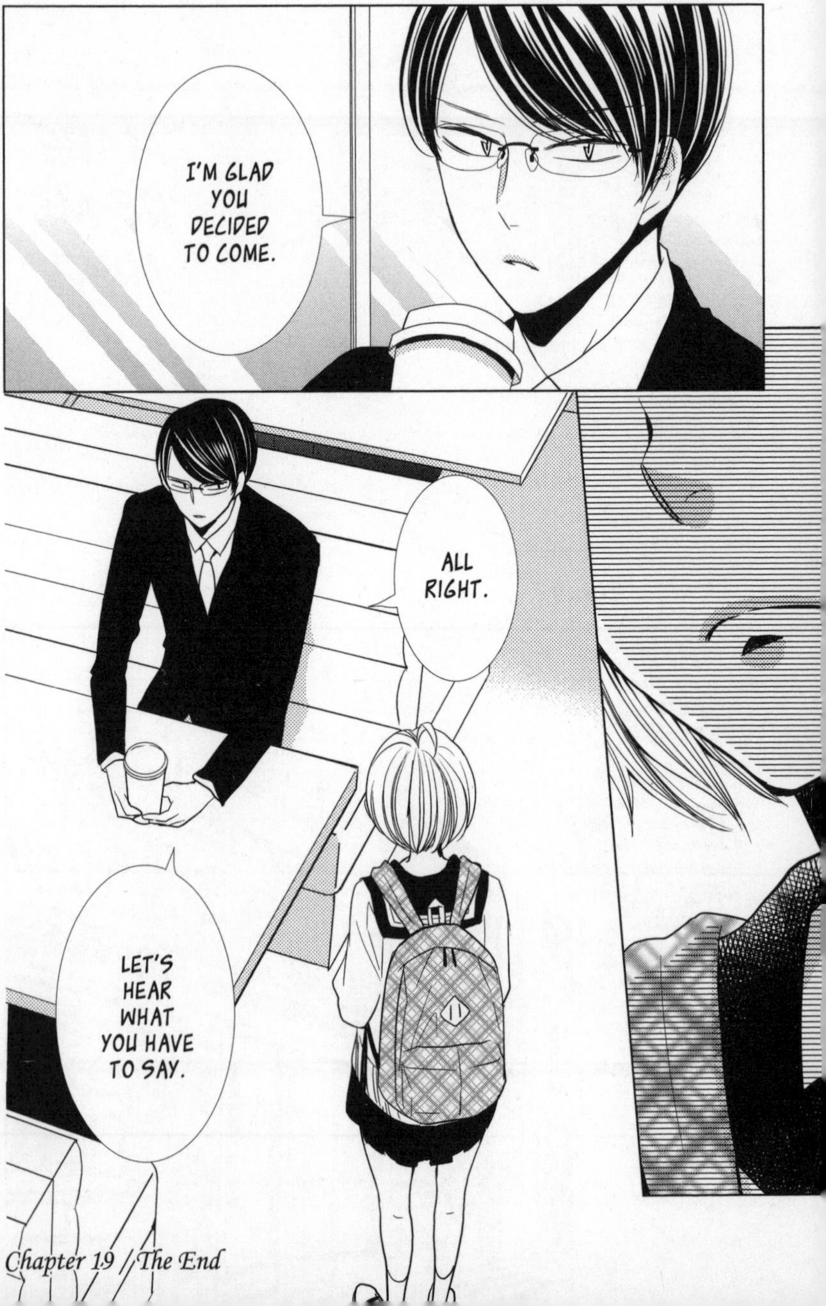
I'M GLAD YOU DECIDED TO COME.
ALL RIGHT.
LET'S HEAR WHAT YOU HAVE TO SAY.

Chapter 19 / The End

Ciao

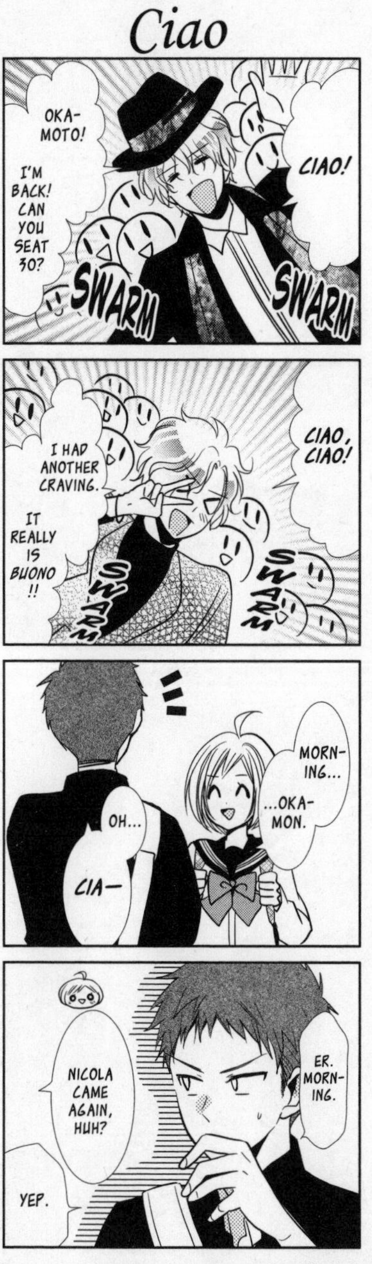
CIAO!
OKA-MOTO!
I'M BACK! CAN YOU SEAT 30?
SWARM
SWARM
CIAO, CIAO!
I HAD ANOTHER CRAVING.
IT REALLY IS BUONO!!
SWARM
SWARM
MORN-ING...
...OKA-MON.
OH...
CIA—
ER. MORN-ING.
NICOLA CAME AGAIN, HUH?
YEP.

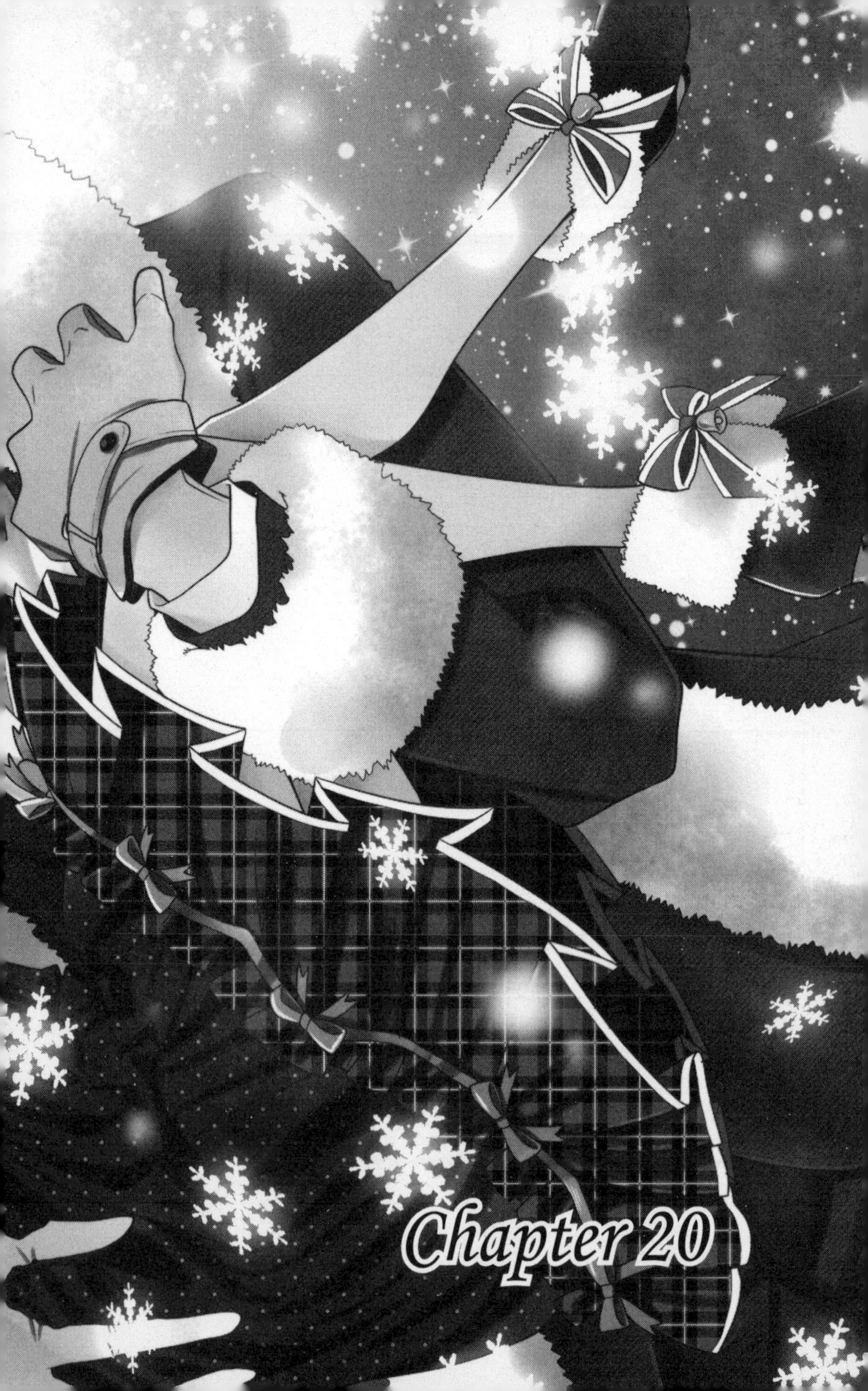
Chapter 20

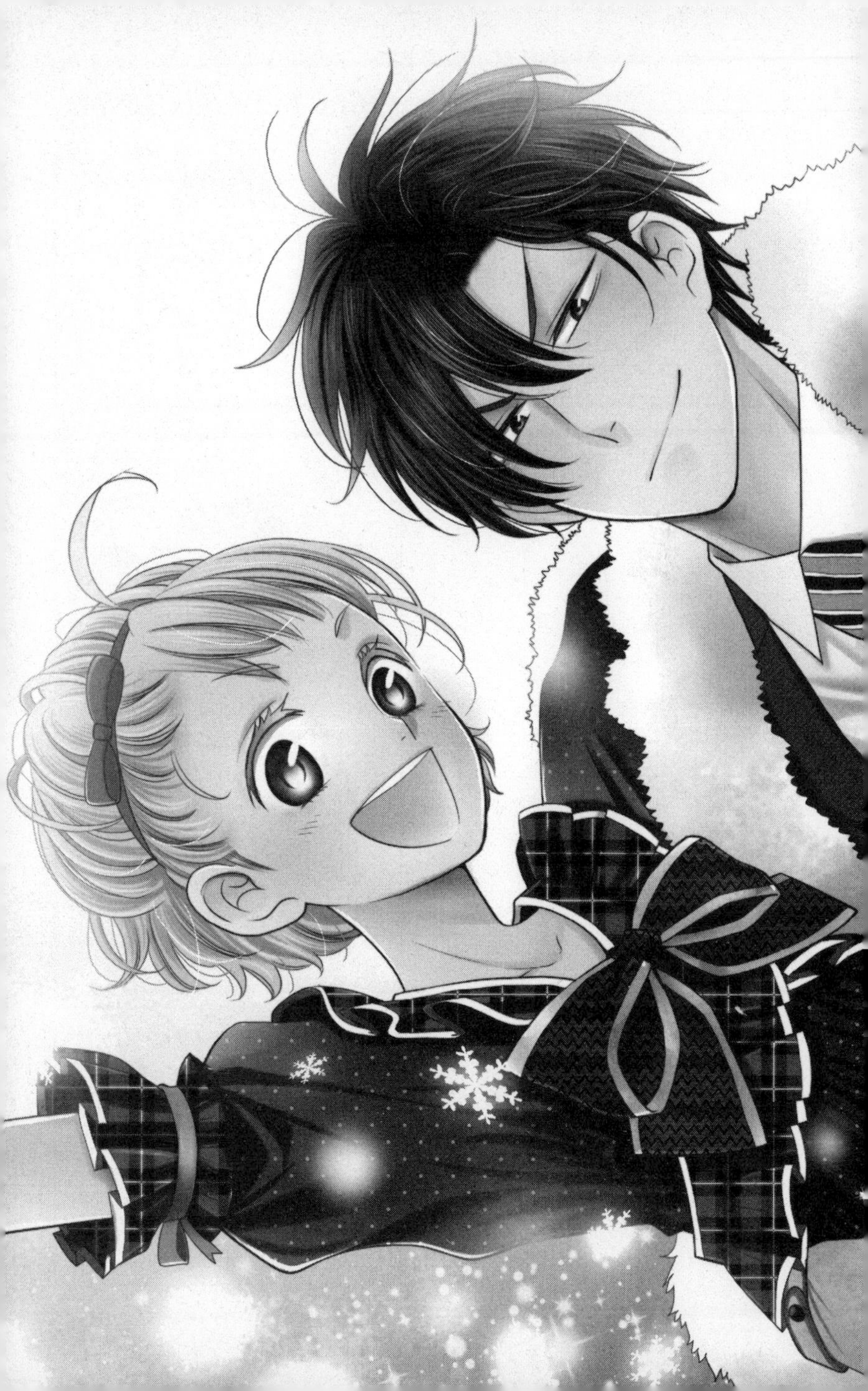

How to Make Hikune

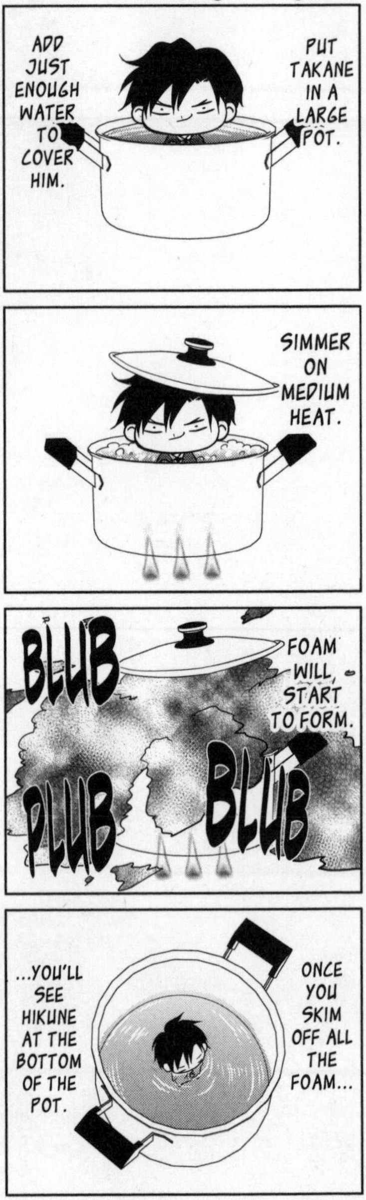
PUT TAKANE IN A LARGE POT.
ADD JUST ENOUGH WATER TO COVER HIM.
SIMMER ON MEDIUM HEAT.
FOAM WILL START TO FORM.
BLUB
BLUB
PLUB
ONCE YOU SKIM OFF ALL THE FOAM...
...YOU'LL SEE HIKUNE AT THE BOTTOM OF THE POT.

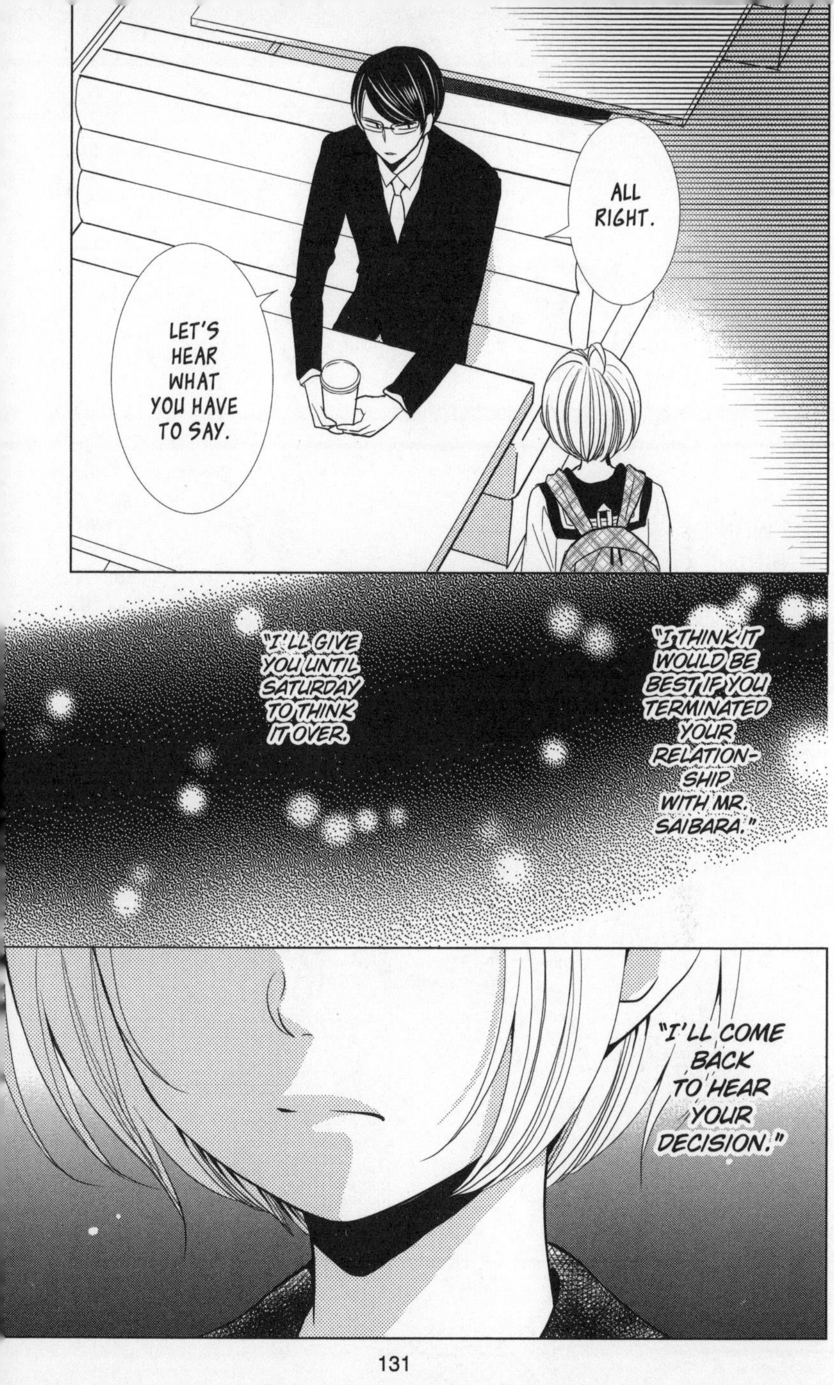
ALL RIGHT.
LET'S HEAR WHAT YOU HAVE TO SAY.
"I THINK IT WOULD BE BEST IF YOU TERMINATED YOUR RELATION-SHIP WITH MR. SAIBARA."
"I'LL GIVE YOU UNTIL SATURDAY TO THINK IT OVER.
"I'LL COME BACK TO HEAR YOUR DECISION."

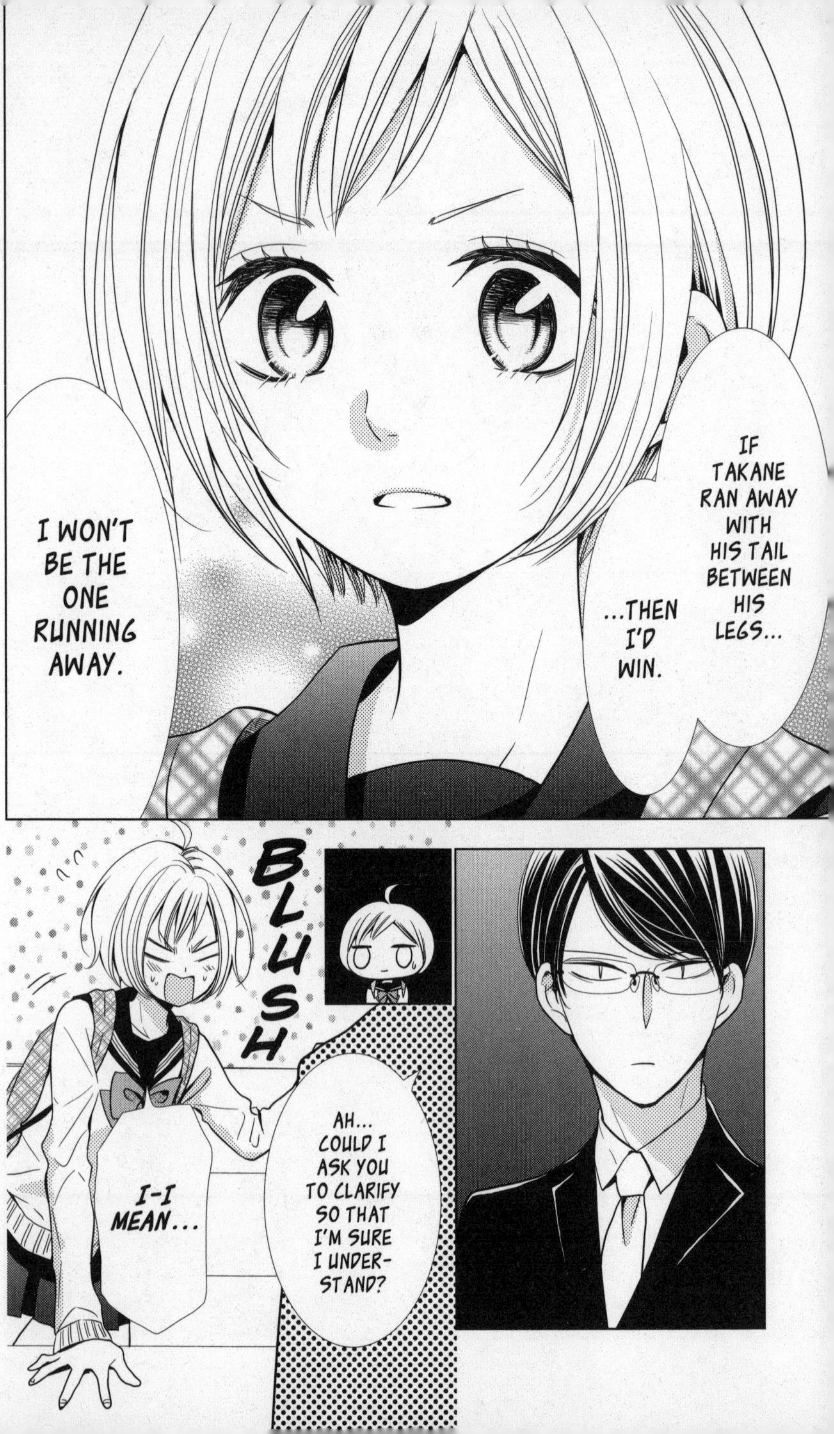
IF TAKANE RAN AWAY WITH HIS TAIL BETWEEN HIS LEGS...
...THEN I'D WIN.
I WON'T BE THE ONE RUNNING AWAY.
AH... COULD I ASK YOU TO CLARIFY SO THAT I'M SURE I UNDER-STAND?
BLUSH
I-I MEAN...

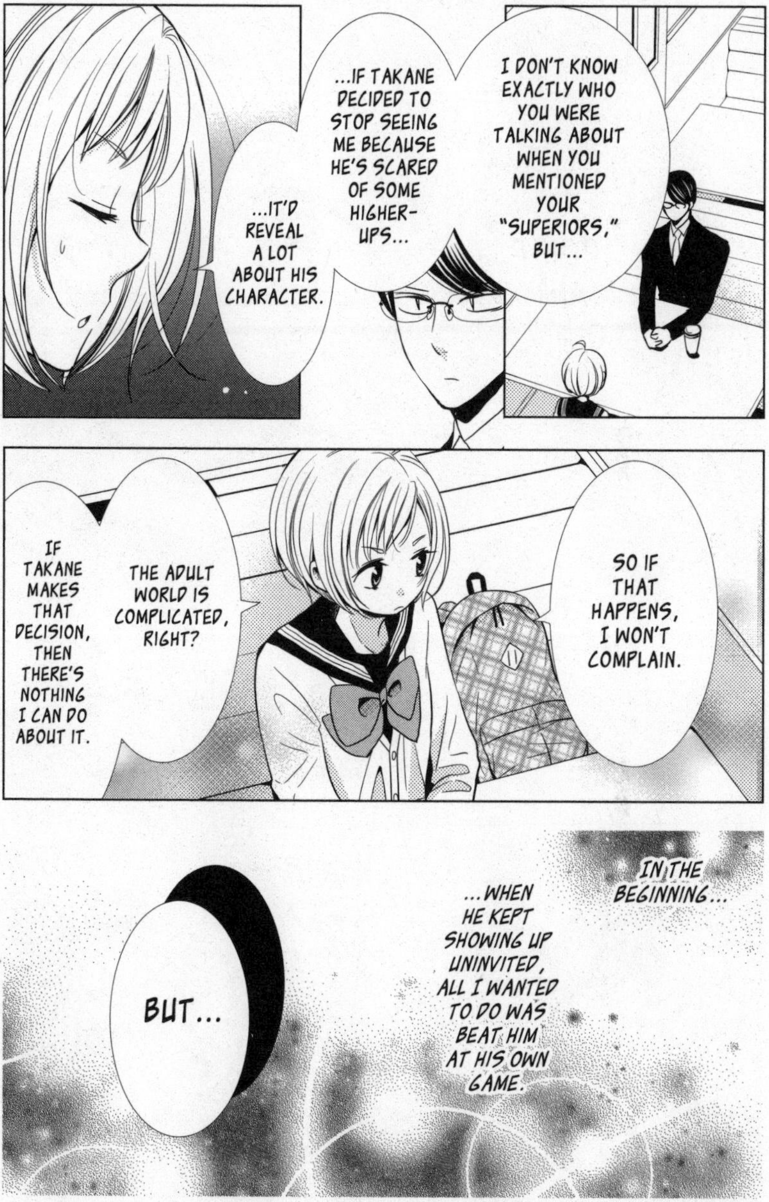
I DON'T KNOW EXACTLY WHO YOU WERE TALKING ABOUT WHEN YOU MENTIONED YOUR "SUPERIORS," BUT...
...IF TAKANE DECIDED TO STOP SEEING ME BECAUSE HE'S SCARED OF SOME HIGHER-UPS...
...IT'D REVEAL A LOT ABOUT HIS CHARACTER.
SO IF THAT HAPPENS, I WON'T COMPLAIN.
THE ADULT WORLD IS COMPLICATED, RIGHT?
IF TAKANE MAKES THAT DECISION, THEN THERE'S NOTHING I CAN DO ABOUT IT.
IN THE BEGINNING...
...WHEN HE KEPT SHOWING UP UNINVITED, ALL I WANTED TO DO WAS BEAT HIM AT HIS OWN GAME.
BUT...

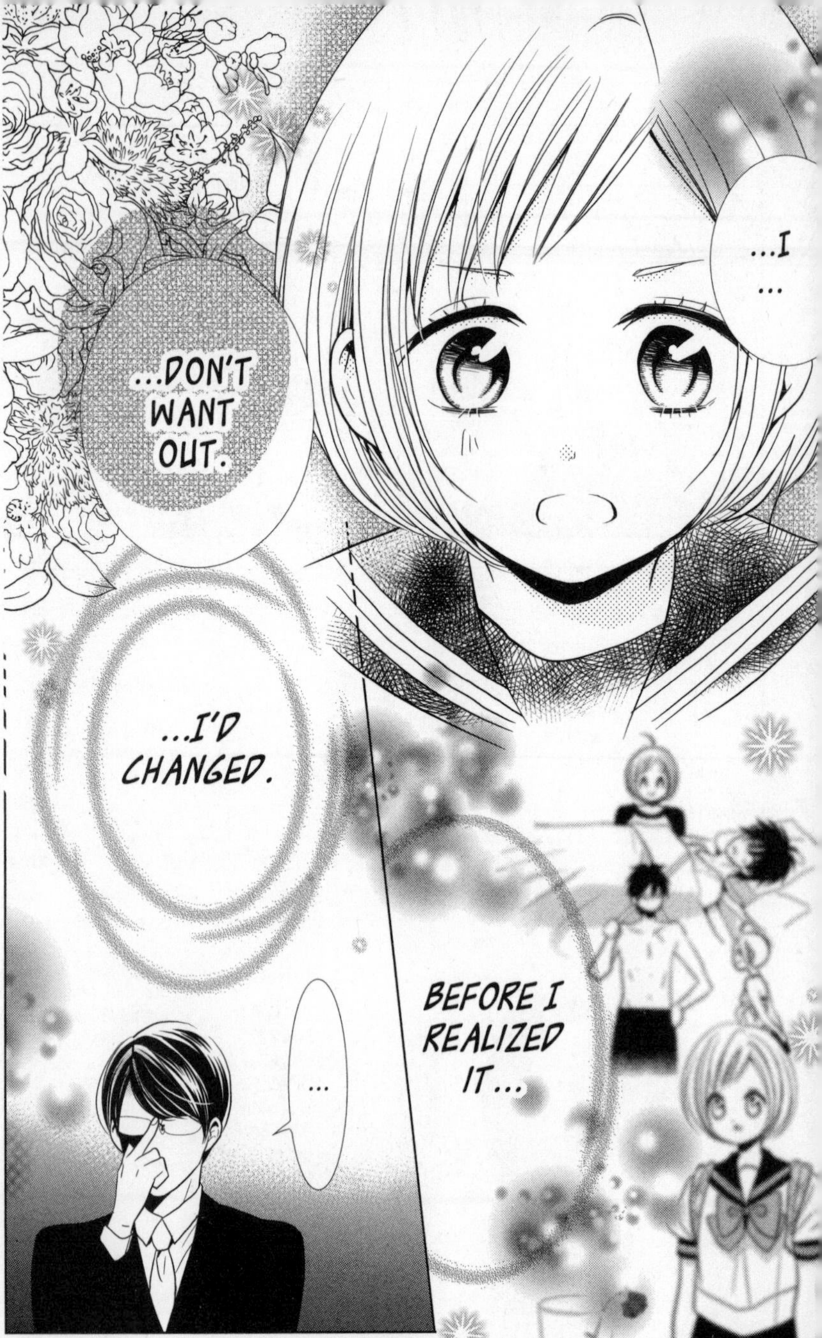
...I
...
...DON'T WANT OUT.
BEFORE I REALIZED IT...
...I'D CHANGED.
...

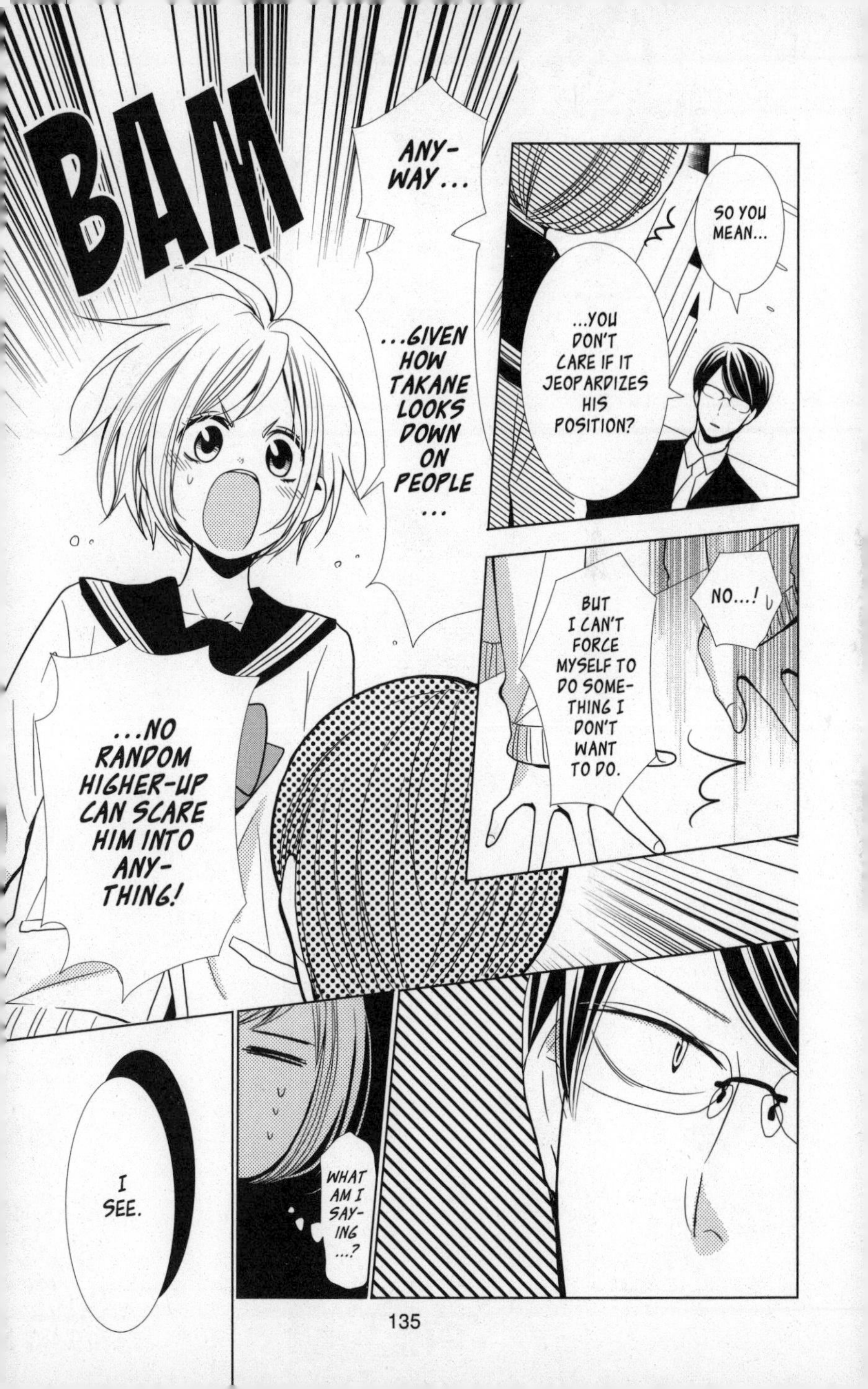
SO YOU MEAN...
...YOU DON'T CARE IF IT JEOPARDIZES HIS POSITION?
NO...!
BUT I CAN'T FORCE MYSELF TO DO SOMETHING I DON'T WANT TO DO.
BAM
ANYWAY...
...GIVEN HOW TAKANE LOOKS DOWN ON PEOPLE...
...NO RANDOM HIGHER-UP CAN SCARE HIM INTO ANYTHING!
WHAT AM I SAYING...?
I SEE.

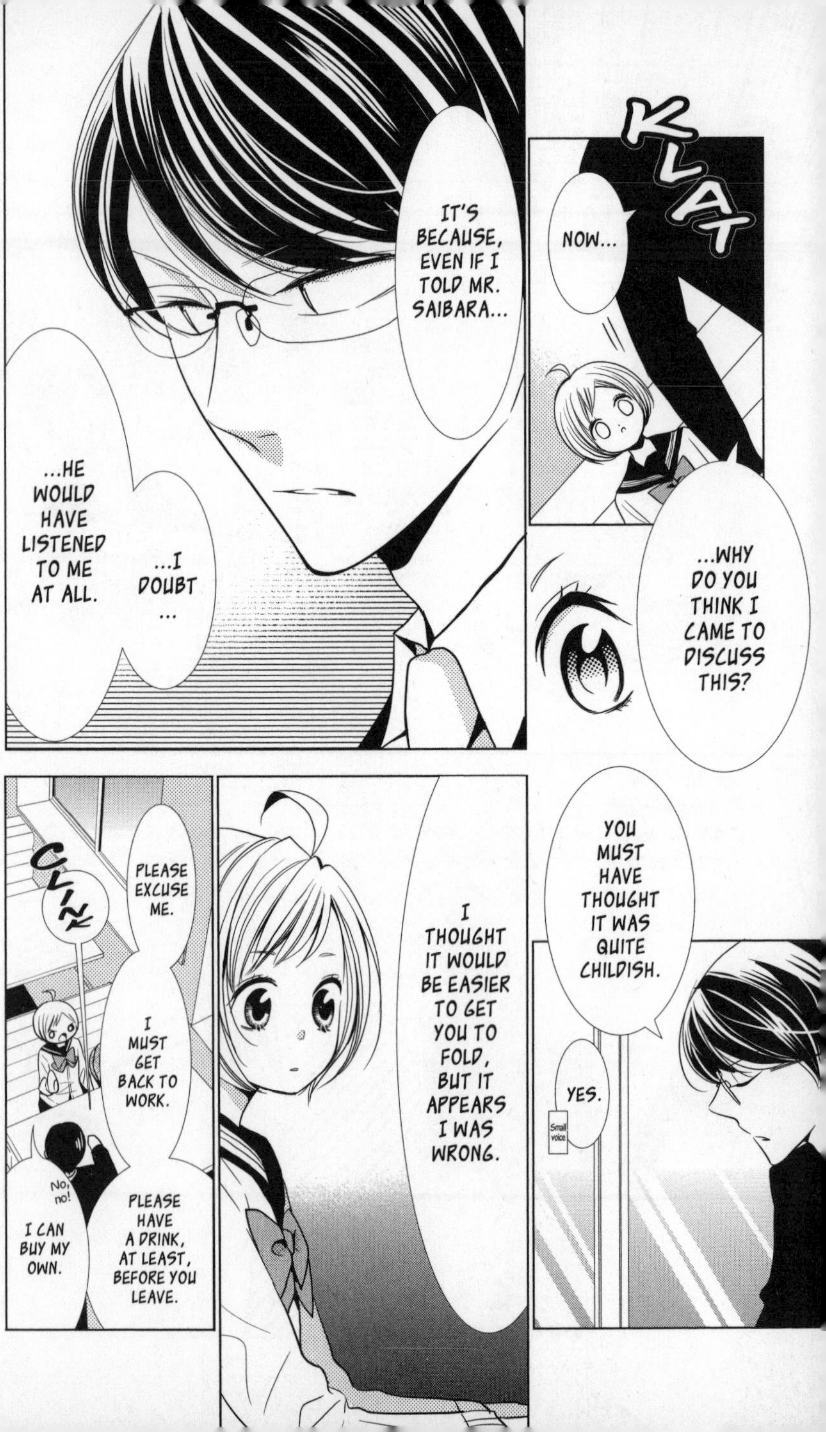
KLAK
NOW...
...WHY DO YOU THINK I CAME TO DISCUSS THIS?
IT'S BECAUSE, EVEN IF I TOLD MR. SAIBARA...
...I DOUBT ...
...HE WOULD HAVE LISTENED TO ME AT ALL.
YOU MUST HAVE THOUGHT IT WAS QUITE CHILDISH.
YES.
Small voice
I THOUGHT IT WOULD BE EASIER TO GET YOU TO FOLD, BUT IT APPEARS I WAS WRONG.
PLEASE EXCUSE ME.
CLINK
I MUST GET BACK TO WORK.
PLEASE HAVE A DRINK, AT LEAST, BEFORE YOU LEAVE.
No, no!
I CAN BUY MY OWN.

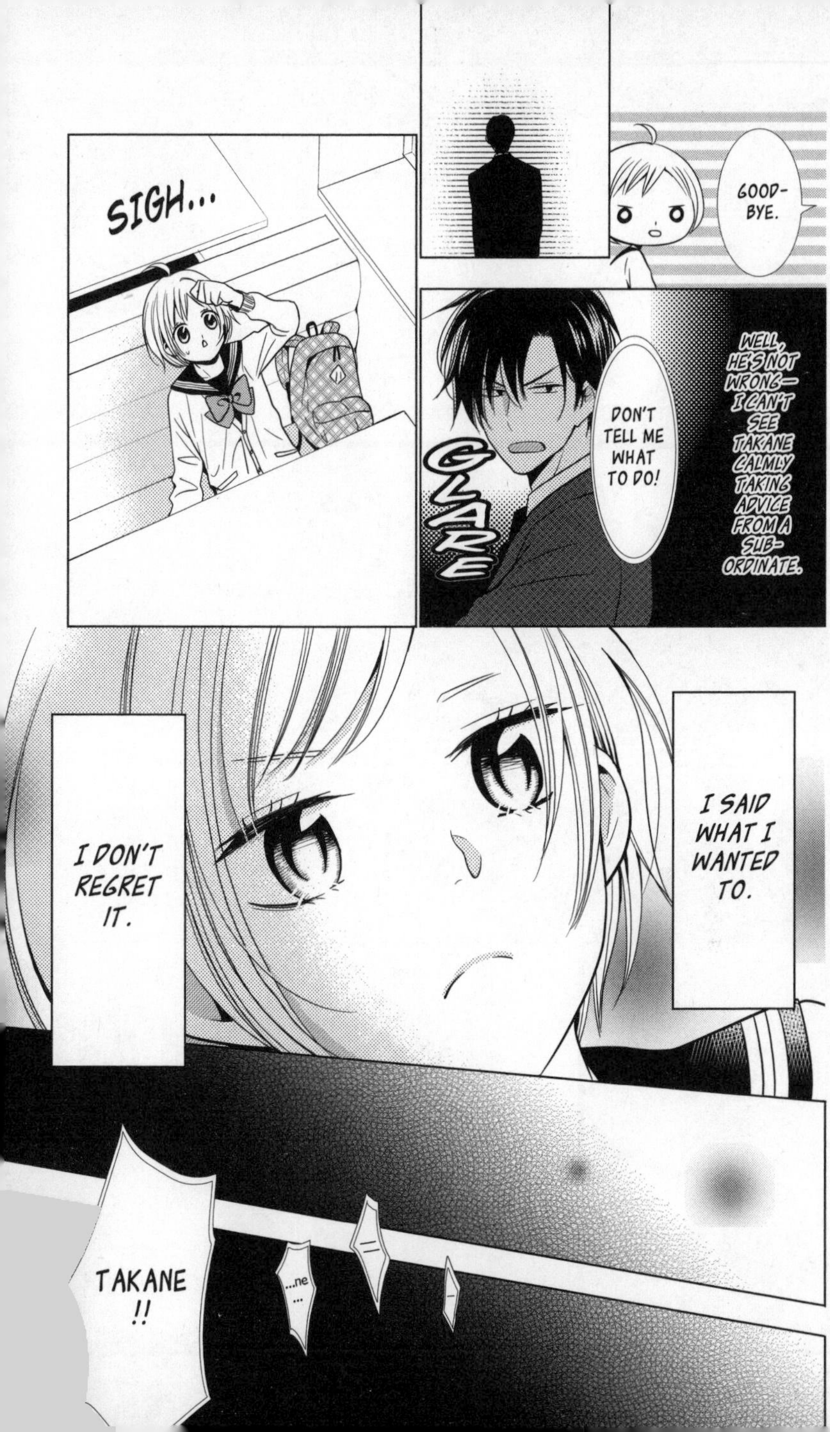
GOOD-BYE.
WELL, HE'S NOT WRONG—I CAN'T SEE TAKANE CALMLY TAKING ADVICE FROM A SUBORDINATE.
DON'T TELL ME WHAT TO DO!
GLARE
SIGH...
I SAID WHAT I WANTED TO.
I DON'T REGRET IT.
—
—
...ne...
TAKANE!!

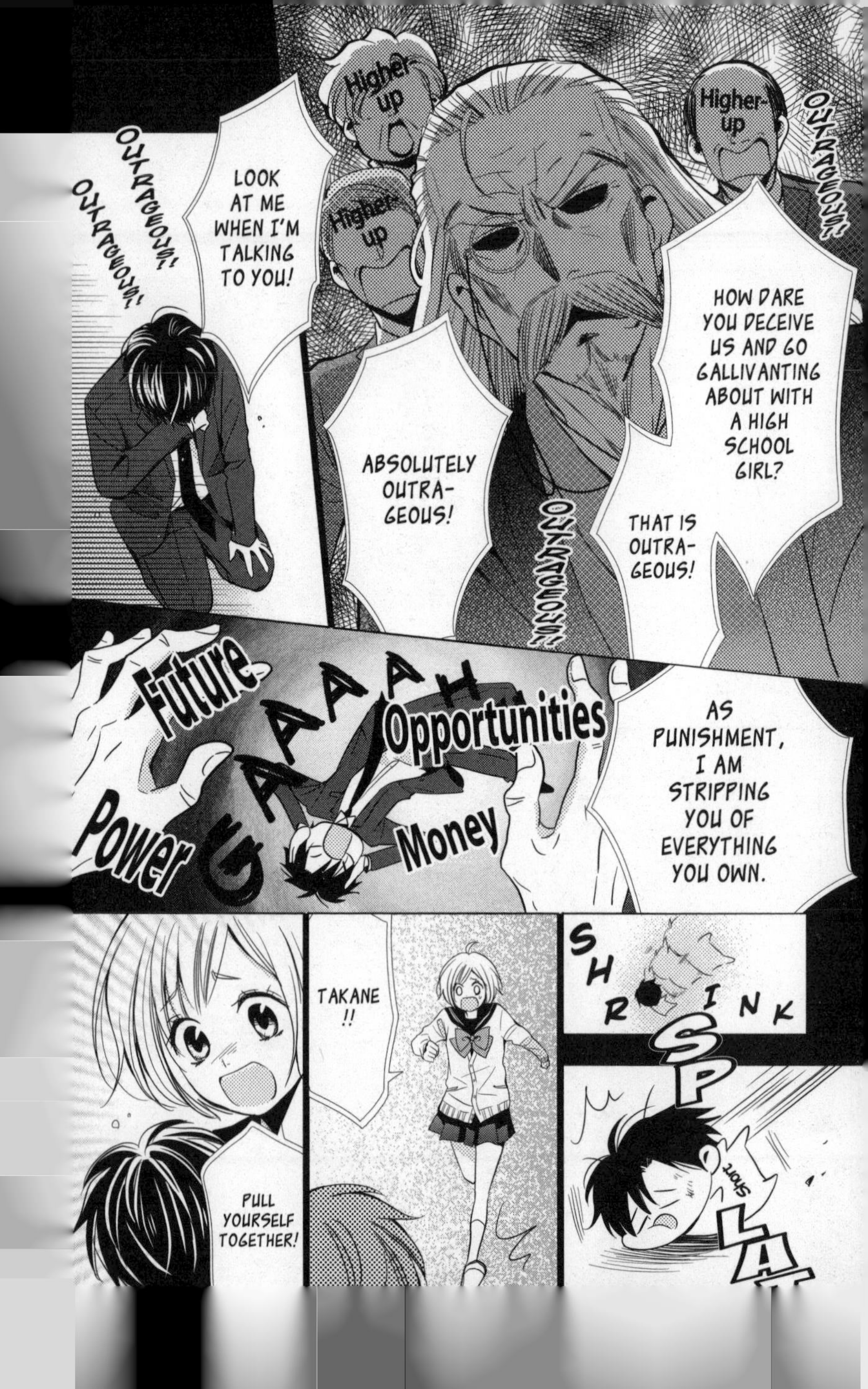
Higher-up
Higher-up
Higher-up
OUTRAGEOUS!
HOW DARE YOU DECEIVE US AND GO GALLIVANTING ABOUT WITH A HIGH SCHOOL GIRL?
THAT IS OUTRAGEOUS!
OUTRAGEOUS!
ABSOLUTELY OUTRAGEOUS!
LOOK AT ME WHEN I'M TALKING TO YOU!
OUTRAGEOUS!
OUTRAGEOUS!
AS PUNISHMENT, I AM STRIPPING YOU OF EVERYTHING YOU OWN.
AAAAH
Opportunities
Future
Money
Power
SHRINK
Short
TAKANE !!
PULL YOURSELF TOGETHER!

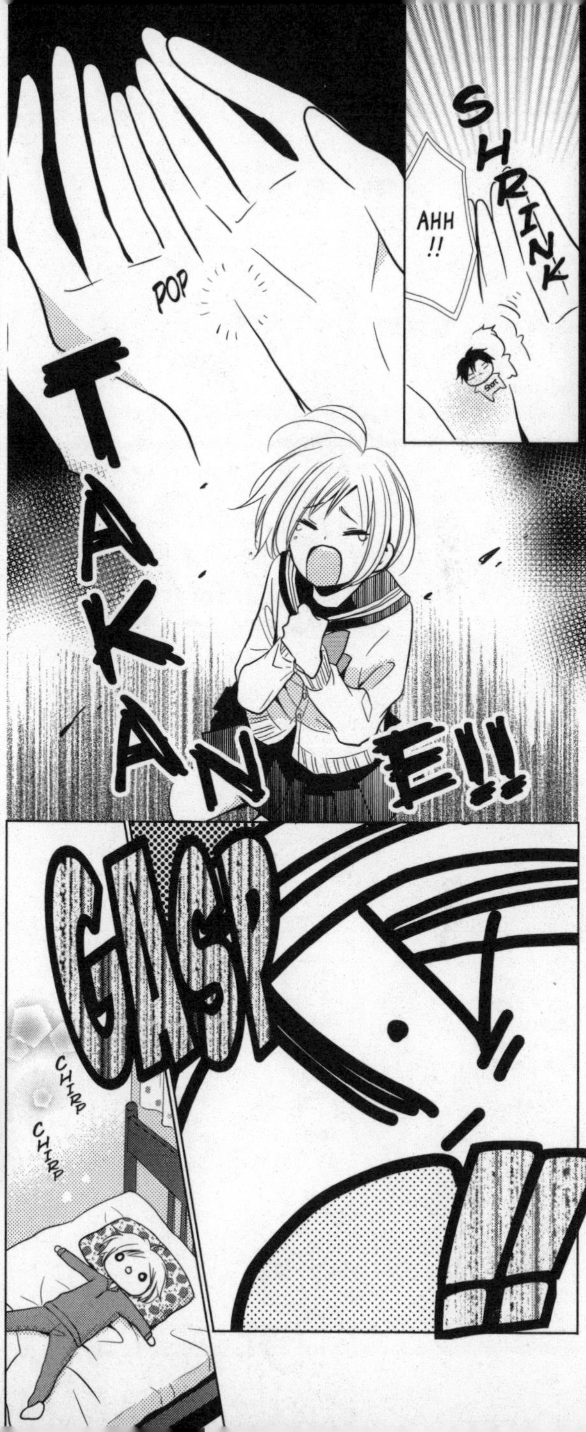
SHRINK
AHH!!
POP
TAKANE!!
GASP
CHIRP
CHIRP
!!

•Eiji Kirigasaki•

He's named Kirigasaki because he's neat and smart. I used the character "ei" in his given name, because for some reason names with that kanji character sound intelligent to me.

Since he has black hair and wears a suit, I wanted to make sure he didn't look like Takane, so I made his eyes look different. I've never drawn eyes like these before. He has the easiest haircut I've ever drawn out of all my characters. It almost made me think that if I drew all my characters with their hair parted to one side, I'd be able to finish work much more quickly.

He prefers having coffee at a café over drinks at a bar. He'll do just about anything as long as he sees it as part of his job.

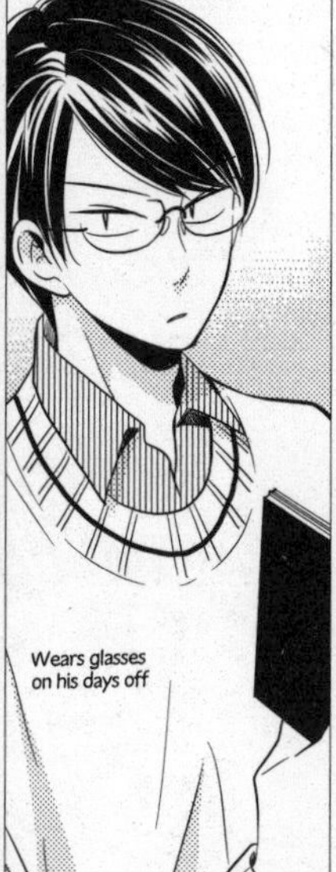
Wears glasses on his days off

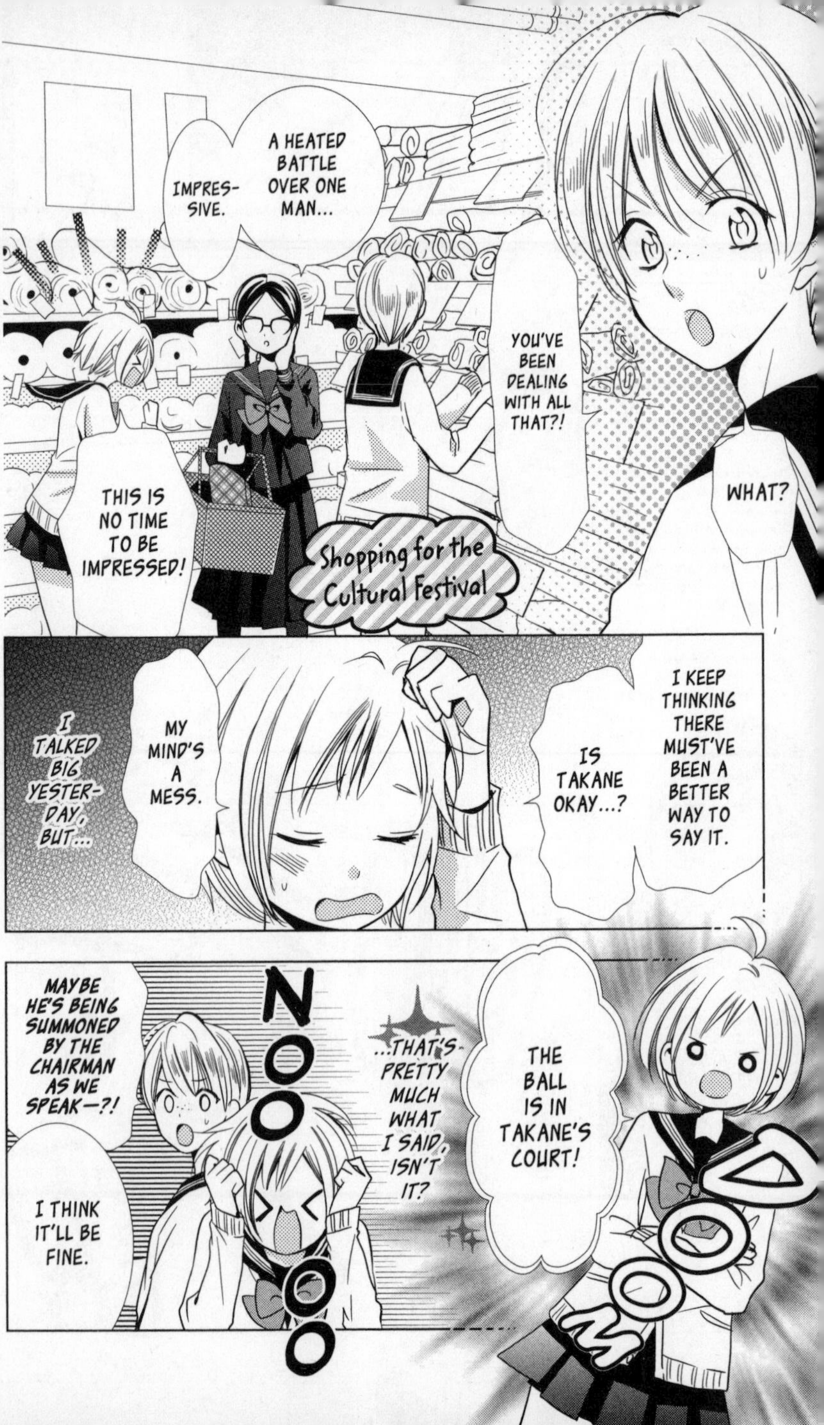
WHAT?
YOU'VE BEEN DEALING WITH ALL THAT?!
A HEATED BATTLE OVER ONE MAN...
IMPRES-SIVE.
THIS IS NO TIME TO BE IMPRESSED!
Shopping for the Cultural Festival
I KEEP THINKING THERE MUST'VE BEEN A BETTER WAY TO SAY IT.
IS TAKANE OKAY...?
MY MIND'S A MESS.
I TALKED BIG YESTER-DAY, BUT...
THE BALL IS IN TAKANE'S COURT!
DOOOM
...THAT'S PRETTY MUCH WHAT I SAID, ISN'T IT?
NOOOOO
MAYBE HE'S BEING SUMMONED BY THE CHAIRMAN AS WE SPEAK—?!
I THINK IT'LL BE FINE.

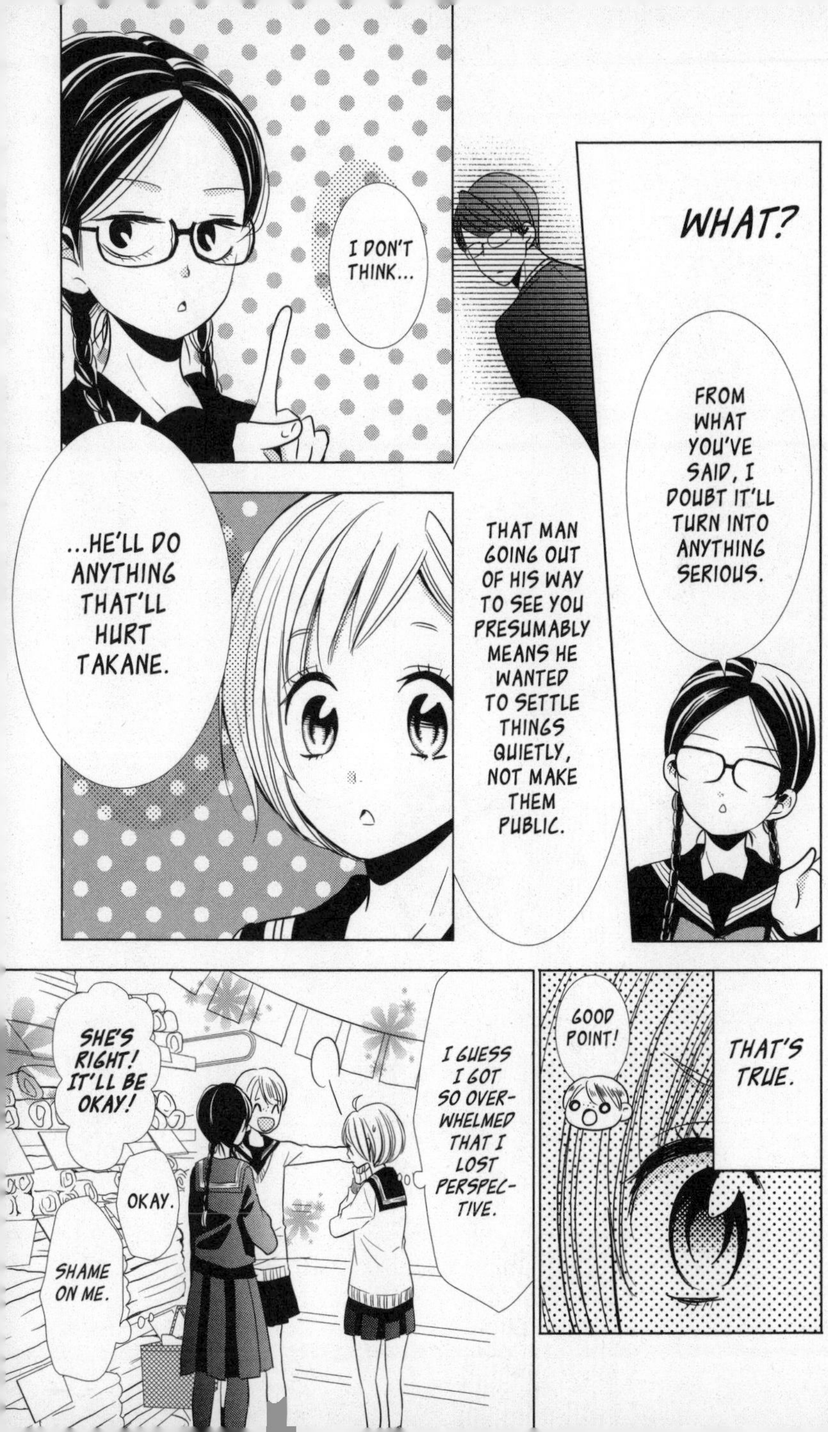
WHAT?
FROM WHAT YOU'VE SAID, I DOUBT IT'LL TURN INTO ANYTHING SERIOUS.
THAT MAN GOING OUT OF HIS WAY TO SEE YOU PRESUMABLY MEANS HE WANTED TO SETTLE THINGS QUIETLY, NOT MAKE THEM PUBLIC.
I DON'T THINK...
...HE'LL DO ANYTHING THAT'LL HURT TAKANE.
THAT'S TRUE.
GOOD POINT!
I GUESS I GOT SO OVER-WHELMED THAT I LOST PERSPEC-TIVE.
SHE'S RIGHT! IT'LL BE OKAY!
OKAY.
SHAME ON ME.

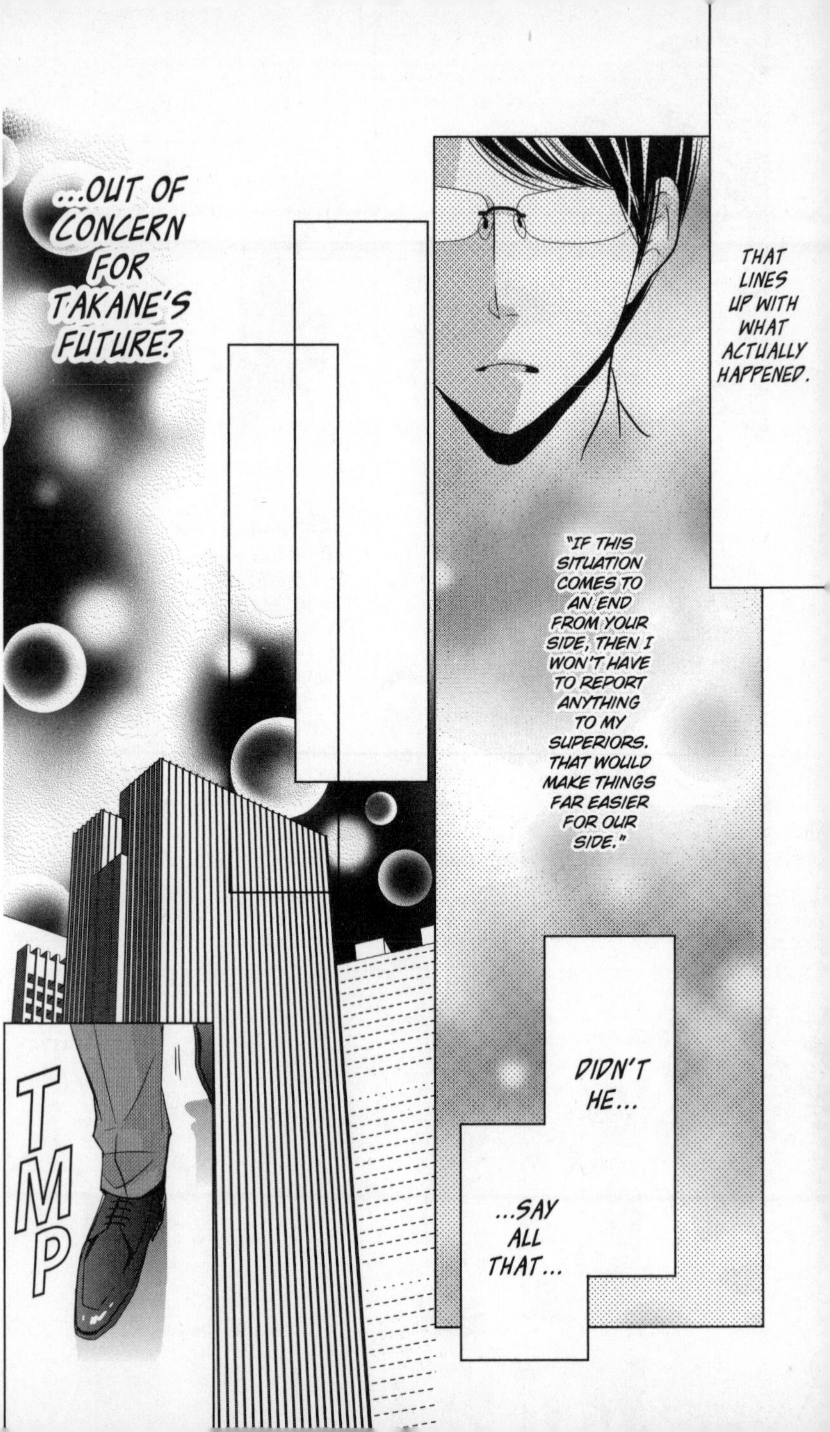
THAT LINES UP WITH WHAT ACTUALLY HAPPENED.
"IF THIS SITUATION COMES TO AN END FROM YOUR SIDE, THEN I WON'T HAVE TO REPORT ANYTHING TO MY SUPERIORS. THAT WOULD MAKE THINGS FAR EASIER FOR OUR SIDE."
DIDN'T HE...
...SAY ALL THAT...
...OUT OF CONCERN FOR TAKANE'S FUTURE?
TMP

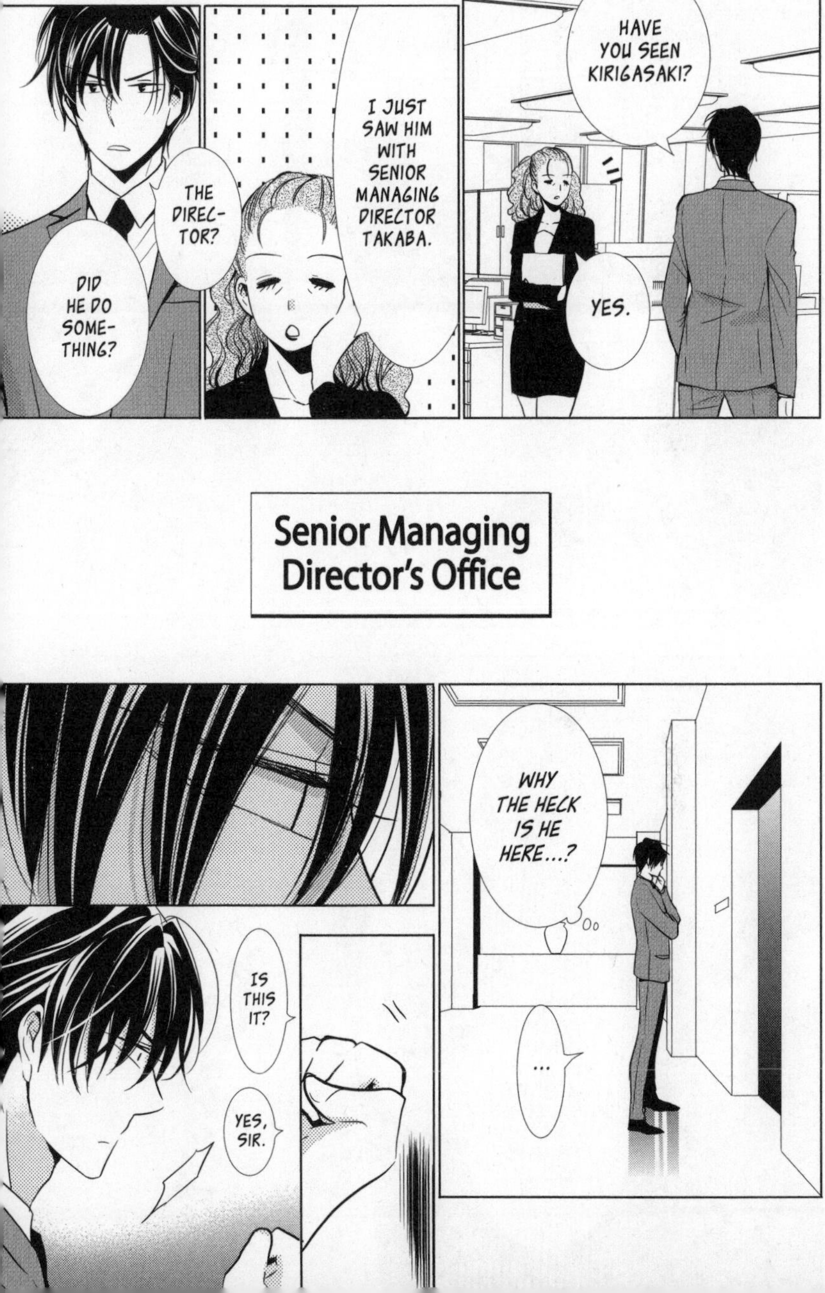
HAVE YOU SEEN KIRIGASAKI?
YES.
I JUST SAW HIM WITH SENIOR MANAGING DIRECTOR TAKABA.
THE DIREC-TOR?
DID HE DO SOME-THING?
Senior Managing Director's Office
WHY THE HECK IS HE HERE...?
...
IS THIS IT?
YES, SIR.

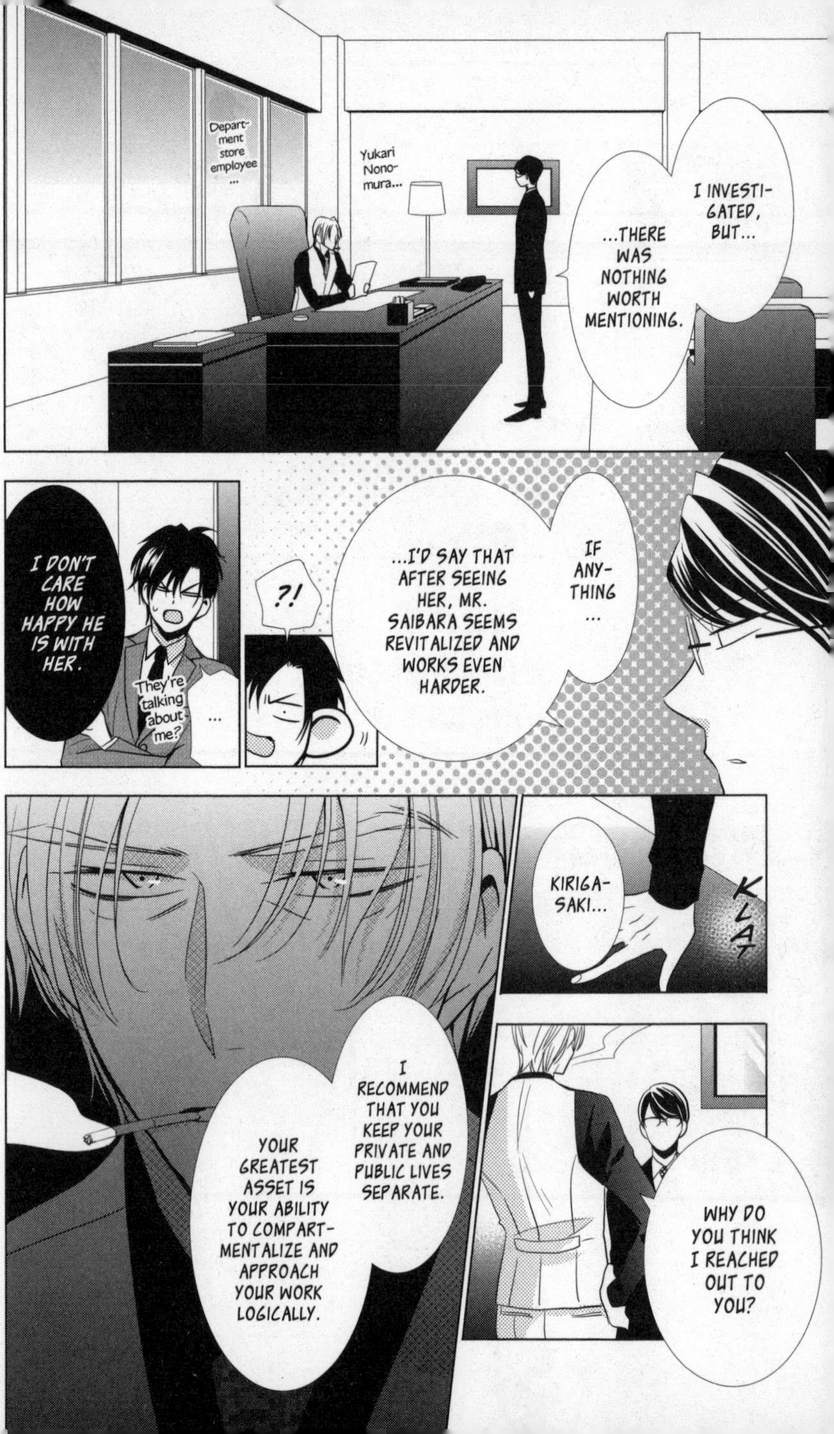
I INVESTIGATED, BUT...
...THERE WAS NOTHING WORTH MENTIONING.
Yukari Nonomura...
Department store employee...
IF ANYTHING...
...I'D SAY THAT AFTER SEEING HER, MR. SAIBARA SEEMS REVITALIZED AND WORKS EVEN HARDER.
?!
They're talking about me?
...
I DON'T CARE HOW HAPPY HE IS WITH HER.
KLAT
KIRIGASAKI...
WHY DO YOU THINK I REACHED OUT TO YOU?
I RECOMMEND THAT YOU KEEP YOUR PRIVATE AND PUBLIC LIVES SEPARATE.
YOUR GREATEST ASSET IS YOUR ABILITY TO COMPARTMENTALIZE AND APPROACH YOUR WORK LOGICALLY.

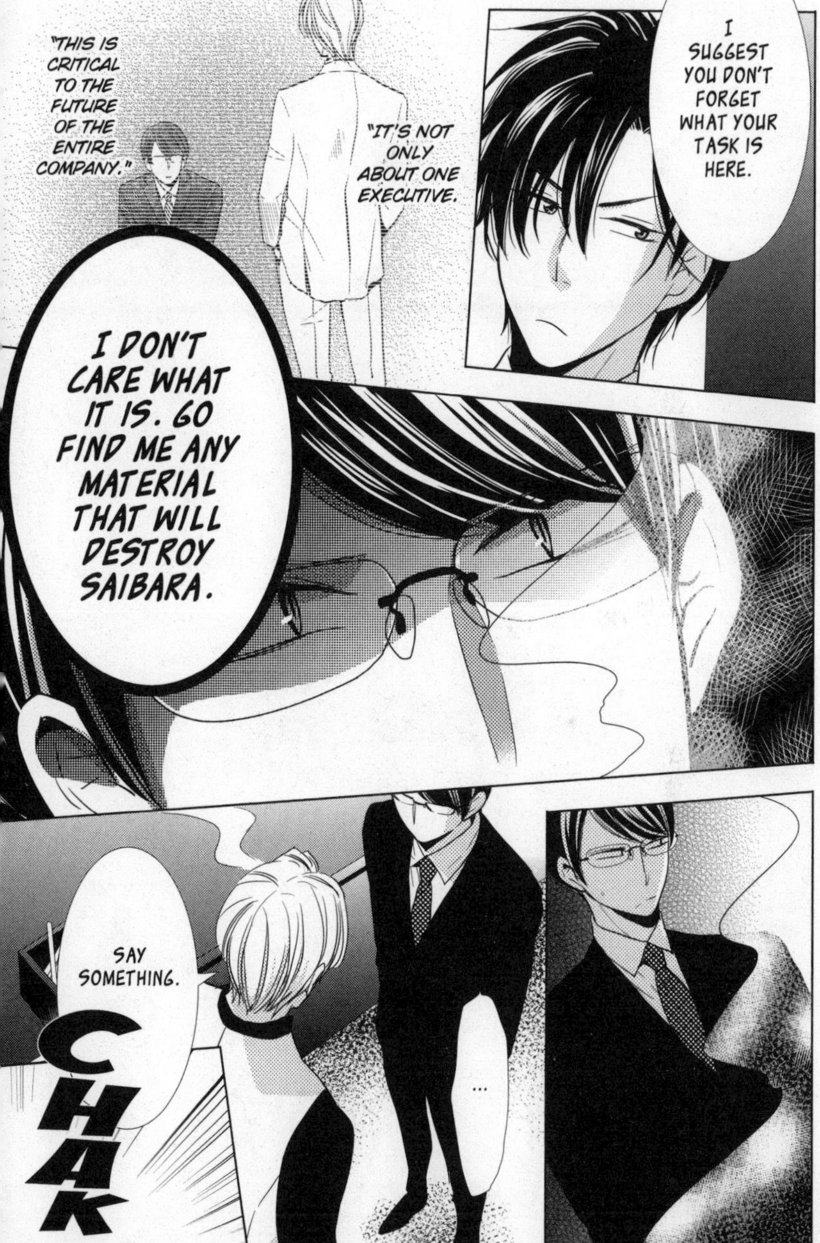
I SUGGEST YOU DON'T FORGET WHAT YOUR TASK IS HERE.
"IT'S NOT ONLY ABOUT ONE EXECUTIVE.
"THIS IS CRITICAL TO THE FUTURE OF THE ENTIRE COMPANY."
I DON'T CARE WHAT IT IS. GO FIND ME ANY MATERIAL THAT WILL DESTROY SAIBARA.
SAY SOMETHING.
CHAK
...

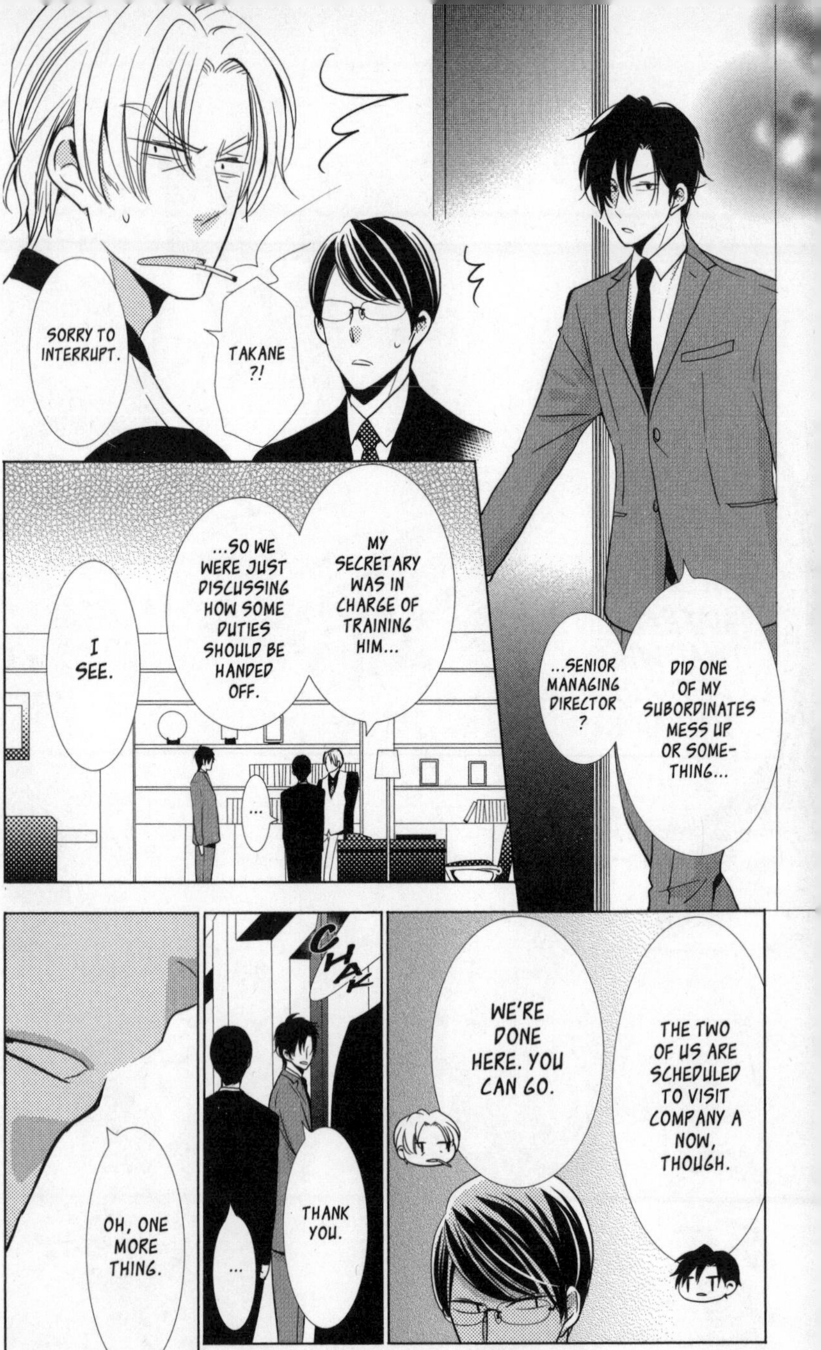
SORRY TO INTERRUPT.
TAKANE?!
...SENIOR MANAGING DIRECTOR?
DID ONE OF MY SUBORDINATES MESS UP OR SOMETHING...
MY SECRETARY WAS IN CHARGE OF TRAINING HIM...
...SO WE WERE JUST DISCUSSING HOW SOME DUTIES SHOULD BE HANDED OFF.
I SEE.
...
THE TWO OF US ARE SCHEDULED TO VISIT COMPANY A NOW, THOUGH.
WE'RE DONE HERE. YOU CAN GO.
CHAK
THANK YOU.
...
OH, ONE MORE THING.

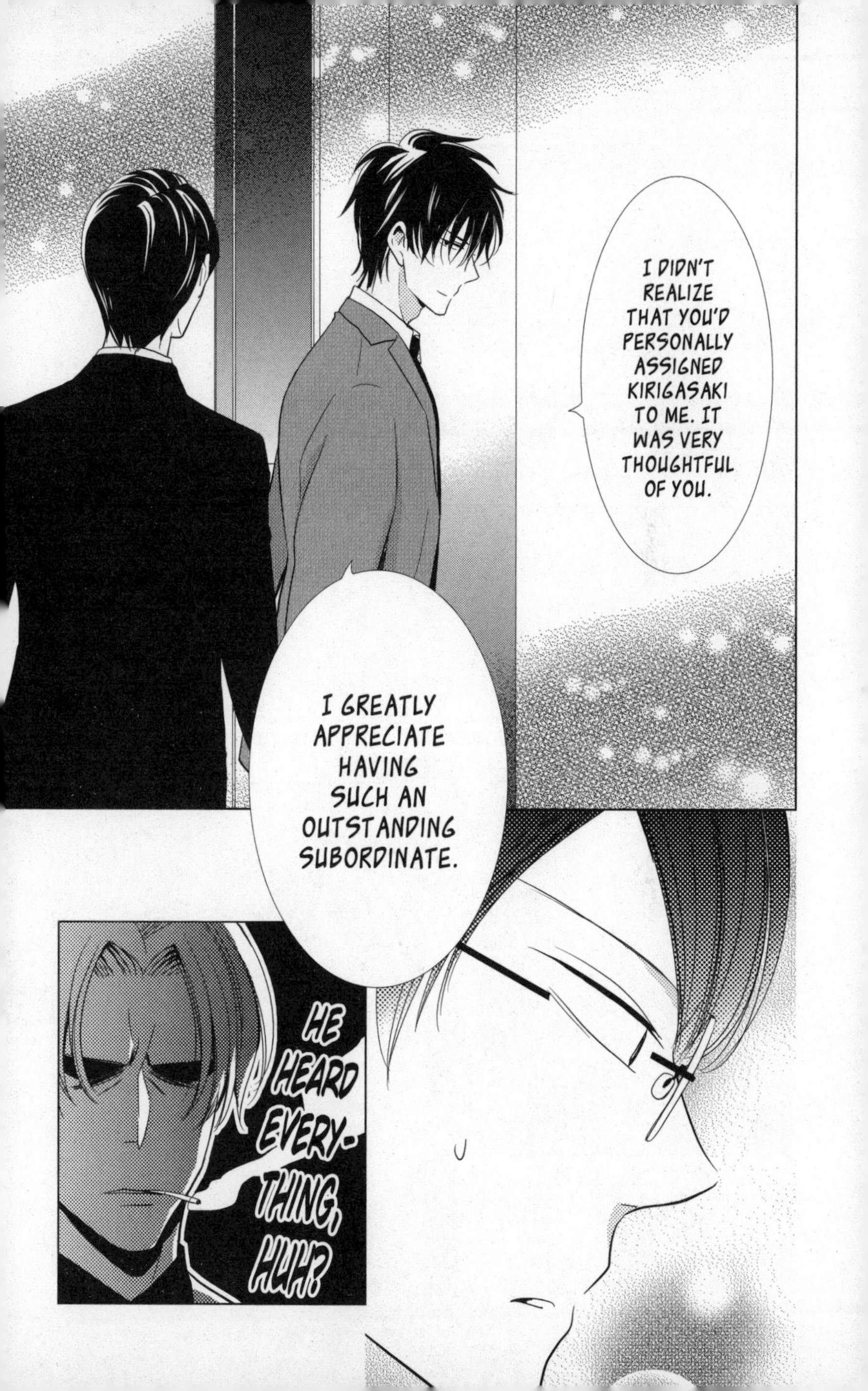
I DIDN'T REALIZE THAT YOU'D PERSONALLY ASSIGNED KIRIGASAKI TO ME. IT WAS VERY THOUGHTFUL OF YOU.
I GREATLY APPRECIATE HAVING SUCH AN OUTSTANDING SUBORDINATE.
HE HEARD EVERY-THING, HUH?

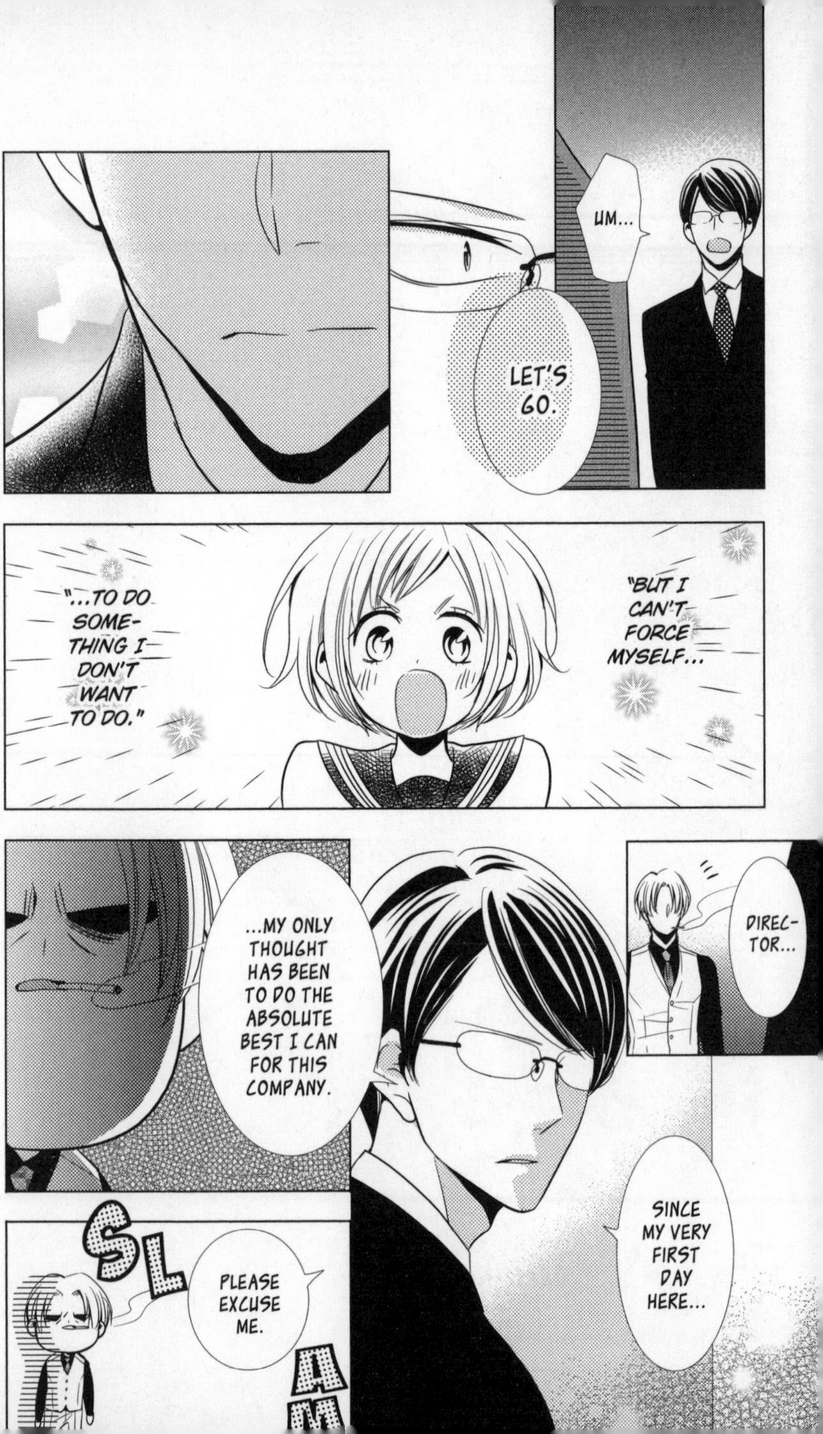
UM...
LET'S GO.
"BUT I CAN'T FORCE MYSELF...
"...TO DO SOMETHING I DON'T WANT TO DO."
DIRECTOR...
SINCE MY VERY FIRST DAY HERE...
...MY ONLY THOUGHT HAS BEEN TO DO THE ABSOLUTE BEST I CAN FOR THIS COMPANY.
PLEASE EXCUSE ME.
SLAM

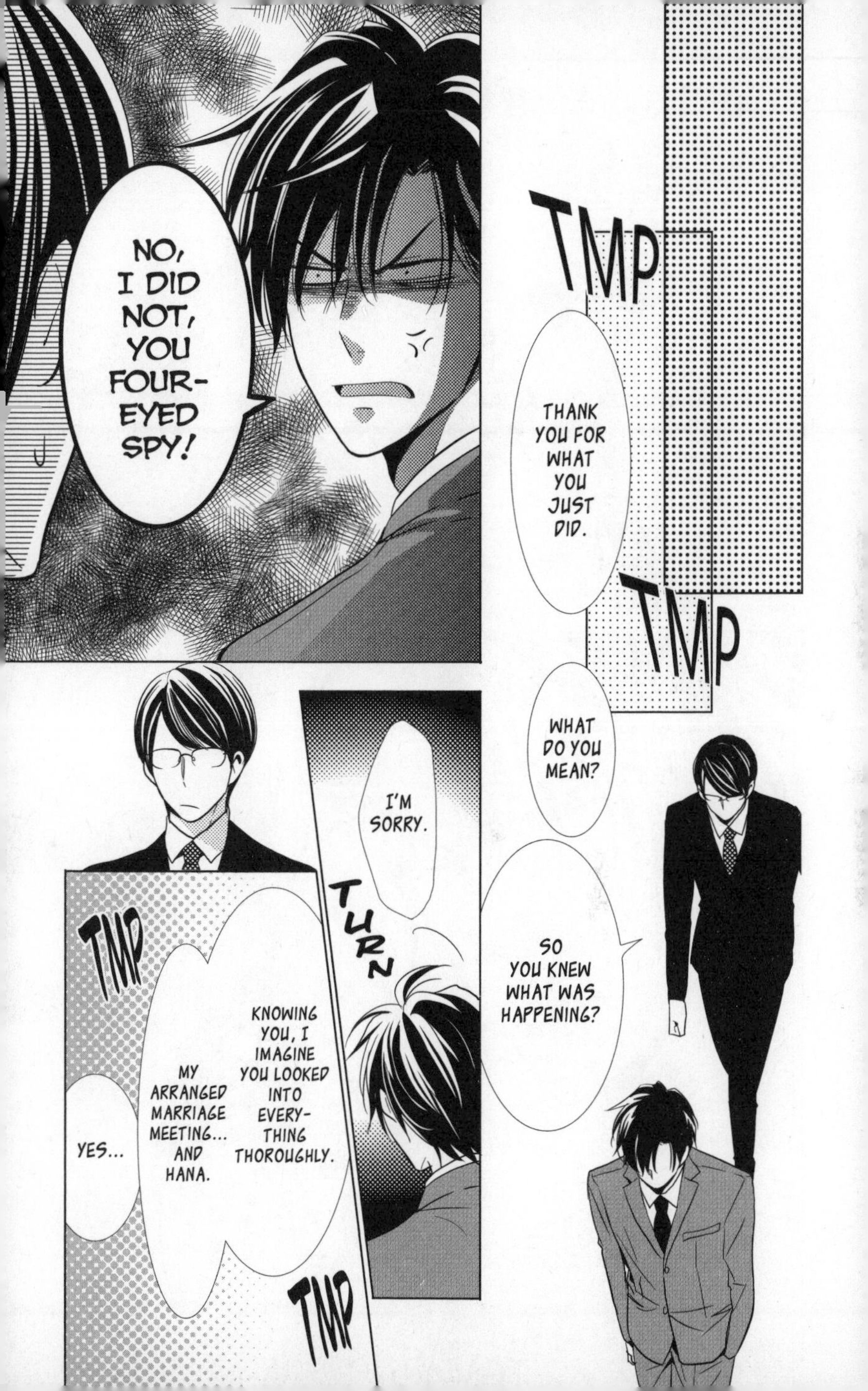
TMP
THANK YOU FOR WHAT YOU JUST DID.
TMP
WHAT DO YOU MEAN?
SO YOU KNEW WHAT WAS HAPPENING?
NO, I DID NOT, YOU FOUR-EYED SPY!
I'M SORRY.
TURN
KNOWING YOU, I IMAGINE YOU LOOKED INTO EVERY-THING THOROUGHLY.
MY ARRANGED MARRIAGE MEETING... AND HANA.
YES...
TMP
TMP

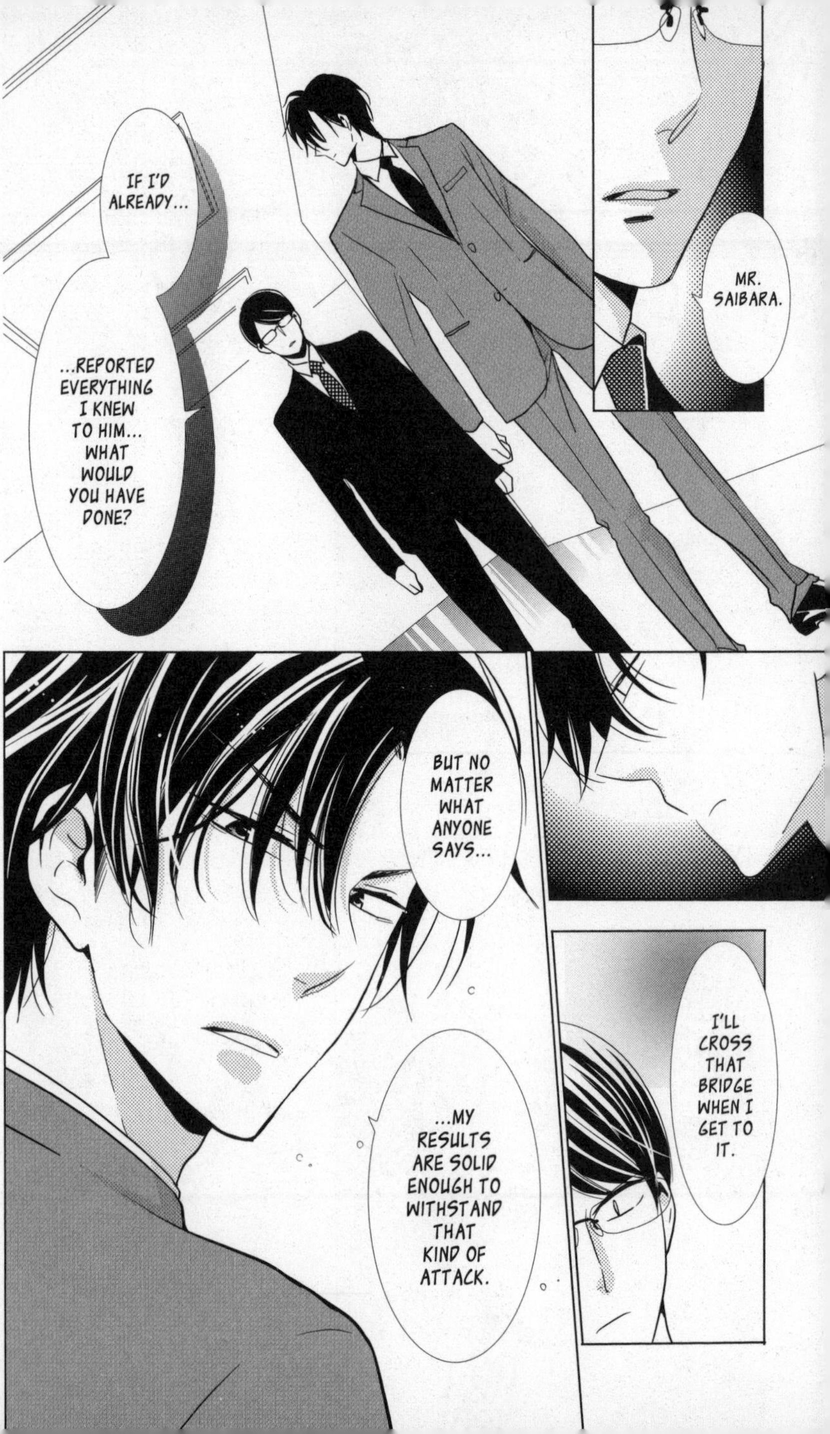
MR. SAIBARA.
IF I'D ALREADY...
...REPORTED EVERYTHING I KNEW TO HIM... WHAT WOULD YOU HAVE DONE?
I'LL CROSS THAT BRIDGE WHEN I GET TO IT.
BUT NO MATTER WHAT ANYONE SAYS...
...MY RESULTS ARE SOLID ENOUGH TO WITHSTAND THAT KIND OF ATTACK.

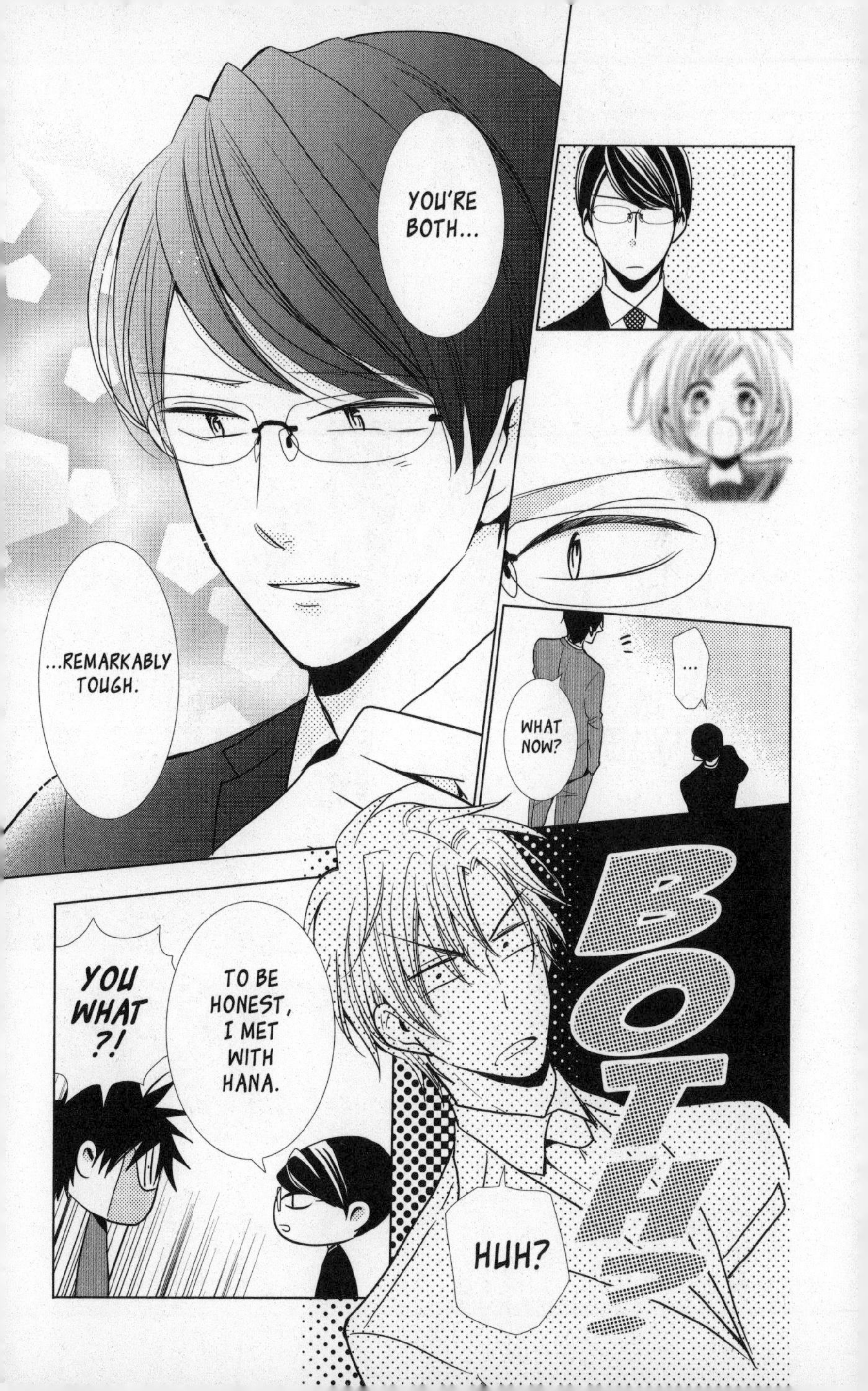
...
WHAT NOW?
YOU'RE BOTH...
...REMARKABLY TOUGH.
BOTH!!
HUH?
TO BE HONEST, I MET WITH HANA.
YOU WHAT?!

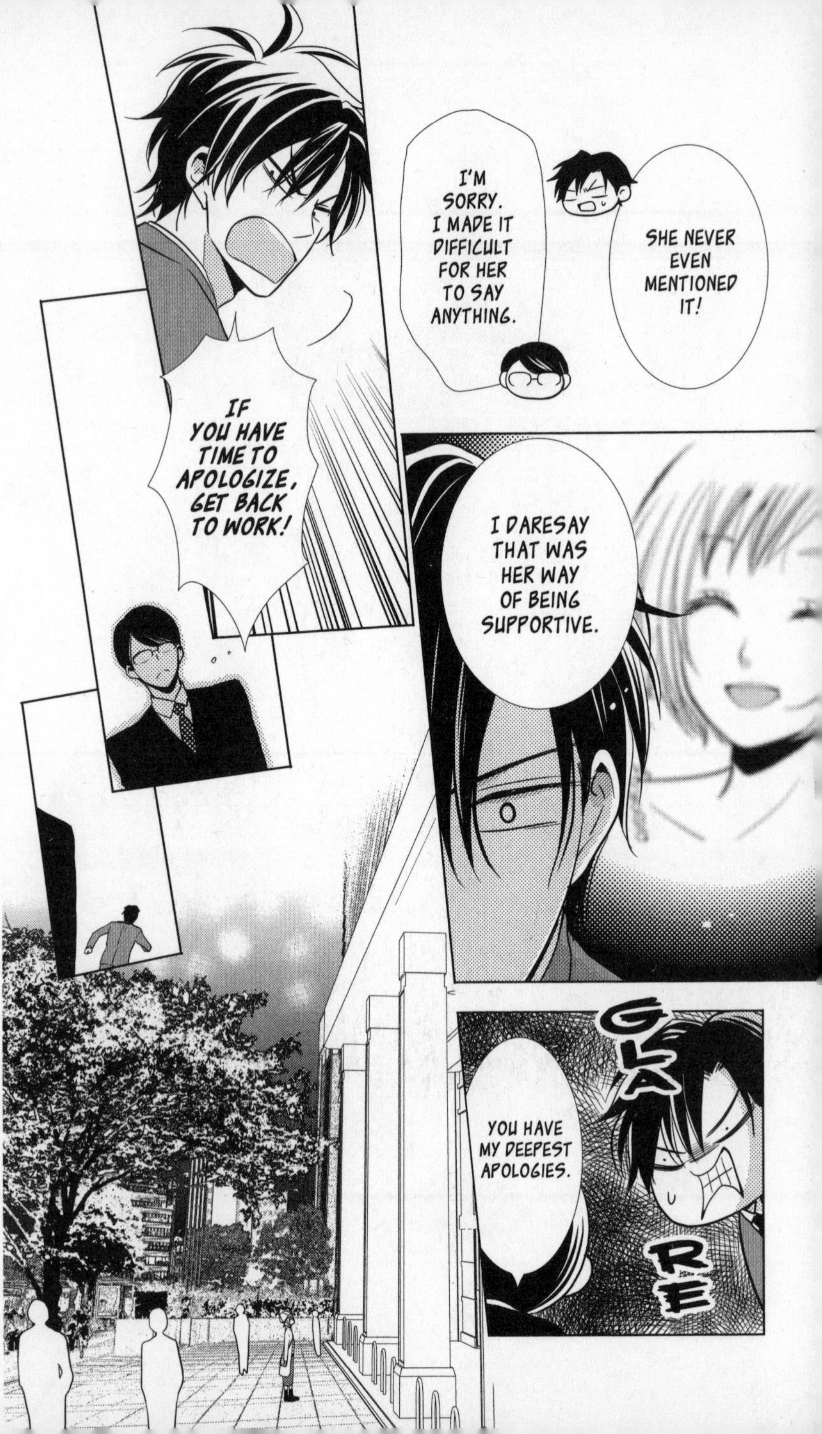
SHE NEVER EVEN MENTIONED IT!
I'M SORRY. I MADE IT DIFFICULT FOR HER TO SAY ANYTHING.
IF YOU HAVE TIME TO APOLOGIZE, GET BACK TO WORK!
I DARESAY THAT WAS HER WAY OF BEING SUPPORTIVE.
YOU HAVE MY DEEPEST APOLOGIES.
GLARE

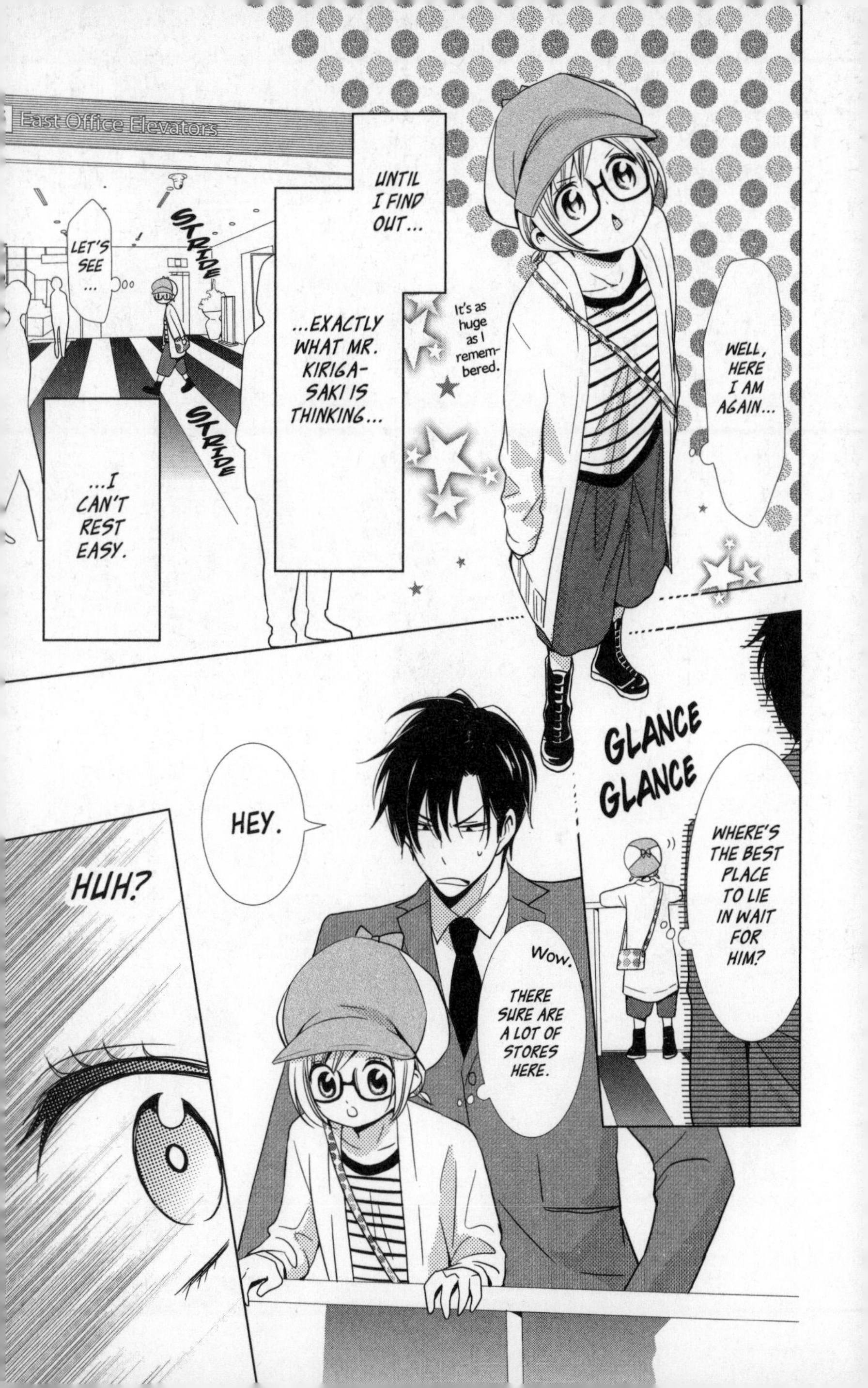
WELL, HERE I AM AGAIN...
It's as huge as I remembered.
UNTIL I FIND OUT...
...EXACTLY WHAT MR. KIRIGA-SAKI IS THINKING...
East Office Elevators
LET'S SEE...
STRIDE
STRIDE
...I CAN'T REST EASY.
GLANCE GLANCE
WHERE'S THE BEST PLACE TO LIE IN WAIT FOR HIM?
Wow.
THERE SURE ARE A LOT OF STORES HERE.
HEY.
HUH?

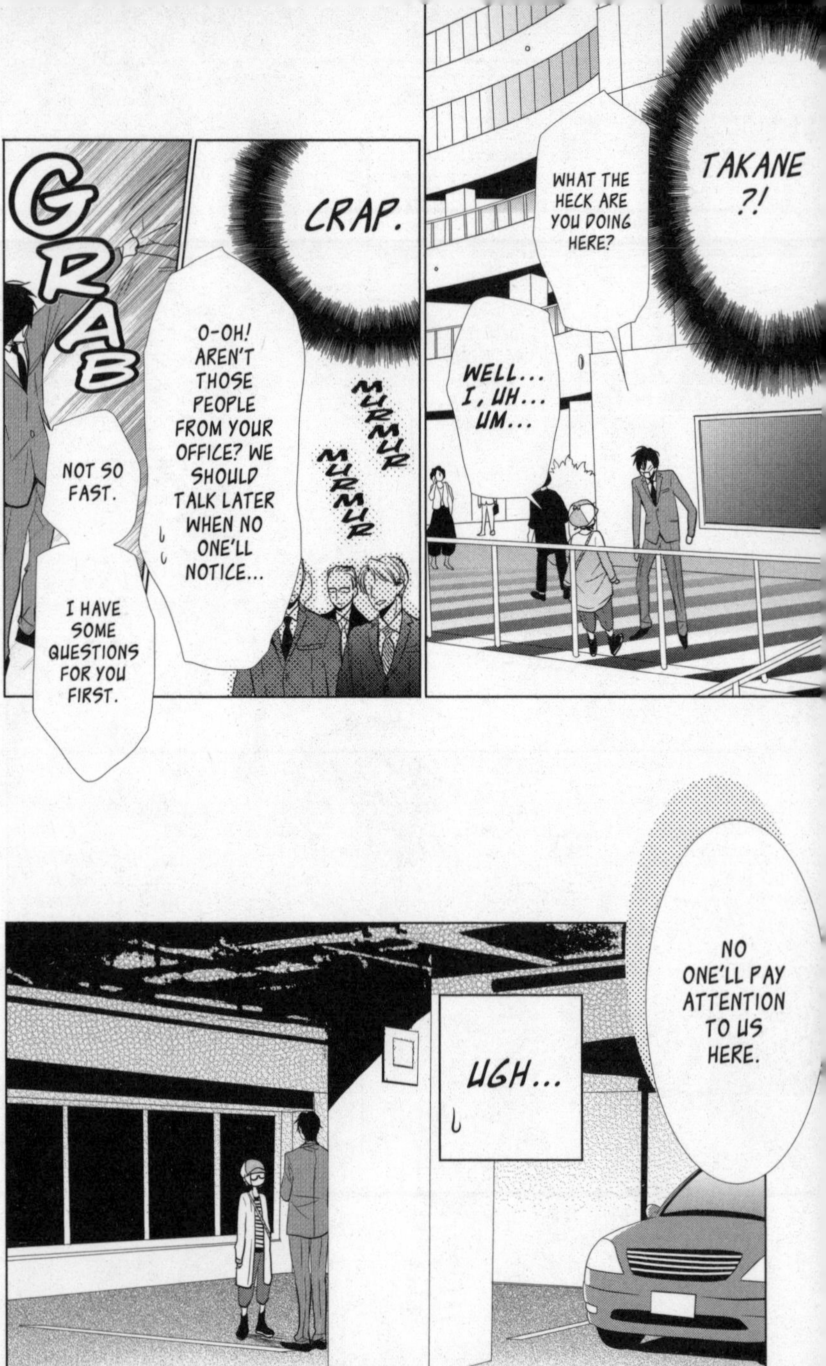
TAKANE ?!
WHAT THE HECK ARE YOU DOING HERE?
WELL... I, UH... UM...
CRAP.
O-OH! AREN'T THOSE PEOPLE FROM YOUR OFFICE? WE SHOULD TALK LATER WHEN NO ONE'LL NOTICE...
MURMUR
MURMUR
GRAB
NOT SO FAST.
I HAVE SOME QUESTIONS FOR YOU FIRST.
NO ONE'LL PAY ATTENTION TO US HERE.
UGH...

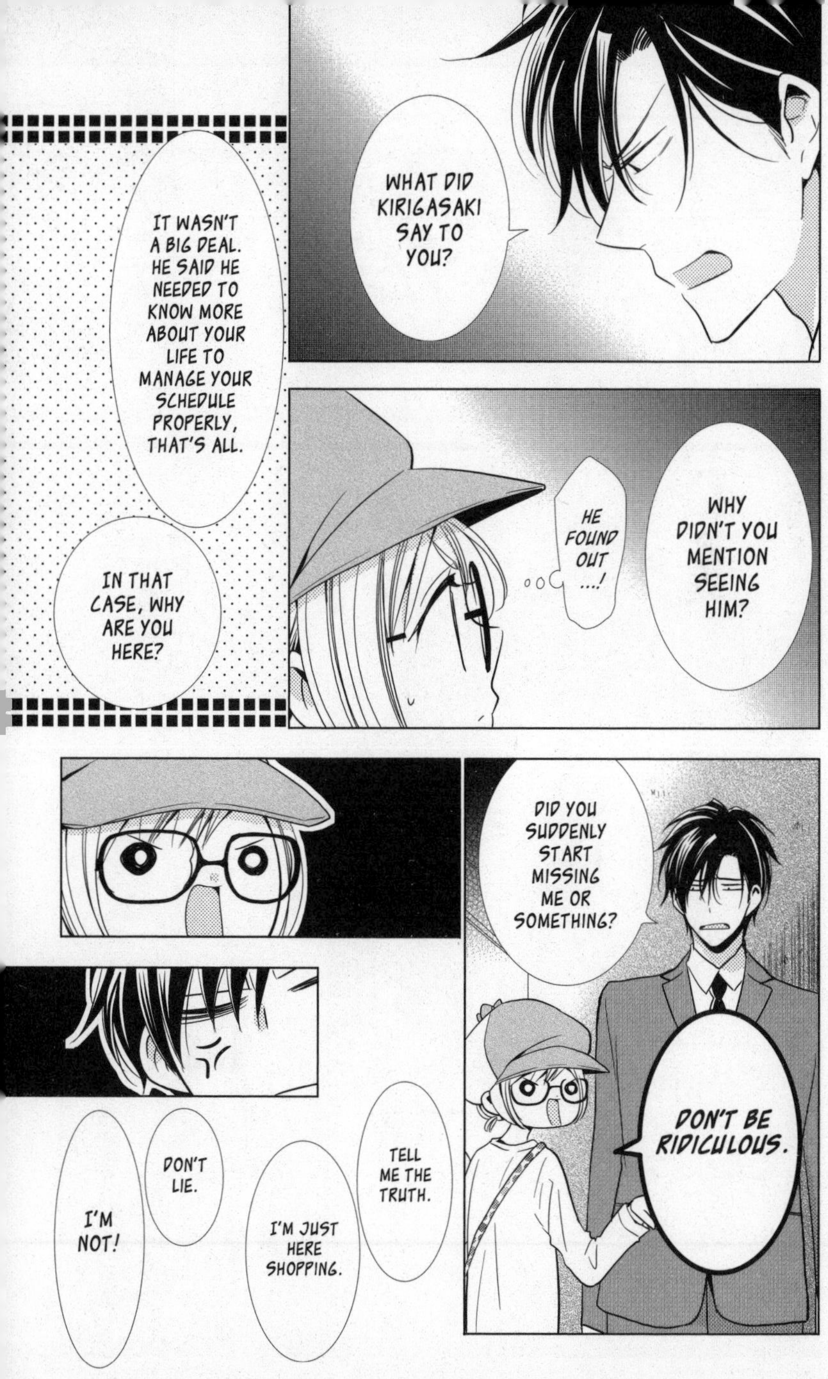
WHAT DID KIRIGASAKI SAY TO YOU?
IT WASN'T A BIG DEAL. HE SAID HE NEEDED TO KNOW MORE ABOUT YOUR LIFE TO MANAGE YOUR SCHEDULE PROPERLY, THAT'S ALL.
WHY DIDN'T YOU MENTION SEEING HIM?
HE FOUND OUT ...!
IN THAT CASE, WHY ARE YOU HERE?
DID YOU SUDDENLY START MISSING ME OR SOMETHING?
DON'T BE RIDICULOUS.
TELL ME THE TRUTH.
I'M JUST HERE SHOPPING.
DON'T LIE.
I'M NOT!

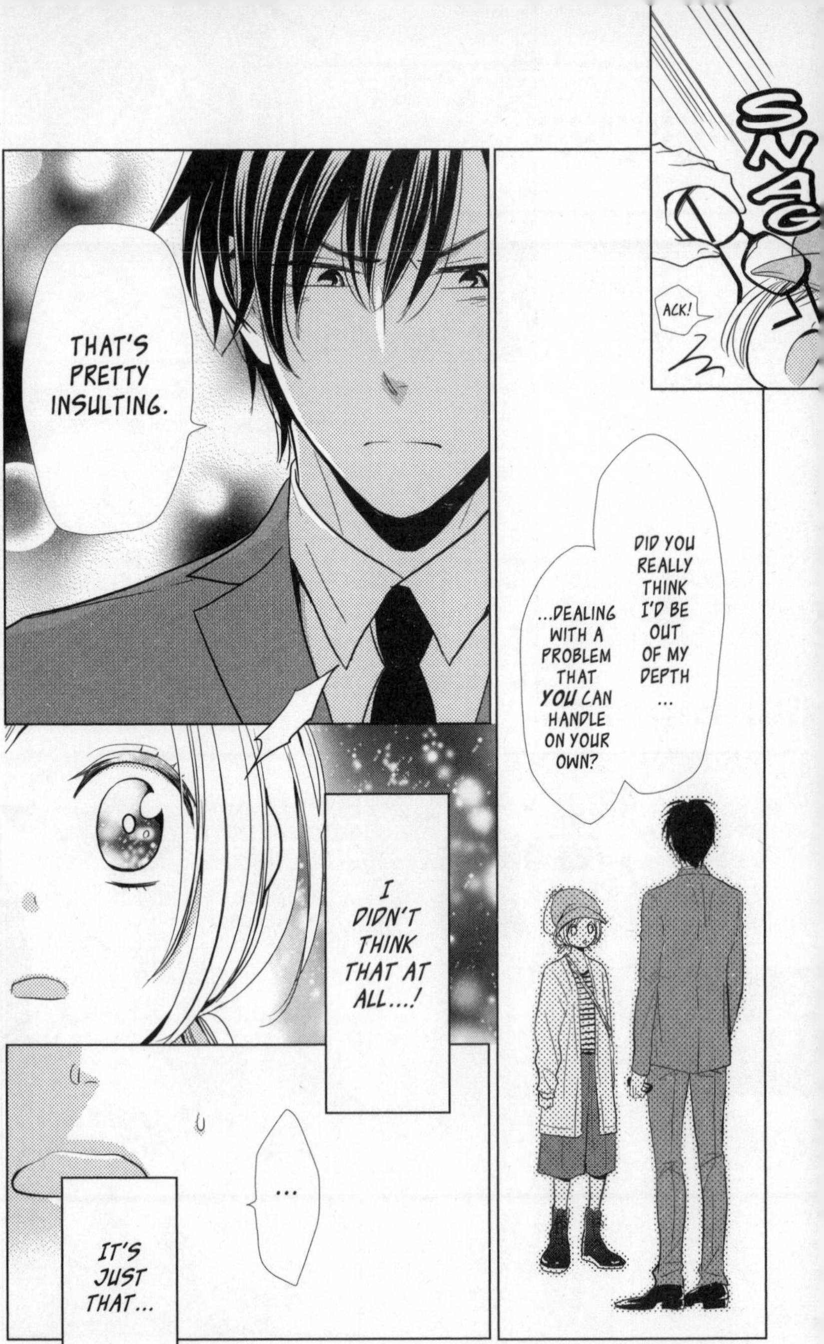
SNAG
ACK!
DID YOU REALLY THINK I'D BE OUT OF MY DEPTH...
...DEALING WITH A PROBLEM THAT YOU CAN HANDLE ON YOUR OWN?
THAT'S PRETTY INSULTING.
I DIDN'T THINK THAT AT ALL...!
...
IT'S JUST THAT...

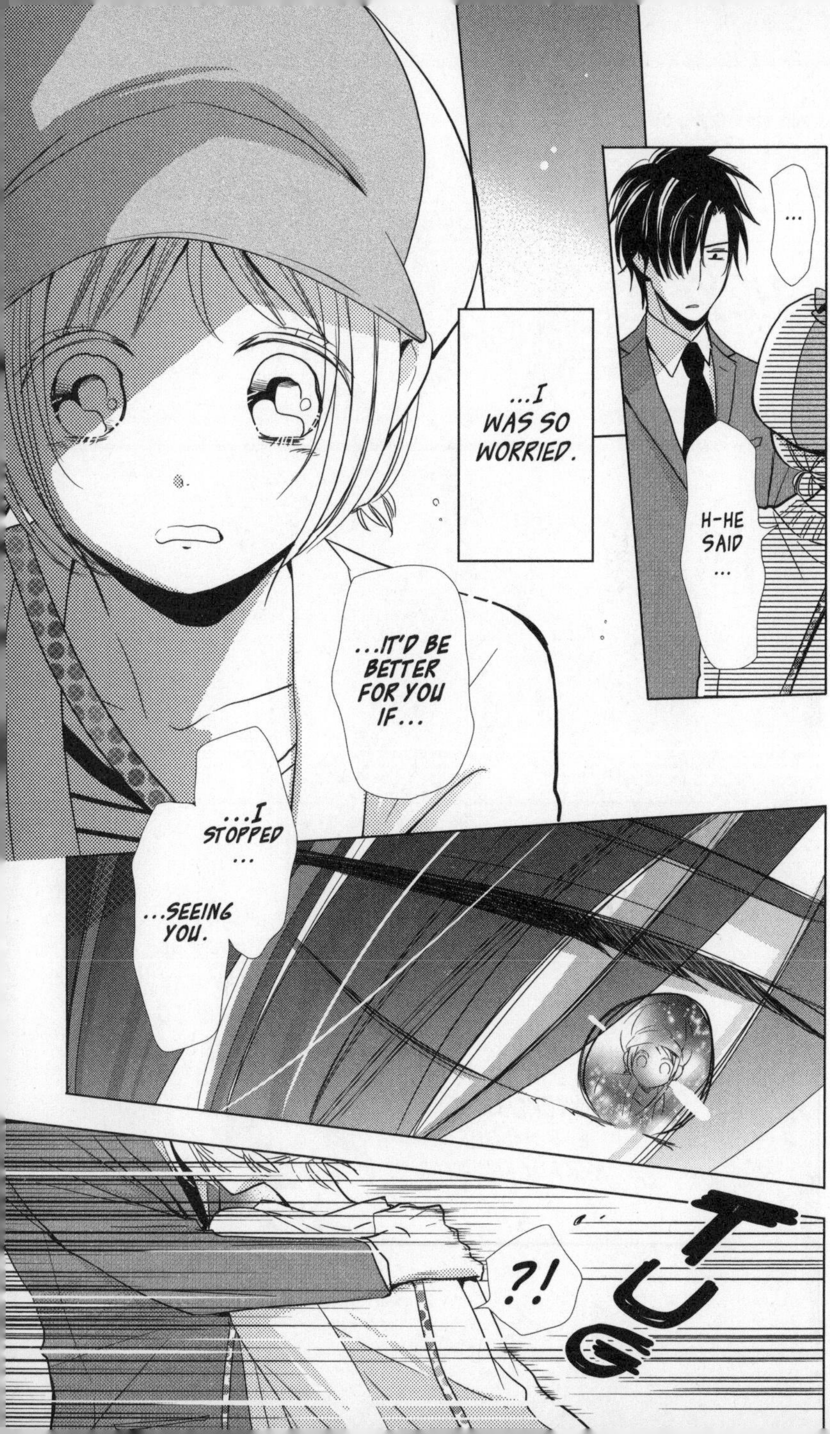
...
H-HE SAID ...
...I WAS SO WORRIED.
...IT'D BE BETTER FOR YOU IF...
...I STOPPED ...
...SEEING YOU.
?!
TUG

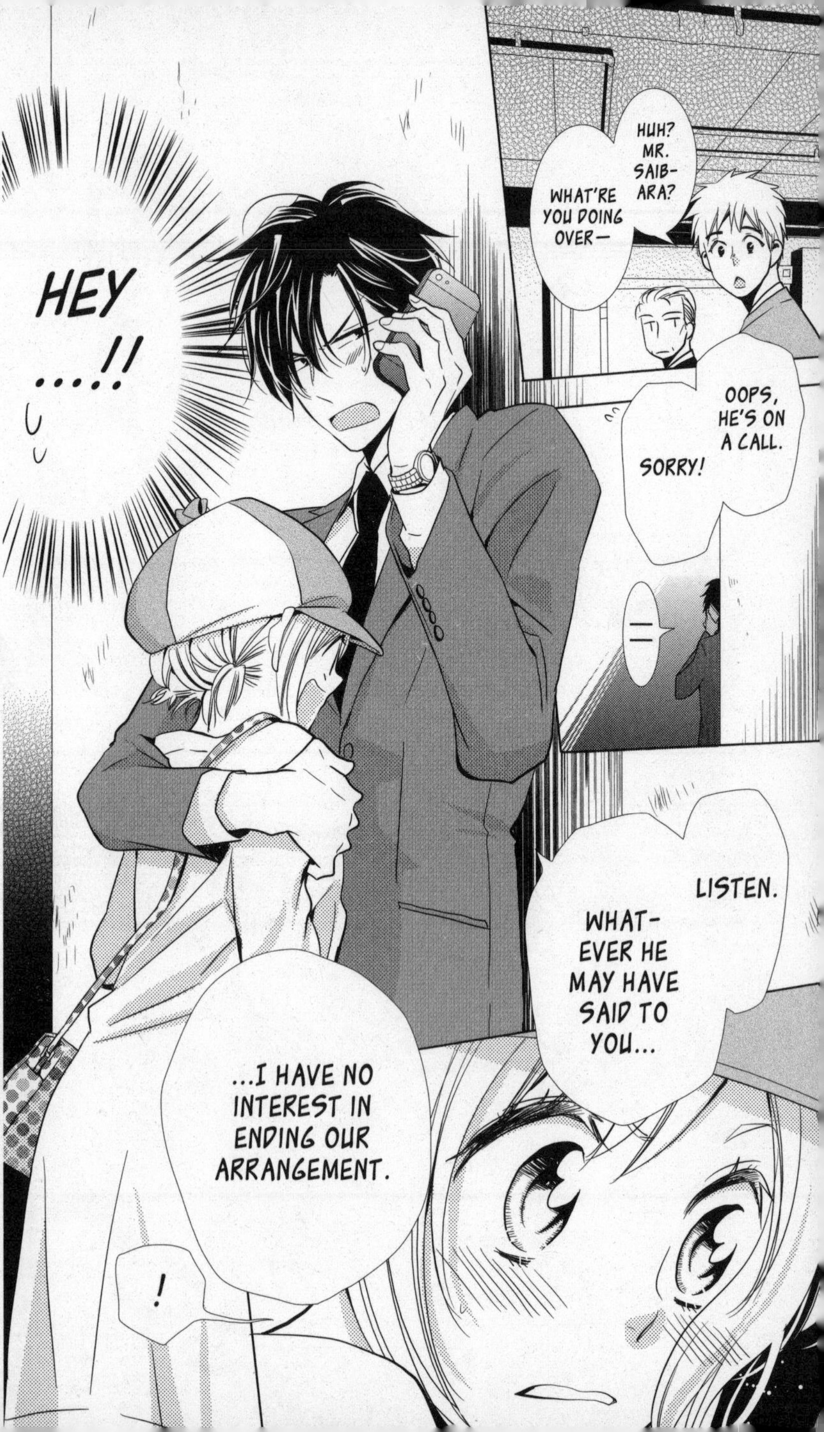
HUH? MR. SAIB-ARA?
WHAT'RE YOU DOING OVER—
OOPS, HE'S ON A CALL.
SORRY!
—
HEY
...!!
LISTEN.
WHAT-EVER HE MAY HAVE SAID TO YOU...
...I HAVE NO INTEREST IN ENDING OUR ARRANGEMENT.
!

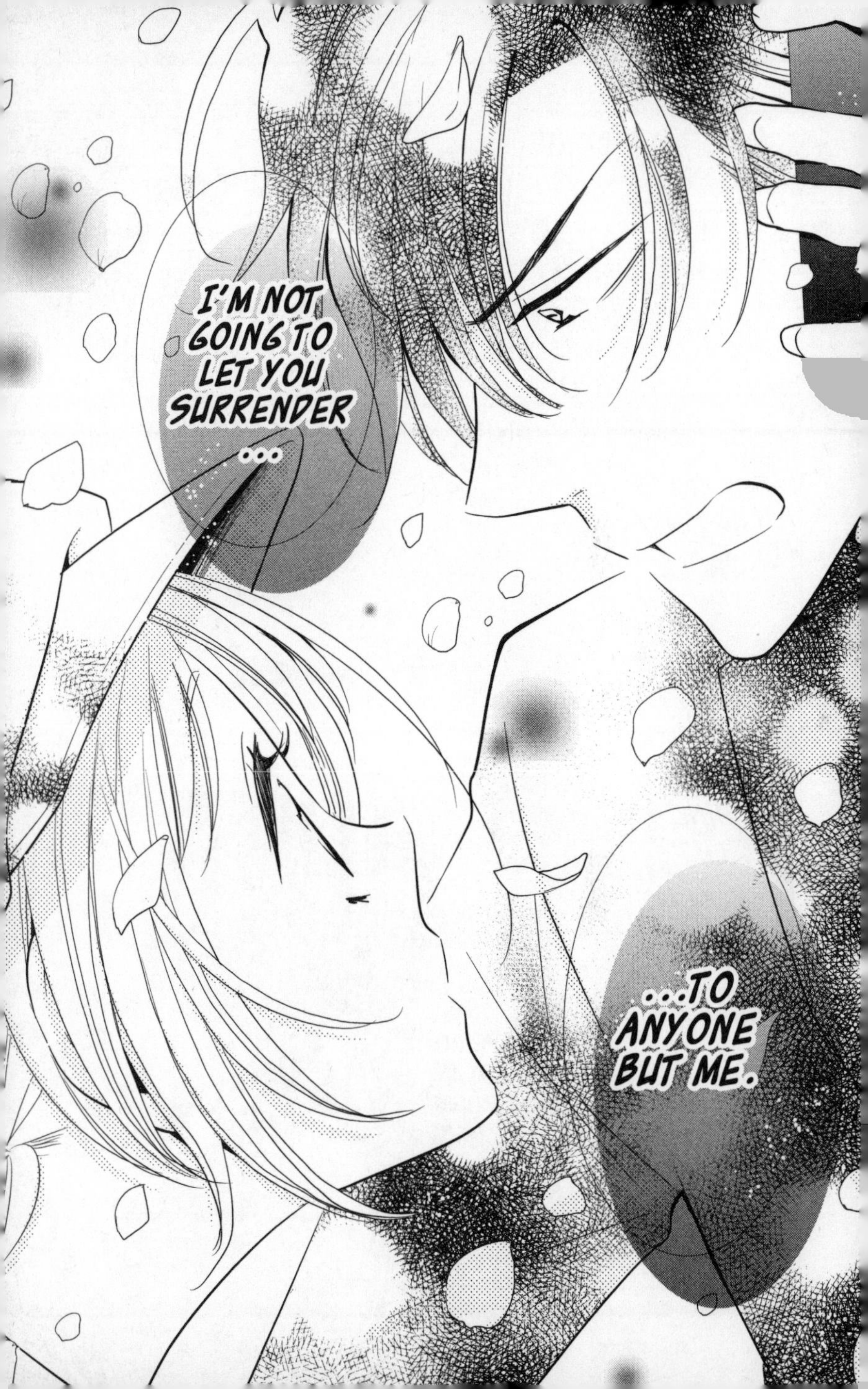
I'M NOT GOING TO LET YOU SURRENDER...
...TO ANYONE BUT ME.

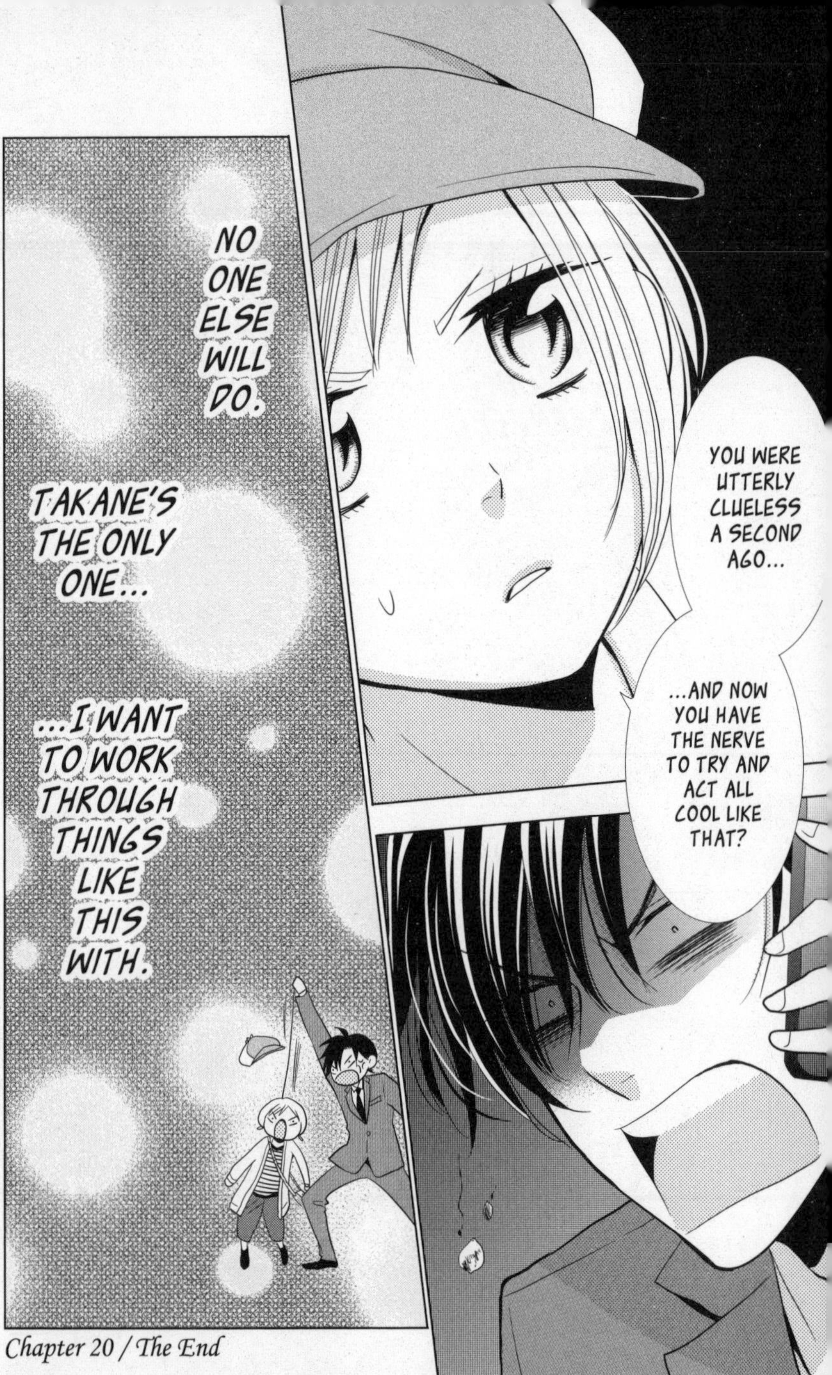
YOU WERE UTTERLY CLUELESS A SECOND AGO...
...AND NOW YOU HAVE THE NERVE TO TRY AND ACT ALL COOL LIKE THAT?
NO ONE ELSE WILL DO.
TAKANE'S THE ONLY ONE...
...I WANT TO WORK THROUGH THINGS LIKE THIS WITH.

Chapter 20 / The End

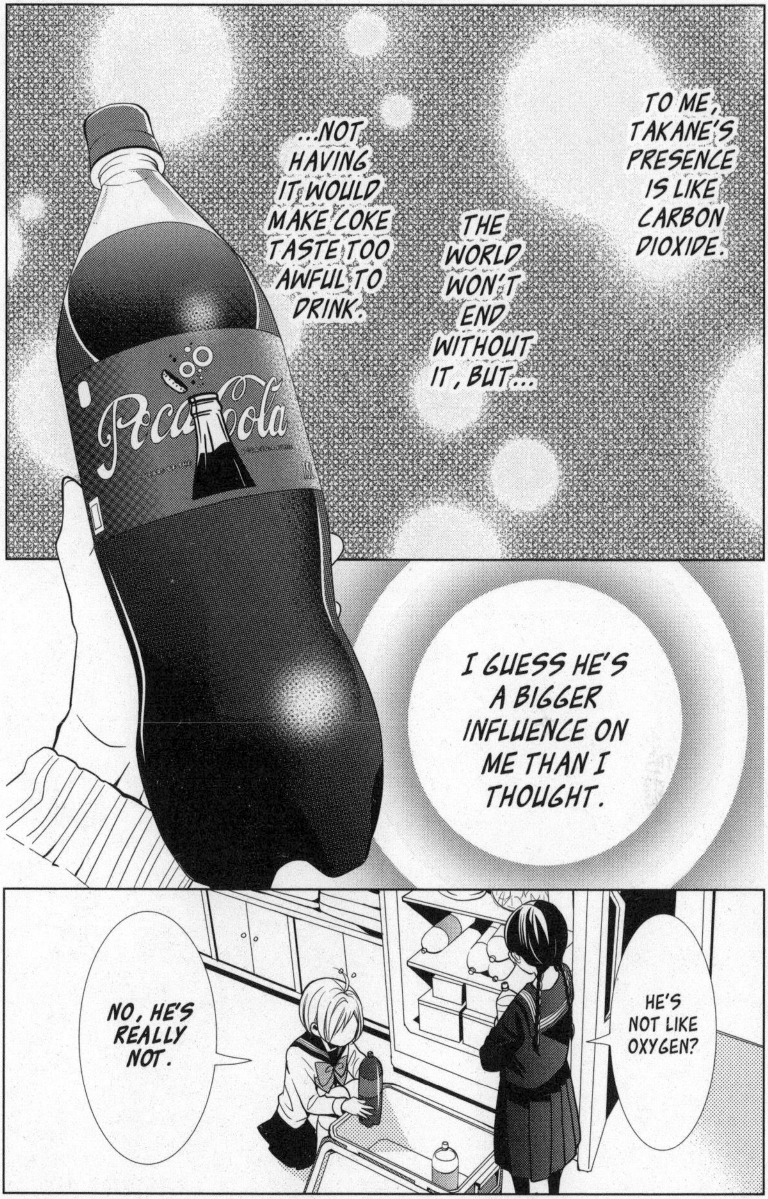
TO ME, TAKANE'S PRESENCE IS LIKE CARBON DIOXIDE.
THE WORLD WON'T END WITHOUT IT, BUT...
...NOT HAVING IT WOULD MAKE COKE TASTE TOO AWFUL TO DRINK.
I GUESS HE'S A BIGGER INFLUENCE ON ME THAN I THOUGHT.
HE'S NOT LIKE OXYGEN?
NO, HE'S REALLY NOT.

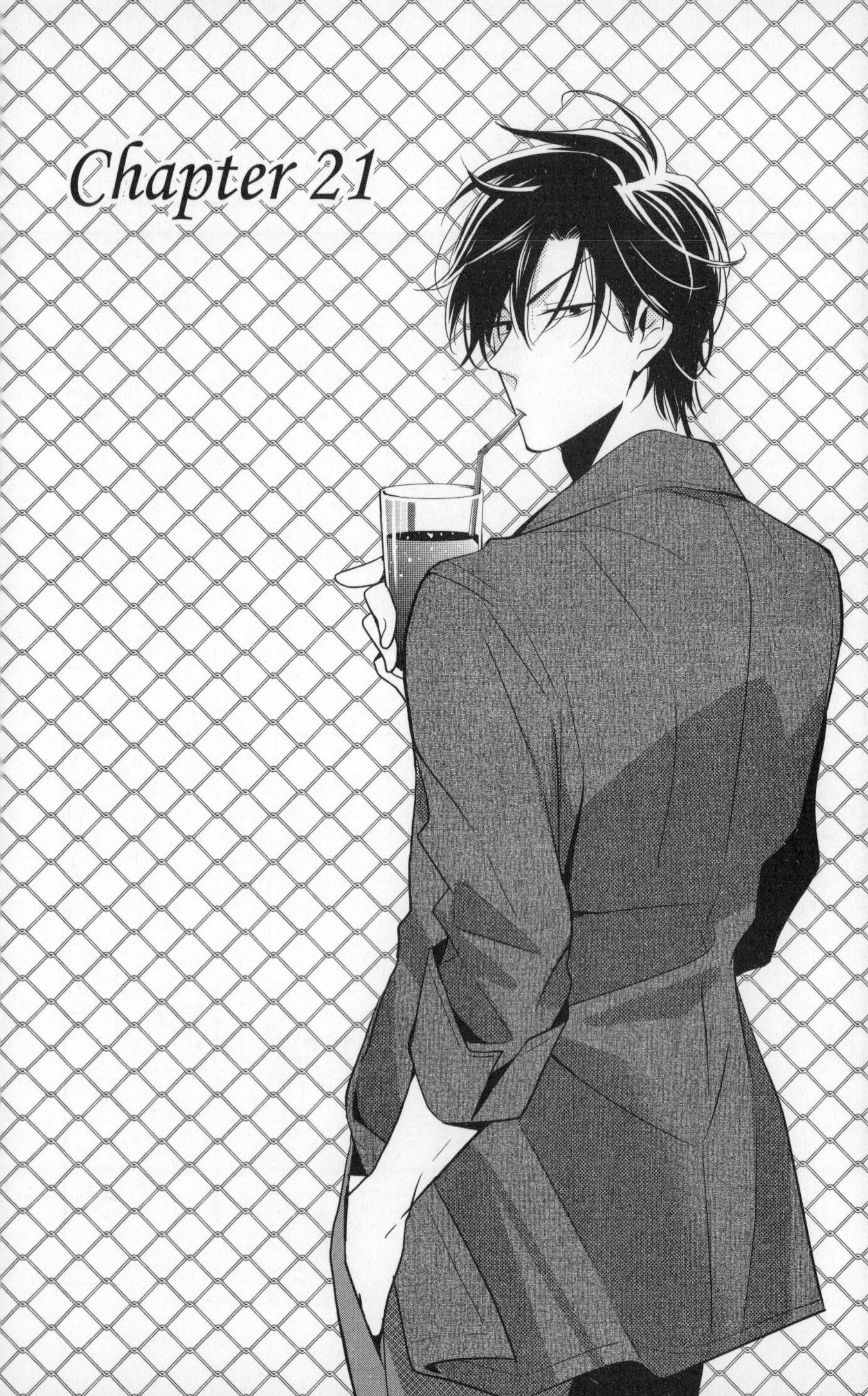
Chapter 21

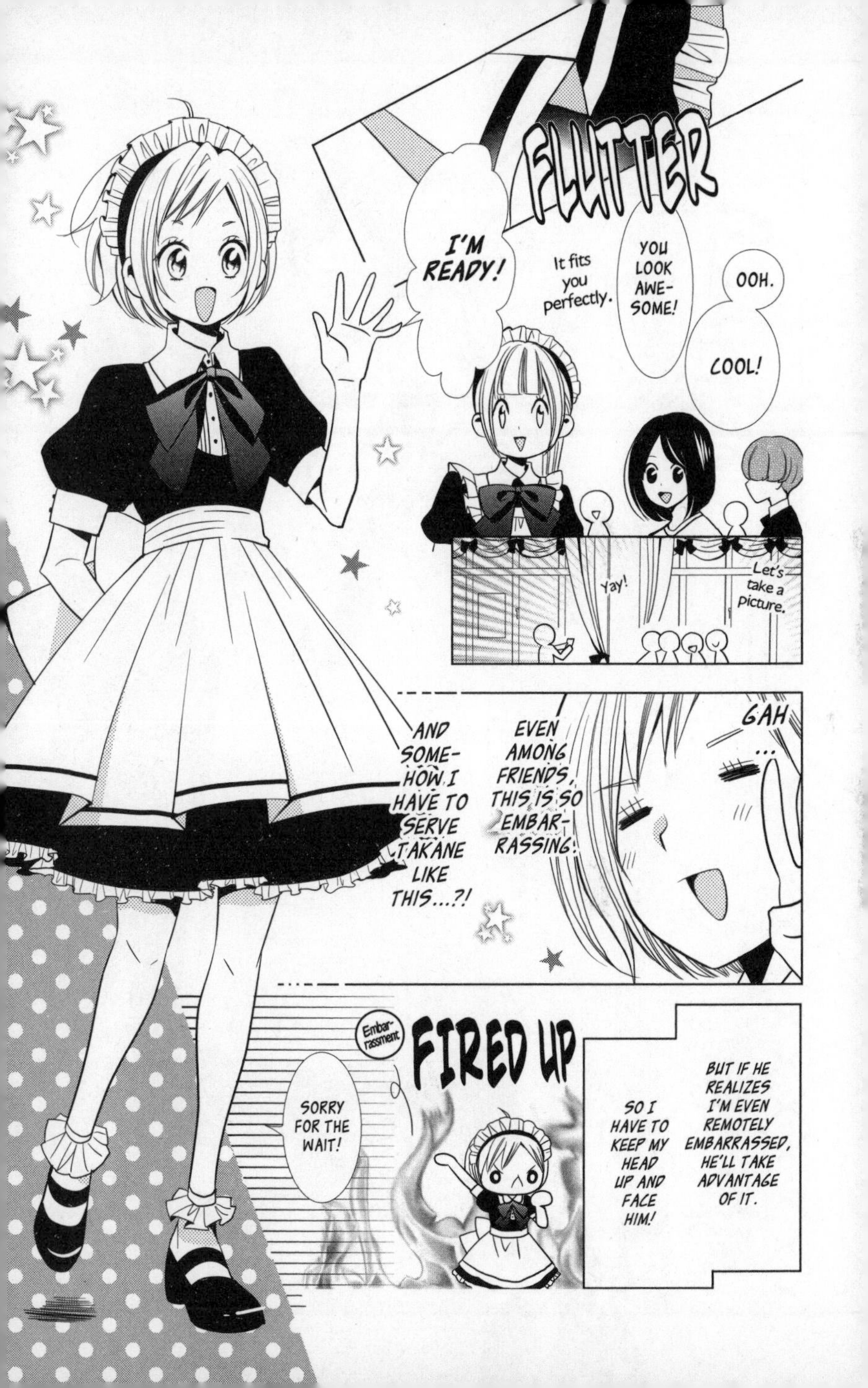
FLUTTER
I'M READY!
OOH.
COOL!
YOU LOOK AWESOME!
It fits you perfectly.
Let's take a picture.
Yay!
GAH...
EVEN AMONG FRIENDS, THIS IS SO EMBARRASSING!
AND SOMEHOW I HAVE TO SERVE TAKANE LIKE THIS...?!
BUT IF HE REALIZES I'M EVEN REMOTELY EMBARRASSED, HE'LL TAKE ADVANTAGE OF IT.
SO I HAVE TO KEEP MY HEAD UP AND FACE HIM!
Embarrassment
FIRED UP
SORRY FOR THE WAIT!

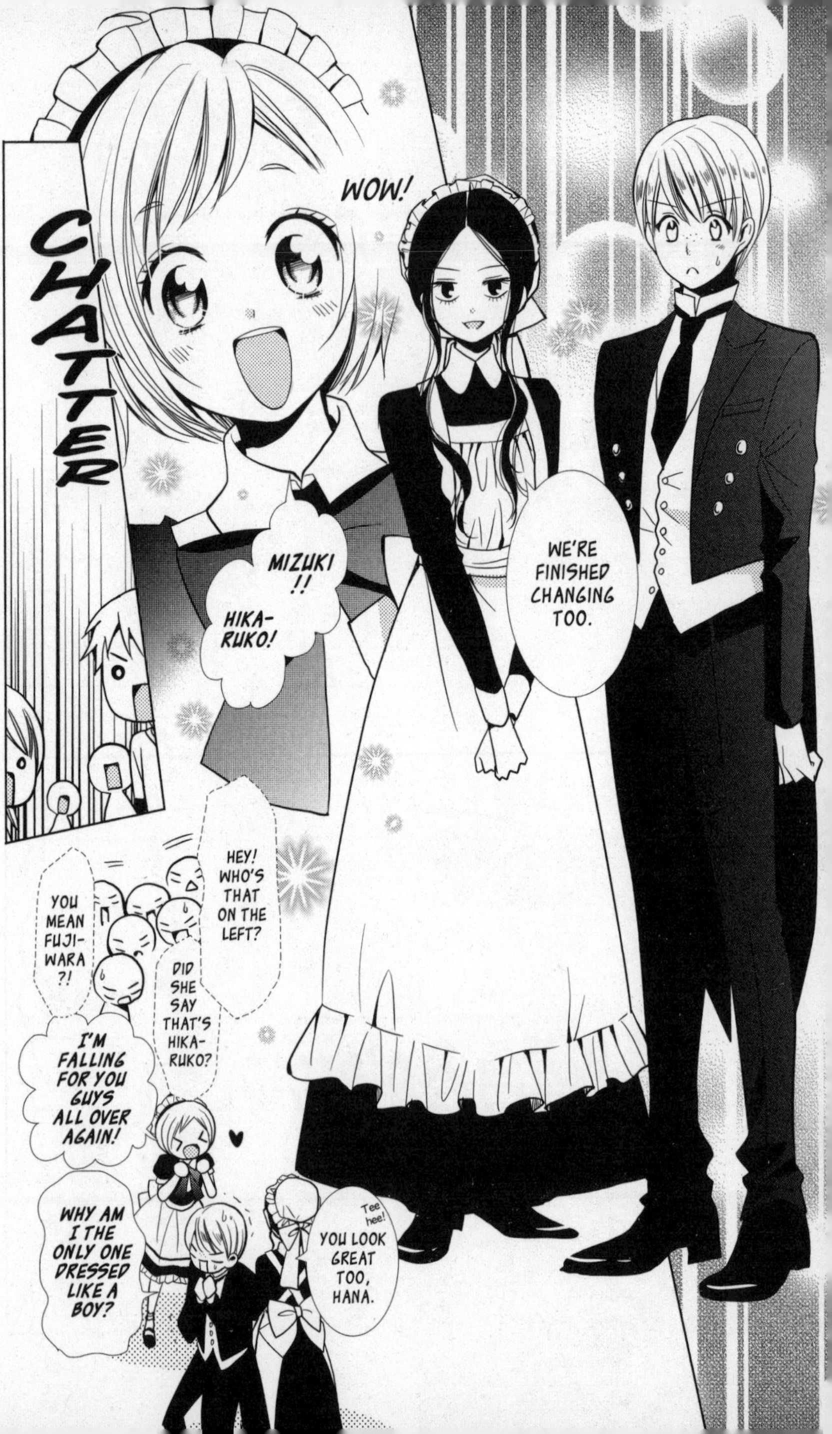

WOW!
WE'RE FINISHED CHANGING TOO.
MIZUKI!!
HIKA-RUKO!
CHATTER
HEY! WHO'S THAT ON THE LEFT?
YOU MEAN FUJI-WARA?!
DID SHE SAY THAT'S HIKA-RUKO?
I'M FALLING FOR YOU GUYS ALL OVER AGAIN!
Tee hee!
YOU LOOK GREAT TOO, HANA.
WHY AM I THE ONLY ONE DRESSED LIKE A BOY?

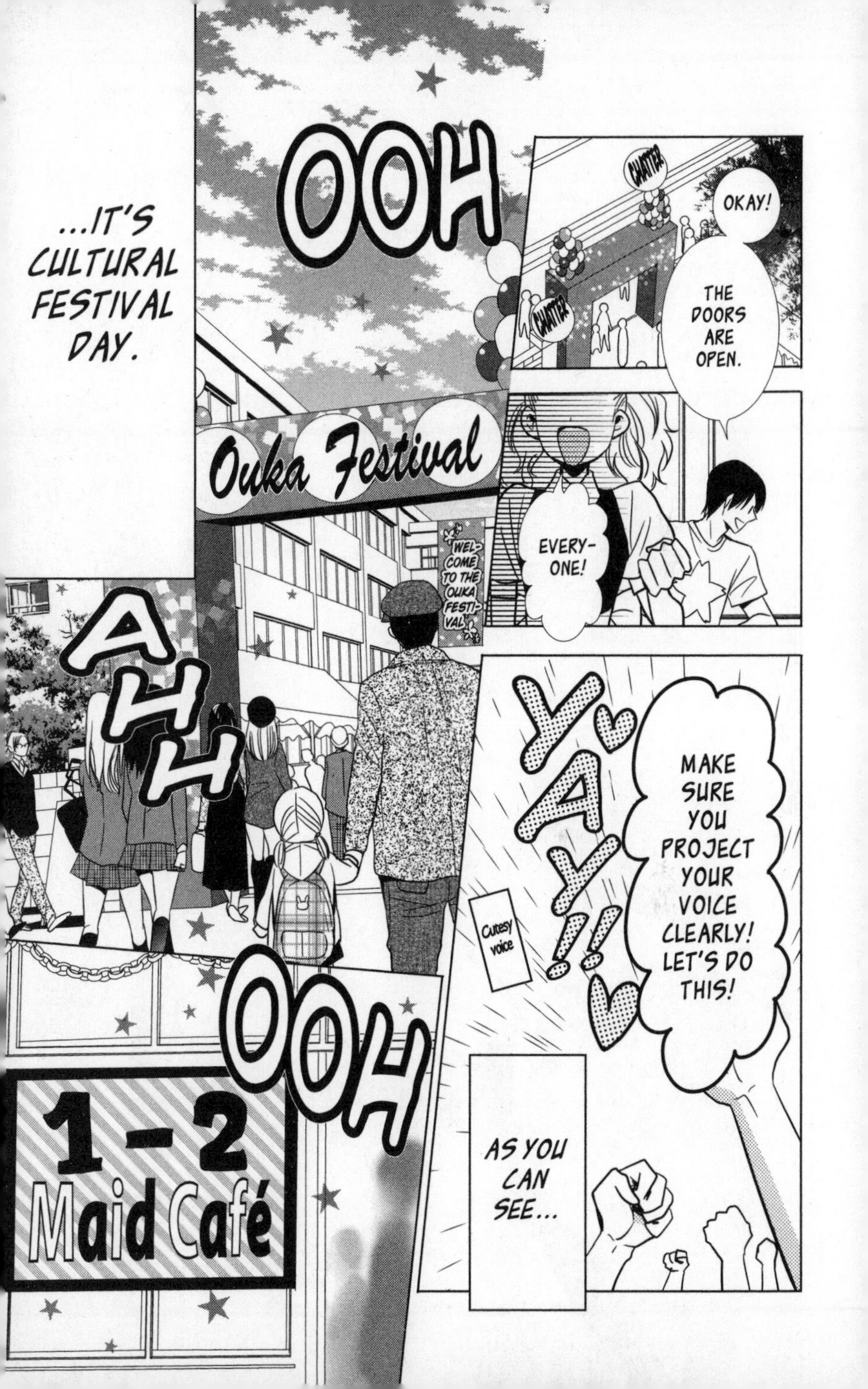
CHATTER
CHATTER
OKAY!
THE DOORS ARE OPEN.
EVERY-ONE!
YAY!!
MAKE SURE YOU PROJECT YOUR VOICE CLEARLY! LET'S DO THIS!
Cutesy voice
AS YOU CAN SEE...
...IT'S CULTURAL FESTIVAL DAY.
OOH
Ouka Festival
WELCOME TO THE OUKA FESTIVAL
AHH
OOH
1-2 Maid Café

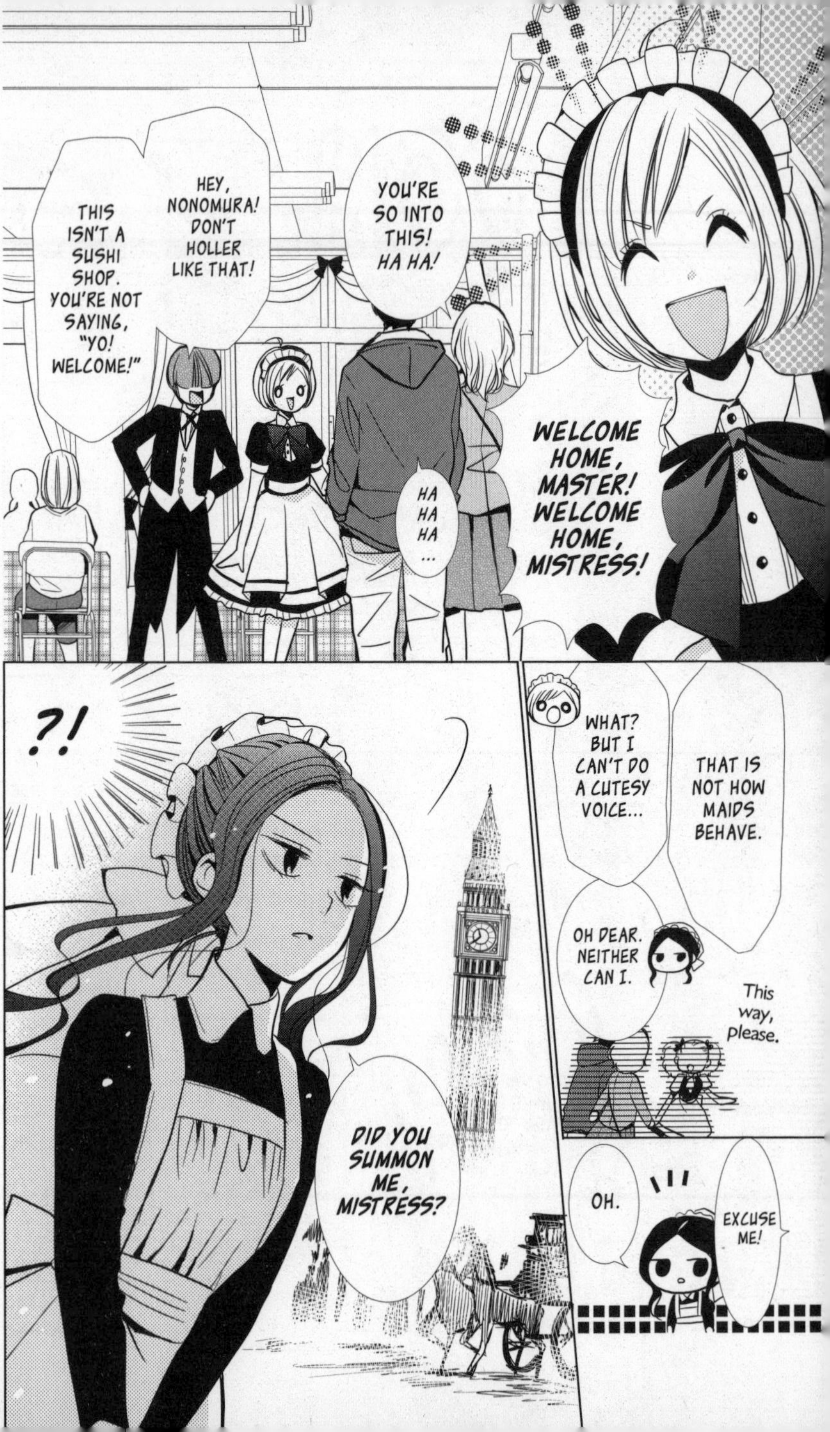
WELCOME HOME, MASTER! WELCOME HOME, MISTRESS!
YOU'RE SO INTO THIS! HA HA!
HEY, NONOMURA! DON'T HOLLER LIKE THAT!
THIS ISN'T A SUSHI SHOP. YOU'RE NOT SAYING, "YO! WELCOME!"
HA HA HA ...
THAT IS NOT HOW MAIDS BEHAVE.
WHAT? BUT I CAN'T DO A CUTESY VOICE...
OH DEAR. NEITHER CAN I.
This way, please.
EXCUSE ME!
OH.
?!
DID YOU SUMMON ME, MISTRESS?

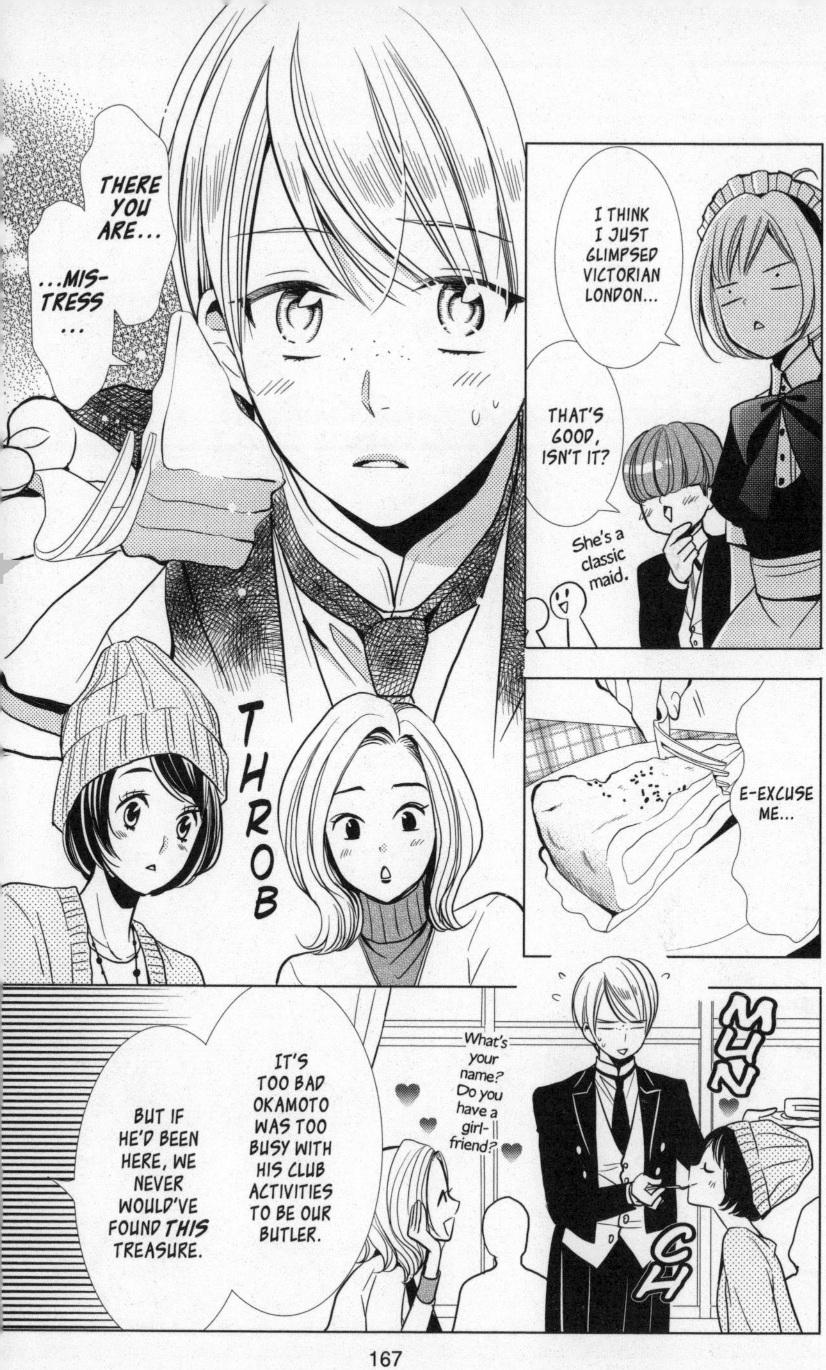

I THINK I JUST GLIMPSED VICTORIAN LONDON...
THAT'S GOOD, ISN'T IT?
She's a classic maid.
E-EXCUSE ME...
THERE YOU ARE...
...MIS-TRESS...
THROB
MUNCH
What's your name? Do you have a girl-friend?
IT'S TOO BAD OKAMOTO WAS TOO BUSY WITH HIS CLUB ACTIVITIES TO BE OUR BUTLER.
BUT IF HE'D BEEN HERE, WE NEVER WOULD'VE FOUND THIS TREASURE.

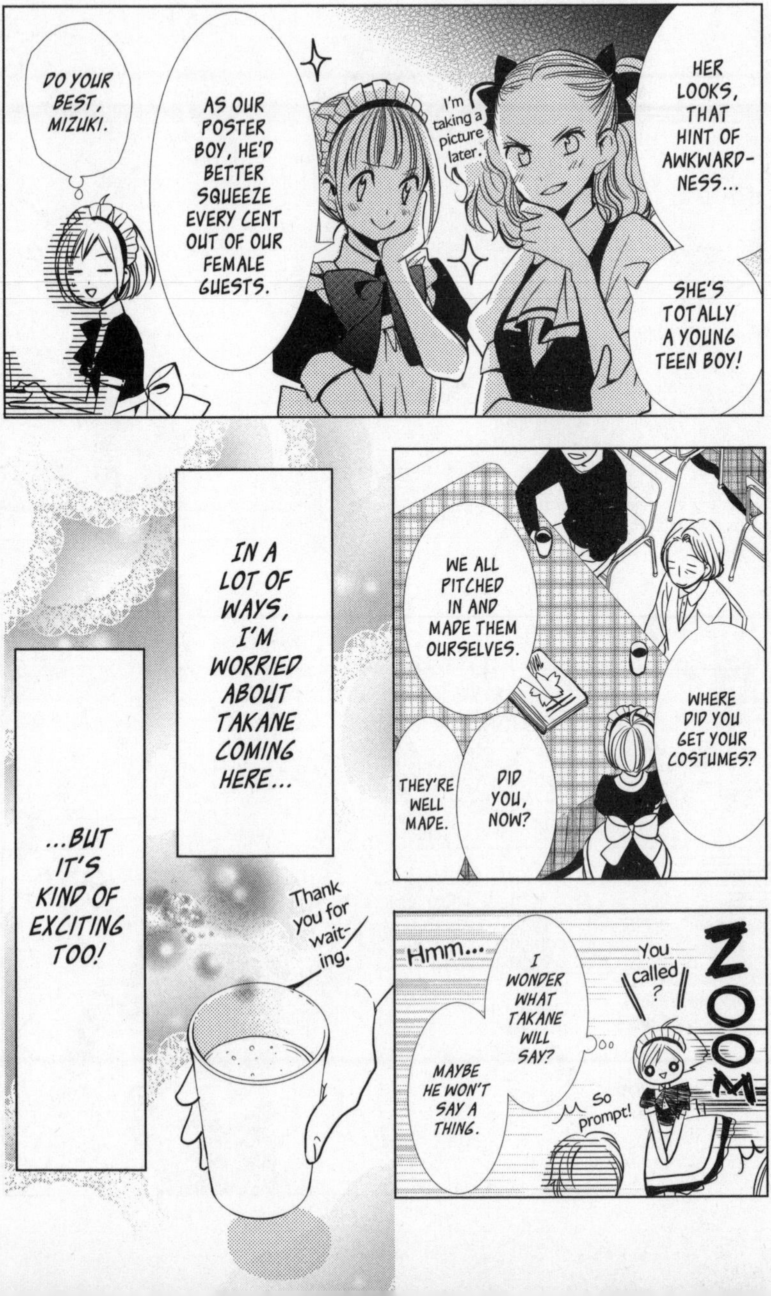
HER LOOKS, THAT HINT OF AWKWARDNESS...
SHE'S TOTALLY A YOUNG TEEN BOY!
I'm taking a picture later.
AS OUR POSTER BOY, HE'D BETTER SQUEEZE EVERY CENT OUT OF OUR FEMALE GUESTS.
DO YOUR BEST, MIZUKI.
WHERE DID YOU GET YOUR COSTUMES?
WE ALL PITCHED IN AND MADE THEM OURSELVES.
DID YOU, NOW?
THEY'RE WELL MADE.
ZOOM
You called?
So prompt!
I WONDER WHAT TAKANE WILL SAY?
Hmm...
MAYBE HE WON'T SAY A THING.
IN A LOT OF WAYS, I'M WORRIED ABOUT TAKANE COMING HERE...
...BUT IT'S KIND OF EXCITING TOO!
Thank you for waiting.

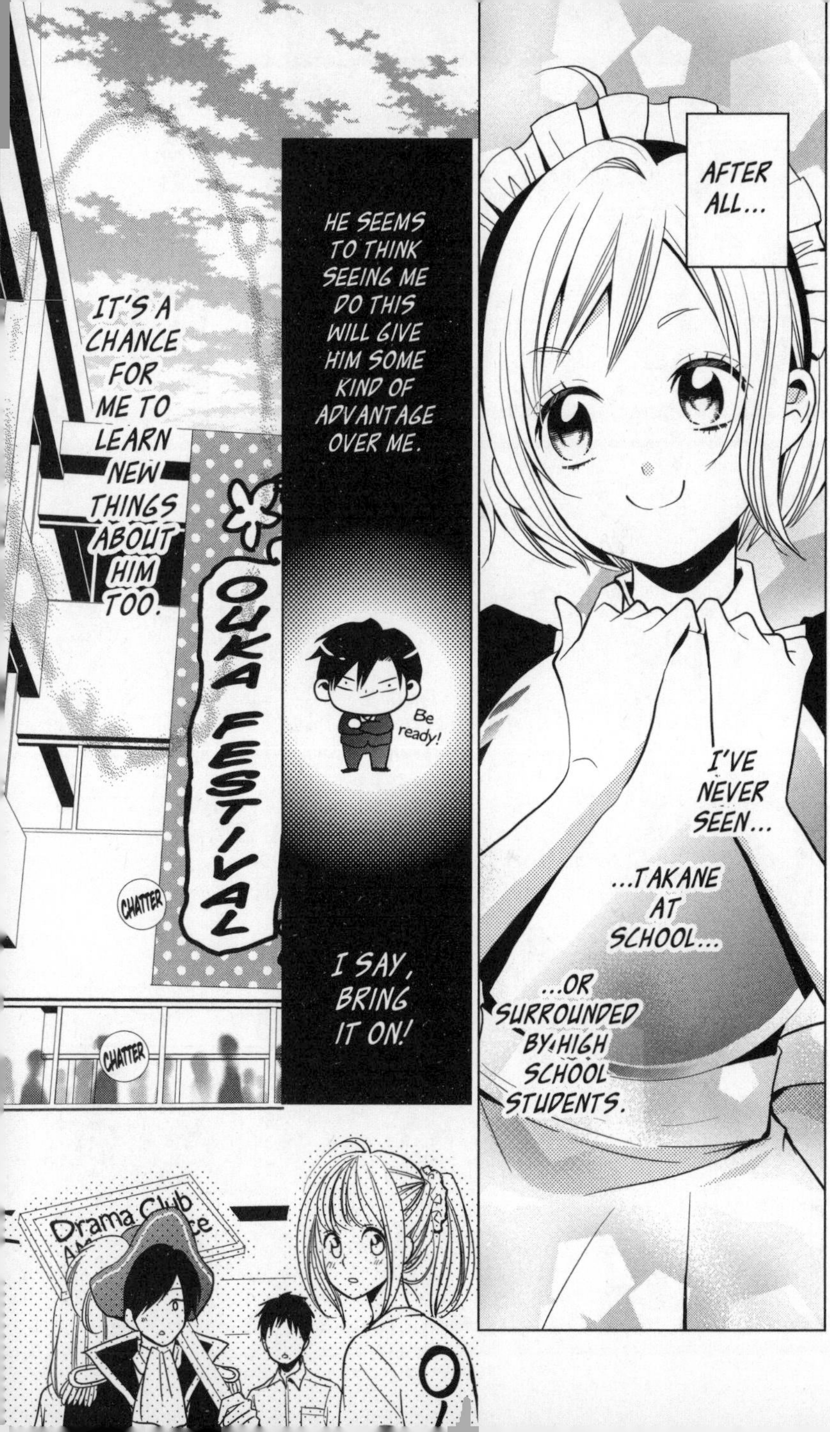
AFTER ALL...
I'VE NEVER SEEN...
...TAKANE AT SCHOOL...
...OR SURROUNDED BY HIGH SCHOOL STUDENTS.
HE SEEMS TO THINK SEEING ME DO THIS WILL GIVE HIM SOME KIND OF ADVANTAGE OVER ME.
Be ready!
I SAY, BRING IT ON!
IT'S A CHANCE FOR ME TO LEARN NEW THINGS ABOUT HIM TOO.
OUKA FESTIVAL
CHATTER
CHATTER
Drama Club

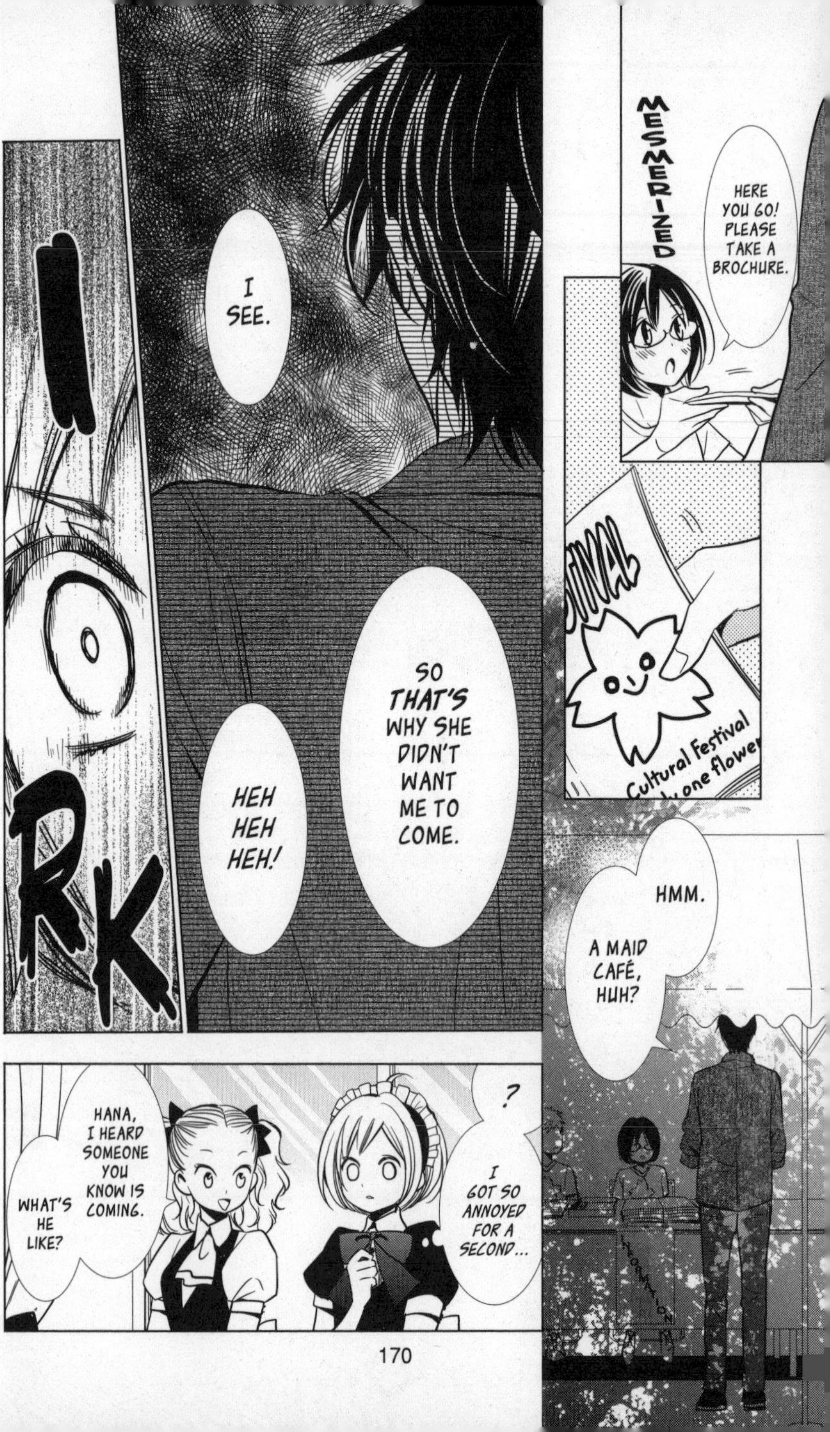
MESMERIZED
HERE YOU GO! PLEASE TAKE A BROCHURE.
STIVAL
Cultural Festival
one flower
HMM.
A MAID CAFÉ, HUH?
I SEE.
SO *THAT'S* WHY SHE DIDN'T WANT ME TO COME.
HEH HEH HEH!
IRK
?
I GOT SO ANNOYED FOR A SECOND...
HANA, I HEARD SOMEONE YOU KNOW IS COMING.
WHAT'S HE LIKE?

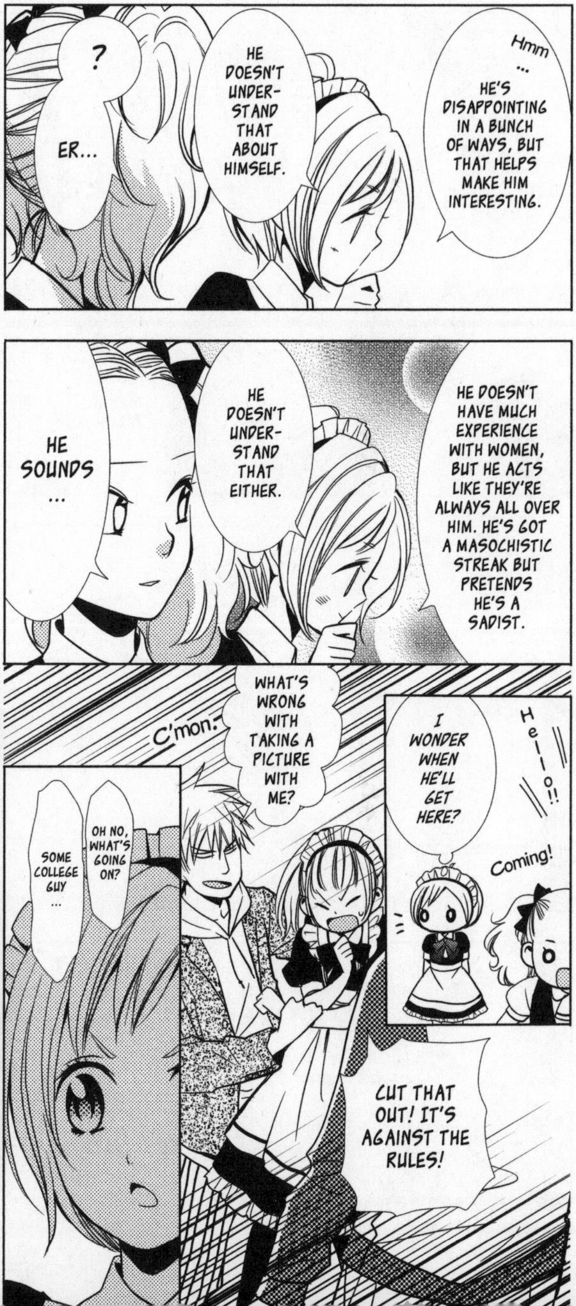
Hmm ...
HE'S DISAPPOINTING IN A BUNCH OF WAYS, BUT THAT HELPS MAKE HIM INTERESTING.
HE DOESN'T UNDER-STAND THAT ABOUT HIMSELF.
?
ER...
HE DOESN'T HAVE MUCH EXPERIENCE WITH WOMEN, BUT HE ACTS LIKE THEY'RE ALWAYS ALL OVER HIM. HE'S GOT A MASOCHISTIC STREAK BUT PRETENDS HE'S A SADIST.
HE DOESN'T UNDER-STAND THAT EITHER.
HE SOUNDS ...
Hello!!
I WONDER WHEN HE'LL GET HERE?
Coming!
WHAT'S WRONG WITH TAKING A PICTURE WITH ME?
C'mon.
CUT THAT OUT! IT'S AGAINST THE RULES!
OH NO, WHAT'S GOING ON?
SOME COLLEGE GUY ...

• Special Thanks •

-My chief editor, "S"
-Everyone who handles sales and marketing
-The editor in charge of the cover design
-Naht Co. Ltd.
-Everyone who had a hand in making this book a reality
-Readers, family and friends
-All of you who have written me letters

• Please Send Your Thoughts and Impressions •

Yuki Shiwasu
c/o Takane & Hana Editor
VIZ Media
P.O. Box 77010
San Francisco, CA 94107

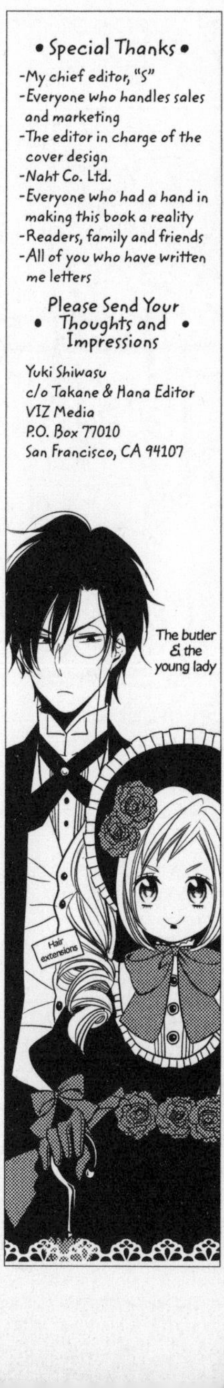
The butler & the young lady
Hair extensions

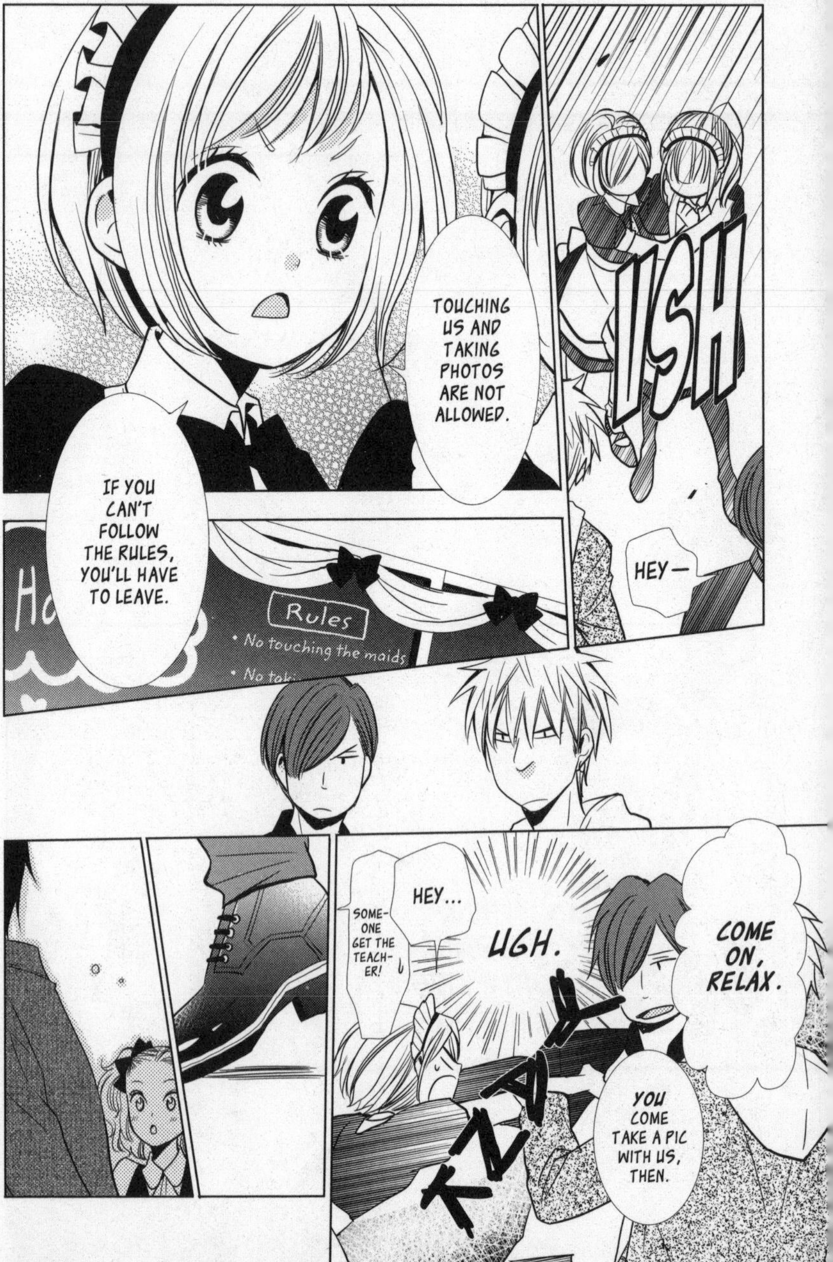
USH
HEY—
TOUCHING US AND TAKING PHOTOS ARE NOT ALLOWED.
IF YOU CAN'T FOLLOW THE RULES, YOU'LL HAVE TO LEAVE.
Rules
• No touching the maids
COME ON, RELAX.
YOU COME TAKE A PIC WITH US, THEN.
UGH.
KZAY
HEY...
SOME-ONE GET THE TEACH-ER!

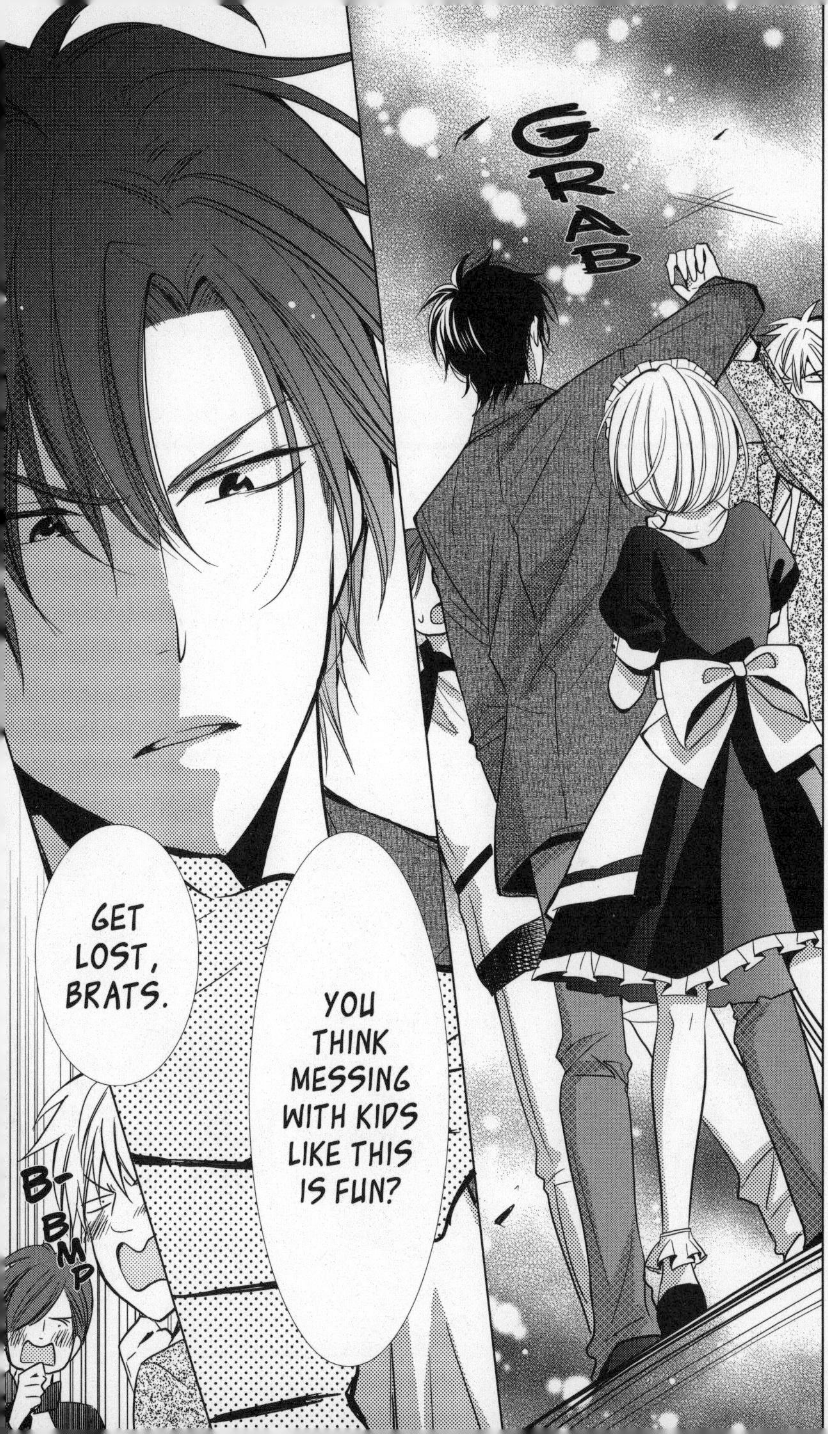
GRAB
YOU THINK MESSING WITH KIDS LIKE THIS IS FUN?
GET LOST, BRATS.
B-BMP

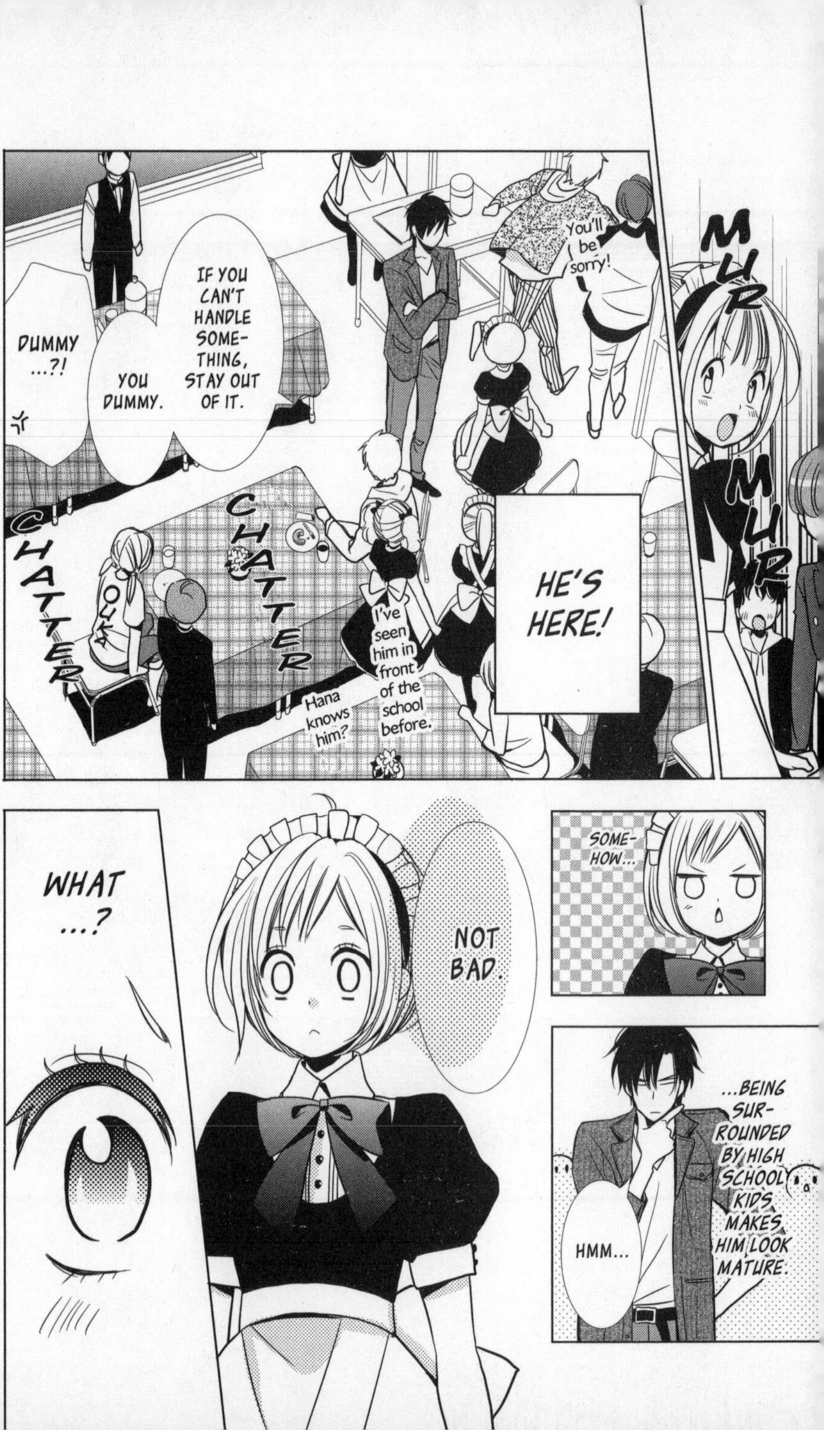
MUR MUR
HE'S HERE!
You'll be sorry!
I've seen him in front of the school before.
Hana knows him?
CHATTER CHATTER
IF YOU CAN'T HANDLE SOMETHING, STAY OUT OF IT.
YOU DUMMY.
DUMMY ...?!
SOME-HOW...
...BEING SURROUNDED BY HIGH SCHOOL KIDS MAKES HIM LOOK MATURE.
HMM...
NOT BAD.
WHAT ...?

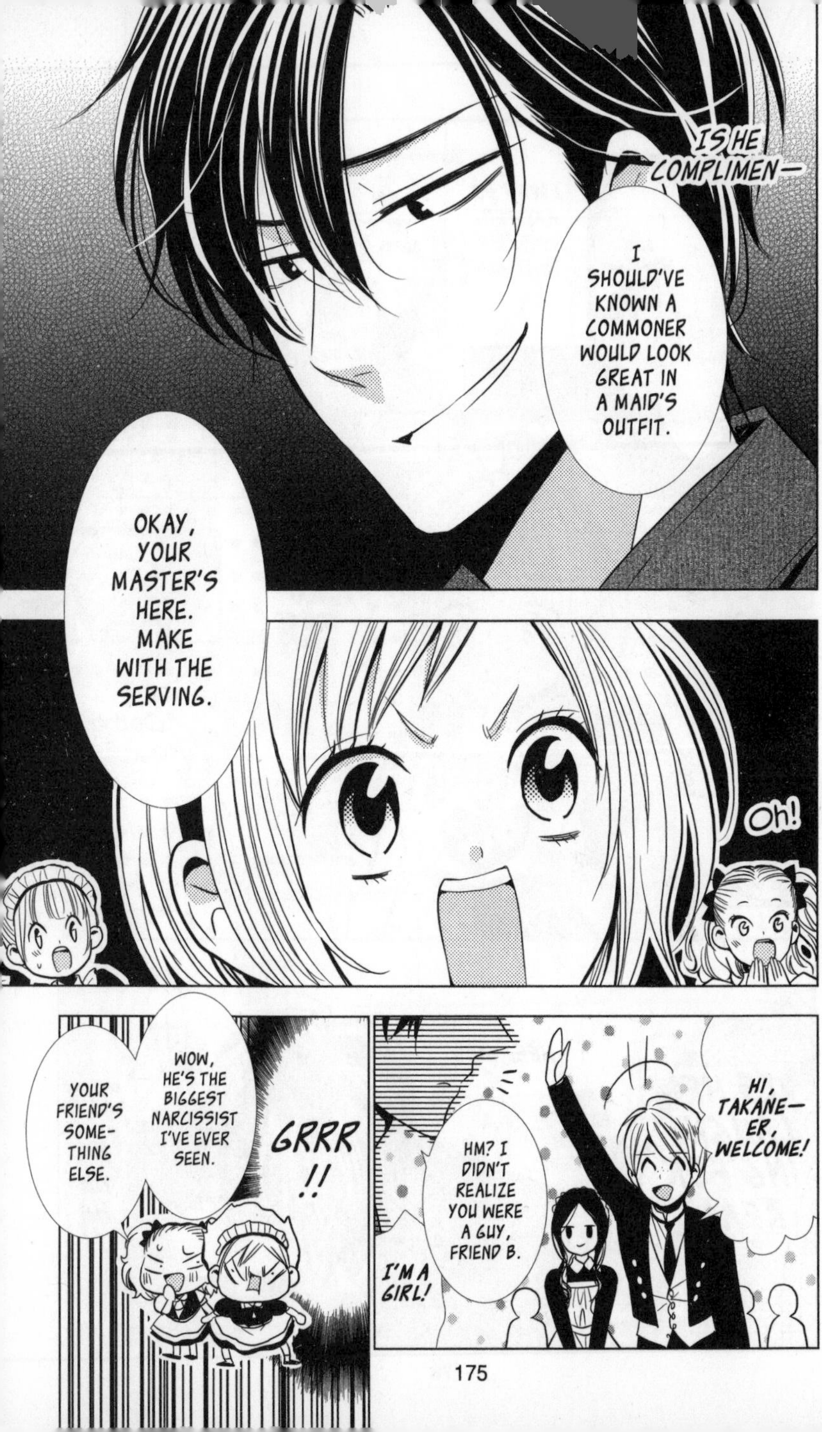
IS HE COMPLIMEN—
I SHOULD'VE KNOWN A COMMONER WOULD LOOK GREAT IN A MAID'S OUTFIT.
OKAY, YOUR MASTER'S HERE. MAKE WITH THE SERVING.
Oh!
HI, TAKANE-ER, WELCOME!
HM? I DIDN'T REALIZE YOU WERE A GUY, FRIEND B.
I'M A GIRL!
GRRR !!
WOW, HE'S THE BIGGEST NARCISSIST I'VE EVER SEEN.
YOUR FRIEND'S SOME-THING ELSE.

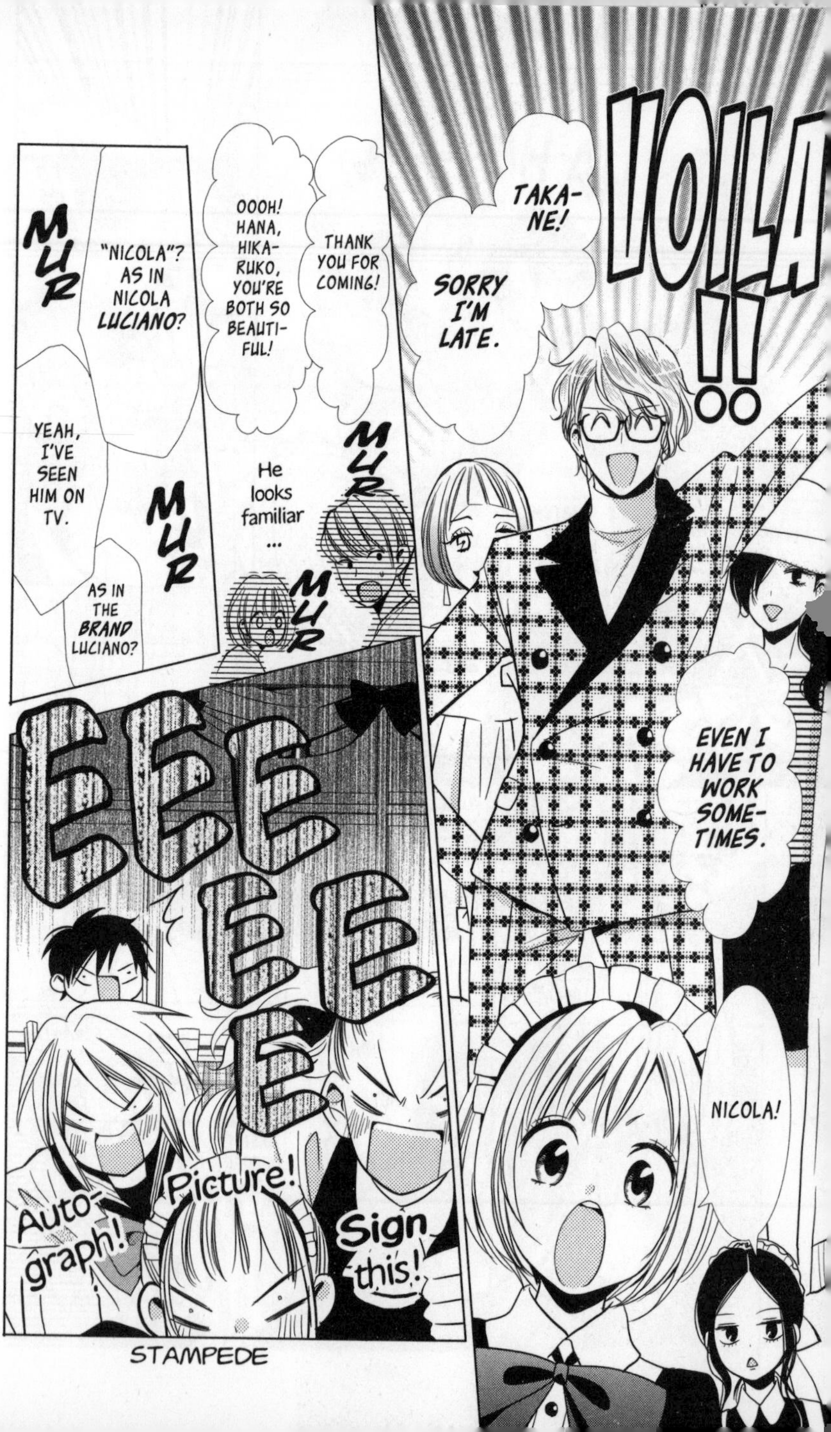
VOILA!!
TAKANE!
SORRY I'M LATE.
EVEN I HAVE TO WORK SOMETIMES.
NICOLA!
THANK YOU FOR COMING!
OOOH! HANA, HIKARUKO, YOU'RE BOTH SO BEAUTIFUL!
MUR
He looks familiar...
MUR
MUR
"NICOLA"? AS IN NICOLA LUCIANO?
MUR
YEAH, I'VE SEEN HIM ON TV.
AS IN THE BRAND LUCIANO?
EEEEEE
Sign this!
Picture!
Autograph!
STAMPEDE

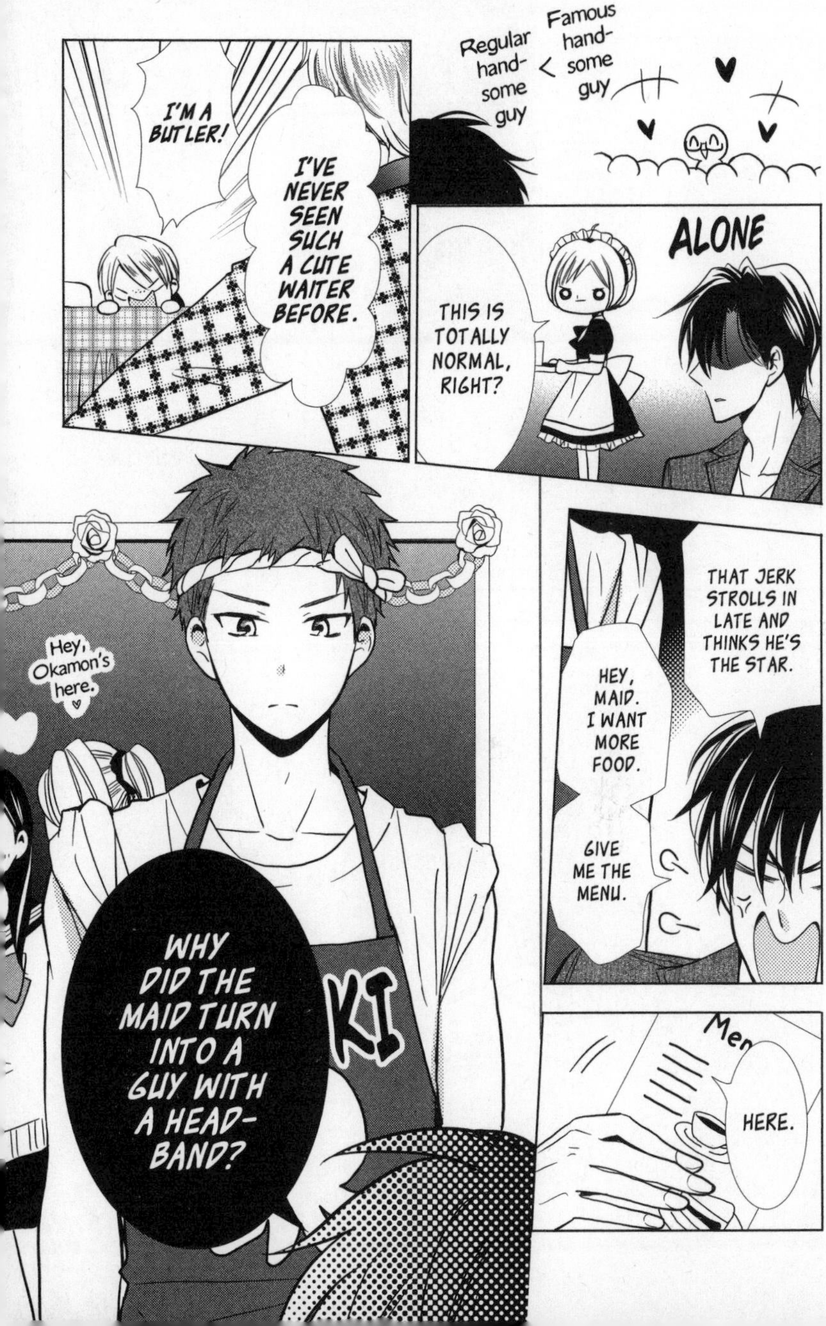
Regular hand-some guy < Famous hand-some guy
ALONE
THIS IS TOTALLY NORMAL, RIGHT?
I'M A BUTLER!
I'VE NEVER SEEN SUCH A CUTE WAITER BEFORE.
THAT JERK STROLLS IN LATE AND THINKS HE'S THE STAR.
HEY, MAID. I WANT MORE FOOD.
GIVE ME THE MENU.
Men
HERE.
Hey, Okamon's here.
WHY DID THE MAID TURN INTO A GUY WITH A HEAD-BAND?
KI

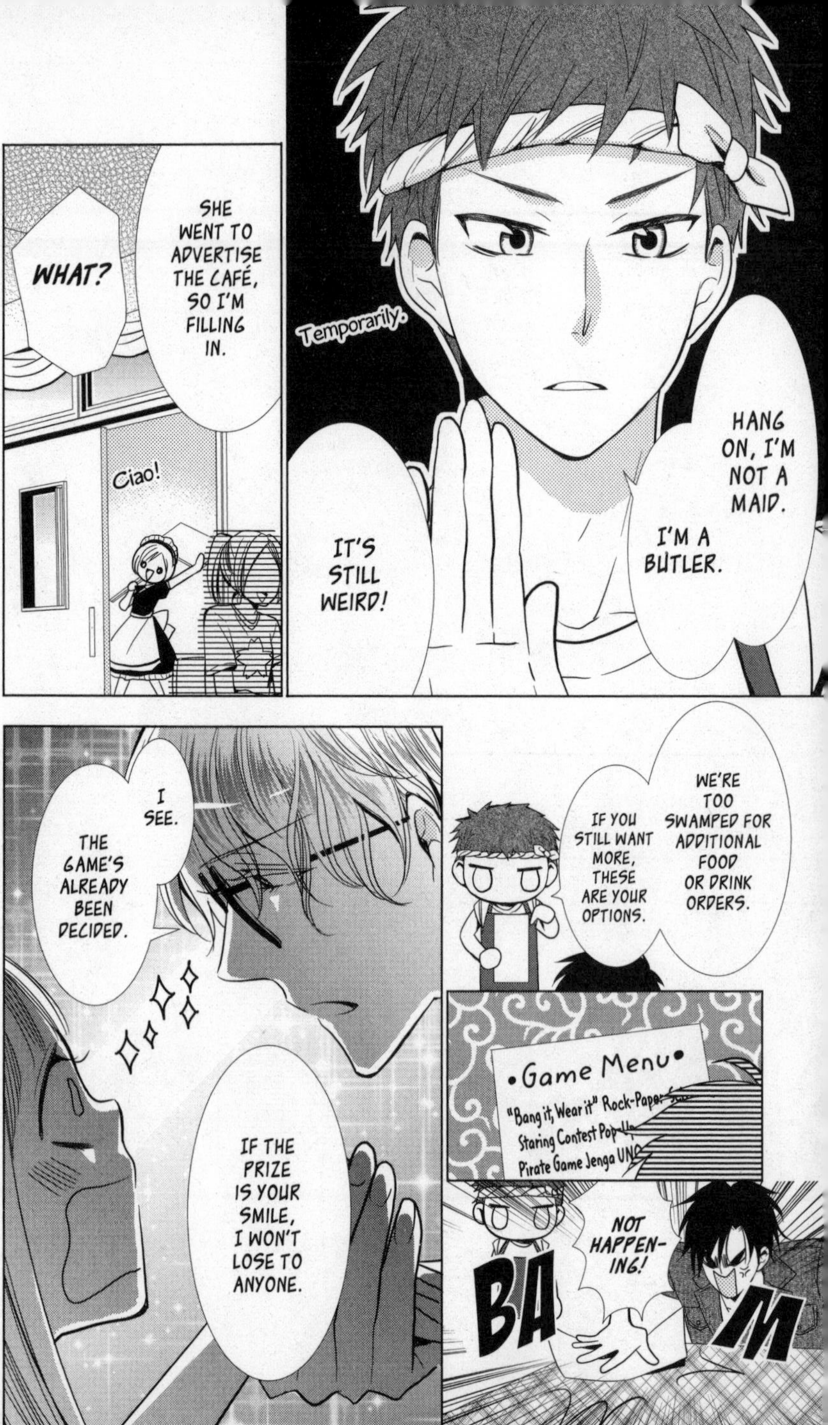
HANG ON, I'M NOT A MAID.
I'M A BUTLER.
IT'S STILL WEIRD!
Temporarily.
SHE WENT TO ADVERTISE THE CAFÉ, SO I'M FILLING IN.
WHAT?
Ciao!
WE'RE TOO SWAMPED FOR ADDITIONAL FOOD OR DRINK ORDERS.
IF YOU STILL WANT MORE, THESE ARE YOUR OPTIONS.
•Game Menu•
"Bang it, Wear it" Rock-Paper-
Staring Contest Pop-
Pirate Game Jenga
NOT HAPPEN-ING!
BAM
I SEE.
THE GAME'S ALREADY BEEN DECIDED.
IF THE PRIZE IS YOUR SMILE, I WON'T LOSE TO ANYONE.

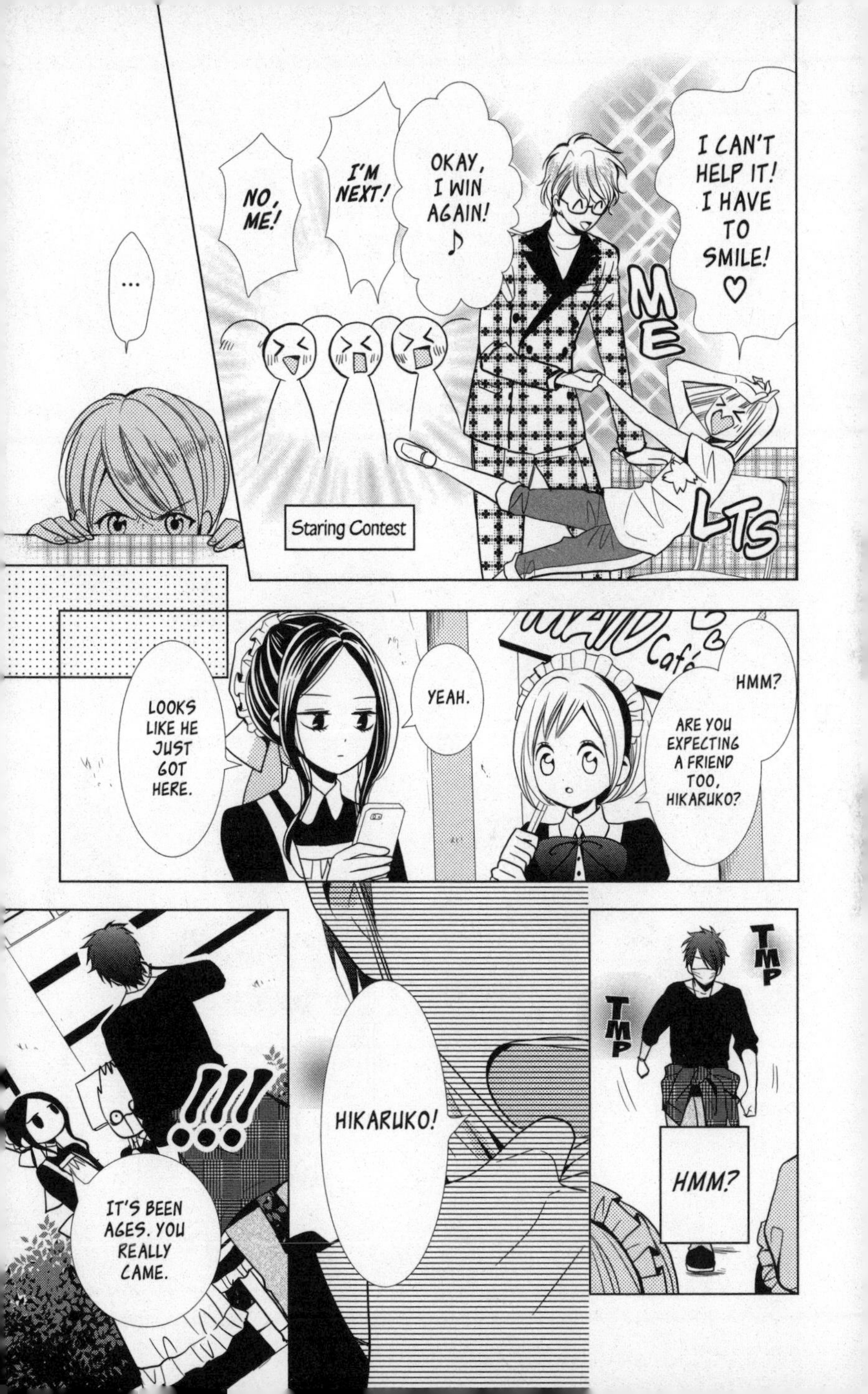

I CAN'T HELP IT! I HAVE TO SMILE! ♡
ME
LTS
OKAY, I WIN AGAIN! ♪
I'M NEXT!
NO, ME!
Staring Contest
...
HMM?
ARE YOU EXPECTING A FRIEND TOO, HIKARUKO?
Café
YEAH.
LOOKS LIKE HE JUST GOT HERE.
TMP
TMP
HMM?
HIKARUKO!
!!!
...
IT'S BEEN AGES. YOU REALLY CAME.

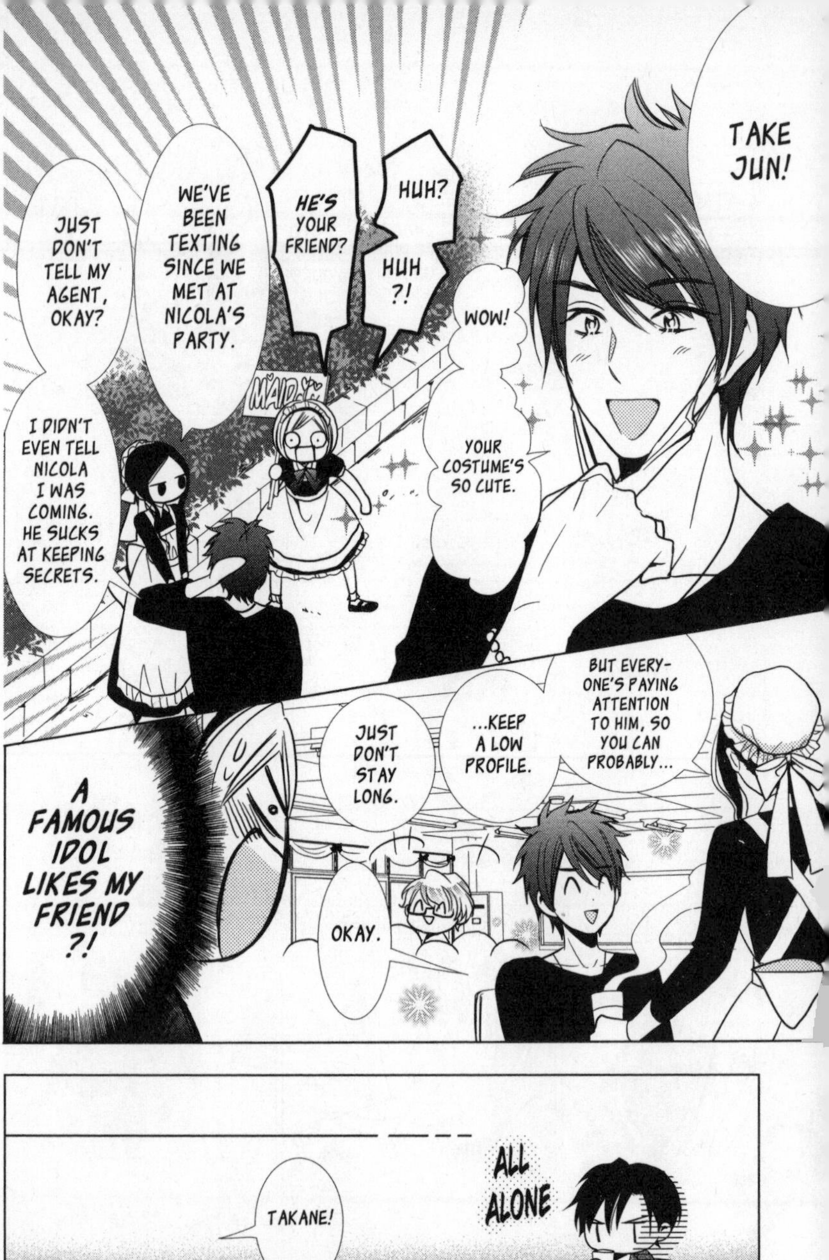
TAKE JUN!
WOW!
YOUR COSTUME'S SO CUTE.
HUH?
HUH?!
HE'S YOUR FRIEND?
WE'VE BEEN TEXTING SINCE WE MET AT NICOLA'S PARTY.
JUST DON'T TELL MY AGENT, OKAY?
I DIDN'T EVEN TELL NICOLA I WAS COMING. HE SUCKS AT KEEPING SECRETS.
BUT EVERYONE'S PAYING ATTENTION TO HIM, SO YOU CAN PROBABLY...
...KEEP A LOW PROFILE.
JUST DON'T STAY LONG.
OKAY.
A FAMOUS IDOL LIKES MY FRIEND?!
ALL ALONE
TAKANE!

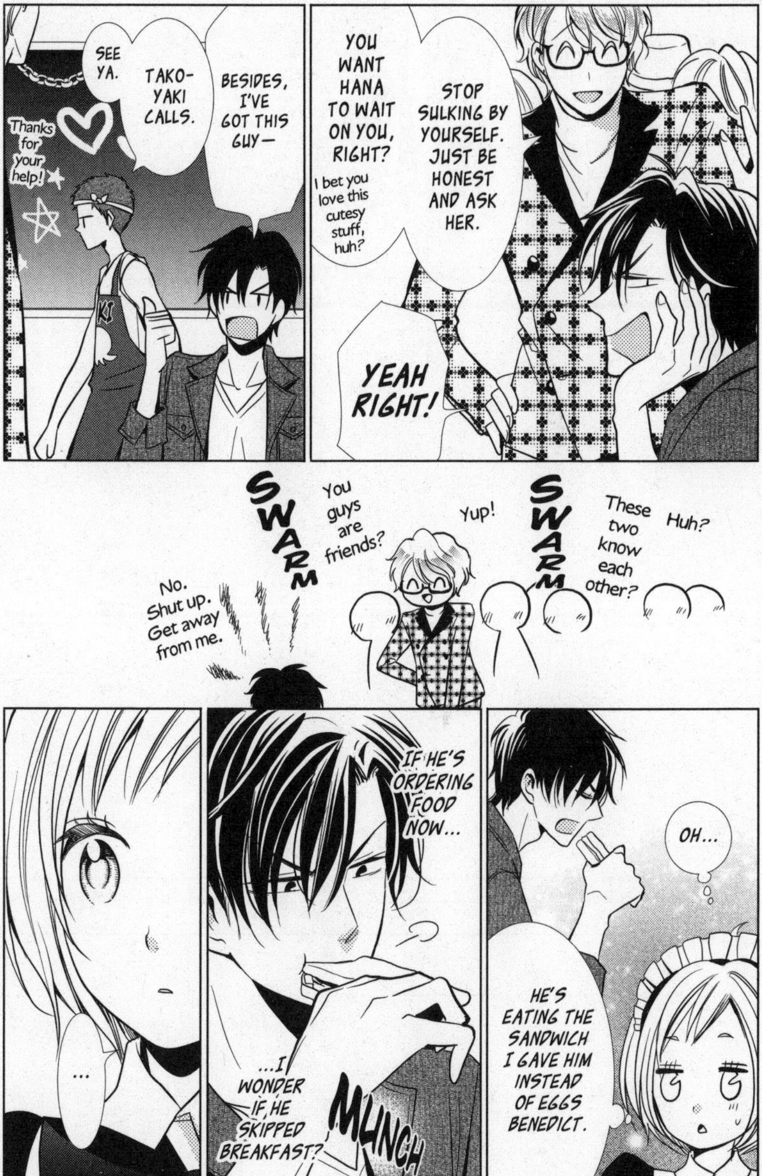
STOP SULKING BY YOURSELF. JUST BE HONEST AND ASK HER.
YOU WANT HANA TO WAIT ON YOU, RIGHT?
I bet you love this cutesy stuff, huh?
YEAH RIGHT!
BESIDES, I'VE GOT THIS GUY—
TAKO-YAKI CALLS.
SEE YA.
Thanks for your help!
Huh?
These two know each other?
SWARM
Yup!
You guys are friends?
SWARM
No. Shut up. Get away from me.
OH...
HE'S EATING THE SANDWICH I GAVE HIM INSTEAD OF EGGS BENEDICT.
IF HE'S ORDERING FOOD NOW...
...I WONDER IF HE SKIPPED BREAKFAST?
MUNCH
...

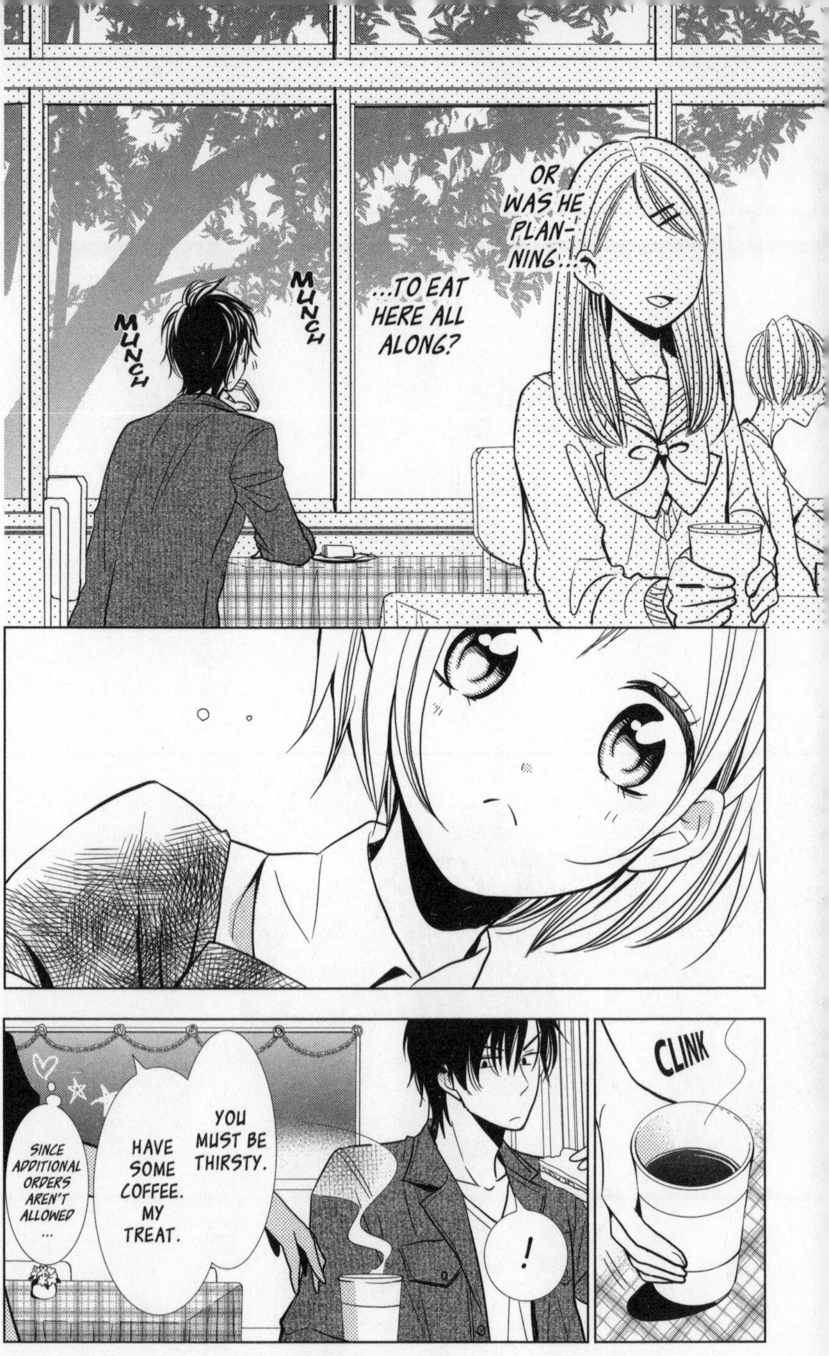
OR WAS HE PLAN-NING...
...TO EAT HERE ALL ALONG?
MUNCH
MUNCH
CLINK
!
YOU MUST BE THIRSTY.
HAVE SOME COFFEE. MY TREAT.
SINCE ADDITIONAL ORDERS AREN'T ALLOWED ...

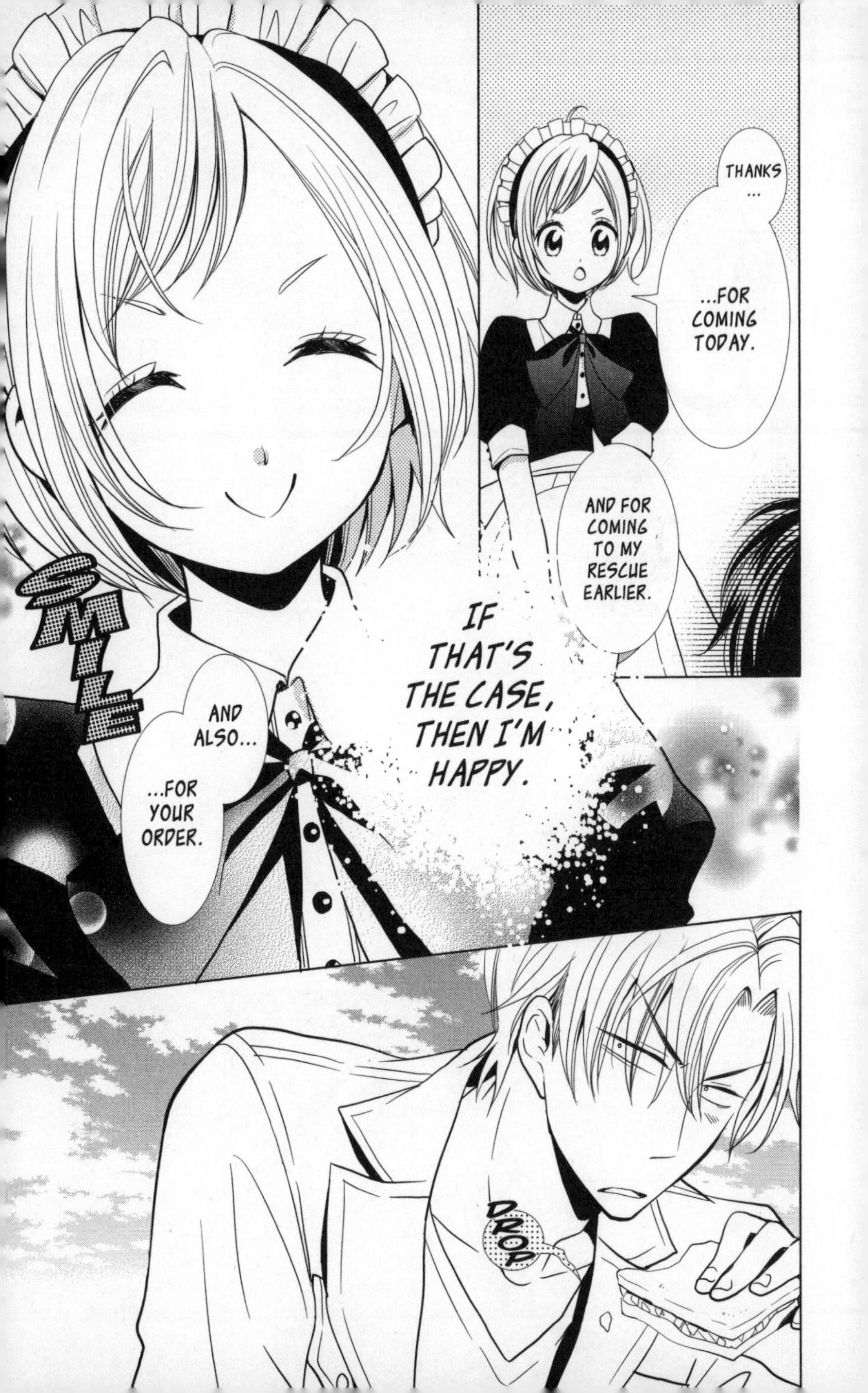
THANKS ...
...FOR COMING TODAY.
AND FOR COMING TO MY RESCUE EARLIER.
SMILE
AND ALSO...
...FOR YOUR ORDER.
IF THAT'S THE CASE, THEN I'M HAPPY.
DROP

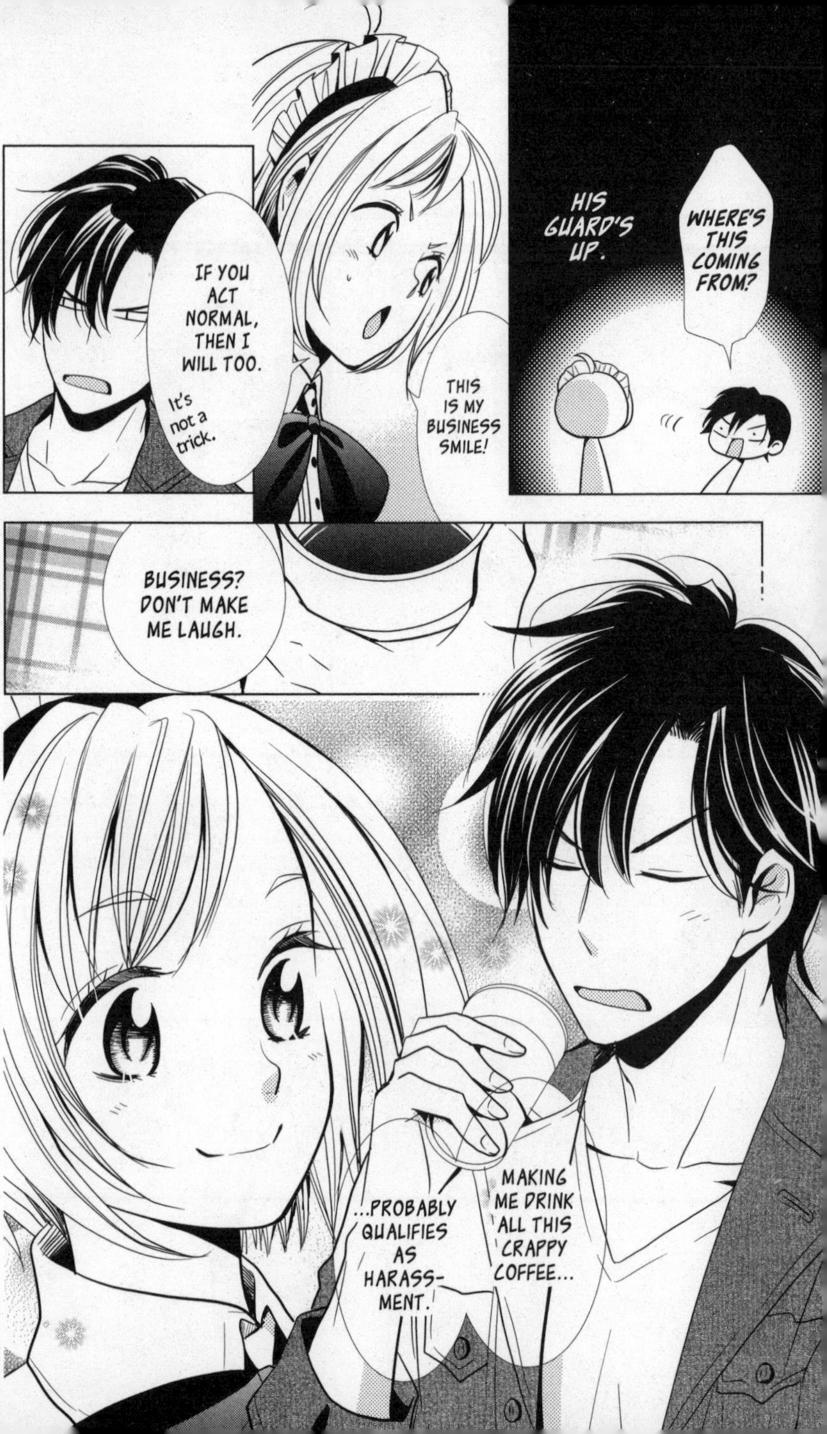
WHERE'S THIS COMING FROM?
HIS GUARD'S UP.
IF YOU ACT NORMAL, THEN I WILL TOO.
It's not a trick.
THIS IS MY BUSINESS SMILE!
BUSINESS? DON'T MAKE ME LAUGH.
MAKING ME DRINK ALL THIS CRAPPY COFFEE...
...PROBABLY QUALIFIES AS HARASS-MENT.

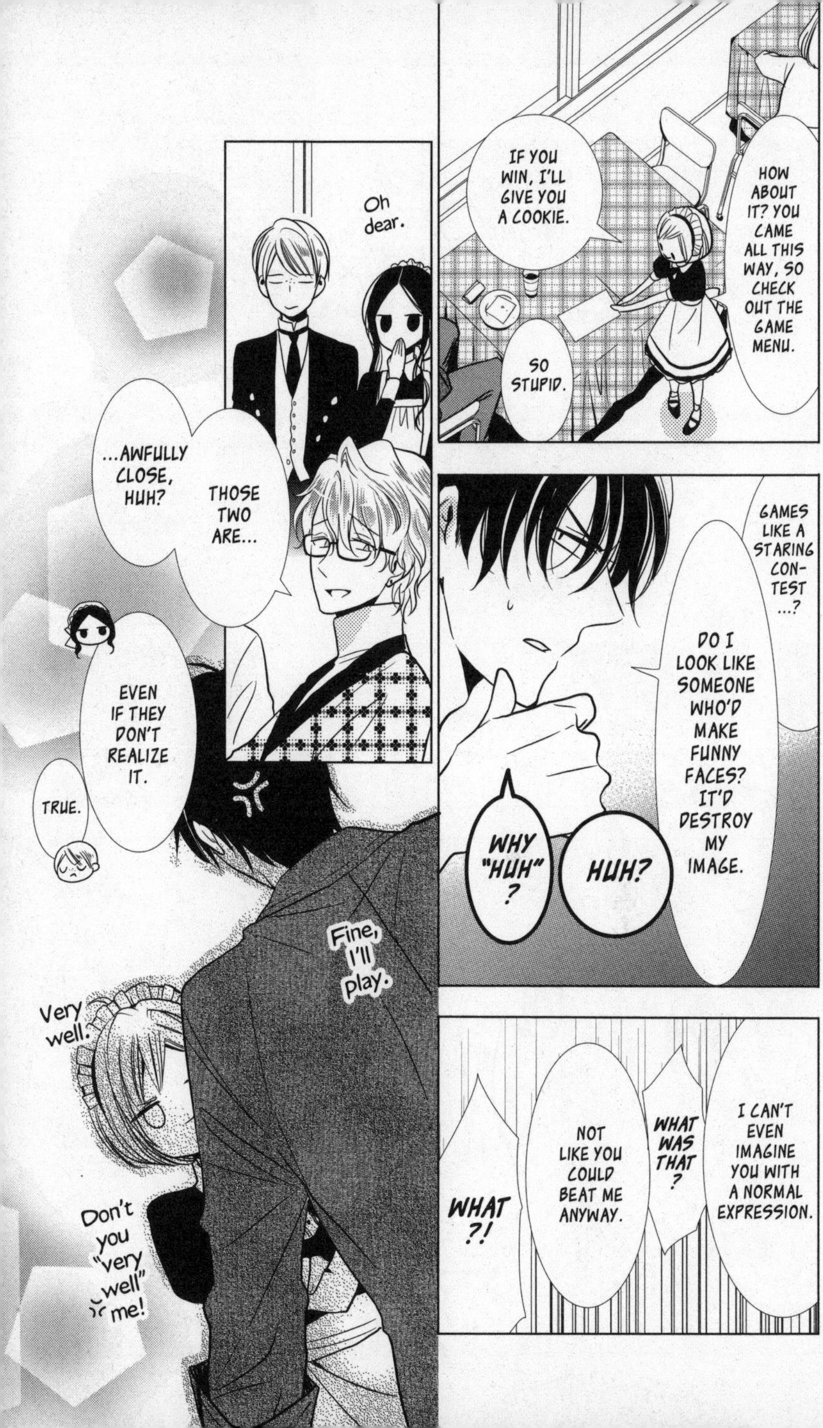
HOW ABOUT IT? YOU CAME ALL THIS WAY, SO CHECK OUT THE GAME MENU.
IF YOU WIN, I'LL GIVE YOU A COOKIE.
SO STUPID.
GAMES LIKE A STARING CON-TEST ...?
DO I LOOK LIKE SOMEONE WHO'D MAKE FUNNY FACES? IT'D DESTROY MY IMAGE.
HUH?
WHY "HUH"?
I CAN'T EVEN IMAGINE YOU WITH A NORMAL EXPRESSION.
WHAT WAS THAT?
NOT LIKE YOU COULD BEAT ME ANYWAY.
WHAT?!
Oh dear.
THOSE TWO ARE...
...AWFULLY CLOSE, HUH?
EVEN IF THEY DON'T REALIZE IT.
TRUE.
Fine, I'll play.
Very well.
Don't you "very well" me!

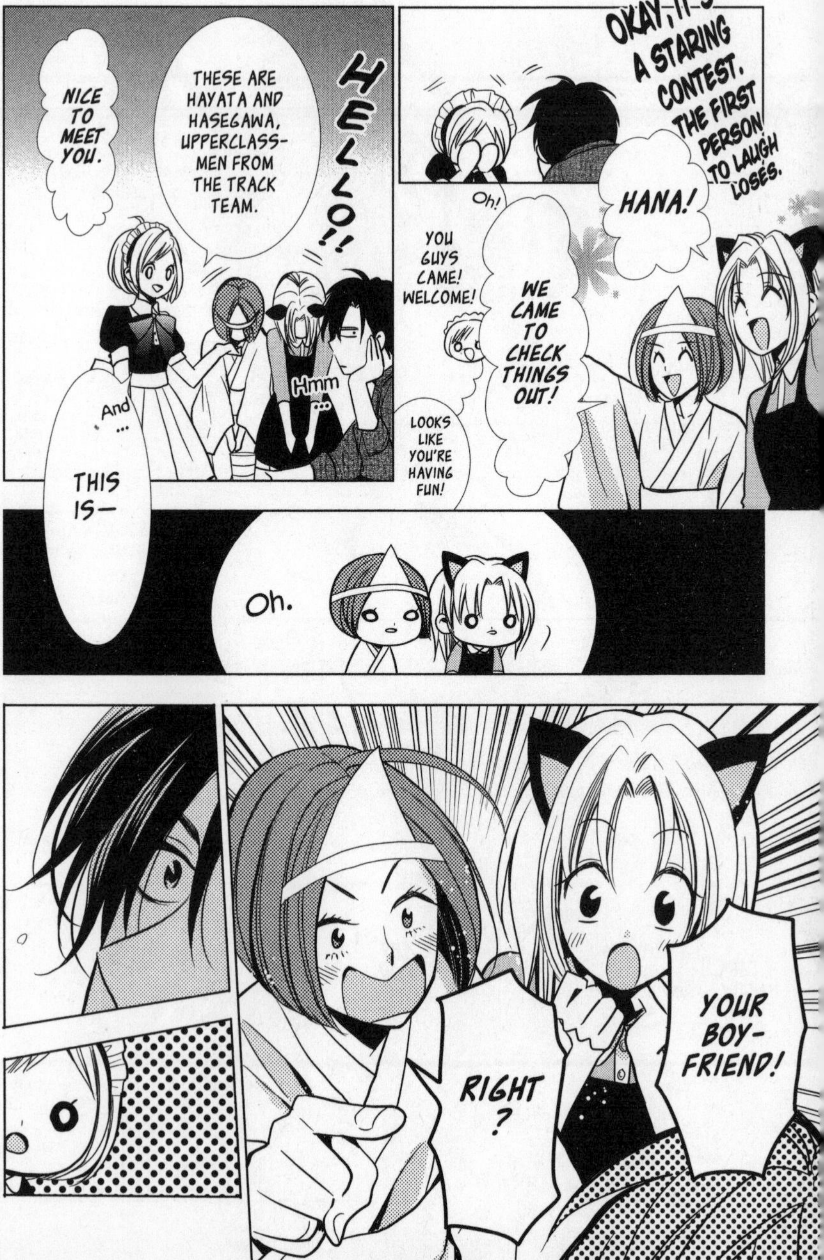
OKAY, IT'S A STARING CONTEST. THE FIRST PERSON TO LAUGH LOSES.
HANA!
Oh!
YOU GUYS CAME! WELCOME!
WE CAME TO CHECK THINGS OUT!
LOOKS LIKE YOU'RE HAVING FUN!
HELLO!!
THESE ARE HAYATA AND HASEGAWA, UPPERCLASSMEN FROM THE TRACK TEAM.
NICE TO MEET YOU.
Hmm...
And...
THIS IS—
Oh.
YOUR BOYFRIEND!
RIGHT?

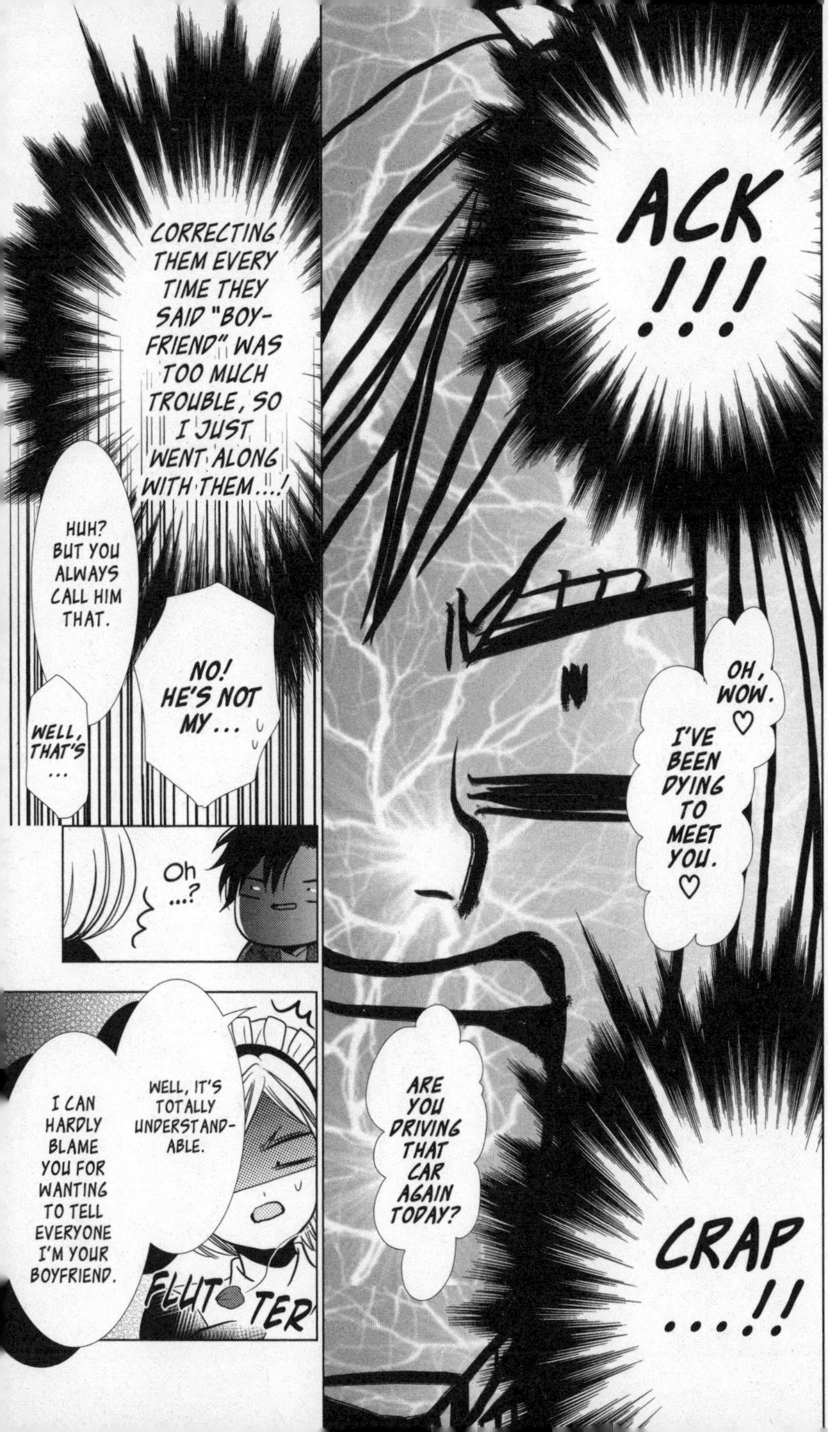
ACK !!!
OH, WOW. ♡ I'VE BEEN DYING TO MEET YOU. ♡
ARE YOU DRIVING THAT CAR AGAIN TODAY?
CRAP ...!!
CORRECTING THEM EVERY TIME THEY SAID "BOY-FRIEND" WAS TOO MUCH TROUBLE, SO I JUST WENT ALONG WITH THEM...!
HUH? BUT YOU ALWAYS CALL HIM THAT.
NO! HE'S NOT MY...
WELL, THAT'S...
Oh ...?
WELL, IT'S TOTALLY UNDERSTAND-ABLE.
I CAN HARDLY BLAME YOU FOR WANTING TO TELL EVERYONE I'M YOUR BOYFRIEND.
FLUTTER

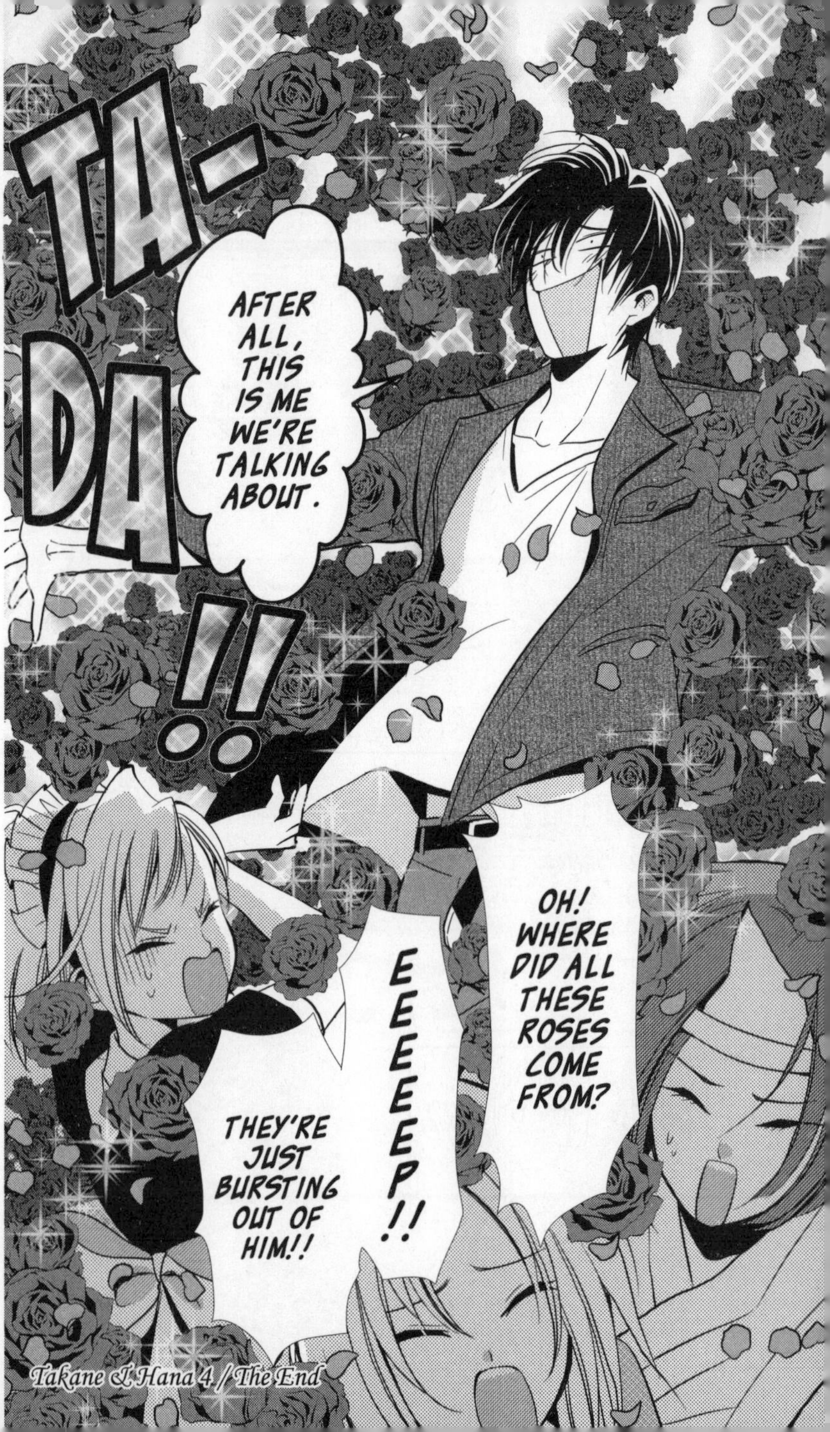
AFTER ALL, THIS IS ME WE'RE TALKING ABOUT.
TA-DA!!
OH! WHERE DID ALL THESE ROSES COME FROM?
EEEEEEP!!
THEY'RE JUST BURSTING OUT OF HIM!!

Takane & Hana 4 / The End

Takane Café

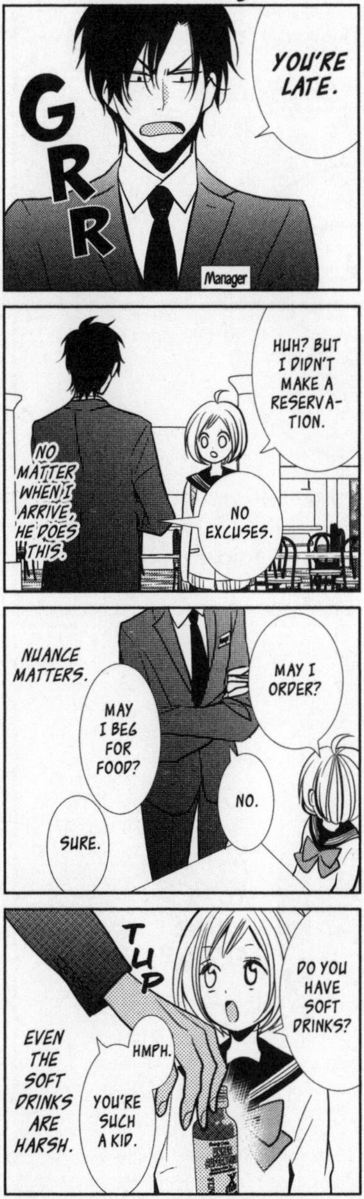
YOU'RE LATE.
GRR
Manager
HUH? BUT I DIDN'T MAKE A RESERVATION.
NO EXCUSES.
NO MATTER WHEN I ARRIVE, HE DOES THIS.
MAY I ORDER?
NO.
NUANCE MATTERS.
MAY I BEG FOR FOOD?
SURE.
DO YOU HAVE SOFT DRINKS?
TUP
HMPH.
YOU'RE SUCH A KID.
EVEN THE SOFT DRINKS ARE HARSH.

For the "bury the cover with stuff" theme, I found a loophole by using roses of different colors.

—YUKI SHIWASU

Born on March 7 in Fukuoka Prefecture, Japan, Yuki Shiwasu began her career as a manga artist after winning the top prize in the Hakusensha Athena Newcomers' Awards from *Hana to Yume* magazine. She is also the author of *Furou Kyoudai* (Immortal Siblings), which was published by Hakusensha in Japan.

Takane & Hana

VOLUME 4
SHOJO BEAT EDITION

STORY & ART BY **YUKI SHIWASU**

ENGLISH ADAPTATION **Ysabet Reinhardt MacFarlane**
TRANSLATION **JN Productions**
TOUCH-UP ART & LETTERING **Freeman Wong**
DESIGN **Shawn Carrico**
EDITOR **Amy Yu**

Takane to Hana by Yuki Shiwasu
© Yuki Shiwasu 2016
All rights reserved.
First published in Japan in 2016 by HAKUSENSHA, Inc., Tokyo.
English language translation rights arranged with HAKUSENSHA, Inc., Tokyo.

Published by VIZ Media, LLC
P.O. Box 77010
San Francisco, CA 94107

10 9 8 7 6 5 4 3 2 1
First printing, August 2018

viz.com

shojobeat.com

IDOL dreams

STORY & ART BY
ARINA TANEMURA

At age 31, office worker Chikage Deguchi feels she missed her chances at love and success. When word gets out that she's a virgin, Chikage is humiliated and wishes she could turn back time to when she was still young and popular. She takes an experimental drug that changes her appearance back to when she was 15. Now Chikage is determined to pursue everything she missed out on all those years ago—including becoming a star!

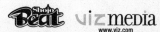

Thirty One Idream © Arina Tanemura 2014/HAKUSENSHA, Inc.

Behind the Scenes!!

STORY AND ART BY BISCO HATORI

From the creator of Ouran High School Host Club

Ranmaru Kurisu comes from a family of hardy, rough-and-tumble fisherfolk and he sticks out at home like a delicate, artistic sore thumb. It's given him a raging inferiority complex and a permanently pessimistic outlook. Now that he's in college, he's hoping to find a sense of belonging. But after a whole life of being left out, does he even know how to fit in?!

FROM THE
CREATOR OF
**VAMPIRE
KNIGHT**

Shuriken
and Pleats

When the master she has sworn to protect is killed, Mikage Kirio, a skilled ninja, travels to Japan to start a new, peaceful life for herself. But as soon as she arrives, she finds herself fighting to protect the life of Mahito Wakashimatsu, a man who is under attack by a band of ninja. From that time on, Mikage is drawn deeper into the machinations of his powerful family.

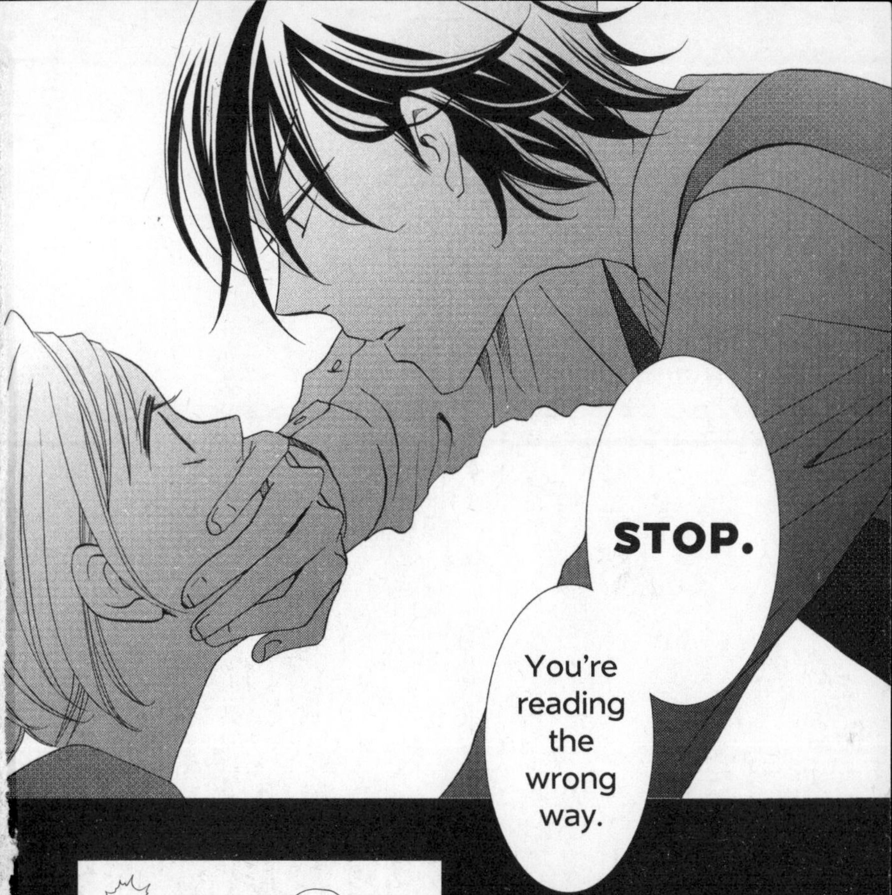
STOP.
You're reading the wrong way.

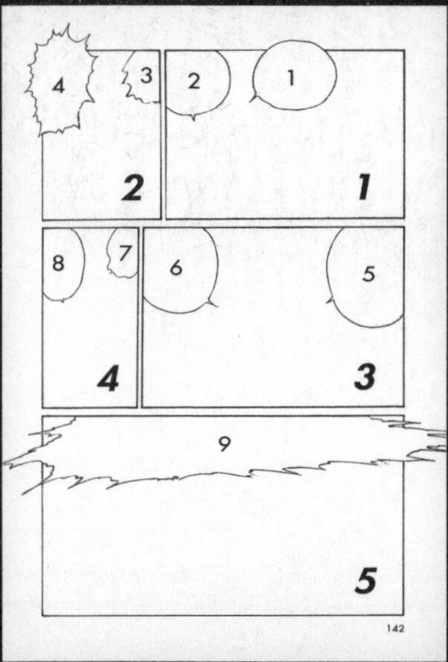
1
2
3
4
5
6
7
8
9
1
2
3
4
5
142

In keeping with the original Japanese comic format, this book reads from right to left—so action, sound effects and word balloons are completely reversed to preserve the orientation of the original artwork.

Check out the diagram shown here to get the hang of things, and then turn to the other side of the book to get started!

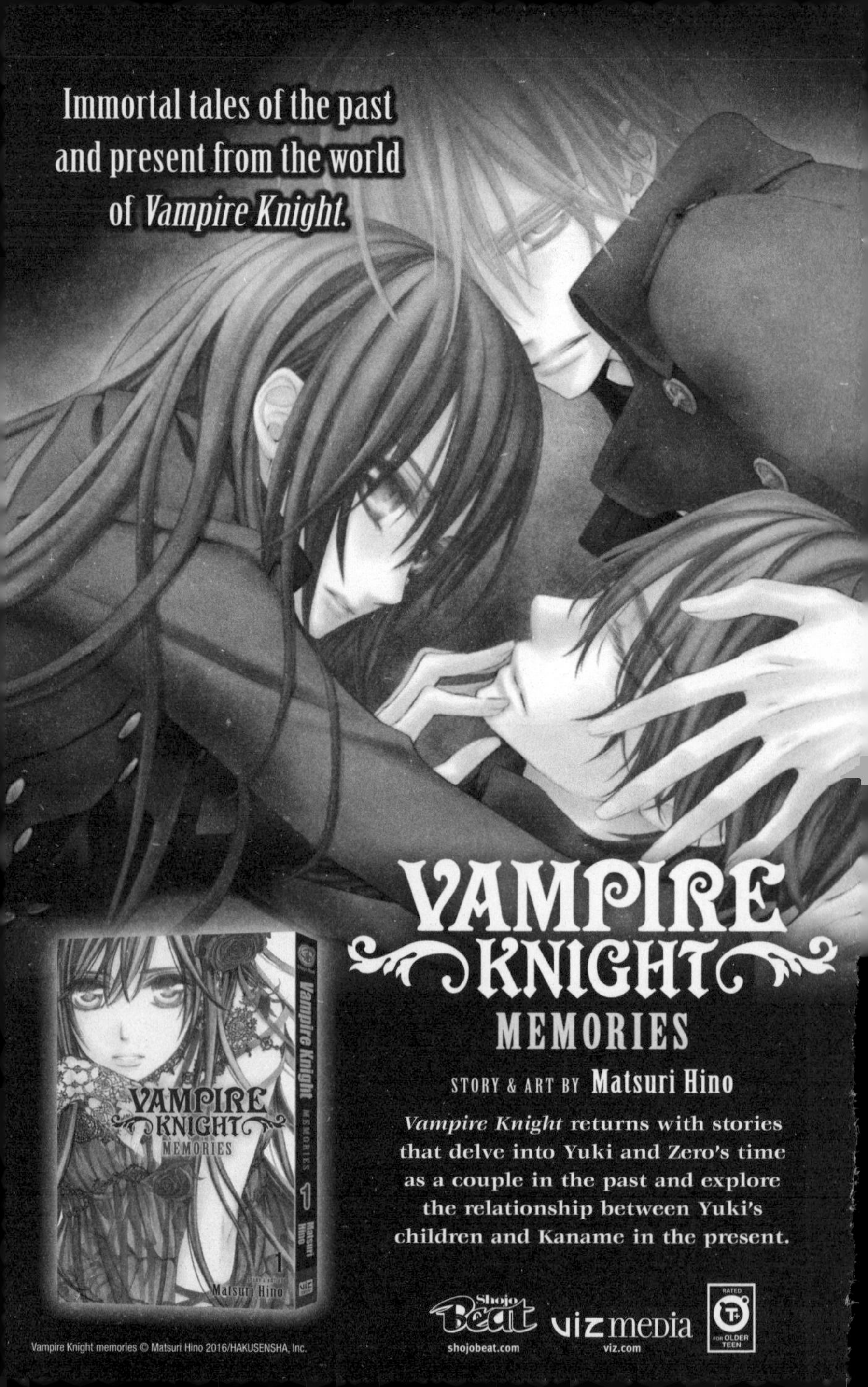
Immortal tales of the past and present from the world of *Vampire Knight*.
VAMPIRE KNIGHT
MEMORIES
STORY & ART BY Matsuri Hino
Vampire Knight returns with stories that delve into Yuki and Zero's time as a couple in the past and explore the relationship between Yuki's children and Kaname in the present.
Vampire Knight
MEMORIES
1
Matsuri Hino
VAMPIRE KNIGHT MEMORIES
Matsuri Hino
Shojo Beat
shojobeat.com
viz media
viz.com
RATED T+ FOR OLDER TEEN
Vampire Knight memories © Matsuri Hino 2016/HAKUSENSHA, Inc.

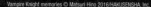